The Domestic Life
of
Thomas Jefferson

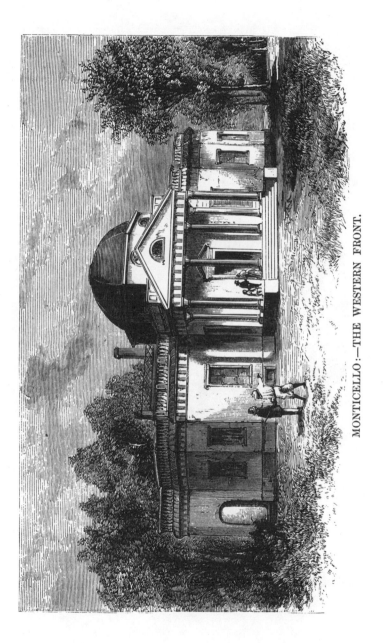

MONTICELLO:—THE WESTERN FRONT.

THOMAS JEFFERSON.
From Portrait by Gilbert Stuart.

THE DOMESTIC LIFE

OF

THOMAS JEFFERSON.

COMPILED FROM

FAMILY LETTERS AND REMINISCENCES,

BY HIS GREAT-GRANDDAUGHTER,

SARAH N. RANDOLPH.

PUBLISHED FOR
THE THOMAS JEFFERSON MEMORIAL FOUNDATION
BY THE UNIVERSITY PRESS OF VIRGINIA
CHARLOTTESVILLE

THE UNIVERSITY PRESS OF VIRGINIA
Copyright © 1978 by the Rector and Visitors
of the University of Virginia

This edition
First published 1978

Library of Congress Cataloging in Publication Data

Randolph, Sarah Nicholas, 1839–1892.
   The domestic life of Thomas Jefferson.

   Reprint of the 1871 ed. published by Harper, New York.
   Includes index.
   1. Jefferson, Thomas, Pres. U.S., 1743–1826.
2. Presidents—United States—Biography. I. Title.
E332.25.R2 1978 973.4'6'0924 [B] 78–14312
ISBN 0–8139–0718–7

Printed in the United States of America

PREFACE.

I DO not in this volume write of Jefferson either as of the great man or as of the statesman. My object is only to give a faithful picture of him as he was in private life— to show that he was, as I have been taught to think of him by those who knew and loved him best, a beautiful domestic character. With this view I have collected the reminiscences of him which have been written by his daughter and grandchildren. From his correspondence, published and unpublished, I have culled his family letters, and here reproduce them as being the most faithful witnesses of the warmth of his affections, the elevation of his character, and the scrupulous fidelity with which he discharged the duties of every relation in life.

I am well aware that the tale of Jefferson's life, both public and private, has been well told by the most faithful of biographers in "Randall's Life of Jefferson," and that much of what is contained in these pages will be found in that admirable work, which, from the author's zealous devotion to truth, and his indefatigable industry in collecting his materials, must ever stand chief among the most valuable contributions to American history. I propose, however, to give a sketch of Jefferson's private life in a briefer form than it can be found in either the thirteen volumes of the two editions of his published correspondence, or in the three stout octavo volumes of his Life by Randall. To give a bird's-eye view of his whole career, and to preserve unbroken the thread of this narrative, I quote freely from his Memoir, and from such of his letters as cast any light upon the subject, filling up the blanks with my own pen.

Jefferson's executor having a few months ago recovered from the United States Government his family letters and private papers, which had been exempted from the sale of his public manuscripts, I am enabled to give in these pages many interesting letters never before published.

No man's private character has been more foully assailed than Jefferson's, and none so wantonly exposed to the public gaze, nor more fully vindicated. I shall be more than rewarded for my labors should I succeed in imparting to my readers a tithe of that esteem and veneration which I have been taught to feel for him by the person with whom he was most intimate during life—the grandson who, as a boy, played upon his knee, and, as a man, was, as he himself spoke of him, "the staff" of his old age.

The portrait of Jefferson is from a painting by Gilbert Stuart, in the possession of his family, and by them considered as the best likeness of him. The portrait of his daughter, Martha Jefferson Randolph, is from a painting by Sully. The view of Monticello represents the home of Jefferson as it existed during his lifetime, and not as it now is—a ruin.

THE AUTHOR.

June, 1871.

CONTENTS.

CHAPTER I.

CHAPTER II.

CHAPTER III.

CHAPTER IV.

CHAPTER V.

CHAPTER VI.

CHAPTER VII.

CHAPTER VIII.

CHAPTER IX.

CHAPTER XVI.

CHAPTER XVII.

CHAPTER XVIII.

CHAPTER XIX.

CHAPTER XX.

CHAPTER XXI.

CHAPTER XXII.

ILLUSTRATIONS.

THE
DOMESTIC LIFE OF JEFFERSON.

CHAPTER I.

On a long, gently sloping hill five miles east of Charlottesville, Virginia, the traveller, passing along the county road of Albemarle; has pointed out to him the spot where Thomas Jefferson was born, April 13th, 1743. A few aged locust-trees are still left to mark the place, and two or three sycamores stretch out their long majestic arms over the greensward beneath, once the scene of young Jefferson's boyish games, but now a silent pasture, where cattle and sheep browse, undisturbed by the proximity of any dwelling. The trees are all that are left of an avenue planted by him on his twenty-first birthday, and, as such, are objects of peculiar interest to those who love to dwell upon the associations of the past.

The situation is one well suited for a family mansion—offering from its site a landscape view rarely surpassed. To the south are seen the picturesque valley and banks of the Rivanna, with an extensive, peaceful-looking horizon view, lying like a sleeping beauty, in the east; while long rolling

B

hills, occasionally rising into mountain ranges until at last they are all lost in the gracefully-sweeping profile of the Blue Ridge, stretch westward, and the thickly - wooded Southwest Mountains, with the highly-cultivated fields and valleys intervening, close the scene on the north, and present landscapes whose exquisite enchantment must ever charm the beholder.

A brief sketch of Jefferson's family and early life is given in the following quotation from his Memoir, written by himself:

January 6, 1821.—At the age of 77, I begin to make some memoranda, and state some recollections of dates and facts concerning myself, for my own more ready reference, and for the information of my family.

The tradition in my father's family was, that their ancestor came to this country from Wales, and from near the mountain of Snowden, the highest in Great Britain. I noted once a case from Wales in the law reports, where a person of our name was either plaintiff or defendant; and one of the same name was Secretary to the Virginia Company. These are the only instances in which I have met with the name in that country. I have found it in our early records; but the first particular information I have of any ancestor was of my grandfather, who lived at the place in Chesterfield called Osborne's, and owned the lands afterwards the glebe of the parish. He had three sons: Thomas, who died young; Field, who settled on the waters of the Roanoke, and left numerous descendants; and Peter, my father, who settled on the lands I still own, called Shadwell, adjoining my present residence. He was born February 29th, 1708, and intermarried 1739 with Jane Randolph, of the age of 19, daughter of Isham Randolph, one of the seven sons of that name and family settled at Dungeness, in Goochland. They trace their pedigree far back in England and Scotland, to which let every one ascribe the faith and merit he chooses.

My father's education had been quite neglected; but being of a strong mind, sound judgment, and eager after information, he read much, and improved himself; insomuch that he was chosen, with Joshua Fry, Professor of Mathematics in

William and Mary College, to run the boundary-line between Virginia and North Carolina, which had been begun by Colonel Byrd, and was afterwards employed with the same Mr. Fry to make the first map of Virginia which had ever been made, that of Captain Smith being merely a conjectural sketch. They possessed excellent materials for so much of the country as is below the Blue Ridge, little being then known beyond that ridge. He was the third or fourth settler, about the year 1737, of the part of the country in which I live. He died August 17th, 1757, leaving my mother a widow, who lived till 1776, with six daughters and two sons, myself the elder.

To my younger brother he left his estate on James River, called Snowden, after the supposed birthplace of the family; to myself, the lands on which I was born and live. He placed me at the English school at five years of age, and at the Latin at nine, where I continued until his death. My teacher, Mr. Douglas, a clergyman from Scotland, with the rudiments of the Latin and Greek languages, taught me the French; and on the death of my father I went to the Rev. Mr. Maury, a correct classical scholar, with whom I continued two years.

The talents of great men are frequently said to be derived from the mother. If they are inheritable, Jefferson was entitled to them on both the paternal and maternal side. His father was a man of most extraordinary vigor, both of mind and body. His son never wearied of dwelling with all the pride of filial devotion and admiration on the noble traits of his character. To the regular duties of his vocation as a land-surveyor (which, it will be remembered, was the profession of Washington also) were added those of county surveyor, colonel of the militia, and member of the House of Burgesses.

Family tradition has preserved several incidents of the survey of the boundary-line between Virginia and North Carolina, which prove him to have been a man of remarkable powers of endurance, untiring energy, and indomitable courage. The perils and toils of running that line across

the Blue Ridge were almost incredible, and were not surpassed by those encountered by Colonel Byrd and his party
in forcing the same line through the forests and marshes of
the Dismal Swamp in the year 1728. On this expedition
Colonel Jefferson and his companions had often to defend
themselves against the attacks of wild beasts during the
day, and at night found but a broken rest, sleeping—as
they were obliged to do for safety—in trees. At length
their supply of provisions began to run low, and his com-
rades, overcome by hunger and exhaustion, fell fainting be-
side him. Amid all these hardships and difficulties, Jefferson's courage did not once flag, but living upon raw flesh, or
whatever could be found to sustain life, he pressed on and
persevered until his task was accomplished.

So great was his physical strength, that when standing
between two hogsheads of tobacco lying on their sides, he
could raise or "head" them both up at once. Perhaps it
was because he himself rejoiced in such gigantic strength
that it was his frequent remark that "it is the strong in
body who are both the strong and free in mind." This, too,
made him careful to have his young son early instructed in
all the manly sports and exercises of his day; so that while
still a school-boy he was a good rider, a good swimmer, and
an ardent sportsman, spending hours and days wandering in
pursuit of game along the sides of the beautiful Southwest
Mountains — thus strengthening his body and his health,
which must otherwise have given way under the intense
application to study to which he soon afterwards devoted
himself.

The Jeffersons were among the earliest immigrants to the
colony, and we find the name in the list of the twenty-two
members who composed the Assembly that met in James-
town in the year 1619—the first legislative body that was
ever convened in America.* Colonel Jefferson's father-in-
law, Isham Randolph, of Dungeness, was a man of consider-

---

* The Jeffersons first emigrated to Virginia in 1612.

able eminence in the colony, whose name associated itself in his day with all that was good and wise. In the year 1717 he married, in London, Jane Rogers. Possessing the polished and courteous manners of a gentleman of the colonial days, with a well-cultivated intellect, and a heart in which every thing that is noble and true was instinctive, he charmed and endeared himself to all who were thrown into his society. He devoted much time to the study of science; and we find the following mention of him in a quaint letter from Peter Collinson, of London, to Bartram, the naturalist, then on the eve of visiting Virginia to study her flora:

When thee proceeds home, I know no person who will make thee more welcome than Isham Randolph. He lives thirty or forty miles above the falls of James River, in Goochland, above the other settlements. Now, I take his house to be a very suitable place to make a settlement at, for to take several days' excursions all round, and to return to his house at night...... One thing I must desire of thee, and do insist that thee must oblige me therein: that thou make up that drugget clothes, to go to Virginia in, and not appear to disgrace thyself or me; for though I should not esteem thee the less to come to me in what dress thou wilt, yet these Virginians are a very gentle, well-dressed people, and look, perhaps, more at a man's outside than his inside. For these and other reasons, pray go very clean, neat, and handsomely-dressed to Virginia. Never mind thy clothes; I will send thee more another year.

In reply to Bartram's account of the kind welcome which he received from Isham Randolph, he writes: "As for my friend Isham, who I am also personally known to, I did not doubt his civility to thee. I only wish I had been there and shared it with thee." Again, after Randolph's death, he writes to Bartram that "the good man is gone to his long home, and, I doubt not, is happy."

Such was Jefferson's maternal grandfather. His mother, from whom he inherited his cheerful and hopeful temper and disposition, was a woman of a clear and strong understanding, and, in every respect, worthy of the love of such a man as Peter Jefferson.

Isham Randolph's nephew, Colonel William Randolph, of Tuckahoe, was Peter Jefferson's most intimate friend. A pleasing incident preserved in the family records proves how warm and generous their friendship was. Two or three days before Jefferson took out a patent for a thousand acres of land on the Rivanna River, Randolph had taken out one for twenty-four hundred acres adjoining. Jefferson, not finding a good site for a house on his land, his friend sold him four hundred acres of his tract, the price paid for these four hundred acres being, as the deed still in the possession of the family proves, "Henry Weatherbourne's biggest bowl of arrack punch."

Colonel Jefferson called his estate "Shadwell," after the parish in England where his wife was born, while Randolph's was named "Edgehill," in honor of the field on which the Cavaliers and Roundheads first crossed swords. By an intermarriage between their grandchildren, these two estates passed into the possession of descendants common to them both, in whose hands they have been preserved down to the present day.

On the four hundred acres thus added by Jefferson to his original patent, he erected a plain weather-boarded house, to which he took his young bride immediately after his marriage, and where they remained until the death of Colonel William Randolph, of Tuckahoe, in 1745.

It was the dying request of Colonel Randolph, that his friend Peter Jefferson should undertake the management of his estates and the guardianship of his young son, Thomas Mann Randolph. Being unable to fulfill this request while living at Shadwell, Colonel Jefferson removed his family to Tuckahoe, and remained there seven years, sacredly guarding, like a Knight of the Round Table, the solemn charge intrusted to him, without any other reward than the satisfaction of fully keeping the promise made to his dying friend. That he refused to receive any other compensation for his services as guardian is not only proved by the frequent assertion of his son in after years, but by his accounts as executor, which have ever remained unchallenged.*

Thomas Jefferson was not more than two years old when his father moved to Tuckahoe, yet he often declared that his earliest recollection in life was of being, on that occasion, handed up to a servant on horseback, by whom he was carried on a pillow for a long distance. He also remembered that later, when five years old, he one day became impatient for his school to be out, and, going out, knelt behind the house, and there repeated the Lord's Prayer, hoping thereby to hurry up the desired hour.

Colonel Jefferson's house at Shadwell was near the public highway, and in those days of primitive hospitality was the stopping-place for all passers-by, and, in the true spirit of Old Virginia hospitality, was thrown open to every guest. Here, too, the great Indian Chiefs stopped, on their journeys to and from the colonial capital, and it was thus that young Jefferson first became acquainted with and interested in them and their people. More than half a century later we find him writing to John Adams:

I know much of the great Ontasseté, the warrior and orator of the Cherokees; he was always the guest of my father on his journeys to and from Williamsburg. I was in his camp when he made his great farewell oration to his people, the evening before his departure for England. The moon was in full splendor, and to her he seemed to address himself in his prayers for his own safety on the voyage, and that of his people during his absence; his sounding voice, distinct articulation, animated action, and the solemn silence of his people at their several fires, filled me with awe and veneration.

The lives led by our forefathers were certainly filled with ease and leisure. One of Thomas Jefferson's grandsons asked him, on one occasion, how the men of his father's day

---

* In spite of these facts, however, some of Randolph's descendants, with more arrogance than gratitude, speak of Colonel Jefferson as being a paid agent of their ancestor.

spent their time.   He smiled, and, in reply, said, " My father
had a devoted friend, to whose house he would go, dine,
spend the night, dine with him again on the second day, and
return to Shadwell in the evening.   His friend, in the course
of a day or two, returned the visit, and spent the same length
of time at his house.   This occurred once every week; and
thus, you see, they were together four days out of the
seven."

This is, perhaps, a fair picture of the ease and leisure of the
life of an old Virginian, and to the causes which produced
this style of life was due, also, the great hospitality for which
Virginians have ever been so renowned.   The process of
farming was then so simple that the labor and cultivation
of an estate were easily and most profitably carried on by
an overseer and the slaves, the master only riding occasionally over his plantation to see that his general orders were
executed.

In the school of such a life, however, were reared and developed the characters of the men who rose to such eminence in the struggles of the Revolution, and who, as giants
in intellect and virtue, must ever be a prominent group
among the great historical characters of the world.   Their
devotion to the chase, to horsemanship, and to all the manly sports of the day, and the perils and adventures to be
encountered in a new country, developed their physical
strength, and inspired them with that bold and dashing
spirit which still characterizes their descendants, while the
leisure of their lives gave them time to devote to study and
reflection.

The city of Williamsburg, being the capital of the colony
and the residence of the governor, was the seat of intelligence, refinement, and elegance, and offered every advantage for social intercourse.   There it was that those graceful manners were formed which made men belonging to the
old colonial school so celebrated for the cordial ease and
courtesy of their address.   As there were no large towns in
the colony, the inducements and temptations offered for the

accumulation of wealth were few, while the abundance of the good things of the earth found on his own plantation rendered the Virginian lavish in his expenditures, and hence his unbounded hospitality. Of this we have ample proof in the accounts which have been handed down to us of their mode of life. Thomas Mann Randolph, of Tuckahoe, it is said, consumed annually a thousand barrels of corn at his family stable; while the princely abode of Colonel Byrd, of Westover, with its offices, covered a space of two acres. The prices of corn were what seem to us now fabulously low. The old chroniclers tell us that one year the price rose to the enormous sum of thirty-three cents a bushel, and that year was ever after known as the "ten-shilling year"— ten shillings being the price per barrel.

In looking over Colonel Peter Jefferson's account-books, one can not refrain from smiling to see the small amount paid for his young son's school education. To the Rev. William Douglas he paid sixteen pounds sterling per annum for his board and tuition, and Mr. Maury received for the same twenty pounds. Colonel Jefferson's eagerness for information was inherited to an extraordinary degree by his son, who early evinced that thirst for knowledge which he preserved to the day of his death. He made rapid progress in his studies, and soon became a proficient in mathematics and the classics. In after years he used often to say, that had he to decide between the pleasure derived from the classical education which his father had given him and the estate he had left him, he would decide in favor of the former.

Jefferson's father died, as we have seen, when he was only fourteen years old. The perils and wants of his situation, deprived as he was so early in life of the guidance and influence of such a father, were very touchingly described by him years afterwards, in a letter written to his eldest grandson,* when the latter was sent from home to school for the first time. He writes:

---

* Thomas Jefferson Randolph.

When I recollect that at fourteen years of age the whole care and direction of myself was thrown on myself entirely, without a relative or friend qualified to advise or guide me, and recollect the various sorts of bad company with which I associated from time to time, I am astonished that I did not turn off with some of them, and become as worthless to society as they were. I had the good-fortune to become acquainted very early with some characters of very high standing, and to feel the incessant wish that I could ever become what they were. Under temptations and difficulties, I would ask myself—What would Dr. Small, Mr. Wythe, Peyton Randolph, do in this situation? What course in it will insure me their approbation? I am certain that this mode of deciding on my conduct tended more to correctness than any reasoning powers I possessed. Knowing the even and dignified lives they pursued, I could never doubt for a moment which of two courses would be in character for them; whereas, seeking the same object through a process of moral reasoning, and with the jaundiced eye of youth, I should often have erred. From the circumstances of my position, I was often thrown into the society of horse-racers, card-players, fox-hunters, scientific and professional men, and of dignified men; and many a time have I asked myself, in the enthusiastic moment of the death of a fox, the victory of a favorite horse, the issue of a question eloquently argued at the bar, or in the great council of the nation, Well, which of these kinds of reputation should I prefer—that of a horse-jockey, a fox-hunter, an orator, or the honest advocate of my country's rights? Be assured, my dear Jefferson, that these little returns into ourselves, this self-catechising habit, is not trifling nor useless, but leads to the prudent selection and steady pursuit of what is right.

After leaving Mr. Maury's school, we find him writing the following letter to a gentleman who was at the time his guardian. It was written when he was seventeen years old, and is the earliest production which we have from his pen:

Shadwell, January 14th, 1760.

Sir—I was at Colo. Peter Randolph's about a fortnight ago, and my Schooling falling into Discourse, he said he thought it would be to my Advantage to go to the College, and was desirous I should go, as indeed I am myself for several Reasons. In the first place as long as I stay at the Mountain, the loss of one fourth of my Time is inevitable, by Company's coming here and detaining me from School. And likewise my Absence will in a great measure, put a Stop to so much Company, and by that Means lessen the Expenses of the Estate in House-keeping. And on the other Hand by going to the College, I shall get a more universal Acquaintance, which may hereafter be serviceable to me; and I suppose I can pursue my Studies in the Greek and Latin as well there as here, and likewise learn something of the Mathematics. I shall be glad of your opinion, and remain, Sir, your most humble servant,

THOMAS JEFFERSON JR:

To Mr. John Hervey, at Bellemont.

We find no traces, in the above school-boy's letter, of the graceful pen which afterwards won for its author so high a rank among the letter-writers of his own, or, indeed, of any day.

It was decided that he should go to William and Mary College, and thither he accordingly went, in the year 1760. We again quote from his Memoir, to give a glance at this period of his life:

It was my great good-fortune, and what, perhaps, fixed the destinies of my life, that Dr. William Small, of Scotland, was the Professor of Mathematics, a man profound in most of the useful branches of science, with a happy talent of communication, correct and gentlemanly manners, and an enlarged and liberal mind. He, most happily for me, became soon attached to me, and made me his daily companion, when not engaged in the school; and from his conversation I got my first views of the expansion of science, and of the system of things in which we are placed. Fortunately, the philosophical chair became vacant soon after my arrival at college, and he was appointed to fill it *per interim;* and he was the first who ever gave, in that college, regular lectures in Ethics, Rhetoric, and Belles Lettres. He returned to Europe in 1762, having previously filled up the measure of his goodness to me, by procuring for me, from his most intimate friend, George Wythe, a reception as a student of law under his direction, and introduced me to the acquaintance and familiar table of Governor Fauquier, the ablest man who had ever filled that office. With him and at his table, Dr. Small and Mr. Wythe, his *amici omnium horarum*, and myself formed a *partie quarrée*, and to the habitual conversations on these occasions I owed much instruction. Mr. Wythe continued to be my faithful and beloved mentor in youth, and my most affectionate friend through life.

There must indeed have been some very great charm and attraction about the young student of seventeen, to have won for him the friendship and esteem of such a profound scholar as Small, and a seat at the family table of the elegant and accomplished Fauquier.

We have just quoted Jefferson's finely-drawn character of Small, and give now the following brilliant but sad picture, as drawn by the Virginia historian, Burke, of the able and generous Fauquier, and of the vices which he introduced into the colony:

With some allowance, he was every thing that could have been wished for by Virginia under a royal government. Generous, liberal, elegant in his manners and acquirements; his example left an impression of taste, refinement and erudition on the character of the colony, which eminently contributed to its present high reputation in the arts. It is stated, on evidence sufficiently authentic, that on the return of Anson from his circumnavigation of the earth, he accidentally fell in with Fauquier, from whom, in a single night's play, he won at cards the whole of his patrimony; that afterwards, being captivated by the striking graces of this gentleman's person and conversation, he procured for him the government of Virginia. Unreclaimed by the former subversion of his fortune, he introduced the same fatal propensity to gaming into Virginia; and the example of so many virtues and accomplishments, alloyed but by a single vice, was but too successful in extending the influence of this pernicious and ruinous practice. He found among the people of his new government a character compounded of the same elements as his own; and he found little difficulty in rendering fashionable a practice which had, before his arrival, already prevailed to an alarming extent. During the recess of the courts of judicature and of the assemblies, he visited the most distinguished landholders of the colonies, and the rage of playing deep, reckless of time, health or money, spread like a contagion among a class proverbial for their hospitality, their politeness and fondness for expense. In every thing besides, Fauquier was the ornament and the delight of Virginia.

Happy it was for young Jefferson, that "the example of so many virtues and accomplishments" in this brave gentleman failed to give any attraction, for him at least, to the vice which was such a blot on Fauquier's fine character. Jefferson never knew one card from another, and never allowed the game to be played in his own house.

Turning from the picture of the gifted but dissipated royal Governor, it is a relief to glance at the character given by Jefferson of the equally gifted but pure and virtuous George Wythe. We can not refrain·from giving the conclusion of his sketch of Wythe, completing, as it does, the picture of the "*partie quarrée*" which so often met at the Governor's hospitable board:

No man ever left behind him a character more venerated than George Wythe. His virtue was of the purest tint; his integrity inflexible, and his justice exact; of warm patriotism, and, devoted as he was to liberty, and the natural and equal rights of man, he might truly be called the Cato of his country, without the avarice of the Roman; for a more disinterested man never lived. Temperance and regularity in all his habits gave him general good health, and his unaffected modesty and suavity of manners endeared him to every one. He was of easy elocution; his language chaste, methodical in the arrangement of his matter, learned and logical in the use of it, and of great urbanity in debate; not quick of apprehension, but, with a little time, profound in penetration and sound in conclusion. In his philosophy he was firm; and neither troubling, nor, perhaps, trusting, any one with his religious creed, he left the world to the conclusion that that religion must be good which could produce a life of such exemplary virtue. His stature was of the middle size, well formed and proportioned, and the features of his face were manly, comely, and engaging. Such was George Wythe, the honor of his own and the model of future times.

CHAPTER II.

Intense Application as a Student.—Habits of Study kept up during his Vaca-
tions.—First Preparations made for Building at Monticello.—Letters to his
College Friend, John Page.—Anecdote of Benjamin Harrison.—Jefferson's
Devotion to his eldest Sister.—He witnesses the Debate on the Stamp
Act.—First Meeting with Patrick Henry.—His Opinion of him.—His su-
perior Education.—Always a Student.—Wide Range of Information.—
Anecdote.—Death of his eldest Sister.—His Grief.—Buries himself in his
Books.—Finishes his Course of Law Studies.—Begins to practise.—Col-
lection of Vocabularies of Indian Languages.—House at Shadwell burnt.
—Loss of his Library.—Marriage.—Anecdote of his Courtship.—Wife's
Beauty.—Bright Prospects.—Friendship for Dabney Carr.—His Talents.
—His Death.—Jefferson buries him at Monticello.—His Epitaph.

GREAT as were the charms and delights of the society
into which Jefferson was thrown in Williamsburg, they had
not the power to draw him off from his studies. On the
contrary, he seemed to find from his intercourse with such
men as Wythe and Small, fresh incentives to diligence in his
literary pursuits; and these, together with his natural taste
for study, made his application to it so intense, that had he
possessed a less vigorous and robust constitution, his health
must have given way. He studied fifteen hours a day.
During the most closely occupied days of his college life it
was his habit to study until two o'clock at night, and rise at
dawn; the day he spent in close application—the only recreation being a run at twilight to a certain stone which stood
at a point a mile beyond the limits of the town. His habits
of study were kept up during his vacations, which were
spent at Shadwell; and though he did not cut himself off
from the pleasures of social intercourse with his friends and
family, yet he still devoted nearly three-fourths of his time
to his books. He rose in the morning as soon as the hands
of a clock placed on the mantle-piece in his chamber could
be distinguished in the gray light of early dawn. After

sunset he crossed the Rivanna in a little canoe, which was kept exclusively for his own use, and walked up to the summit of his loved Monticello, where he was having the apex of the mountain levelled down, preparatory to building.

The following extracts from letters written to his friends while he was a college-boy, give a fair picture of the sprightliness of his nature and his enjoyment of society.

To John Page—a friend to whom he was devotedly attached all through life—he writes, Dec. 25, 1762:

You can not conceive the satisfaction it would give me to have a letter from you. Write me very circumstantially every thing which happened at the wedding. Was she* there? because if she was, I ought to have been at the devil for not being there too. If there is any news stirring in town or country, such as deaths, courtships, or marriages, in the circle of my acquaintance, let me know it. Remember me affectionately to all the young ladies of my acquaintance, particularly the Miss Burwells, and Miss Potters; and tell them that though that heavy earthly part of me, my body, be absent, the better half of me, my soul, is ever with them, and that my best wishes shall ever attend them. Tell Miss Alice Corbin that I verily believe the rats knew I was to win a pair of garters from her, or they never would have been so cruel as to carry mine away. This very consideration makes me so sure of the bet, that I shall ask every body I see from that part of the world, what pretty gentleman is making his addresses to her. I would fain ask the favor of Miss Becca Burwell to give me another watch-paper of her own cutting, which I should esteem much more, though it were a plain round one, than the nicest in the world cut by other hands; however, I am afraid she would think this presumption, after my suffering the other to get spoiled.

A few weeks later, he writes to Page, from Shadwell:

To tell you the plain truth, I have not a syllable to write to you about. For I do not conceive that any thing can happen in my world which you would give a curse to know,

---

* His lady-love, doubtless—Rebecca Burwell.

or I either. All things here appear to me to trudge on in one and the same round: we rise in the morning that we may eat breakfast, dinner, and supper; and go to bed again that we may get up the next morning and do the same; so that you never saw two peas more alike than our yesterday and to-day. Under these circumstances, what would you have me say? Would you that I should write nothing but truth? I tell you, I know nothing that is true. Or would you rather that I should write you a pack of lies? Why, unless they are more ingenious than I am able to invent, they would furnish you with little amusement. What can I do, then? Nothing but ask you the news in your world. How have you done since I saw you? How did Nancy look at you when you danced with her at Southall's? Have you any glimmering of hope? How does R. B. do? Had I better stay here and do nothing, or go down and do less? or, in other words, had I better stay here while I am here, or go down that I may have the pleasure of sailing up the river again in a full-rigged flat? Inclination tells me to go, receive my sentence, and be no longer in suspense; but reason says, If you go, and your attempt proves unsuccessful, you will be ten times more wretched than ever...... I have some thoughts of going to Petersburg if the actors go there in May. If I do, I do not know but I may keep on to Williamsburg, as the birth-night will be near. I hear that Ben Harrison* has been to Wilton: let me know his success.

In his literary pursuits and plans for the future, Jefferson found a most congenial and sympathizing companion, as well

---

* This Ben Harrison afterwards married Miss Randolph, of Wilton, and was a signer of the Declaration of Independence. He was fond of the good things of this life, and was a high liver. Mr. Madison used to tell, with great glee, the following good story about him: While a member of the first Congress, which met in Philadelphia, he was on one occasion joined by a friend as he left the congressional hall. Wishing to ask his friend to join him in a bumper, he took him to a certain place where supplies were furnished to the members of Congress, and called for two glasses of brandy-and-water. The man in charge replied that liquors were not included in the supplies furnished to Congressmen.

"Why," asked Harrison, "what is it, then, that I see the New England members come here and drink?"

"Molasses and water, which they have charged as *stationery*," was the reply.

"Very well," said Harrison, "give me the brandy-and-water, and charge it as *fuel*."

C

as a loving friend, in his highly-gifted young sister, Jane Jefferson. Three years his senior, and a woman of extraordinary vigor of mind, we can well imagine with what pride and pleasure she must have watched the early development and growth of her young brother's genius and learning. When five years old, he had read all the books contained in his father's little library, and we have already found him sought out by the royal Governor, and chosen as one of his favorite companions, when but a college-boy. Like himself, his sister was devoted to music, and they spent many hours together cultivating their taste and talent for it. Both were particularly fond of sacred music, and she often gratified her young brother by singing for him hymns.

We have seen, from his letters to his friend Page, that, while a student in Williamsburg, Jefferson fell in love with Miss Rebecca Burwell—one of the beauties of her day. He was indulging fond dreams of success in winning the young lady's heart and hand, when his courtship was suddenly cut short by her, to him, unexpected marriage to another.

In the following year, 1765, there took place in the House of Burgesses the great debate on the Stamp Act, in which Patrick Henry electrified his hearers by his bold and sublime flights of oratory. In the lobby of the House was seen the tall, thin figure of Jefferson, bending eagerly forward to witness the stirring scene—his face paled from the effects of hard study, and his eyes flashing with the fire of latent genius, and all the enthusiasm of youthful and devoted patriotism. In allusion to this scene, he writes in his Memoir:

When the famous resolutions of 1765 against the Stamp Act were proposed, I was yet a student of law in Williamsburg. I attended the debate, however, at the door of the lobby of the House of Burgesses, and heard the splendid display of Mr. Henry's talents as a popular orator. They were indeed great; such as I have never heard from any other man. He appeared to me to speak as Homer wrote.

It was when on his way to Williamsburg to enter William and Mary College, that Jefferson first met Henry. They spent a fortnight together on that occasion, at the house of Mr. Dandridge, in Hanover, and there began the acquaintance and friendship between them which lasted through life. While not considering Henry a man of education or a well-read lawyer, Jefferson often spoke with enthusiasm to his friends and family of the wonders and beauties of his eloquence, and also of his great influence and signal services in bringing about unanimity among the parties which were found in the colony at the commencement of the troubles with the mother-country. He frequently expressed admiration for his intrepid spirit and inflexible courage. Two years before his death we find him speaking of Henry thus:

Wirt says he read Plutarch's Lives once a year. I don't believe he ever read two volumes of them. On his visits to court, he used always to put up with me. On one occasion of the breaking up in November, to meet again in the spring, as he was departing in the morning, he looked among my books, and observed, " Mr. Jefferson, I will take two volumes of Hume's Essays, and try to read them this winter." On his return, he brought them, saying he had not been able to get half way into one of them.

His great delight was to put on his hunting-shirt, collect a parcel of overseers and such-like people, and spend weeks together hunting in the " piny woods," camping at night and cracking jokes round a light-wood fire.

It was to him that we were indebted for the unanimity that prevailed among us. He would address the assemblages of the people at which he was present in such strains of native eloquence as Homer wrote in. I never heard any thing that deserved to be called by the same name with what flowed from him; and where he got that torrent of language from is inconceivable. I have frequently shut my eyes while he spoke, and, when he was done, asked myself what he had said, without being able to recollect a word of it. He was no logician. He was truly a great man, however—one of enlarged views.

Mr. Jefferson furnished anecdotes, facts, and documents for Wirt's Life of Henry, and Mr. Wirt submitted his manuscript to him for criticism and review, which he gave, and also suggested alterations that were made. We find, from his letters to Mr. Wirt, that when the latter flagged and hesitated as to the completion and publication of his work, it was Jefferson who urged him on. In writing of Henry's supposed inattention to ancient charters, we find him expressing himself thus: "He drew all natural rights from a purer source—the feelings of his own breast."*

In connection with this subject, we can not refrain from quoting from Wirt the following fine description of Henry in the great debate on the Stamp Act:

It was in the midst of this magnificent debate, while he (Henry) was descanting on the tyranny of the obnoxious act, that he exclaimed, in a voice of thunder, and with the look of a god, " Cæsar had his Brutus, Charles the First his Cromwell, and George the Third—" ("Treason !" cried the Speaker. "Treason! treason!" echoed from every part of the House. It was one of those trying moments which are so decisive of character. Henry faltered not an instant ; but rising to a loftier altitude, and fixing on the Speaker an eye of the most determined fire, he finished his sentence with the firmest emphasis)—" may profit by their example. If this be treason, make the most of it."†

When we think of the wonderful powers of this great man, whose heaven-born eloquence so stirred the hearts of men, how touching the meekness with which, at the close of an eventful and honorable career, he thus writes of himself: " Without any classical education, without patrimony, without what is called the influence of family connection, and without solicitation, I have attained the highest offices of my country. I have often contemplated it as a rare and extraordinary instance, and pathetically exclaimed, ' Not unto me, not unto me, O Lord, but unto thy name be the praise !' "‡

---

* Kennedy's "Life of Wirt," vol. i., p. 367.
† Wirt's Life of Henry.   ‡ Ibid.

Jefferson continued to prosecute his studies at William and Mary, and we have in the following incident a pleasing proof of his generosity:

While at college, he was one year quite extravagant in his dress, and in his outlay in horses. At the end of the year he sent his account to his guardian; and thinking that he had spent more of the income from his father's estate than was his share, he proposed that the amount of his expenses should be deducted from his portion of the property. His guardian, however, replied good-naturedly, " No, no ; if you have sowed your wild oats in this manner, Tom, the estate can well afford to pay your expenses."

When Jefferson left college, he had laid the broad and solid foundations of that fine education which in learning placed him head and shoulders above his contemporaries. A fine mathematician, he was also a finished Greek, Latin, French, Spanish, and Italian scholar. He carried with him to Congress in the year 1775 a reputation for great literary acquirements. John Adams, in his diary for that year, thus speaks of him: "Duane says that Jefferson is the greatest rubber-off of dust that he has met with ; that he has learned French, Italian, and Spanish, and wants to learn German."

His school and college education was considered by him as only the vestibule to that palace of learning which is reached by "no royal road." He once told a grandson that from the time when, as a boy, he had turned off wearied from play and first found pleasure in books, he had never sat down in idleness. And when we consider the vast fund of learning and wide range of information possessed by him, and which in his advanced years won for him the appellation of a "walking encyclopædia," we can well understand how this must have been the case. His thirst for knowledge was insatiable, and he seized eagerly all means of obtaining it. It was his habit, in his intercourse with all classes of men—the mechanic as well as the man of science—to turn the conversation upon that subject with which the man was best acquainted, whether it was the construction of a wheel or the anatomy of an extinct species of animals; and after having drawn from him all the information which he possessed, on returning home or retiring to his private apartments, it was all set down by him in writing—thus arranging it methodically and fixing it in his mind.

An anecdote which has been often told of him will give the reader an idea of the varied extent of his knowledge. On one occasion, while travelling, he stopped at a country inn. A stranger, who did not know who he was, entered into conversation with this plainly-dressed and unassuming traveller. He introduced one subject after another into the conversation, and found him perfectly acquainted with each. Filled with wonder, he seized the first opportunity to inquire of the landlord who his guest was, saying that, when he spoke of the law, he thought he was a lawyer; then turning the conversation on medicine, felt sure he was a physician; but having touched on theology, he became convinced that he was a clergyman. "Oh," replied the landlord, "why I thought you knew the Squire." The stranger was then astonished to hear that the traveller whom he had found so affable and simple in his manners was Jefferson.

The family circle at Shadwell consisted of six sisters, two brothers, and their mother. Of the sisters, two married early, and left the home of their youth—Mary as the wife of Thomas Bolling, and Martha as that of the generous and highly-gifted young Dabney Carr, the brilliant promise of whose youth was so soon to be cut short by his untimely death.

In the fall of the year 1765, the whole family was thrown into mourning, and the deepest distress, by the death of Jane Jefferson—so long the pride and ornament of her house. She died in the twenty-eighth year of her age. The eldest of her family, and a woman who, from the noble qualities of her head and heart, had ever commanded their love and admiration, her death was a great blow to them all, but was felt by none so keenly as by Jefferson himself. The loss of such a sister to such a brother was irreparable; his grief for her was deep and constant; and there are, perhaps, few incidents in the domestic details of history more beautiful than his devotion to her during her life, and the tenderness of the love with which he cherished her memory to the last days of his long and eventful career. He frequently spoke of her to his grandchildren, and even in his extreme old age said that often in church some sacred air which her sweet voice had made familiar to him in youth recalled to him sweet visions of this sister whom he had loved so well and buried so young.

Among his manuscripts we find the following touching epitaph which he wrote for her:

> "Ah, Joanna, puellarum optima,
> Ah, ævi virentis flore prærepta,
> Sit tibi terra lævis;
> Longe, longeque valeto!"

After the death of his sister Jane, Jefferson had no congenial intellectual companion left in the family at Shadwell; his other sisters being all much younger than himself, except one, who was rather deficient in intellect. It is curious to remark the unequal distribution of talent in this family— each gifted member seeming to have been made so at the expense of one of the others.

In the severe affliction caused by the death of his sister, Jefferson sought consolation in renewed devotion to his books. After a five years' course of law studies, he was, as we have seen from his Memoir, introduced to its practice, at the bar of the General Court of Virginia, in the year 1767, by his "beloved friend and mentor," George Wythe. Of the extent of his practice during the eight years that it lasted, we have ample proof in his account-books. These show that during that time, in the General Court alone, he was engaged in nine hundred and forty-eight cases, and that he was employed as counsel by the first men in the colonies, and even in the mother-country.

An idea of the impression made by him as an advocate in the court-room is given in the following anecdote, which we have from his eldest grandson, Mr. Jefferson Randolph. Anxious to learn how his grandfather had stood as a pleader, Mr. Randolph once asked an old man of good sense who in his youth had often heard Jefferson deliver arguments in court, how he ranked as a speaker, " Well," said the old gentleman, in reply, " it is hard to tell, because he always took the right side." Few speakers, we imagine, would desire a greater compliment than that which the old man unconsciously paid in his reply.

The works which Jefferson has left behind him as his share in the revision of the laws of the State, place his erudition as a lawyer beyond question, while to no man does Virginia owe more for the preservation of her ancient records than to him. In this last work he was indefatigable. The manuscripts and materials for the early history of the State had been partially destroyed and scattered by the burning of State buildings and the ravages of war. These Jefferson, as far as it was possible, collected and restored, and it is to him that we owe their preservation at the present day.

While in the different public offices which he held during his life, Jefferson availed himself of every opportunity to get information concerning the language of the Indians of North America, and to this end he made a collection of the vocabularies of all the Indian languages, intending, in the leisure of his retirement from public life, to analyze them, and see if he could trace in them any likeness to other languages. When he left Washington, after vacating the presidential chair, these valuable papers were packed in a trunk and sent, with the rest of his baggage, around by Richmond, whence they were to be sent up the James and Rivanna Rivers to Monticello. Two negro boatmen who had charge of them, and who, in the simplicity of their ignorance, took it for granted that the ex-President was returning from office with untold wealth, being deceived by the weight of the trunk, broke into it, thinking that it contained gold. On discovering their mistake, the papers were scattered to the wind; and

Know all men by these presents that we, Thomas Jefferson and Francis Eppes are held and firmly bound to our sovereign lord the king his heirs and successors in the sum of fifty pounds current money of Virginia, to the paiment of which well and truly to be made we bind ourselves jointly and severally, our joint and several heirs executors and administrators in witness whereof we have hereto set our hands and seals this twenty third day of December in the year of our lord one thousand seven hundred and seventy one.

The condition of the above obligation is such that if there be no lawful cause to obstruct a marriage intended to be had and solemnized between the above bound Thomas Jefferson and Martha Skelton of the county of Charles city, widow, for which a licence is desired, then this obligation is to be null and void; otherwise to remain in full force.

thus were lost literary treasures which might have been a rich feast to many a philologist.

In the year 1770 the house at Shadwell was destroyed by fire, and Jefferson then moved to Monticello, where his preparations for a residence were sufficiently advanced to enable him to make it his permanent abode. He was from home when the fire took place at Shadwell, and the first inquiry he made of the negro who carried him the news was after his books. "Oh, my young master," he replied, carelessly, "they were all burnt; but, ah! we saved your fiddle."

In 1772 Jefferson married Martha Skelton, the widow of Bathurst Skelton, and the daughter of John Wayles, of whom he speaks thus in his Memoir

Mr. Wayles was a lawyer of much practice, to which he was introduced more by his industry, punctuality, and practical readiness, than by eminence in the science of his profession. He was a most agreeable companion, full of pleasantry and humor, and welcomed in every society. He acquired a handsome fortune, and died in May, 1773, leaving three daughters. The portion which came on that event to Mrs. Jefferson, after the debts were paid, which were very considerable, was about equal to my own patrimony, and consequently doubled the ease of our circumstances.

The marriage took place at "The Forest," in Charles City County. The bride having been left a widow when very young, was only twenty-three when she married a second time.* She is described as having been very beautiful. A little above middle height, with a lithe and exquisitely formed figure, she was a model of graceful and queenlike carriage. Nature, so lavish with her charms for her, to great personal attractions, added a mind of no ordinary calibre. She was well educated for her day, and a constant reader; she inher-

---

* The license-bond for the marriage, demanded by the laws of Virginia, of which a fac-simile is given on the opposite page, written by Jefferson's own hand, is signed by him and by Francis Eppes, whose son afterwards married Jefferson's daughter. It will be noticed that the word "spinster" is erased, and "widow" inserted in another hand-writing.

ited from her father his method and industry, as the accounts, kept in her clear handwriting, and still in the hands of her descendants, testify. Her well-cultivated talent for music served to enhance her charms not a little in the eyes of such a musical devotee as Jefferson.

So young and so beautiful, she was already surrounded by suitors when Jefferson entered the lists and bore off the prize. A pleasant anecdote about two of his rivals has been preserved in the tradition of his family. While laboring under the impression that the lady's mind was still undecided as to which of her suitors should be the accepted lover, they met accidentally in the hall of her father's house. They were on the eve of entering the drawing-room, when the sound of music caught their ear; the accompanying voices of Jefferson and his lady-love were soon recognized, and the two disconcerted lovers, after exchanging a glance, picked up their hats and left.

The New-year and wedding festivities being over, the happy bridal couple left for Monticello. Their adventures on this journey of more than a hundred miles, made in the dead of the winter, and their arrival at Monticello, were, years afterwards, related as follows, by their eldest daughter, Mrs. Randolph,* who heard the tale from her father's lips:

They left The Forest after a fall of snow, light then, but increasing in depth as they advanced up the country. They were finally obliged to quit the carriage and proceed on horseback. Having stopped for a short time at Blenheim, where an overseer only resided, they left it at sunset to pursue their way through a mountain track rather than a road, in which the snow lay from eighteen inches to two feet deep, having eight miles to go before reaching Monticello. They arrived late at night, the fires all out and the servants retired to their own houses for the night. The horrible drear-

* The manuscript from which I take this account, and from which I shall quote frequently in the following pages, was written by Mrs. Randolph at the request of Mr. Tucker, who desired to have her written reminiscences of her father when he wrote his life.

iness of such a house at the end of such a journey I have often heard both relate.

Too happy in each other's love, however, to be long troubled by the "dreariness" of a cold and dark house, and having found a bottle of wine "on a shelf behind some books," the young couple refreshed themselves with its contents, and startled the silence of the night with song and merry laughter.

Possessing a fine estate and being blessed with a beautiful and accomplished wife, Jefferson seemed fairly launched upon the great ocean of life with every prospect of a prosperous and happy voyage. We find from his account-books that his income was a handsome one for that day, being three thousand dollars from his practice and two thousand from his farms. This, as we have seen, was increased by the receipt of his wife's fortune at her father's death.

Of the many friends by whom he was surrounded in his college days Dabney Carr was his favorite; his friendship for him was strengthened by the ties of family connection, on his becoming his brother-in-law as the husband of his sister Martha. As boys, they had loved each other; and when studying together it was their habit to go with their books to the well-wooded sides of Monticello, and there pursue their studies beneath the shade of a favorite oak. So much attached did the two friends become to this tree, that it became the subject of a mutual promise, that the one who survived should see that the body of the other was buried at its foot. When young Carr's untimely death occurred Jefferson was away from home, and on his return he found that he had been buried at Shadwell. Being mindful of his promise, he had the body disinterred, and removing it, placed it beneath that tree whose branches now bend over such illustrious dead—for this was the origin of the grave-yard at Monticello.

It is not only as Jefferson's friend that Dabney Carr lives in history. The brilliancy of the reputation which he won in his short career, has placed his name among the men who stood first for talent and patriotism in the early days of the Revolution. Jefferson himself, in describing his first appearance in the Virginia House of Burgesses, pays a warm and handsome tribute to his friend. He says:

I well remember the pleasure expressed in the countenance and conversation of the members generally on this début of Mr. Carr, and the hopes they conceived as well from the talents as the patriotism it manifested........ His character was of a high order. A spotless integrity, sound judgment, handsome imagination, enriched by education and reading, quick and clear in his conceptions, of correct and ready elocution, impressing every hearer with the sincerity of the heart from which it flowed. His firmness was inflexible in whatever he thought was right; but when no moral principle stood in the way, never had man more of the milk of human kindness, of indulgence, of softness, of pleasantry of conversation and conduct. The number of his friends and the warmth of their affection, were proofs of his worth, and of their estimate of it.

We have again from Jefferson's pen a charming picture of the domestic character of Carr, in a letter to his friend John Page, written in 1770:

He (Carr) speaks, thinks, and dreams of nothing but his young son. This friend of ours, Page, in a very small house, with a table, half a dozen chairs, and one or two servants, is the happiest man in the universe. Every incident in life he so takes as to render it a source of pleasure. With as much benevolence as the heart of man will hold, but with an utter neglect of the costly apparatus of life, he exhibits to the world a new phenomenon in life—the Samian sage in the tub of the cynic.

The death of this highly-gifted young Virginian, whose early life was so full of promise, took place on the 16th of May, 1773, in the thirtieth year of his age. His wife, a woman of vigorous understanding and earnest warmth of heart, was passionately devoted to him, and his death fell like a blight on her young life. She found in her brother a loving protector for herself and a fatherly affection and guidance for her six children—three sons and three daughters—who were received into his family as his adopted children. Among Jefferson's papers there was found, after his death, the following, written on a sheet of note-paper:

INSCRIPTION ON MY FRIEND D. CARR'S TOMB.

Lamented shade, whom every gift of heaven
Profusely blest; a temper winning mild;
Nor pity softer, nor was truth more bright.
Constant in doing well, he neither sought
Nor shunned applause. No bashful merit sighed
Near him neglected: sympathizing he
Wiped off the tear from Sorrow's clouded eye
With kindly hand, and taught her heart to smile.

MALLET'S *Excursion.*

Send for a plate of copper to be nailed on the tree at the foot of his grave, with this inscription:

Still shall thy grave with rising flowers be dressed
And the green turf lie lightly on thy breast;
There shall the morn her earliest tears bestow,
There the first roses of the year shall blow,
While angels with their silver wings o'ershade
The ground now sacred by thy reliques made.

On the upper part of the stone inscribe as follows:

Here lie the remains of
DABNEY CARR,
Son of John and Jane Carr, of Louisa County,
Who was born ———, 1744.
Intermarried with Martha Jefferson, daughter of Peter
and Jane Jefferson, 1765;
And died at Charlottesville, May 16, 1773,
Leaving six small children.
To his Virtue, Good Sense, Learning, and Friendship
this stone is dedicated by Thomas Jefferson, who, of all men living,
loved him most.

CHAPTER III.

Happy Life at Monticello.—Jefferson's fine Horsemanship.—Birth of his oldest Child.—Goes to Congress.—Death of his Mother.—Kindness to British Prisoners.—Their Gratitude.—His Devotion to Music.—Letter to General De Riedesel.—Is made Governor of Virginia.—Tarleton pursues Lafayette.—Reaches Charlottesville.—The British at Monticello.—Cornwallis's Destruction of Property at Elk Hill.—Jefferson retires at the End of
his Second Term as Governor.—Mrs. Jefferson's delicate Health.—Jefferson meets with an Accident.—Writes his Notes on Virginia.—The Marquis De Chastellux visits Monticello.—His Description of it.—Letter of
Congratulation from Jefferson to Washington.—Mrs. Jefferson's Illness
and Death.—Her Daughter's Description of the Scene.—Jefferson's Grief.

FOLLOWING the course which I have laid down for myself,
I shall give but a passing notice of the political events of
Jefferson's life, and only dwell on such incidents as may
throw out in bold relief the beauties and charms of his domestic character. Except when called from home by duties
imposed upon him by his country, the even tenor of his happy life at Monticello remained unbroken. He prosecuted his
studies with that same ardent thirst for knowledge which he
had evinced when a young student in Williamsburg, master-
ing every subject that he took up.

Much time and expense were devoted by him to orna-
menting and improving his house and grounds. A great
lover of nature, he found his favorite recreations in out-of-
door enjoyments, and it was his habit to the day of his
death, no matter what his occupation, nor what office he
held, to spend the hours between one and three in the afternoon on horseback. Noted for his bold and graceful horsemanship, he kept as riding-horses only those of the best
blood of the old Virginia stock. In the days of his youth
he was very exacting of his groom in having his horses always beautifully kept; and it is said that it was his habit,
when his riding-horse was brought up for him to mount, to

brush his white cambric handkerchief across the animal's shoulders and send it back to the stable if any dust was left on the handkerchief.

The garden-book lying before me shows the interest which he took in all gardening and farming operations. This book, in which he began to make entries as early as the year 1766, and which he continued to keep all through life, except when from home, has every thing jotted down in it, from the date of the earliest peach-blossom to the day when his wheat was ready for the sickle. His personal, household, and farm accounts were kept with the precision of the most rigid accountant, and he was a rare instance of a man of enlarged views and wide range of thought, being fond of details. The price of his horses, the fee paid to a ferryman, his little gifts to servants, his charities—whether great or small—from the penny dropped into the church-box to the handsome donation given for the erection of a church—all found a place in his account-book.

In 1772 his eldest child, Martha, was born; his second daughter, Jane Randolph, died in the fall of 1775, when eighteen months old. He was most unfortunate in his children—out of six that he had, only two, Martha and Mary, surviving the period of infancy.

In the year 1775 Jefferson went to Philadelphia as a member of the first Congress.* In the year 1776 he made the following entry in his little pocket account-book: "*March* 31. My mother died about eight o'clock this morning, in the

---

* A gentleman who had been a frequent visitor at Monticello during Mr. Jefferson's life gave Mr. Randall (Jefferson's biographer) the following amusing incident concerning this venerated body and Declaration of Independence: "While the question of Independence was before Congress, it had its meetings near a livery-stable. The members wore short breeches and silk stockings, and, with handkerchief in hand, they were diligently employed in lashing the flies from their legs. So very vexatious was this annoyance, and to so great an impatience did it arouse the sufferers, that it hastened, if it did not aid, in inducing them to promptly affix their signatures to the great document which gave birth to an empire republic. "This anecdote I had from Mr. Jefferson at Monticello, who seemed to enjoy it very much, as well as to give great credit to the influence of the flies. He told it with much glee, and seemed to retain a vivid recollection of an attack, from which the only relief was signing the paper and flying from the scene."

D

57th year of her age." Thus she did not live to see the great day with whose glory her son's name is indissolubly connected.*

The British prisoners who were surrendered by Burgoyne at the battle of Saratoga were sent to Virginia and quartered in Albemarle, a few miles from Monticello. They had not, however, been settled there many months, before the Governor (Patrick Henry) was urged to have them moved to some other part of the country, on the plea that the provisions consumed by them were more necessary for our own forces. The Governor and Council were on the eve of issuing the order for their removal, when an earnest entreaty addressed to them by Jefferson put a stop to all proceedings on the subject. In this address and petition he says, in speaking of the prisoners,

Their health is also of importance. I would not endeavor to show that their lives are valuable to us, because it would suppose a possibility that humanity was kicked out of doors in America, and interest only attended to.........
But is an enemy so execrable, that, though in captivity, his wishes and comforts are to be disregarded and even crossed? I think not. It is for the benefit of mankind to mitigate the horrors of war as much as possible. The practice, therefore, of modern nations, of treating captive enemies with politeness and generosity, is not only delightful in contemplation, but really interesting to all the world—friends, foes, and neutrals.

This successful effort in their behalf called forth the most earnest expressions of gratitude from the British and German officers among the prisoners. The Baron De Riedesel, their commander, was comfortably fixed in a house not far from Monticello, and he and the baroness received every attention from Jefferson. Indeed, these attentions were ex-

---

* On the opposite page is given a fac-simile of a portion of the original draft of the Declaration of Independence; the greater portion of this paragraph was omitted in the document as finally adopted. The interlineations in this portion are in the handwriting of John Adams.

Nor have we been wanting in attentions to our British brethren: we have
warned them from time to time of attempts by their legislature to extend a juris-
-diction over [these our states]. we have reminded them of the circumstances of
our emigration & settlement here, [no one of which could warrant so strange a
pretension: that these were effected at the expence of our own blood & treasure,
unassisted by the wealth or the strength of Great Britain: that in constituting
indeed our several forms of government, we had adopted one common king, thereby
laying a foundation for perpetual league & amity with them: but that submission to their
parliament was no part of our constitution, nor ever in idea, if history may be
credited: and we appealed to their native justice & magnanimity [as well as to] the ties
of our common kindred to disavow these usurpations which [were likely to] interrupt
our correspondence. they too have been deaf to the voice of justice &
of consanguinity. [& when occasions have been given them, by the regular course of

tended to young officers of the lowest rank. The hospitali-
ties of her house were gracefully and cordially tendered to
these unfortunate strangers by Mrs. Jefferson, and her husband threw open to them his library, whence they got books
to while away the tedium of their captivity. The baroness,
a warm-hearted, intelligent woman, from her immense stature, and her habit of riding on horseback *en cavalier*, was
long remembered as a kind of wonder by the good and sim-
ple-hearted people of Albermarle. The intercourse between
her household and that at Monticello was that of neighbors.

When Phillips, a British officer whom Jefferson characterized as "the proudest man of the proudest nation on earth,"
wrote his thanks to him for his generous kindness, we find
Jefferson replying as follows:

The great cause which divides our countries is not to be
decided by individual animosities. The harmony of private
societies can not weaken national efforts. To contribute by
neighborly intercourse and attention to make others happy,
is the shortest and surest way of being happy ourselves. As
these sentiments seem to have directed your conduct, we
should be as unwise as illiberal, were we not to preserve the
same temper of mind.

He also had some pleasant intercourse and correspondence
with young De Ungar, an accomplished officer, who seems to
have had many literary and scientific tastes congenial with
Jefferson's. He thus winds up a letter to this young officer:

When the course of human events shall have removed you
to distant scenes of action, where laurels not moistened with
the blood of my country may be gathered, I shall urge my
sincere prayers for your obtaining every honor and prefer-
ment which may gladden the heart of a soldier. On the
other hand, should your fondness for philosophy resume its
merited ascendency, is it impossible to hope that this unex-
plored country may tempt your residence, by holding out
materials wherewith to build a fame, founded on the happiness and not the calamities of human nature? Be this as it

may—a philosopher or a soldier—I wish you personally many felicities.

The following extract from a letter, written in 1778 to a friend in Europe, shows Jefferson's extreme fondness of music:

If there is a gratification which I envy any people in this world, it is, to your country, its music. This is the favorite passion of my soul, and fortune has cast my lot in a country where it is in a state of deplorable barbarism. From the line of life in which we conjecture you to be, I have for some time lost the hope of seeing you here. Should the event prove so, I shall ask your assistance in procuring a substitute, who may be a proficient in singing, etc., on the harpsichord. I should be contented to receive such an one two or three years hence, when it is hoped he may come more safely, and find here a greater plenty of those useful things which commerce alone can furnish. The bounds of an American fortune will not admit the indulgence of a domestic band of musicians, yet I have thought that a passion for music might be reconciled with that economy which we are obliged to observe.

From his correspondence for the year 1780 I take the following pleasantly written letter to General De Riedesel. I have elsewhere alluded to the pleasant intercourse between his family and Jefferson's, when he was a prisoner on parole in the neighborhood of Monticello.

To General De Riedesel.

Richmond, May 3d, 1780.

Sir—Your several favors of December 4th, February 10th, and March 30th, are come duly to hand. I sincerely condole with Madame De Riedesel on the birth of a *daughter*,* but receive great pleasure from the information of her recovery, as every circumstance of felicity to her, yourself or family, is interesting to us. The little attentions you are pleased to magnify so much, never deserved a mention or thought. My mortification was, that the peculiar situation in which

---

* Jefferson himself had no son.

we were, put it out of our power to render your stay here more comfortable. I am sorry to learn that the negotiations for the exchange of prisoners have proved abortive, as well from a desire to see the necessary distresses of war alleviated in every possible instance, as I am sensible how far yourself and family are interested in it. Against this, however, is to be weighed the possibility that we may again have a pleasure we should otherwise, perhaps, never have had—that of seeing you again. Be this as it may, opposed as we happen to be in our sentiments of duty and honor, and anxious for contrary events, I shall, nevertheless, sincerely rejoice in every circumstance of happiness or safety which may attend you personally; and when a termination of the present contest shall put it into my power to declare to you more unreservedly how sincere are the sentiments of esteem and respect (wherein Mrs. Jefferson joins me) which I entertain for Madame De Riedesel and yourself, and with which I am, sir, your most obedient and most humble servant,

TH. JEFFERSON.

Jefferson was made Governor of Virginia in 1779; and when Tarleton, in 1781, reached Charlottesville, after his famous pursuit of "the boy" Lafayette, who slipped through his fingers, it was expected that Monticello, as the residence of the Governor, would be pillaged. The conduct of the British was far different.

Jefferson, on being informed that the enemy were close at hand, put Mrs. Jefferson and her children in a carriage and sent them to a neighbor's, where they would be out of harm's way. Having sent his horse to the blacksmith's to be shod, he ordered him to be taken to a certain point of the road between Monticello and Carter's Mountain, while he remained quietly at home collecting his most valuable papers. Two hours after the departure of his family, a gentleman rode up and told him that the British were on the mountain. He then left the house and walked over to Carter's Mountain, whence he had a full view of Charlottesville. He viewed the town through a small telescope which he took with him, and seeing no "red-coats," thought their coming was a false alarm, and turned with the intention of going back to the house. He had not gone far, however, when he found his light sword-cane had dropped from its sheath. He retraced his steps, found the weapon, and, on turning around again, saw that Charlottesville was "alive with British." He then mounted his horse and followed his family.

Captain McLeod commanded the party of British soldiers who were sent to Monticello to seize the Governor, and he went with "strict orders from Tarleton to allow nothing in the house to be injured." When he found that the bird had flown, he called for a servant of the house, asked which were Mr. Jefferson's private apartments, and, being shown the door which led to them, he turned the key in the lock and ordered that every thing in the house should be untouched.

Unprepared for this generous conduct on the part of the British, two faithful slaves, Martin and Cæsar, were busy concealing their master's plate under a floor, a few feet from the ground, when the red-coats made their appearance on the lawn at Monticello. A plank had been removed, and Cæsar, having slipped down through the cavity, stood below to receive the plate as it was handed down by Martin. The last piece had been handed down when the soldiers came in sight. There was not a moment to lose, and Martin, thinking only of his master's plate and not of Cæsar's comfort, clapped the plank down on top of the poor fellow, and there he remained in the dark and without food for three days and three nights. Martin himself on this occasion gave a much more striking proof of fidelity. A brutal soldier placed a pistol to his breast and threatened to fire unless he disclosed his master's retreat. "Fire away then!" was the slave's ready and defiant reply.

The handsome conduct of the British at Monticello afforded a striking contrast to that of their forces under the command of Cornwallis, who visited Elk Hill—Jefferson's James River estate. The commanding general, Cornwallis, had his head-quarters for ten days at the house on the estate. This house, though not often occupied by Jefferson and his family, was furnished, and contained a library. The following is the owner's account of the manner in which the estate was laid waste:

I had time to remove most of the effects out of the house. He destroyed all my growing crops of corn and tobacco; he burned all my barns containing the same articles of the last year, having first taken what corn he wanted; he used, as was to be expected, all my stock of cattle, sheep, and hogs, for the sustenance of his army, and carried off all the horses capable of service; of those too young for service he cut the throats; and he burned all the fences on the plantation, so as to render it an absolute waste. He carried off, also, about thirty slaves. Had this been to give them freedom he would have done right, but it was to consign them to inevitable death from the small-pox and putrid fever then raging in his camp. This I knew afterwards to be the fate of twenty-seven of them. I never had news of the remaining three, but suppose they shared the same fate. When I say that Lord Cornwallis did all this, I do not mean that he carried about the torch in his own hands, but that it was all done under his eye—the situation of the house in which he was commanding a view of every part of the plantation, so that he must have seen every fire.*

Again he writes:

History will never relate the horrors committed by the British army in the Southern States of America. They raged in Virginia six months only, from the middle of April to the middle of October, 1781, when they were all taken prisoners; and I give you a faithful specimen of their transactions for ten days of that time, and on one spot only.†

At the end of the second year of his term Jefferson resigned his commission as Governor. The state of Mrs. Jefferson's health was at this time a source of great anxiety to him, and he promised her, when he left public life on this occasion, that he would never again leave her to accept any

---

* Jefferson to Dr. Gordon.   † Ibid.

office or take part in political life. Saddened by the deaths of her children, and with a constitution weakened by disease, her condition was truly alarming, and wrung the heart of her devoted husband as he watched her failing day by day. He himself met with an accident about this time—a fall from his horse—which, though not attended with serious consequences, kept him, for two or three weeks, more closely confined in the house than it was his habit to be.

It was during this confinement that he wrote the principal part of his "Notes on Virginia." He had been in the habit of committing to writing any information about the State which he thought would be of use to him in any station, public or private; and receiving a letter from M. De Marbois, the French ambassador, asking for certain statistical accounts of the State of Virginia, he embodied the substance of the information he had so acquired and sent it to him in the form of the "Notes on Virginia."

A charming picture of Monticello and its inmates at that day is found in "Travels in North America, by the Marquis De Chastellux." This accomplished French nobleman visited Jefferson in the spring of 1782. After describing his approach to the foot of the southwest range of mountains, he says:

On the summit of one of them we discovered the house of Mr. Jefferson, which stands pre-eminent in these retirements; it was himself who built it, and preferred this situation; for although he possessed considerable property in the neighborhood, there was nothing to prevent him from fixing his residence wherever he thought proper. But it was a debt Nature owed to a philosopher, and a man of taste, that in his own possessions he should find a spot where he might best study and enjoy her. He calls his house *Monticello* (in Italian, Little Mountain), a very modest title, for it is situated upon a very lofty one, but which announces the owner's attachment to the language of Italy; and, above all, to the fine arts, of which that country was the cradle, and is still the asylum. As I had no further occasion for a guide, I separated from the Irishman; and after ascending by a tolerably commodious road for more than half an hour we arrived at Monticello. This house, of which Mr. Jefferson was the architect, and often one of the workmen, is rather elegant, and in the Italian taste, though not without fault; it consists of one large square pavilion, the entrance of which is by two porticoes, ornamented with pillars. The ground-floor consists of a very large lofty saloon, which is to be decorated entirely in the antique style; above it is a library of the same form; two small wings, with only a ground-floor and attic story, are joined to this pavilion, and communicate with the kitchen, offices, etc., which will form a kind of basement story, over which runs a terrace.

My object in this short description is only to show the difference between this and the other houses of the country; for we may safely aver that Mr. Jefferson is the first American who has consulted the fine arts to know how he should shelter himself from the weather.

But it is on himself alone I ought to bestow my time. Let me describe to you a man, not yet forty, tall and with a mild and pleasing countenance, but whose mind and understanding are ample substitutes for every exterior grace. An American, who, without ever having quitted his own country, is at once a musician, skilled in drawing, a geometrician, an astronomer, a natural philosopher, legislator, and statesman. A Senator of America, who sat for two years in that body which brought about the Revolution; and which is never mentioned without respect, though unhappily not without regret, a Governor of Virginia, who filled this difficult station during the invasions of Arnold, of Phillips, and of Cornwallis; a philosopher, in voluntary retirement from the world and public business because he loves the world, in as much only as he can flatter himself with being useful to mankind, and the minds of his countrymen are not yet in a condition either to bear the light or suffer contradiction. A mild and amiable wife, charming children, of whose education he himself takes charge, a house to embellish, great provisions to improve, and the arts and sciences to cultivate; these are what remain to Mr. Jefferson, after having played a principal character on the theatre of the New World, and which he preferred to the honorable commission of Minister Plenipoten tiary in Europe.

The visit which I made him was not unexpected, for he had long since invited me to come and pass a few days with him in the centre of the mountains; notwithstanding which, I found his appearance serious—nay even cold, but before I had been two hours with him, we were as intimate as if we had passed our whole lives together; walking, books, but above all, a conversation always varied and interesting, always supported by the sweet satisfaction experienced by two persons, who, in communicating their sentiments and opinions, are invariably in unison, and who understand each other at the first hint, made four days pass away like so many minutes.

This conformity of opinions and sentiments on which I insist because it constitutes my own eulogium (and self-love must somewhere show itself), this conformity, I say, was so perfect, that not only our taste was similar, but our predilections also; those partialities which cold methodical minds ridicule as enthusiastic, while sensible and animated ones cherish and adopt the glorious appellation. I recollect with pleasure that as we were conversing over a bowl of punch, after Mrs. Jefferson had retired, our conversation turned on the poems of Ossian. It was a spark of electricity which passed rapidly from one to the other; we recollected the passages in those sublime poems which particularly struck us, and entertained my fellow-travellers, who fortunately knew English well, and were qualified to judge of their merits, though they had never read the poems. In our enthusiasm the book was sent for, and placed near the bowl, where, by their mutual aid, the night far advanced imperceptibly upon us.

Sometimes natural philosophy, at others politics or the arts, were the topics of our conversation, for no object had escaped Mr. Jefferson; and it seemed as if from his youth he had placed his mind, as he has done his house, on an elevated situation, from which he might contemplate the universe.*

Mr. Jefferson—continues the Marquis—amused himself by raising a score of these animals (deer) in his park; they are become very familiar, which happens to all the animals of America; for they are in general much easier to tame than

---

* Chastellux's Travels in America, pp. 40–46.

those of Europe. He amuses himself by feeding them with Indian corn, of which they are very fond, and which they eat out of his hand. I followed him one evening into a deep valley, where they are accustomed to assemble towards the close of the day, and saw them walk, run, and bound; but the more I examined their paces, the less I was inclined to annex them to any particular species in Europe. Mr. Jefferson being no sportsman, and not having crossed the seas, could have no decided opinion on this part of natural history; but he has not neglected the other branches.

I saw with pleasure that he had applied himself particularly to meteorological observation, which, in fact, of all the branches of philosophy, is the most proper for Americans to cultivate, from the extent of their country and the variety of their situation, which gives them in this point a great advantage over us, who, in other respects, have so many over them. Mr. Jefferson has made with Mr. Madison, a well-informed professor of mathematics, some correspondent observations on the reigning winds at Williamsburg and Monticello.*

But—says the Marquis—I perceive my journal is something like the conversation I had with Mr. Jefferson; I pass from one object to another, and forget myself as I write, as it happened not unfrequently in his society. I must now quit the friend of nature, but not Nature herself, who expects me, in all her splendor, at the end of my journey; I mean the famous Bridge of Rocks, which unites two mountains, the most curious object I ever beheld, as its construction is the most difficult of solution. Mr. Jefferson would most willingly have conducted me thither, although this wonder is upward of eighty miles from him, and he had often seen it, but his wife being expected every moment to lie in, and himself being as good a husband as he is an excellent philosopher and virtuous citizen, he only acted as my guide for about sixteen miles, to the passage of the little river Mechum, when we parted, and, I presume to flatter myself, with mutual regret."†

The following warm letter of congratulation to General Washington shows the affection felt for him by Jefferson:

* Vol. ii., p. 48. † Vol. ii., p. 55.

To General Washington.

Monticello, October 28th, 1781.

Sir—I hope it will not be unacceptable to your Excellency to receive the congratulations of a private individual on your return to your native country, and, above all things, on the important success which has attended it.* Great as this has been, however, it can scarcely add to the affection with which we have looked up to you. And if, in the minds of any, the motives of gratitude to our good allies were not sufficiently apparent, the part they have borne in this action must amply convince them. Notwithstanding the state of perpetual solicitude to which I am unfortunately reduced,† I should certainly have done myself the honor of paying my respects to you personally; but I apprehend that these visits, which are meant by us as marks of our attachment to you, must interfere with the regulations of a camp, and be particularly inconvenient to one whose time is too precious to be wasted in ceremony.

I beg you to believe me among the sincerest of those who subscribe themselves your Excellency's most obedient and most humble servant,

TH. JEFFERSON.

The delicate condition of Mrs. Jefferson's health, alluded to in the preceding letter, continued to be such as to excite the alarm of her friends, and their worst apprehensions were soon realized. After the birth of her sixth child she sank so rapidly that it was plain there was no hope of her recovery. During her illness Jefferson was untiring in his attentions to her, and the devotion he showed her was constant and touching. The following account of the closing scenes of this domestic tragedy I take from Mrs. Randolph's manuscript:

During my mother's life he (Jefferson) bestowed much time and attention on our education—our cousins, the Carrs, and myself—and after her death, during the first month of desolation which followed, I was his constant companion while we remained at Monticello......

---

* At Yorktown. † On account of Mrs. Jefferson's health.

As a nurse no female ever had more tenderness nor anxiety. He nursed my poor mother in turn with aunt Carr and her own sister—sitting up with her and administering her medicines and drink to the last. For four months that she lingered he was never out of calling; when not at her bedside, he was writing in a small room which opened immediately at the head of her bed. A moment before the closing scene, he was led from the room in a state of insensibility by his sister, Mrs. Carr, who, with great difficulty, got him into the library, where he fainted, and remained so long insensible that they feared he never would revive. The scene that followed I did not witness, but the violence of his emotion, when, almost by stealth, I entered his room by night, to this day I dare not describe to myself. He kept his room three weeks, and I was never a moment from his side. He walked almost incessantly night and day, only lying down occasionally, when nature was completely exhausted, on a pallet that had been brought in during his long fainting-fit. My aunts remained constantly with him for some weeks—I do not remember how many. When at last he left his room, he rode out, and from that time he was incessantly on horseback, rambling about the mountain, in the least frequented roads, and just as often through the woods. In those melancholy rambles I was his constant companion—a solitary witness to many a burst of grief, the remembrance of which has consecrated particular scenes of that lost home* beyond the power of time to obliterate.

Mrs. Jefferson left three children, Martha, Mary, and Lucy Elizabeth—the last an infant. As far as it was possible, their father, by his watchful care and tender love, supplied the place of the mother they had lost. The account of her death just given gives a vivid description of his grief, and so alarming was the state of insensibility into which he fell, that his sister, Mrs. Carr, called to his sister-in-law, who was still bending over her sister's lifeless body, " to leave the dead and come and take care of the living."

---

* Mrs. Randolph wrote this after Monticello had been sold and passed into the hands of strangers.

Years afterwards he wrote the following epitaph for his wife's tomb:

To the Memory of

MARTHA JEFFERSON,

Daughter of John Wayles;
Born October 19th, 1748, O. S.;
Intermarried with

THOMAS JEFFERSON

January 1st, 1772;
Torn from him by Death
September 6th, 1782:
This Monument of his Love is inscribed.

If in the melancholy shades below,
The flames of friends and lovers cease to glow,
Yet mine shall sacred last; mine undecayed
Burn on through death and animate my shade.*

---

* These four lines Mr. Jefferson left in the Greek in the original epitaph.

CHAPTER IV.

A SHORT time after Mrs. Jefferson's death, Jefferson went with his children to Ampthill, in Chesterfield County, the residence of Colonel Archibald Cary. This gentleman had kindly offered his house to him, that he might there have his children inoculated for the small-pox. While engaged as their chief nurse on this occasion, he received notice of his appointment by Congress as Plenipotentiary to Europe, to be associated with Dr. Franklin and Mr. Adams in negotiating peace. Twice before the same appointment had been declined by him, as he had promised his wife never again to enter public life while she lived. Mr. Madison, in alluding to his appointment by Congress, says:

The reappointment of Mr. Jefferson as Minister Plenipotentiary for negotiating peace, was agreed to unanimously, and without a single adverse remark. The act took place in consequence of its being suggested that the death of Mrs. Jefferson had probably changed the sentiments of Mr. Jefferson with regard to public life.*

Jefferson himself, in speaking of this appointment, says in his Memoir:

I had, two months before that, lost the cherished companion of my life, in whose affections, unabated on both sides, I had lived the last ten years in unchequered happiness.

---

* Madison Papers.

With the public interests the state of my mind concurred in recommending the change of scene proposed; and I accepted the appointment.

Writing to the Marquis de Chastellux, he says:

Ampthill, November 26th, 1782.

Dear Sir—I received your friendly letters of —— and June 30th, but the latter not till the 17th of October. It found me a little emerging from the stupor of mind which had rendered me as dead to the world as was she whose loss occasioned it...... Before that event my scheme of life had been determined. I had folded myself in the arms of retirement, and rested all prospects of future happiness on domestic and literary objects. A single event wiped away all my plans, and left me a blank which I had not the spirits to fill up. In this state of mind an appointment from Congress found me, requiring me to cross the Atlantic.

Having accepted the appointment, Mr. Jefferson left his two youngest children with their maternal aunt, Mrs. Eppes, of Eppington, and went North with his daughter Martha, then in her eleventh year. Some delay in his departure for Europe was occasioned by news received from Europe by Congress. During the uncertainty as to the time of his departure he placed the little Martha at school in Philadelphia, under the charge of an excellent and kind lady, Mrs. Hopkinson. From this time we find him writing regularly to his daughters during every separation from them, and it is in the letters written on those occasions that are portrayed most vividly the love and tenderness of the father, and the fine traits of character of the man. That the reader may see what these were, I shall give a number of these letters, and, as far as possible, in their chronological order.

The original of the first of the following letters is now in the possession of the Queen of England. Mr. Aaron Vail, when Chargé d'Affaires of the United States at the Court of St. James, being requested by Princess Victoria to procure her an autograph of Jefferson, applied to a member of Mr. Jefferson's family, who sent him this letter for the princess. Mr. Jefferson was at this time again a member of Congress, which was then holding its sessions in Annapolis.

Thomas Jefferson to Martha Jefferson.

Annapolis, Nov. 28th, 1783.

My dear Patsy—After four days' journey, I arrived here without any accident, and in as good health as when I left Philadelphia. The conviction that you would be more improved in the situation I have placed you than if still with me, has solaced me on my parting with you, which my love for you has rendered a difficult thing. The acquirements which I hope you will make under the tutors I have provided for you will render you more worthy of my love; and if they can not increase it, they will prevent its diminution. Consider the good lady who has taken you under her roof, who has undertaken to see that you perform all your exercises, and to admonish you in all those wanderings from what is right or what is clever, to which your inexperience would expose you: consider her, I say, as your mother, as the only person to whom, since the loss with which Heaven has pleased to afflict you, you can now look up; and that her displeasure or disapprobation, on any occasion, will be an immense misfortune, which should you be so unhappy as to incur by any unguarded act, think no concession too much to regain her good-will. With respect to the distribution of your time, the following is what I should approve:

From 8 to 10, practice music.

From 10 to 1, dance one day and draw another.

From 1 to 2, draw on the day you dance, and write a letter next day.

From 3 to 4, read French.

From 4 to 5, exercise yourself in music.

From 5 till bed-time, read English, write, etc.

Communicate this plan to Mrs. Hopkinson, and if she approves of it, pursue it. As long as Mrs. Trist remains in Philadelphia, cultivate her affection. She has been a valuable friend to you, and her good sense and good heart make her valued by all who know her, and by nobody on earth more than me. I expect you will write me by every post.

Inform me what books you read, what tunes you learn, and inclose me your best copy of every lesson in drawing. Write also one letter a week either to your Aunt Eppes, your Aunt Skipwith, your Aunt Carr, or the little lady* from whom I now inclose a letter, and always put the letter you so write under cover to me. Take care that you never spell a word wrong. Always before you write a word, consider how it is spelt, and, if you do not remember it, turn to a dictionary. It produces great praise to a lady to spell well. I have placed my happiness on seeing you good and accomplished; and no distress which this world can now bring on me would equal that of your disappointing my hopes. If you love me, then strive to be good under every situation and to all living creatures, and to acquire those accomplishments which I have put in your power, and which will go far towards ensuring you the warmest love of your affectionate father,

TH. JEFFERSON.

P.S.—Keep my letters and read them at times, that you may always have present in your mind those things which will endear you to me.

Thomas Jefferson to Martha Jefferson.—[Extract.]†

Annapolis, Dec. 11th, 1783.

I hope you will have good sense enough to disregard those foolish predictions that the world is to be at an end soon. The Almighty has never made known to any body at what time he created it; nor will he tell any body when he will put an end to it, if he ever means to do it. As to preparations for that event, the best way is for you always to be prepared for it. The only way to be so is, never to say or do a bad thing. If ever you are about to say any thing

---

* Her little sister, Mary Jefferson.

† We find the key to this and the letter following it in the following paragraph of a letter from Mrs. Trist to Mr. Jefferson: "Patsy is very hearty; she now and then gives us a call. She seems happy, much more so than I expected. When you write, give her a charge about her dress, which will be a hint to Mrs. H. to be particular with her. De Simitière complains that his pupil is rather inattentive. You can be particular to these matters when you write, but don't let her know you heard any complaints. I fancy the old lady is preparing for the other world, for she conceits the earthquake we had the other night is only a prelude to something dreadful that will happen."

amiss, or to do any thing wrong, consider beforehand you will feel something within you which will tell you it is wrong, and ought not to be said or done. This is your conscience, and be sure and obey it. Our Maker has given us all this faithful internal monitor, and if you always obey it you will always be prepared for the end of the world; or for a much more certain event, which is death. This must happen to all; it puts an end to the world as to us; and the way to be ready for it is never to do a wrong act.

Thomas Jefferson to Martha Jefferson.—[Extract.]

Annapolis, Dec. 22d, 1783.

I omitted in that letter to advise you on the subject of dress, which I know you are a little apt to neglect. I do not wish you to be gaily clothed at this time of life, but that your wear should be fine of its kind. But above all things and at all times let your clothes be neat, whole, and properly put on. Do not fancy you must wear them till the dirt is visible to the eye. You will be the last one who is sensible of this. Some ladies think they may, under the privileges of the *déshabillé*, be loose and negligent of their dress in the morning. But be you, from the moment you rise till you go to bed, as cleanly and properly dressed as at the hours of dinner or tea. A lady who has been seen as a sloven or a slut in the morning, will never efface the impression she has made, with all the dress and pageantry she can afterwards involve herself in. Nothing is so disgusting to our sex as a want of cleanliness and delicacy in yours. I hope, therefore, the moment you rise from bed, your first work will be to dress yourself in such style, as that you may be seen by any gentleman without his being able to discover a pin amiss, or any other circumstance of neatness wanting.

Thomas Jefferson to Martha Jefferson.

Annapolis, Jan. 15th, 1783.

My dear Martha—I am anxious to know what books you read, what tunes you play, and to receive specimens of your drawing. With respect to your meeting M. Simitière* at Mr. Rittenhouse's, nothing could give me more pleasure than

---

* M. Simitière was a Frenchman, from whom, as his letters show, Mr. Jefferson was anxious for his daughter to take drawing lessons.

your being much with that worthy family, wherein you will
see the best examples of rational life, and learn to esteem and
copy them.   But I should be very tender of intruding you
on the family ; as it might, perhaps, be not always convenient for you to be there at your hours of attending M. Simitière.   I can only say, then, that if it has been desired by Mr.
and Mrs. Rittenhouse, in such a manner as that Mrs. Hopkinson shall be satisfied that they will not think it inconvenient, I would have you thankfully accept it; and conduct
yourself with so much attention to the family as that they
may never feel themselves incommoded by it.   I hope Mrs.
Hopkinson will be so good as to act for you in this matter
with that delicacy and prudence of which she is so capable.
I have much at heart your learning to draw, and should be
uneasy at your losing this opportunity, which probably is
your last.

Thomas Jefferson to Martha Jefferson.—[Extract.]

Annapolis, February 18th, 1784.

I am sorry M. Simitière can not attend you, because it is
probable you will never have another opportunity of learning to draw, and it is a pretty and pleasing accomplishment.
With respect to the payment of the guinea, I would wish
him to receive it ; because if there is to be a doubt between
him and me which of us acts rightly, I would wish to remove
it clearly off my own shoulders.   You must thank Mrs.
Hopkinson for me for the trouble she gave herself in this
matter ; from which she will be relieved by paying M. Simitière his demand.

In the spring of this year (1784) Mr. Jefferson received
definite orders from Congress to go to Europe as Minister
Plenipotentiary, and act in conjunction with Dr. Franklin
and Mr. Adams in negotiating treaties of commerce with
foreign nations.   He accordingly sailed in July, taking with
him his young daughter Martha.   The following description
of his voyage, establishment in Paris and life there, is from
her pen.   The other two children, Mary and Lucy Elizabeth,
were left with their good aunt, Mrs. Eppes.   Mrs. Randolph
says, in her manuscript :

He sailed from Boston in a ship of Colonel Tracy's (the Ceres, Capt. St. Barbe); the passengers—only six in number —of whom Colonel Tracy himself was one, were to a certain degree select, being chosen from many applying. The voyage was as pleasant as fine weather, a fine ship, good company, and an excellent table could make it. From land to land they were only nineteen days, of which they were becalmed three on the Banks of Newfoundland, which were spent in cod-fishing. The epicures of the cabin feasted on fresh tongues and sounds, leaving the rest of the fish for the sailors, of which much was thrown overboard for want of salt to preserve it. We were landed at Portsmouth, where he was detained a week by the illness of his little travelling companion, suffering from the effects of the voyage. Nothing worthy of note occurred on the voyage or journey to Paris.

On his first arrival in Paris he occupied rooms in the Hôtel d'Orléans, *Rue des Petits Augustins*, until a house could be got ready for him. His first house was in the Cul-de-sac Têtebout, near the Boulevards. At the end of the year he removed to a house belonging to M. le Comte de L'Avongeac, at the corner of the Grande Route des Champs Elysées and the Rue Neuve de Berry, where he continued as long as he remained in Paris. Colonel Humphreys, the secretary of legation, and Mr. Short, his private secretary, both lived with him. The house was a very elegant one even for Paris, with an extensive garden, court, and outbuildings, in the handsomest style.

He also had rooms in the Carthusian Monastery on Mount Calvary; the boarders, of whom I think there were forty, carried their own servants, and took their breakfasts in their own rooms. They assembled to dinner only. They had the privilege of walking in the gardens, but as it was a hermitage, it was against the rules of the house for any voices to be heard outside of their own rooms, hence the most profound silence. The author of Anacharsis was a boarder at the time, and many others who had reasons for a temporary retirement from the world. Whenever he had a press of business, he was in the habit of taking his papers and going to the hermitage, where he spent sometimes a week or more till he had finished his work. The hermits visited him occasionally in Paris, and the Superior made him a present of an ivory broom that was turned by one of the brothers.

His habits of study in Paris were pretty much what they were elsewhere. He was always a very early riser and the whole morning was spent in business, generally writing till one o'clock, with the exception of a short respite afforded by the breakfast-table, at which he frequently lingered, conversing willingly at such times. At one o'clock he always rode or walked as far as seven miles into the country. Returning from one of these rambles, he was on one occasion joined by some friend, and being earnestly engaged in conversation he fell and broke his wrist. He said nothing at the moment, but holding the suffering limb with the other hand, he continued the conversation until he arrived near to his own house, when, informing his companion of the accident, he left him to send for the surgeon. The fracture was a complicated one and probably much swollen before the arrival of the surgeon; but it was not set, and remained ever after weak and stiff. While disabled by this accident he was in the habit of writing with his left hand, in which he soon became tolerably expert—the writing being well-formed but stiff. A few years before his death another fall deprived him in like manner of the use of his left hand, which rendered him very helpless in his hands, particularly for writing, which latterly became very slow and painful to him...... He kept me with him till I was sent to a convent in Paris, where his visits to me were daily for the first month or two, till in fact I recovered my spirits.

Nothing could have been more congenial or delightful to him than the society in which Jefferson moved in Paris. At the head of an elegant establishment, as an American and the friend of Lafayette, his house was the favorite resort of all the accomplished and gallant young French officers who had enthusiastically taken up arms in defense of the great cause of liberty in the New World; while as a philosopher and the author of the "Notes on Virginia," his society was sought for and enjoyed by the most distinguished savants and men of science, who thronged from all parts of Europe to the great French capital. Nor were the ease and grace of his address, the charms of his eloquent conversation, and the varied extent of his learning, lost upon the witty and handsome women who were found at the court of the amiable young Louis the Sixteenth and of his queen, the lovely Marie Antoinette—so sadly pre-eminent for beauty and misfortune. His social intercourse with them, and the pleasant friendships formed for many, we discover in his gracefully-written letters to them.

Mr. and Mrs. John Adams were in Paris with Jefferson, and Mrs. Adams pays a graceful tribute to his talents and worth in her letters home, and in one of them speaks of him as being one of the " choice ones of the earth." His intercourse with his two colleagues, Dr. Franklin and Mr. Adams, was of the most delightful character, and by both he was sincerely loved and esteemed. The friendship then formed between Mr. Adams and himself withstood, in after years, all the storms and bitterness of political life, at a time when, perhaps, party feeling and prejudice ran higher than ever before.

When Franklin returned home, loaded with all the honors and love that the admiration of the French people could lavish on him, Jefferson was appointed to take his place as Minister from the United States at the Court of St. Germains. " You replace Dr. Franklin," said Count de Vergennes, the French Premier, to him—" I *succeed* him; no one could replace him," was Jefferson's ready reply. Perhaps no greater proof of Jefferson's popularity in Paris could be given, than the fact that he so soon became a favorite in that learned and polished society in which the great Franklin had been the lion of the day. I quote from Jefferson's writings the following anecdotes of Franklin, which the reader will not find out of place here:

When Dr. Franklin went to France on his revolutionary mission, his eminence as a philosopher, his venerable appearance, and the cause on which he was sent, rendered him extremely popular—for all ranks and conditions of men there entered warmly into the American interest. He was, therefore, feasted and invited to all the court parties. At these he sometimes met the old Duchess of Bourbon, who being a chess-player of about his force, they very generally played together. Happening once to put her king into prise, the Doctor took it. "Ah," says she, " we do not take kings so." " We do in America," said the Doctor.

At one of these parties the Emperor Joseph II., then at Paris *incog.* under the title of Count Falkenstein, was over-looking the game in silence, while the company was engaged in animated conversations on the American question. "How happens it, M. le Comte," said the Duchess, "that while we all feel so much interest in the cause of the Americans, you say nothing for them?" "I am a king by trade," said he.

The Doctor told me at Paris the following anecdote of the Abbé Raynal: He had a party to dine with him one day at Passy, of whom one half were Americans, the other half French, and among the last was the Abbé. During the dinner he got on his favorite theory of the degeneracy of animals and even of man in America, and urged it with his usual eloquence. The Doctor, at length noticing the accidental stature and position of his guests at table, "Come," says he, "M. l'Abbé, let us try this question by the fact before us. We are here, one half Americans and one half French, and it happens that the Americans have placed themselves on one side of the table, and our French friends are on the other. Let both parties rise, and we will see on which side nature has degenerated." It happened that his American guests were Carmichael, Harmer, Humphreys, and others of the finest stature and form; while those of the other side were remarkably diminutive, and the Abbé himself, particularly, was a mere shrimp. He parried the appeal, however, by a complimentary admission of exceptions, among which the Doctor himself was a conspicuous one.

The following interesting quotations from Mrs. Adams's letters, in which she alludes to Mr. Jefferson, will be found interesting here. To her sister she writes:

There is now a court mourning, and every foreign minis-

ter, with his family, must go into mourning for a Prince of
eight years old, whose father is an ally to the King of France.
This mourning is ordered by the Court, and is to be worn
eleven days only. Poor Mr. Jefferson had to hie away for a
tailor to get a whole black silk suit made up in two days;
and at the end of eleven days, should another death happen,
he will be obliged to have a new suit of mourning of cloth,
because that is the season when silk must be left off.

To her niece Mrs. Adams writes:

Well, my dear niece, I have returned from Mr. Jefferson's. When I got there I found a pretty large company.
It consisted of the Marquis and Madame de Lafayette; the
Count and Countess de ——; a French Count who had been
a general in America, but whose name I forget; Commodore
Jones; Mr. Jarvis, an American gentleman lately arrived
(the same who married Amelia B——), who says there is so
strong a likeness between your cousin and his lady, that he
is obliged to be upon his guard lest he should think himself
at home, and commit some mistake—he appears a very sensible, agreeable gentleman; a Mr. Bowdoin, an American
also; I ask the Chevalier de la Luzerne's pardon—I had like
to have forgotten him; Mr. Williams, of course, as he always
dines with Mr. Jefferson; and Mr. Short—though one of Mr.
Jefferson's family, as he has been absent some time I name
him. He took a resolution that he would go into a French
family at St. Germain, and acquire the language; and this is
the only way for a foreigner to obtain it. I have often wished that I could not hear a word of English spoken. I think
I have mentioned Mr. Short before, in some of my letters; he
is about the stature of Mr. Tudor; a better figure, but much
like him in looks and manners; consequently a favorite of
mine.

They have some customs very curious here. When company are invited to dine, if twenty gentlemen meet, they seldom or never sit down, but are standing or walking from
one part of the room to the other, with their swords on, and
their *chapeau de bras*, which is a very small silk hat, always
worn under the arm. These they lay aside while they dine,
but reassume them immediately after. I wonder how the

fashion of standing crept in among a nation who really deserve the appellation of polite; for in winter it shuts out all the fire from the ladies; I know I have suffered from it many times.

At dinner, the ladies and gentlemen are mixed, and you converse with him who sits next you, rarely speaking to two persons across the table, unless to ask if they will be served with any thing from your side. Conversation is never general as with us; for, when the company quit the table, they fall into *tête-à-tête* of two and two, when the conversation is in a low voice, and a stranger unacquainted with the customs of the country, would think that every body had private business to transact.

Mrs. Adams writes to her sister:

We see as much company in a formal way as our revenues will admit; and Mr. Jefferson, with one or two Americans, visits us in the social, friendly way. I shall really regret to leave Mr. Jefferson; he is one of the choice ones of the earth. On Thursday, I dine with him at his house. On Sunday he is to dine here. On Monday we all dine with the Marquis.

The intimate and friendly relations which existed between Mr. Jefferson and Mrs. Adams's family is seen from the following playful note from him to her daughter, Mrs. Smith:

Mr. Jefferson has the honor to present his compliments to Mrs. Smith and to send her the two pair of corsets she desired. He wishes they may be suitable, as Mrs. Smith omitted to send her measure. Times are altered since Mademoiselle de Sanson had the honor of knowing her; should they be too small, however, she will be so good as to lay them by a while. There are ebbs as well as flows in this world. When the mountain refused to come to Mahomet, he went to the mountain. Mr. Jefferson wishes Mrs. Smith a happy new-year, and abundance of happier ones still to follow it. He begs leave to assure her of his esteem and respect, and that he shall always be happy to be rendered useful to her by being charged with her commands.

Paris, Jan. 15, 1787.

CHAPTER V.

JEFFERSON's first impressions of Europe and of the French are found in the following extracts from his letters written to America at that time:

Extract from a Letter to Mrs. Trist.

Paris, August 18th, 1785.

I am much pleased with the people of this country. The roughnesses of the human mind are so thoroughly rubbed off with them, that it seems as if one might glide through a whole life among them without a jostle. Perhaps, too, their manners may be the best calculated for happiness to a people in their situation, but I am convinced they fall far short of effecting a happiness so temperate, so uniform, and so lasting as is generally enjoyed with us. The domestic bonds here are absolutely done away, and where can their compensation be found? Perhaps they may catch some moments of transport above the level of the ordinary tranquil joy we experience, but they are separated by long intervals, during which all the passions are at sea without a rudder or a compass. Yet, fallacious as the pursuits of happiness are, they seem, on the whole, to furnish the most effectual abstraction from the contemplation of the hardness of their government. Indeed, it is difficult to conceive how so good a people, with so good a king, so well-disposed rulers in general, so genial a climate, so fertile a soil, should be rendered so ineffectual for producing human happiness by one single curse—that of a bad form of government. But it is a fact in spite of the

mildness of their governors, the people are ground to powder by the vices of the form of government.   Of twenty millions of people supposed to be in France, I am of opinion
there are nineteen millions more wretched, more accursed, in
every circumstance of human existence, than the most con-
spicuously wretched individual of the whole United States.
I beg your pardon for getting into politics.   I will add only
one sentiment more of that character—that is, nourish peace
with their persons, but war against their manners.   Every
step we take towards the adoption of their manners is a step
to perfect misery.

In a fit of homesickness, he writes to the Baron de Geis-
mer, Sept. 6 :

To Baron de Geismer.

I am now of an age which does not easily accommodate
itself to new modes of living and new manners; and I am
savage enough to prefer the woods, the wilds and independence of Monticello, to all the brilliant pleasures of this gay
capital.   I shall, therefore, rejoin myself to my native country with new attachments and exaggerated esteem for its
advantages; for though there is less wealth· there, there is
more freedom, more ease, and less misery.   I should like it
better, however, if it could tempt you once more to visit it;
but that is not to be expected.   Be this as it may, and
whether fortune means to allow or deny me the pleasure
of ever seeing you again, be assured that the worth which
gave birth to my attachment, and which still animates it,
will continue to keep it up while we both live, and that it is
with sincerity I subscribe myself, etc., etc.

Early in the month of March of the following year (1786)
Mr. Jefferson went for a short while to England.   Before
leaving, he wrote a letter of adieu to his daughter Martha,
then at school in a convent in Paris.   The following is an
extract from this letter:

To Martha Jefferson.—[Extract.]

Paris, March 6th, 1786.
I need not tell you what pleasure it gives me to see you

improve in every thing useful and agreeable. The more you learn the more I love you; and I rest the happiness of my life on seeing you beloved by all the world, which you will be sure to be, if to a good heart you join those accomplishments so peculiarly pleasing in your sex. Adieu, my dear child; lose no moment in improving your head, nor any opportunity of exercising your heart in benevolence.

The following letter to his sister proves him to have been as devoted and thoughtful a brother as father:

To Ann S. Jefferson.

London, April 22d, 1786.

My dear Nancy—Being called here for a short time, and finding that I could get some articles on terms here of which I thought you might be in want, I have purchased them for you. They are two pieces of linen, three gowns, and some ribbon. They are done up in paper, sealed, and packed in a trunk, in which I have put some other things for Colonel Nicholas Lewis. They will of course go to him, and he will contrive them to you. I heard from Patsy a few days ago; she was well. I left her in France, as my stay here was to be short. I hope my dear Polly is on her way to me. I desired you always to apply to Mr. Lewis for what you should want; but should you at any time wish any thing particular from France, write to me and I will send it to you. Doctor Currie can always forward your letters. Pray remember me to my sisters Carr and Bolling, to Mr. Bolling and their families, and be assured of the sincerity with which I am, my dear Nancy, your affectionate brother,

TH. JEFFERSON.

While in England, Jefferson visited many places of interest there, and kept a short journal, of which we give the heading, and from which we make one quotation:

Extract from Journal.

A TOUR TO SOME OF THE GARDENS OF ENGLAND.

Memorandums made on a Tour to some of the Gardens in England, described by Whately in his Book on Gardening.

While his descriptions, in point of style, are models of perfect elegance and classical correctness, they are as re-

F

markable for their exactness. I always walked over the
gardens with his book in my hand, examined with attention
the particular spots which he described, found them so justly
characterized by him as to be easily recognized, and saw
with wonder that his fine imagination had never been able
to seduce him from the truth. My inquiries were directed
chiefly to such practical things as might enable me to estimate the expense of making and maintaining a garden in
that style. My journey was in the months of March and
April, 1786......

Blenheim.—Twenty-five hundred acres, of which two hundred is garden, one hundred and fifty water, twelve kitchen-
garden, and the rest park. Two hundred people employed
to keep it in order, and to make alterations and additions.
About fifty of these employed in pleasure-grounds. The
turf is mowed once in ten days. In summer, about two
thousand fallow-deer in the park, and two or three thousand
sheep. The palace of Henry II. was remaining till taken
down by Sarah, widow of the first Duke of Marlborough.
It was on a round spot levelled by art, near what is now
water, and but a little above it. The island was a part of
the high-road leading to the palace. Rosamond's Bower
was near where now is a little grove, about two hundred
yards from the palace. The well is near where the bower
was. The water here is very beautiful and very grand.
The cascade from the lake is a fine one; except this the garden has no great beauties. It is not laid out in fine lawns
.and woods, but the trees are scattered thinly over the
ground, and every here and there small thickets of shrubs,
in oval raised beds, cultivated, and flowers among the
shrubs. The gravelled walks are broad; art appears too
much. There are but a few seats in it, and nothing of architecture more dignified. There is no one striking position in
it. There has been great addition to the length of the river
since Whately wrote.

In a letter written, after his return to Paris, to his old
friend, John Page, of Virginia, Mr. Jefferson speaks thus of
England:

To John Page.

I returned but three or four days ago from a two months' trip to England. I traversed that country much, and must own both town and country fell short of my expectations. Comparing it with this, I have found a much greater proportion of barrens, a soil, in other parts, not naturally so good as this, not better cultivated, but better manured, and therefore more productive. This proceeds from the practice of long leases there, and short ones here. The laboring people are poorer here than in England. They pay about one half of their produce in rent, the English in general about one third. The gardening in that country is the article in which it excels all the earth. I mean their pleasure-gardening. This, indeed, went far beyond my ideas. The city of London, though handsomer than Paris, is not so handsome as Philadelphia. Their architecture is in the most wretched style I ever saw, not meaning to except America, where it is bad, nor even Virginia, where it is worse than any other part of America which I have seen. The mechanical arts in London are carried to a wonderful perfection.

His faithful little pocket account-book informs us that he paid, "for seeing house where Shakspeare was born, 1s.; seeing his tomb, 1s.; entertainment, 4s. 2d.; servants, 2s."

In the fall of this year Jefferson, on behalf of the State of Virginia, presented to the city authorities of Paris a bust of his distinguished friend, the Marquis de Lafayette, which was inaugurated with all due form and ceremony and placed in the Hôtel de Ville. A few months later he wrote the following letter:

To Mrs. Trist.

Dear Madam—I have duly received your friendly letter of July 24, and received it with great pleasure, as I do all those you do me the favor to write me. If I have been long in acknowledging the receipt, the last cause to which it should be ascribed would be want of inclination. Unable to converse with my friends in person, I am happy when I do it in black and white. The true cause of the delay has been an unlucky dislocation of my wrist, which has disabled me from writing three months. I only begin to write a little now, but with pain. I wish, while in Virginia, your curiosity had led you on to James River. At Richmond you would have seen your old friends, Mr. and Mrs. Randolph, and a little farther you would have become acquainted with my friend, Mrs. Eppes, whom you would have found among the most amiable women on earth. I doubt whether you would ever have got away from her. This trip would have made you better acquainted too with my lazy and hospitable countrymen, and you would have found that their character has some good traits mixed with some feeble ones. I often wish myself among them, as I am here burning the candle of life without present pleasure or future object. A dozen or twenty years ago this scene would have amused me; but I am past the age for changing habits. I take all the fault on myself, as it is impossible to be among a people who wish more to make one happy—a people of the very best character it is possible for one to have. We have no idea in America of the real French character; with some true samples we have had many false ones......

Living from day to day, without a plan for four-and-twenty hours to come, I form no catalogue of impossible events. Laid up in port for life, as I thought myself at one time, I am thrown out to sea, and an unknown one to me. By so slender a thread do all our plans of life hang! My hand denies itself farther, every letter admonishing me, by a pain, that it is time to finish, but my heart would go on in expressing to you all its friendship. The happiest moments it knows are those in which it is pouring forth its affections to a few esteemed characters. I will pray you to write to me often. I wish to know that you enjoy health and that you are happy. Present me in the most friendly terms to your mother and brother, and be assured of the sincerity of the esteem with which I am, dear madam, your affectionate friend and humble servant,

TH. JEFFERSON.

Among the many pleasant friendships formed by Jefferson in Paris, there was none that he prized more than that of Mr. and Mrs. Cosway. Both were artists; but the husband was an Englishman, while the wife was born under the more genial skies of Italy. Possessing all that grace and beauty which seem to be the unfailing birthright of an Italian, she united to a bright and well-cultivated intellect great charms of manner and sweetness of disposition. Her Southern warmth of manner, and the brilliancy of her wit and conversation, were fascinations which few could resist, and which made her one of the queens of Parisian society. In Jefferson she found a congenial friend, and held his worth, his genius, and his learning in the highest estimation. When her husband and herself left Paris, she opened a correspondence with him, and it was at the beginning of this correspondence that he addressed to her that beautiful and gracefully written letter, called the " Dialogue between the Head and Heart," which is found in both editions of his published correspondence. Mrs. Cosway's own letters are sprightly and entertaining. I have lying before me the originals of some that she wrote to Jefferson, from which I give the following extracts, only reminding the reader that they are written in a language which to her was foreign, though the Italian idiom adds grace and freshness to the sweet simplicity of these letters. Many of them are without date.

Mrs. Cosway to Thomas Jefferson.

Paris, ——, 1786.

You don't always judge by appearances, or it would be much to my disadvantage this day, without deserving it; it has been the day of contradiction. I meant to have seen you twice, and I have appeared a monster for not having sent to know how you were the whole day.* I have been more uneasy than I can express. This morning my husband killed my project I had proposed to him, by burying himself among pictures and forgetting the hours. Though we were near your house, coming to see you, we were obliged to come back, the time being much past that we were to be at St. Cloud, to dine with the Duchess of

---

* Mr. Jefferson, the reader will remember, was at this time suffering with his broken wrist.

Kingston. Nothing was to hinder us from coming in the evening, but, alas! my good intentions proved only a disturbance to your neighbors, and just late enough to break the rest of all your servants, and perhaps yourself. I came home with the disappointment of not having been able to make my apologies *in propria persona.* I hope you feel my distress instead of accusing me; the one I deserve, the other not. We will come to see you to-morrow morning, if nothing happens to prevent it. Oh! I wish you were well enough to come to us to-morrow to dinner, and stay the evening. I won't tell you what I shall have; temptations now are cruel for your situation. I only mention my wishes. If the executing them should be possible, your merit will be greater, as my satisfaction the more flattered. I would serve you and help you at dinner, and divert your pain after with good music. Sincerely your friend,

                                        MARIA COSWAY.

Mrs. Cosway to Thomas Jefferson.

I am very sorry indeed, and blame myself for having been the cause of your pains in the wrist. Why would you go, and why was I not more friendly to you, and less so to myself by preventing your giving me the pleasure of your company? You repeatedly said it would do you no harm. I felt interested and did not insist. We shall go, I believe, this morning. Nothing seems ready, but Mr. Cosway seems more disposed than I have seen him all this time. I shall write to you from England; it is impossible to be wanting to a person who has been so excessively obliging. I don't attempt to make compliments—there can be none for you, but I beg you will think us sensible to your kindness, and that it will be with exquisite pleasure I shall remember the charming days we have passed together, and shall long for next spring.

You will make me very happy if you would send a line to the *poste restante* at Antwerp, that I may know how you are. Believe me, dear sir, your most obliged, affectionate servant,

                                        MARIA COSWAY.

The letter from Mr. Jefferson to Mrs. Cosway containing

the "Dialogue between the Head and Heart," though too long to be given here in full, is too beautiful to be omitted altogether. I accordingly give the following extracts:

Thomas Jefferson to Mrs. Cosway.

Paris, October 12, 1786.

My dear Madam—Having performed the last sad office of handing you into your carriage at the Pavillon de St. Denis, and seen the wheels get actually in motion, I turned on my heel and walked, more dead than alive, to the opposite door, where my own was awaiting me. M. Danguerville was missing. He was sought for, found, and dragged down stairs. We were crammed into the carriage like recruits for the Bastile, and not having soul enough to give orders to the coachman, he presumed Paris our destination, and drove off. After a considerable interval, silence was broken, with a "*Je suis vraiment affligé du depart de ces bons gens.*" This was a signal for a mutual confession of distress. He began immediately to talk of Mr. and Mrs. Cosway, of their goodness, their talents, their amiability; and though we spoke of nothing else, we seemed hardly to have entered into the matter, when the coachman announced the Rue St. Denis, and that we were opposite M. Danguerville's. He insisted on descending there and traversing a short passage to his lodgings. I was carried home. Seated by my fireside, solitary and sad, the following dialogue took place between my Head and my Heart.

Head. Well, friend, you seem to be in a pretty trim.

Heart. I am, indeed, the most wretched of all earthly beings. Overwhelmed with grief, every fibre of my frame distended beyond its natural powers to bear, I would willingly meet whatever catastrophe should leave me no more to feel, or to fear.........

Head. It would have been happy for you if my diagrams and crotchets had gotten you to sleep on that day, as you are pleased to say they eternally do......... While I was occupied with these objects, you were dilating with your new acquaintances, and contriving how to prevent a separation from them. Every soul of you had an engagement for the day. Yet all these were to be sacrificed, that you might dine together. Lying messages were to be dispatched into every quarter of the city, with apologies for your breach of engagement. You, particularly, had the effrontery to send word to the Duchess Danville, that on the moment we were setting out to dine with her, dispatches came to hand which required immediate attention. You wanted me to invent a more ingenious excuse, but I knew you were getting into a scrape, and I would have nothing to do with it. Well; after dinner to St. Cloud, from St. Cloud to Ruggieri's, from Ruggieri's to Krum-foltz; and if the day had been as long as a Lapland summer day, you would still have contrived means among you to have filled it.

Heart. Oh! my dear friend, how you have revived me, by recalling to my mind the transactions of that day! How well I remember them all, and that when I came home at night, and looked back to the morning, it seemed to have been a month agone. Go on, then, like a kind comforter, and paint to me the day we went to St. Germains. How beautiful was every object! the Pont de Renilly, the hills along the Seine, the rainbows of the machine of Marly, the terras of St. Germains, the chateaux, the gardens, the statues of Marly, the pavillon of Lucienne. Recollect, too, Madrid, Bagatelle, the King's Garden, the Dessert. How grand the idea excited by the remains of such a column. The spiral staircase, too, was beautiful.........

Heart. God only knows what is to happen. I see nothing impossible in that proposition :* and I see things wonderfully contrived sometimes, to make us happy. Where could they find such objects as in America for the exer-cise of their enchanting art? especially the lady, who paints landscapes so inimitably. She wants only subjects worthy of immortality to render her pencil immortal. The Falling Spring, the Cascade of Niagara, the Passage of the Potomac through the Blue Mountains, the Natural Bridge; it is worth a voyage across the Atlantic to see these objects; much more to paint, and make them, and thereby ourselves, known to all ages. And our own dear Monticello—where has Nature spread so rich a mantle under the eye?— mountains, forests, rocks, rivers. With what majesty do we ride above the storms! How sublime to look down into the workhouse of Nature, to see her clouds, hail, snow, rain, thunder, all fabricated at our feet! and the glo-rious sun, when rising as if out of a distant water, just gilding the tops of the mountains, and giving life to all nature! I hope in God no circumstance may ever make either seek an asylum from grief!......... Deeply practiced in the school of affliction, the human heart knows no joy which I have not lost, no sorrow of which I have not drunk! Fortune can present no grief of unknown form to me! Who, then, can so softly bind up the wound of an-other as he who has felt the same wound himself?..........

I thought this a favorable proposition whereon to rest the issue of the dialogue. So I put an end to it by calling for my night-cap. Methinks I hear you wish to Heaven I had called a little sooner, and so spared you the ennui of such a sermon...... We have had incessant rains since your de-parture. These make me fear for your health, as well as that you had an uncomfortable journey. The same cause has prevented me from being able to give you an account of your friends here. This voyage to Fontainebleau will probably send the Count de Moustier and the Marquis de

---

* That is, Mr. and Mrs. Cosway to visit America.

Brehan to America. Danguerville promised to visit me but has not done it yet. De la Tude comes sometimes to take family soup with me, and entertains me with anecdotes of his five-and-thirty years' imprisonment. How fertile is the mind of man, which can make the Bastile and dungeon of Vincennes yield interesting anecdotes! You know this was for making four verses on Madame De Pompadour. But I think you told me you did not know the verses. They were these :

> "Sans ésprit, sans sentiment,
>   Sans être belle, ni neuve,
> En France on peut avoir le premier amant:
>   Pompadour en est l'épreuve."

I have read the memoir of his three escapes. As to myself, my health is good, except my wrist, which mends slowly, and my mind, which mends not at all, but broods constantly over your departure. The lateness of the season obliges me to decline my journey into the South of France. Present me in the most friendly terms to Mr. Cosway, and receive me into your own recollection with a partiality and warmth, proportioned not to my own poor merit, but to the sentiments of sincere affection and esteem, with which I have the honor to be, my dear Madam, your most obedient, humble servant,

TH. JEFFERSON.

The following letter, written in a sprightly and artless style, will be found more than usually interesting, from the allusion in it to Sheridan's great speech in the trial of Warren Hastings—that scene of which Macaulay's enchanted pen has left so brilliant a picture. A few awkward expressions in this charming letter remind us that its author wrote in a foreign language.

Mrs. Cosway to Thomas Jefferson.

London, February 15th, 1788.

I have the pleasure of receiving two letters from you, and though very short I must content myself, and lament much the reason that deprived me of their usual length. I must confess that the beginning of your correspondence has made me an *enfant-gâtée.* I shall never learn to be reasonable in my expectations, and shall feel disappointed whenever your letters are not as long as the first was; thus you are the occasion of a continual reproaching disposition in me. It is a disagreeable one, and it will tease you into a hatred towards me, notwithstanding the partiality you have had for me till now, for nothing disobliges more than a dissatisfied mind, and that my fault is occasioned by yourself you will be the most distant to allow. I trust your friendship would wish to see me perfect and mine to be so, but defects are, or are not, most conspicuous according to the feelings which we have for the objects which possess them........

I feel at present an inclination to make you an endless letter, but have not yet determined what subject to begin with. Shall I continue this reproaching style, quote all the whats and whys out of Jeremiah's Lamentations, and then present you with some outlines of Job for consolation? Of all torments, temptations, and wearinesses, the female has always been the principal and most powerful, and this is to be felt by you at present from my pen. Are you to be painted in future ages, sitting solitary and sad on the beautiful Monticello, tormented by the shadow of a woman, who will present you a deformed rod, broken and twisted, instead of the emblematical instrument belonging to the Muses, held by Genius, inspired by Wit; and with which all that is beautiful and happy can be described so as to entertain a mind capable of the highest enjoyments?........

I have written this *in memoria* of the many pages of scrawls addressed to you by one whose good intentions repay you for your beautiful allegories with such long, insipid chit-chat.*...... Allegories, however, are always far-fetched, and I don't like to follow the subject, though I might find something which would explain my ideas.

Suppose I turn to the debates of Parliament? Were I a good politician, I could entertain you much. What do you think of a famous speech Sheridan has made, which lasted four hours, which has astonished every body, and which has been the subject of conversation and admiration of the whole town? Nothing has been talked of for many days but this speech. The whole House applauded him at the moment,

---

* An allusion to the "Dialogue between the Head and Heart."

each member complimented him when they rose, and Pitt
made him the highest encomiums. Only poor Mr. Hastings
suffered for the power of his eloquence, though nothing can
be decided yet. Mr. H. was with Mr. Cosway at the very
moment the trial was going on; he seemed perfectly easy—
talking on a variety of subjects with great tranquillity and
cheerfulness. The second day he was the same, but on the
third seemed very much affected and agitated. All his
friends give him the greatest character of humanity, generosity, and feeling; amiable in his manner, he seems, in short,
totally different from the disposition of cruelty they accuse
him of. Turning from parliamentary discussions, it is time
to tell you that I have been reading with great pleasure your
descriptions of America;* it is writen by *you*, but Nature
represents all the scenes to me in reality, therefore do not
take any thing to yourself; I must refer to your name to
make it the more valuable to me, but *she* is your rival—you
her usurper. Oh! how I wish myself in those delightful
places! those enchanted grottoes! those magnificent mountains, rivers, etc., etc., etc.! Why am I not a man, that I
might set out immediately, satisfy my curiosity, and indulge
my sight with wonders?

I go to very few parties. I have a dislike for them, and I
have grown so excessively indolent that I do not go out for
months together. All the morning I paint whatever presents itself most pleasing to me. Sometimes I have beautiful objects to paint from, and add historical characters to
make them more interesting. Female and infantine beauty
is the most perfect to see. Sometimes I indulge in those
melancholy subjects in which History often represents herself—the horrid, the grand, the sublime, the sentimental, or
the pathetic. I attempt, I exercise in them all, and end by
being witness of my own disappointment and incapacity for
executing the Poet, the Historian, or the conceptions of my
own imagination. Thus the mornings are spent regretting
they are not longer, to have more time to attempt again in
search of better success, or thinking they have been too long,
as they have afforded me many moments of uneasiness and
anxiety, and a testimony of my not being able to do any thing.

---

* Meaning, doubtless, his "Notes on Virginia."

I devote my evenings to music, and then I am much visited by the first Professors, who come to play, often every evening, something new, and are all perfect in their kind. To complete the pleasure, a small society of agreeable friends frequently come to see me, and in this manner you see that I am more attached to my home than to going in search of amusement out, where there are nothing but crowded assemblies, uncomfortable heat, and not the least pleasure in meeting any body, not being able to enjoy any conversation. The Operas are very bad, tho' Zubenelli and Madame Mosa are the first singers; the dancers, too, are very bad; all this I say from report, as I have not been yet. Pray tell me something about Madame De Polignac; they make a great deal about it here; we hardly hear any thing else, and the stories are so different from one another that it is impossible to guess the real one. She is expected in England.

I send this letter by a gentleman whom I think you will like. He is a Spaniard. I am partial to that nation, as I know several who are very agreeable. He is going to Paris as Secretary of Embassy at that Court. He has travelled much, and talks well. If I should be happy enough to come again in the summer to Paris, I hope we shall pass many agreeable days. I am in a million fears about it; Mr. Cosway still keeps to his intentions, but how many chances from our inclinations to the gratification of our wishes. Poor D'Ancarville has been very ill. I received a long letter from him appointing himself my *correspondent* at Paris. I know a gentleman who causes my faith to be weak on this occasion, for *he* flattered me with hopes that I have seen fail; nevertheless I have accepted this offer, and shall see if I find a second disappointment.

Is it not time to finish my letter? Perhaps I might go on, but I must send this to the gentleman who is to take it.

I hope you are quite well by this time, and that your hand will tell me so by a line. I must be reasonable, but give me leave to remind you how much pleasure you will give by remembering sometimes with friendship one who will be as sensible and grateful of it as is, yours sincerely,

MARIA COSWAY.

In a letter to Colonel Edward Carrington, written early in

January, 1787, Jefferson thus notices the meeting of the Notables:

To Colonel Carrington.

In my letter to Mr. Jay I have mentioned the meeting of the Notables, appointed for the 29th instant. It is now put off to the 7th or 8th of next month. This event, which will hardly excite any attention in America, is deemed here the most important one which has taken place in their civil line during the present century. Some promise their country great things from it, some nothing. Our friend De Lafayette was placed on the list originally. Afterwards his name disappeared; but finally was reinstated. This shows that his character here is not considered as an indifferent one; and that it excites agitation. His education in our school has drawn on him a very jealous eye from a court whose principles are the most absolute despotism. But I hope he has nearly passed his crisis. The King, who is a good man, is favorably disposed towards him; and he is supported by powerful family connections, and by the public good-will. He is the youngest man of the Notables, except one whose office placed him on the list.

In a letter written to Madison a few days later, he gives a few sketches of character which we quote, only reminding the reader of Jefferson's great intimacy with Madison, to whom he consequently wrote more freely of men and measures than to any one else.

To James Madison.

Paris, January 30th, 1787.

As you have now returned to Congress, it will become of importance that you should form a just estimate of certain public characters, on which, therefore, I will give you such notes as my knowledge of them has furnished me with. You will compare them with the materials you are otherwise possessed of, and decide on a view of the whole.

You know the opinion I formerly entertained of my friend Mr. Adams...... A seven months' intimacy with him here, and as many weeks in London, have given me opportunities of studying him closely. He is vain, irritable, and a bad cal-

culator of the force and probable effect of the motives which
govern men. This is all the ill which can possibly be said
of him. He is as disinterested as the Being who made him;
he is profound in his views and accurate in his judgment,
except where knowledge of the world is necessary to form a
judgment. He is so amiable, that I pronounce you will love
him if ever you become acquainted with him. He would
be, as he was, a great man in Congress......

The Marquis de Lafayette is a most valuable auxiliary
to me. His zeal is unbounded, and his weight with those in
power great. His education having been merely military,
commerce was an unknown field to him. But, his good sense
enabling him to comprehend perfectly whatever is explained to him, his agency has been very efficacious. He has a
great deal of sound genius, is well remarked by the king,
and is rising in popularity. He has nothing against him
but a suspicion of republican principles. I think he will one
day be of the ministry. His foible is a canine appetite for
popularity and fame; but he will get over this. The Count
de Vergennes is ill. The possibility of his recovery renders
it dangerous for us to express a doubt of it; but he is in
danger. He is a great minister in European affairs, but has
very imperfect ideas of our institutions, and no confidence in
them. His devotion to the principles of pure despotism renders him unaffectionate to our governments. But his fear
of England makes him value us as a make-weight. He is
cool, reserved in political conversations, but free and familiar
on other subjects, and a very attentive, agreeable person to
do business with. It is impossible to have a clearer, better
organized head; but age has chilled his heart.

Nothing should be spared on our part to attach this
country to us. It is the only one on which we can rely for
support under every event. Its inhabitants love us more, I
think, than they do any other nation on earth. This is very
much the effect of the good dispositions with which the
French officers returned. In a former letter I mentioned to
you the dislocation of my wrist. I can make not the least
use of it except for the single article of writing, though it is
going on five months since the accident happened. I have
great anxieties lest I should never recover any considerable
use of it. I shall, by the advice of my surgeons, set out in a

fortnight for the waters of Aix, in Provence. I chose these out of several they proposed to me, because if they fail to be effectual, my journey will not be useless altogether. It will give me an opportunity of examining the canal of Langue-doc, and of acquiring knowledge of that species of naviga-tion, which may be useful hereafter...... I shall be absent between two and three months, unless any thing happens to recall me here sooner; which may always be effected in ten days, in whatever part of my route I may be.

In speaking of characters, I omitted those of Rayneval and Hennin, the two eyes of the Count de Vergennes. The former is the most important character, because possessing the most of the confidence of the Count. He is rather cun-ning than wise, his views of things being neither great nor liberal. He governs himself by principles which he has learned by rote, and is fit only for the details of execution. His heart is susceptible of little passions, but not of good ones. He is brother-in-law to M. Gerard, from whom he re-ceived disadvantageous impressions of us which can not be effaced. He has much duplicity. Hennin is a philosopher, sincere, friendly, liberal, learned, beloved by every body; the other by nobody. I think it a great misfortune that the United States are in the department of the former. As par-ticulars of this kind may be useful to you in your present situation, I may hereafter continue the chapter. I know it will be safely lodged in your discretion. I send you by Colonel Franks your pocket-telescope, walking-stick, and chemical-box. The two former could not be combined to-gether. The latter could not be had in the form you refer-red to. Having a great desire to have a portable copying-machine, and being satisfied, from some experiments, that the principle of the large machine might be applied in a small one, I planned one when in England, and had it made. It answers perfectly. I have since set a workman to making them here, and they are in such demand that he has his hands full. Being assured that you will be pleased to have one, when you shall have tried its convenience, I send you one by Colonel Franks. The machine costs ninety-six livres, the appendages twenty-four livres, and I send you paper and ink for twelve livres; in all one hundred and thirty-two li-vres. There is a printed paper of directions; but you must expect to make many essays before you succeed perfectly. A soft brush like a shaving-brush is more convenient than the sponge. You can get as much paper and ink as you please from London. The paper costs a guinea a ream. I am, dear sir, with sincere esteem and affection, your most humble and obedient servant,

TH. JEFFERSON.

The following charmingly written letter to one of his lady friends gives a spirited picture of the life of a Parisian belle:

To Mrs. Bingham.

Paris, February 7th, 1787.

I know, Madam, that the twelvemonth is not yet expired; but it will be, nearly, before this will have the honor of being put into your hands. You are then engaged to tell me, truly and honestly, whether you do not find the tranquil pleasures of America preferable to the empty bustle of Paris. For to what does the bustle tend? At eleven o'clock it is day, *chez madame.* The curtains are drawn. Propped on bolsters and pillows, and her head scratched into a little order, the bulletins of the sick are read, and the billets of the well. She writes to some of her acquaintances, and receives the visits of others. If the morning is not very thronged, she is able to get out and hobble around the cage of the Palais Royal; but she must hobble quickly, for the coiffeur's turn is come; and a tremendous turn it is! Happy if he does not make her arrive when dinner is half over! The torpitude of digestion a little passed, she flutters for half an hour through the streets, by way of paying visits, and then to the spectacles. These finished, another half-hour is devoted to dodging in and out of the doors of her very sincere friends, and away to supper. After supper, cards; and after cards, bed—to rise at noon the next day, and to tread, like a mill-horse, the same trodden circle over again. Thus the days of life are consumed, one by one, without an object beyond the present moment; ever flying from the ennui of that, yet carrying it with us; eternally in pursuit of happiness, which keeps eternally before us. If death or bankruptcy happen to trip us out of the circle, it is matter for the buzz of the evening, and is completely forgotten by the next morning. In America, on the other hand, the society of your husband, the fond cares for the children, the arrangements of the house, the improvements of the grounds, fill every moment with a useful and healthy activity. Every exertion is encouraging, because to present amusement it joins the promise of some future good. The intervals of leisure are filled by the society of real friends, whose affections are not thinned to cobweb, by being spread over a thousand objects. This is the picture, in the light it is presented to my mind; now let me have it in yours. If we do not concur this year, we shall the next; or if not then, in a year or two more. You see I am determined not to suppose myself mistaken.

To let you see that Paris is not changed in its pursuits since it was honored with your presence, I send you its monthly history. But this relating only to the embellishments of their persons, I must add, that those of the city go on well also. A new bridge, for example, is begun at the Place Louis Quinze; the old ones are clearing of the rubbish which encumbered them in the form of houses; new hospitals erecting; magnificent walls of inclosure, and custom-houses at their entrances, etc., etc. I know of no interesting change among those whom you have honored with your acquaintance, unless Monsieur de Saint James was of that number. His bankruptcy, and taking asylum in the Bastile, have furnished matter of astonishment. His garden at the Pont de Neuilly, where, on seventeen acres of ground, he had laid out fifty thousand louis, will probably sell for somewhat less money. The workmen of Paris are making rapid strides towards English perfection. Would you believe that, in the course of the last two years, they have learned even to surpass their London rivals in some articles? Commission me to have you a phaeton made, and if it is not as much handsomer than a London one as that is than a fiacre, send it back to me. Shall I fill the box with caps, bonnets, etc.? —not of my own choosing, but—I was going to say—of Mademoiselle Bertin's, forgetting for the moment that she too is bankrupt. They shall be chosen, then, by whom you please; or, if you are altogether nonplused by her eclipse, we will call an Assemblée des Notables, to help you out of the difficulty, as is now the fashion. In short, honor me with your commands of any kind, and they shall be faithfully executed. The packets now established from Havre to New York furnish good opportunities of sending whatever you wish.

I shall end where I began, like a Paris day, reminding you of your engagement to write me a letter of respectable length, an engagement the more precious to me, as it has furnished me the occasion, after presenting my respects to Mr. Bingham, of assuring you of the sincerity of those sentiments of esteem and respect with which I have the honor to be, dear Madam, your most obedient and most humble servant,

TH. JEFFERSON.

Mrs. Bingham to Thomas Jefferson.

June 1st, 1787.

I am too much flattered by the honor of your letter from Paris not to acknowledge it by the earliest opportunity, and to assure you that I am very sensible of your attentions. The candor with which you express your sentiments merits a sincere declaration of mine. I agree with you that many of the fashionable pursuits of the Parisian ladies are rather frivolous, and become uninteresting to a reflective mind; but the picture you have exhibited is rather overcharged; you have thrown a strong light upon all that is ridiculous in their characters, and you have buried their good qualities in the shade. It shall be my task to bring them forward, or at least to attempt it. The state of society in different countries requires corresponding manners and qualifications. Those of the French women are by no means calculated for the meridian of America, neither are they adapted to render the sex so amiable or agreeable in the English acceptation of those words. But you must confess that they are more accomplished, and understand the intercourse of society better, than in any other country. We are irresistibly pleased with them, because they possess the happy art of making us pleased with ourselves. Their education is of a higher cast, and by great cultivation they procure a happy variety of genius, which forms their conversation to please either the fop or the philosopher.

In what other country can be found a Marquise de Coigny, who, young and handsome, takes a lead in all the fashionable dissipations of life, and at more serious moments collects at her house an assembly of the literati, whom she charms with her knowledge and her *bel esprit.* The women of France interfere with the politics of the country, and often give a decided turn to the fate of empires. Either by the gentle arts of persuasion, or the commanding force of superior attractions and address, they have obtained that rank and consideration in society which the sex are entitled to, and which they in vain contend for in other countries. We are therefore bound in gratitude to admire and revere them for asserting our privileges, as much as the friends of the liberties of mankind reverence the successful struggles of the American patriots.

The agreeable resources of Paris must certainly please and instruct every class of characters. The arts of elegance are there considered as essential, and are carried to a state of perfection, and there the friend of art is continually gratified by the admiration for works of taste. I have the pleasure of knowing you too well to doubt of your subscribing to this opinion. With respect to my native country, I assure you that I am fervently attached to it, as well as to my friends and connections in it; there, perhaps, there is more sincerity in professions, and a stronger desire of rendering real services, and when the mouth expresses the heart speaks.

I am sensible that I shall tire you to death with the length of this letter, and had almost forgotten that you are in Paris, and that every instant of your time is valuable, and might be much better employed than I can possibly do it. However, I shall reserve a further examination of this subject to the period when I can have the happiness of meeting you, when we will again resume it. I feel myself under many obligations for your kind present of *les modes de Paris.* They have furnished our ladies with many hints for the decoration of their persons, and I have informed them to whom they are indebted. I shall benefit by your obliging offer of service, whenever I shall have occasion for a fresh importation of fashions; at present I am well stocked, having lately received a variety of articles from Paris.

Be so kind as to remember me with affection to Miss Jefferson. Tell her she is the envy of all the young ladies in America, and that I should wish nothing so much as to place my little girl under her inspection and protection, should she not leave Paris before I revisit it. I shall hope for the pleasure of hearing from you, and if you accompany another book of fashions with any new operas or comedies you will infinitely oblige me. It is quite time I bade you adieu; but remember this first of June I am constant to my former opinion, nor can I believe that any length of time will change it. I am determined to have some merit in your eyes, if not for taste and judgment, at least for consistency. Allow me to say, my dear sir, that I am sincerely and respectfully yours,

A. BINGHAM.

CHAPTER VI.

Death of Count de Vergennes.—Jefferson is ordered to Aix by his Surgeon.—
Death of his youngest Child.—Anxiety to have his Daughter Mary with
him.—Her Reluctance to leave Virginia.—Her Letters to and from her Fa-
ther.—Jefferson's Letters to Mrs. and Mr. Eppes.—To Lafayette.—To the
Countess de Tesse.—To Lafayette.—Correspondence with his Daughter
Martha.

In a letter written to Mr. Jay on the 23d of February,
1787, Mr. Jefferson says:

The event of the Count de Vergennes's death, of which I
had the honor to inform you in a letter of the 4th instant,
the appointment of the Count Montmorin, and the propriety
of my attending at his first audience, which will be on the
27th, have retarded the journey I proposed a few days.

The journey above mentioned was a trip to Aix, whither
he was ordered by his surgeon, in order to try the effect of
its mineral-waters on his dislocated wrist. In the letters
which he wrote to his daughter Martha, while absent on
this occasion, he alludes frequently to his youngest daughter, Mary, or Polly, as she was sometimes called. As I
have before mentioned, she and her younger sister, Lucy,
were left by their father in Virginia, with their kind uncle
and aunt, Mr. and Mrs. Eppes. Lucy died in the fall of the
year 1784, and her death was announced to her father in a
letter from Mr. Eppes, who writes:

I am sorry to inform you that my fears about the welfare
of our children, which I mentioned in my last, were too well
founded. Yours, as well as our dear little Lucy, have fallen
sacrifices to the most horrible of all disorders, the whooping-
cough. They both suffered as much pain, indeed more than
ever I saw two of their ages experience. We were happy

in having had every experience this country afforded ; however, they were beyond the reach of medicine.*

The death of this child was felt keenly by Jefferson. After getting established in Paris, he became impatient to have his little daughter Mary with him. She did not join him, however, until the year 1787, her uncle and aunt being loath to part with her, and no good opportunity occurring for getting her across the Atlantic. The child herself could not bear the thought of being torn from the kind uncle and aunt, whom she had learned to love so devotedly, to go to a strange land. I have lying before me a package of her letters to her father, whose sweet, childish prattle must be excuse enough for their appearing here, trivial though they seem. The first was written for her by her aunt. The others are in the huge, grotesque-looking letters of a child just beginning to write. The following was written before her father had left Philadelphia :

Mary Jefferson to Thomas Jefferson.

Eppington, April 11th, 1784.

My dear Papa—I want to know what day you are going to come and see me, and if you will bring sister Patsy and my baby with you. I was mighty glad of my sashes, and gave Cousin Bolling one. I can almost read.

Your affectionate daughter,

POLLY JEFFERSON.

---

* With the tender sensibility of a mother, Mrs. Eppes announced this event to Jefferson in the following touching lettter :

Eppington, October 13th, 1784.

Dear Sir—It is impossible to paint the anguish of my heart on this melancholy occasion. A most unfortunate whooping-cough has deprived you and us of two sweet Lucys within a week. Ours was the first that fell a sacrifice. She was thrown into violent convulsions, lingered out a week, and then died. Your dear angel was confined a week to her bed, her sufferings were great, though nothing like a fit; she retained her senses perfectly, called me a few minutes before she died and asked distinctly for water. Dear Polly has had it most violently, though always kept about, and is now quite recovered. ......
Life is scarcely supportable under such severe afflictions. Be so good as to remember me most affectionately to my dear Patsy, and beg she will excuse my not writing till the gloomy scene is a little forgotten. I sincerely hope you are both partaking of every thing that can in the smallest degree entertain and make you happy. ·Our warmest affections attend you both.

Your sincere friend,   E. EPPES.

It is touching to see how gently her father tries to reconcile her, in the following letter, to her separation from her good uncle and aunt, and how he attempts to lure her to France with the promise that she shall have in Paris " as many dolls and playthings " as she wants.

Thomas Jefferson to Mary Jefferson.

Paris, Sept. 20th, 1785.

My dear Polly—I have not received a letter from you since I came to France. If you knew how much I love you and what pleasure the receipt of your letters gave me at Philadelphia, you would have written to me, or at least have told your aunt what to write, and her goodness would have induced her to take the trouble of writing it. I wish so much to see you, that I have desired your uncle and aunt to send you to me. I know, my dear Polly, how sorry you will be, and ought to be, to leave them and your cousins; .but your sister and myself can not live without you, and after a while we will carry you back again to see your friends in Virginia. In the mean time you shall be taught here to play on the harpsichord, to draw, to dance, to read and talk French, and such other things as will make you more worthy of the love of your friends; but above all things, by our care and love of you, we will teach you to love us more than you will do if you stay so far from us. I have had no opportunity since Colonel Le Maire went, to send you any thing; but when you come here you shall have as many dolls and playthings as you want for yourself, or to send to your cousins whenever you shall have opportunities. I hope you are a very good girl, that you love your uncle and aunt very much, and are very thankful to them for all their goodness to you; that you never suffer yourself to be angry with any body, that you give your playthings to those who want them, that you do whatever any body desires of you that is right, that you never tell stories, never beg for any thing, mind your books and your work when your aunt tells you, never play but when she permits you, nor go where she forbids you; remember, too, as a constant charge, not to go out without your bonnet, because it will make you very ugly, and then we shall not love you so much. If you always practice these lessons we shall continue to love you as we do now, and it is impossible to love you any more. We shall hope to have you with us next summer, to find you a very good girl, and to assure you of the truth of our affection for you. Adieu, my dear child. Yours affectionately,

TH. JEFFERSON.

Mary Jefferson to Thomas Jefferson.

Dear Papa—I long to see you, and hope that you and sister Patsy are well; give my love to her and tell her that I long to see her, and hope that you and she will come very soon to see us. I hope that you will send me a doll. I am very sorry that you have sent for me. I don't want to go to France, I had rather stay with Aunt Eppes. Aunt Carr, Aunt Nancy and Cousin Polly Carr are here. Your most happy and dutiful daughter,

POLLY JEFFERSON.

Dear Papa—I should be very happy to see you, but I can not go to France, and hope that you and sister Patsy are well. Your affectionate daughter. Adieu.

MARY JEFFERSON.

Dear Papa—I want to see you and sister Patsy, but you must come to Uncle Eppes's house.

POLLY JEFFERSON.

Mr. Jefferson's anxieties about his little daughter crossing the ocean, and his impatience to fold her once more in his arms, are vividly portrayed in the following letter:

Thomas Jefferson to Mrs. Eppes.

Paris, Sept. 22d, 1785.

Dear Madam — The Mr. Fitzhughs having staid here longer than they expected, I have (since writing my letter of Aug. 30, to Mr. Eppes) received one from Dr. Currie, of August 5, by which I have the happiness to learn you are all well, and my Poll also. Every information of this kind is like gaining another step, and seems to say we "have got so far safe." Would to God the great step was taken and taken safely; I mean that which is to place her on this side of the Atlantic. No event of your life has put it into your power to conceive how I feel when I reflect that such a child, and so dear to me, is to cross the ocean, is to be exposed to all the sufferings and risks, great and small, to which a situation on board a ship exposes every one. I drop my pen at the thought—but she must come. My affections would leave me balanced between the desire to have her with me, and the fear of exposing her; but my reason tells me the dangers are not great, and the advantages to her will be considerable.

I send by Mr. Fitzhugh some garden and flower seed and bulbs; the latter, I know, will fall in your department. I wish the opportunity had admitted the sending more, as well as some things for the children; but Mr. Fitzhugh being to pass a long road both here and in America, I could not ask it of him. Pray write to me, and write me long letters. Currie has sent me one worth a great deal for the details of small news it contains. I mention this as an example for you. You always know facts enough which would be interesting to me to fill sheets of paper. I pray you, then, to give yourself up to that kind of inspiration, and to scribble on as long as you recollect any thing unmentioned, without regarding whether your lines are straight or your letters even. Remember me affectionately to Mr. Skipwith, and to the little ones of both houses; kiss dear Polly for me, and encourage her for the journey. Accept assurances of unchangeable affection from, dear Madam, your sincere friend and servant,

TH. JEFFERSON.

In the letter to Mr. Eppes of August 30th, which Mr. Jefferson alludes to in the preceding, he writes:

Thomas Jefferson to Mr. Eppes.

I must now repeat my wish to have Polly sent to me next summer. This, however, must depend on the circumstance of a good vessel sailing from Virginia in the months of April, May, June, or July. I would not have her set out sooner or later on account of the equinoxes. The vessel should have performed one voyage at least, but not be more than four or five years old. We do not attend to this circumstance till we have been to sea, but there the consequence of it is felt. I think it would be found that all the vessels which are lost are either on their first voyage or after they are five years old; at least there are few exceptions to this. With respect to the person to whose care she should be trusted, I must leave it to yourself and Mrs. Eppes altogether. Some good lady passing from America to France, or even England, would be most eligible; but a careful gentleman who would be so kind as to superintend her would do. In this case some woman who has had the small-pox must attend her. A careful negro woman, as Isabel, for instance, if she has had the small-pox, would suffice under the patronage of a gentleman. The woman need not come farther than Havre, l'Orient, Nantes, or whatever port she should land at, because I could go there for the child myself, and the person could return to Virginia directly. My anxieties on this subject could induce me to endless details, but your discretion and that of Mrs. Eppes saves me the necessity. I will only add that I would rather live a year longer without her than have her trusted to any but a good ship and a summer passage. Patsy is well. She speaks French as easily as English; while Humphries, Short, and myself are scarcely better at it than when we landed........

I look with impatience to the moment when I may rejoin you. There is nothing to tempt me to stay here. Present me with the most cordial affection to Mrs. Eppes, the children, and the family at Hors-du-monde. I commit to Mrs. Eppes my kisses for dear Poll, who hangs on my mind night and day.

Had he been the mother instead of the father of the little girl who was to cross the Atlantic, he could not have shown more anxiety about her welfare and safety on the passage. In a letter of Jan. 7th, 1786, to Mr. Eppes, he writes:

I wrote you last on the 11th of December, by the way of London. That conveyance being uncertain, I write the present chiefly to repeat a prayer I urged in that, that you would confide my daughter only to a French or English vessel having a Mediterranean *pass*. This attention, though of little consequence in matters of merchandise, is of weight in the

mind of a parent which sees even possibilities of capture beyond the reach of any estimate. If a peace be concluded
with the Algerines in the mean time, you shall be among
the first to hear it from myself. I pray you to believe it
from nobody else, as far as respects the conveyance of my
daughter to me.

A few weeks later he writes:

I know that Mrs. Eppes's goodness will make her feel a
separation from an infant who has experienced so much of
her tenderness. My unlimited confidence in her has been
the greatest solace possible under my own separation from
Polly. Mrs. Eppes's good sense will suggest to her many
considerations which render it of importance to the future
happiness of the child that she should neither forget nor be
forgotten by her sister and myself.

In concluding the same letter, he says:

How much should I prize one hour of your fireside, where
I might indulge that glow of affection which the recollection
of Mrs. Eppes and her little ones excites in me, and give you
personal assurances of the sincere esteem with which I am,
dear Sir, your affectionate friend and servant.

In a letter written to Mr. Eppes a year later, he says, " My
dear Poll, I hope, is on the way to me. I endeavor not to
think of her till I hear she is landed." His reasons for in-
sisting upon his little daughter being sent to him are found
in the following letter:

To Mrs. Eppes.

Paris, Dec. 14th, 1786.

Dear Madam—I perceive, indeed, that our friends are kind-
er than we have sometimes supposed them, and that their
letters do not come to hand. I am happy that yours of
July 30th has not shared the common fate. I received it
about a week ago, together with one from Mr. Eppes announcing to me that my dear Polly will come to me the ensuing summer. Though I am distressed when I think of this
voyage, yet I know it is necessary for her happiness. She is

better with you, my dear Madam, than she could be anywhere else in the world, except with those whom nature has allied still more closely to her. It would be unfortunate through life, both to her and us, were those affections to be loosened which ought to bind us together, and which should be the principal source of our future happiness. Yet this would be too probably the effect of absence at her age. This is the only circumstance which has induced me to press her joining us...... I am obliged to cease writing. An unfortunate dislocation of my right wrist has disabled me from writing three months. I have as yet no use of it, except that I can write a little, but slowly and in great pain. I shall set out in a few days to the South of France, to try the effect of some mineral-waters there. Assure Mr. and Mrs. Skipwith of my warm affections. Kiss the little ones for me. I suppose Polly not to be with you. Be assured yourself of my sincere love and esteem.

Yours affectionately,

TH. JEFFERSON.

On the eve of his departure for the South of France, we find him writing the following letter to his devoted friend, Lafayette. In the advice which he gives of keeping England for a model, we see, on his part, an apprehension of the dangers ahead in the proceedings of the Assemblée des Notables.

To Lafayette.

Paris, February 28th, 1787.

Dear Sir—I am just now in the moment of my departure. Monsieur de Montmorin having given us audience at Paris yesterday, I missed the opportunity of seeing you once more. I am extremely pleased with his modesty, the simplicity of his manners, and his dispositions towards us. I promise myself a great deal of satisfaction in doing business with him. I hope he will not give ear to any unfriendly suggestions. I flatter myself I shall hear from you sometimes. Send your letters to my hotel, as usual, and they will be forwarded to me. I wish you success in your meeting. I should form better hopes of it, if it were divided into two Houses instead of seven. Keeping the good model of your neighboring country before your eyes, you may get on, step by step, towards a good constitution. Though that model is not perfect, yet, as it would unite more suffrages than any new one which could be proposed, it is better to make that the object. If every advance is to be purchased by filling the royal coffers with gold, it will be gold well employed. The King, who means so well, should be encouraged to repeat these Assemblies. You see how we republicans are apt to preach when we get on politics. Adieu, my dear friend.

Yours affectionately,

TH. JEFFERSON.

While on this tour though the southern part of France, Jefferson wrote some of his most charming letters to his daughter and his friends; among the latter the two most agreeable were to Lafayette and the Comtesse de Tesse, which we now give:

*To the Comtesse de Tesse.**

Nismes, March 20th, 1787.

Here I am, Madam, gazing whole hours at the Maison Quarrée, like a lover at his mistress. The stocking-weavers and silk-spinners around it consider me as a hypochondriac Englishman, about to write with a pistol the last chapter of his history. This is the second time I have been in love since I left Paris. The first was with a Diana at the Château de Laye-Epinaye in Beaujolais, a delicious morsel of sculpture, by M. A. Slodtz. This, you will say, was in rule, to fall in love with a female beauty; but with a house! It is out of all precedent. No, Madam, it is not without a precedent in my own history. While in Paris, I was violently smitten with the Hôtel de Salm, and used to go to the Tuileries almost daily to look at it. The *loueuse des chaises*—inattentive to my passion—never had the complaisance to place a chair there, so that sitting on the parapet, and twisting my neck around to see the object of my admiration, I generally left it with a *torti-colli*.

From Lyons to Nismes I have been nourished with the remains of Roman grandeur. They have always brought you

---

* This lady was an aunt of Madame Lafayette, and an intimate friend of Jefferson's.

to my mind, because I know your affection for whatever is Roman and noble. At Vienne I thought of you. But I am glad you were not there; for you would have seen me more angry than, I hope, you will ever see me. The Prætorian palace, as it is called—comparable, for its fine proportions, to the Maison Quarrée—defaced by the barbarians who have converted it to its present purpose, its beautiful, fluted Corinthian columns cut out, in part, to make space for Gothic windows, and hewed down, in the residue, to the plane of the building, was enough, you must admit, to disturb my composure. At Orange, too, I thought of you. I was sure you had seen with pleasure the sublime triumphal arch of Marius at the entrance of the city. I went then to the Arenæ. Would you believe, Madam, that in this eighteenth century, in France, under the reign of Louis XVI., they are at this moment pulling down the circular wall of this superb remain, to pave a road? And that, too, from a hill which is itself an entire mass of stone, just as fit, and more accessible! A former intendant, a Monsieur de Basville, has rendered his memory dear to the traveller and amateur, by the pains he took to preserve and restore these monuments of antiquity. The present one (I do not know who he is) is demolishing the object, to make a good road to it. I thought of you again, and I was then in great good-humor, at the Pont du Gard, a sublime antiquity and well preserved. But most of all here, where Roman taste, genius, and magnificence excite ideas analogous to yours at every step. I could no longer oppose the inclination to avail myself of your permission to write to you, a permission given with too much complaisance by you, and used by me with too much indiscretion. Madame de Tott did me the same honor. But, she being only the descendant of some of those puny heroes who boiled their own kettles before the walls of Troy, I shall write to her from a Grecian, rather than a Roman canton; when I shall find myself, for example, among her Phocian relations at Marseilles.

Loving as you do, Madam, the precious remains of antiquity, loving architecture, gardening, a warm sun and a clear sky, I wonder you have never thought of moving Chaville to Nismes. This, as you know, has not always been deemed impracticable; and therefore, the next time a *Sur-intendant des batiments du roi*, after the example of M. Colbert, sends

persons to Nismes to move the Maison Quarrée to Paris, that
they may not come empty-handed, desire them to bring Chaville with them, to replace it.   Apropos of Paris.   I have
now been three weeks from there, without knowing any
thing of what has passed.   I suppose I shall meet it all at
Aix, where I have directed my letters to be lodged *poste restante.*   My journey has given me leisure to reflect on the Assemblée des Notables.   Under a good and a young king, as
the present, I think good may be made of it.   I would have
the deputies, then, by all means, so conduct themselves as to
encourage him to repeat the calls of this Assembly.   Their
first step should be to get themselves divided into two Chambers instead of seven—the Noblesse and the Commons sep-
arately.   The second, to persuade the King, instead of choosing the deputies of the Commons himself, to summon those
chosen by the people for the provincial administrations.
The third, as the Noblesse is too numerous to be all of the
Assemblée, to obtain permission for that body to choose its
own deputies.   Two Houses, so elected, would contain a
mass of wisdom which would make the people happy and
the King great—would place him in history where no other
act could possibly place him.   They would thus put themselves in the track of the best guide they can follow; they
would soon overtake it, become its guide in turn, and lead to
the wholesome modifications wanting in that model, and
necessary to constitue a rational government.   Should they
attempt more than the established habits of the people are
ripe for, they may lose all, and retard indefinitely the ultimate object of their aim.   These, Madam, are my opinions;
but I wish to know yours, which, I am sure will be better.

From a correspondent at Nismes you will not expect
news.   Were I to attempt to give you news, I should tell
you stories one thousand years old.   I should detail to you
the intrigues of the courts of the Cæsars—how they affect us
here, the oppressions of their prætors, prefects, etc.   I am
immersed in antiquities from morning to night.   For me
the city of Rome is actually existing in all the splendor of
its empire.   I am filled with alarms for the event of the ir-
ruptions daily making on us by the Goths, Visigoths, Os-
trogoths, and Vandals, lest they should reconquer us to our
original barbarism.   If I am sometimes induced to look for-

ward to the eighteenth century, it is only when recalled to it by the recollection of your goodness and friendship, and by those sentiments of sincere esteem and respect, with which I have the honor to be, Madam, your most obedient and most humble servant,

TH. JEFFERSON.

To Lafayette.

Nice, April 11th, 1787.

Your head, my dear friend, is full of Notable things; and being better employed, therefore, I do not expect letters from you. I am constantly roving about to see what I have never seen before, and shall never see again. In the great cities, I go to see what travellers think alone worthy of being seen; but I make a job of it, and generally gulp it all down in a day. On the other hand, I am never satiated with rambling through the fields and farms, examining the culture and cultivators with a degree of curiosity which makes some take me to be a fool, and others to be much wiser than I am. I have been pleased to find among the people a less degree of physical misery than I had expected. They are generally well clothed, and have a plenty of food, not animal, indeed, but vegetable, which is as wholesome.......

From the first olive-fields of Pierrelatte to the orangeries of Hières has been continued rapture to me. I have often wished for you. I think you have not made this journey. It is a pleasure you have to come, and an improvement to be added to the many you have already made. It will be a great comfort to you to know, from your own inspection, the condition of all the provinces of your own country, and it will be interesting to them, at some future day, to be known to you. This is, perhaps, the only moment of your life in which you can acquire that knowledge. And to do it most effectually, you must be absolutely incognito, you must ferret the people out of their hovels, as I have done, look into their kettles, eat their bread, loll on their beds under pretense of resting yourself, but in fact to find if they are soft. You will feel a sublime pleasure in the course of this investigation, and a sublimer one hereafter, when you shall be able to apply your knowledge to the softening of their beds, or the throwing a morsel of meat into their kettle of vegetables.

You will not wonder at the subjects of my letter; they are the only ones which have been presented to my mind for some time past, and the waters must always be what are the fountains from which they flow. According to this, indeed, I should have intermingled, from beginning to end, warm expressions of friendship to you. But, according to the ideas of our country, we do not permit ourselves to speak even truths, when they have the air of flattery. I content myself, therefore, with saying once more for all, that I love you, your wife and children. Tell them so, and adieu.   Yours affectionately,

TH. JEFFERSON.

The following correspondence between Jefferson and his daughter Martha will be found unusually interesting. Her letters were written from the convent of Panthemont, in Paris, where she was at school. She was at the time fifteen years old, and the artlessness, intelligence, and warm affection with which she writes to her father render her letters inexpressibly charming.

Martha Jefferson to Thomas Jefferson.

Being disappointed in my expectation of receiving a letter from my dear papa, I have resolved to break so painful a silence by giving you an example that I hope you will follow, particularly as you know how much pleasure your letters give me. I hope your wrist is better, and I am inclined to think that your voyage is rather for your pleasure than your health; however, I hope it will answer both purposes. I will now tell you how I go on with my masters. I have begun a beautiful tune with Balbastre, done a very pretty landscape with Pariseau—a little man playing on the violin —and begun another beautiful landscape. I go on slowly with my *Tite Live*,* it being in such ancient Italian that I can not read without my master, and very little with him even. As for the dancing-master, I intend to leave him off as soon as my month is finished. Tell me if you are still de-

---

* Livy.

H

termined that I shall dine at the abbess's table. If you are, I shall at the end of my quarter. The King's speech and that of the Eveque de Narbonne have been copied all over the convent. As for Monsieur, he rose up to speak, but sat down again without daring to open his lips. I know no news, but suppose Mr. Short will write you enough for him and me too. Madame Thaubeneu desires her compliments to you. Adieu, my dear papa. I am afraid you will not be able to read my scrawl, but I have not the time of copying it over again; and therefore I must beg your indulgence, and assure you of the tender affection of yours,

M. JEFFERSON.

Pray write often, and long letters.

Panthemont, February 8th, 1787.

Martha Jefferson to Thomas Jefferson.

My dear Papa—Though the knowledge of your health gave me the greatest pleasure, yet I own I was not a little disappointed in not receiving a letter from you. However, I console myself with the thought of having one very soon, as you promised to write to me every week. Until now you have not kept your word the least in the world, but I hope you will make up for your silence by writing me a fine, long letter by the first opportunity. *Titus Livius* puts me out of my wits. I can not read a word by myself, and I read of it very seldom with my master; however, I hope I shall soon be able to take it up again. All my other masters go on much the same—perhaps better. Every body here is very well, particularly Madame L'Abbesse, who has visited almost a quarter of the new building—a thing that she has not done for two or three years before now. I have not heard any thing of my harpsichord, and I am afraid it will not come before your arrival. They make every day some new history on the Assemblée des Notables. I will not tell you any, for fear of taking a trip to the Bastile for my pains, which I am by no means disposed to do at this moment. I go on pretty well with Thucydides, and hope I shall very soon finish it. I expect Mr. Short every instant for my letter, therefore I must leave you. Adieu, my dear papa; be assured you are never a moment absent from my thoughts, and believe me to be, your most affectionate child,

M. JEFFERSON.

March 25th, 1787.

Thomas Jefferson to Martha Jefferson.

Aix en Provence, March 28th, 1787.

I was happy, my dear Patsy, to receive, on my arrival here, your letter, informing me of your good health and occupation. I have not written to you sooner because I have been almost constantly on the road. My journey hitherto has been a very pleasing one. It was undertaken with the hope that the mineral-waters of this place might restore strength to my wrist. Other considerations also concurred—instruction, amusement, and abstraction from business, of which I had too much at Paris. I am glad to learn that you are employed in things new and good, in your music and drawing. You know what have been my fears for some time past—that you do not employ yourself so closely as I could wish. You have promised me a more assiduous attention, and I have great confidence in what you promise. It is your future happiness which interests me, and nothing can contribute more to it (moral rectitude always excepted) than the contracting a habit of industry and activity. Of all the cankers of human happiness none corrodes with so silent, yet so baneful an influence, as indolence. Body and mind both unemployed, our being becomes a burthen, and every object about us loathsome, even the dearest. Idleness begets ennui, ennui the hypochondriac, and that a diseased body. No laborious person was ever yet hysterical. Exercise and application produce order in our affairs, health of body and cheerfulness of mind, and these make us precious to our friends. It is while we are young that the habit of industry is formed. If not then, it never is afterwards. The fortune of our lives, therefore, depends on employing well the short period of youth. If at any moment, my dear, you catch yourself in idleness, start from it as you would from the precipice of a gulf. You are not, however, to consider yourself as unemployed while taking exercise. That is necessary for your health, and health is the first of all objects. For this reason, if you leave your dancing-master for the summer, you must increase your other exercise.

I do not like your saying that you are unable to read the ancient print of your Livy but with the aid of your master. We are always equal to what we undertake with resolution.

A little degree of this will enable you to decipher your Livy. If you always lean on your master, you will never be able to proceed without him. It is a part of the American character to consider nothing as desperate; to surmount every difficulty by resolution and contrivance. In Europe there are shops for every want; its inhabitants, therefore, have no idea that their wants can be supplied otherwise. Remote from all other aid, we are obliged to invent and to execute; to find means within ourselves, and not to lean on others. Consider, therefore, the conquering your Livy as an exercise in the habit of surmounting difficulties; a habit which will be necessary to you in the country where you are to live, and without which you will be thought a very helpless animal, and less esteemed. Music, drawing, books, invention, and exercise, will be so many resources to you against ennui. But there are others which, to this object, add that of utility. These are the needle and domestic economy. The latter you can not learn here, but the former you may. In the country life of America there are many moments when a woman can have recourse to nothing but her needle for employment. In a dull company, and in dull weather, for instance, it is ill-manners to read, it is ill-manners to leave them; no card-playing there among genteel people — that is abandoned to blackguards. The needle is then a valuable resource. Besides, without knowing how to use it herself, how can the mistress of a family direct the work of her servants?

You ask me to write you long letters. I will do it, my dear, on condition you will read them from time to time, and practice what they inculcate. Their precepts will be dictated by experience, by a perfect knowledge of the situation in which you will be placed, and by the fondest love for you. This it is which makes me wish to see you more qualified than common. My expectations from you are high, yet not higher than you may attain. Industry and resolution are all that are wanting. Nobody in this world can make me so happy, or so miserable, as you. Retirement from public life will ere long become necessary for me. To your sister and yourself I look to render the evening of my life serene and contented. Its morning has been clouded by loss after loss, till I have nothing left but you. I do not doubt either your affections or dispositions. But great exertions are necessary, and you have little time left to make them. Be industrious, then, my dear child. Think nothing insurmountable by resolution and application, and you will be all that I wish you to be.

You ask if it is my desire that you should dine at the Abbess's table? It is. Propose it as such to Madame de Frauleinheim, with my respectful compliments, and thanks for her care of you. Continue to love me with all the warmth with which you are beloved by, my dear Patsy,

Yours affectionately,

TH. JEFFERSON.

Martha Jefferson to Thomas Jefferson.

My dear Papa—I am very glad that the beginning of your voyage has been so pleasing, and I hope that the rest will not be less so, as it is a great consolation for me, being deprived of the pleasure of seeing you, to know at least that you are happy. I hope your resolution of returning in the end of April is always the same. I do not doubt but what Mr. Short has written you word that my sister sets off with Fulwar Skipwith in the month of May, and she will be here in July. Then, indeed, shall I be the happiest of mortals; united to what I have the dearest in the world, nothing more will be requisite to render my happiness complete. I am not so industrious as you or I would wish, but I hope that in taking pains I very soon shall be. I have already begun to study more. I have not heard any news of my harpsichord; it will be really very disagreeable if it is not here before your arrival. I am learning a very pretty thing now, but it is very hard. I have drawn several little flowers, all alone, that the master even has not seen; indeed, he advised me to draw as much alone as possible, for that is of more use than all I could do with him. I shall take up my Livy, as you desire it. I shall begin it again, as I have lost the thread of the history. As for the hysterics, you may be quiet on that head, as I am not lazy enough to fear them. Mrs. Barett has wanted me out, but Mr. Short told her that you had forgotten to tell Madame L'Abbesse to let me go out with her. There was a gentleman, a few days ago, that killed himself because he thought that his wife did not love him. They had been married ten years. I believe that if every husband in Paris was to do as much, there would be nothing but widows left. I shall speak to Madame Thaubeneu about dining at the Abbess's table. As for needlework, the only kind that I could learn here would be embroidery, indeed netting also; but I could not do much of those in America, because of the impossibility of having proper silks; however, they will not be totally useless. You say your expectations for me are high, yet not higher than I can attain. Then be assured, my dear papa, that you shall be satisfied in that, as well as in any thing else that lies in my power; for what I hold most precious is your satisfaction, indeed I should be miserable without it. You wrote me a long letter, as I asked you; however, it would have been much more so without so wide a margin. Adieu, my dear papa. Be assured of the tenderest affection of your loving daughter,

M. JEFFERSON.

Pray answer me very soon—a long letter, without a margin. I will try to follow the advice they contain with the most scrupulous exactitude.

Panthemont, April 9th, 1787.

Thomas Jefferson to Martha Jefferson.

Toulon, April 7th, 1787.

My dear Patsy—I received yesterday, at Marseilles, your letter of March 25th, and I received it with pleasure, because it announced to me that you were well. Experience learns us to be always anxious about the health of those whom we love. I have not been able to write to you as often as I expected, because I am generally on the road, and when I stop anywhere I am occupied in seeing what is to be seen. It will be some time now, perhaps three weeks, before I shall be able to write you again. But this need not slacken your writing to me, because you have leisure, and your letters come regularly to me. I have received letters which inform me that our dear Polly will certainly come to us this summer. By the time I return it will be time to expect her. When she arrives she will become a precious charge on your hands. The difference of your age, and your common loss of a mother, will put that office on you. Teach her above all things to be good, because without that we can neither be valued by others nor set any value on ourselves. Teach her to be always true; no vice is so mean as the want of truth, and at the same time so useless. Teach her never to be angry; anger only serves to torment ourselves, to divert others, and alienate their esteem. And teach her industry, and application to useful pursuits. I will venture to assure you that, if you inculcate this in her mind, you will make her a happy being in herself, a most inestimable friend to you, and precious to all the world. In teaching her these dispositions of mind, you will be more fixed in them yourself, and render yourself dear to all your acquaintances. Practice them, then, my dear, without ceasing. If ever you find yourself in difficulty, and doubt how to extricate yourself, do what is right, and you will find it the easiest way of getting out of the difficulty. Do it for the additional incitement of increasing the happiness of him who loves you infinitely, and who is, my dear Patsy, yours affectionately,

TH. JEFFERSON.

Martha Jefferson to Thomas Jefferson.

My dear Papa—I was very sorry to see, by your letter to Mr. Short, that your return would be put off. However, I hope not much, as you must be here for the arrival of my sister. I wish I was myself all that you tell me to make her; however, I will try to be as near like it as I can. I have another landscape since I wrote to you last, and have begun another piece of music. I have not been able to do more, having been confined some time to my bed with a violent headache and a pain in my side, which afterwards blistered up and made me suffer a great deal, but I am now much better. I have seen a physician who had just drawn two of my companions out of a most dreadful situation, which gave me a great deal of trust in him. But the most disagreeable thing is, that I have been obliged to discontinue all my masters, and am able now to take only some of them that are the least fatiguing. However, I hope to take them all very soon. Madame L'Abbesse has just had a *fluxion de poitrine*, and has been at the last extremity, but now is better. The *pays bas* have revolted against the Emperor, who is gone to Prussia to join with the Empress and the Venetians to war against the Turks. The plague is in Spain. A Virginia ship coming to Spain met with a corsair of the same strength. They fought, and the battle lasted an hour and a quarter. The Americans gained and boarded the corsair, where they found chains that had been prepared for them. They took them, and made use of them for the Algerians themselves. They returned to Virginia, from whence they are to go back to Algiers to change the prisoners, to which, if the Algerians will not consent, the poor creatures will be sold as slaves. Good God! have we not enough? I wish with all my soul that the poor negroes were all freed...... A coach-and-six, well shut up, was seen to go to the Bastile, and the Baron de Breteuil went two hours before to prepare an apartment. They suppose it to be Madame de Polignac and her sister; however, no one knows. The King asked M. D'Harcourt how much a year was necessary for the Dauphin. M. D'Harcourt having looked over the accounts, told him two millions; upon which the King could not help expressing his astonishment, because each of his daughters cost him more; so Madame de Polignac had pocketed the rest. Mr. Smith is at Paris. That is all the news I know; they told me a great deal more, but I have forgotten it. Adieu, my dear papa, and believe me to be for life your most tender and affectionate child,

M. JEFFERSON.

Paris, May 3d, 1787.

Thomas Jefferson to Martha Jefferson.

Marseilles, May 5th, 1787.

My dear Patsy—I got back to Aix the day before yesterday, and found there your letter of the 9th of April—from which I presume you to be well, though you do not say so. In order to exercise your geography, I will give you a detail of my journey. You must therefore take your map and trace out the following places: Dijon, Lyons, Pont St. Esprit, Nismes, Arles, St. Remis, Aix, Marseilles, Toulon, Hières, Fréjus, Antibes, Nice, Col de Tende, Coni, Turin, Vercelli, Milan, Pavia, Tortona, Novi, Genoa, by sea to Albenga, by land to Monaco, Nice, Antibes, Fréjus, Brignolles, Aix, and Marseilles. The day after to-morrow, I set out hence for

Aix, Avignon, Pont du Gard, Nismes, Montpellier, Narbonne, along the Canal of Languedoc to Toulouse, Bordeaux, Rochefort, Rochelle, Nantes, L'Orient, Nantes, Tours, Orléans, and Paris—where I shall arrive about the middle of June, after having travelled something upwards of a thousand leagues.

From Genoa to Aix was very fatiguing—the first two days having been at sea, and mortally sick—two more clambering the cliffs of the Apennines, sometimes on foot, sometimes on a mule, according as the path was more or less difficult—and two others travelling through the night as well as day without sleep. I am not yet rested, and shall therefore shortly give you rest by closing my letter, after mentioning that I have received a letter from your sister, which, though a year old, gave me great pleasure. I inclose it for your perusal, as I think it will be pleasing for you also. But take care of it, and return it to me when I shall get back to Paris, for, trifling as it seems, it is precious to me.

When I left Paris, I wrote to London to desire that your harpsichord might be sent during the months of April and May, so that I am in hopes it will arrive a little before I shall, and give me an opportunity of judging whether you have got the better of that want of industry which I began to fear would be the rock on which you would split. Determine never to be idle. No person will have occasion to complain of the want of time who never loses any. It is wonderful how much may be done if we are always doing. And that you may be always doing good, my dear, is the ardent prayer of, yours affectionately,

TH. JEFFERSON.

Martha Jefferson to Thomas Jefferson.

My dear Papa—I was very glad to see by your letter that you were on your return, and I hope that I shall very soon have the pleasure of seeing you. My sister's letter gave me a great deal of happiness. I wish she would write to me; but as I shall enjoy her presence very soon, it will make up for a neglect that I own gives me the greatest pain. I still remember enough of geography to know where the places marked in your letter are. I intend to copy over my extracts and learn them by heart. I have learnt several new pieces on the harpsichord, drawn five landscapes and three flowers, and hope to have done something more by the time you come. I go on pretty well with my history, and as for *Tite Live* I have begun it three or four times, and go on so slowly with it that I believe I never shall finish it. It was in vain that I took courage; it serves to little good in the execution of a thing almost impossible. I read a little of it with my master who tells me almost all the words, and, in fine, it makes me lose my time. I begin to have really great difficulty to write English; I wish I had some pretty letters to form my style. Pray tell me if it is certain that my sister comes in the month of July, because if it is, Madame De Taubenheim will keep a bed for her. My harpsichord is not come yet. Madame L'Abbesse is better, but she still keeps her bed. Madame De Taubenheim sends her compliments to you. Pray how does your arm go? I am very well now. Adieu, my dear papa; as I do not know any news, I must finish in assuring you of the sincerest affection of your loving child,

Paris, May 27th, 1787.   M. JEFFERSON.

Thomas Jefferson to Martha Jefferson.

May 21st, 1787.

I write you, my dear Patsy, from the canal of Languedoc, on which I am at present sailing, as I have been for a week past, cloudless skies above, limpid waters below, and on each hand, a row of nightingales in full chorus. This delightful bird had given me a rich treat before, at the fountain of Vaucluse. After visiting the tomb of Laura at Avignon, I went to see this fountain—a noble one of itself, and rendered famous forever by the songs of Petrarch, who lived near it. I arrived there somewhat fatigued, and sat down by the fountain to repose myself. It gushes, of the size of a river, from a secluded valley of the mountain, the ruins of Petrarch's château being perched on a rock two hundred feet perpendicular above. To add to the enchantment of the scene, every tree and bush was filled with nightingales in full song. I think you told me that you had not yet noticed this bird. As you have trees in the garden of the convent, there might be nightingales in them, and this is the season of their song. Endeavor, my dear, to make yourself acquainted with the music of this bird, that when you return to your own country you may be able to estimate its merit in comparison with that of the mocking-bird. The latter has the advantage of singing through a great part of the year, whereas the nightingale sings but about five or six weeks in the spring, and a still shorter term, and with a more feeble voice, in the fall.

I expect to be at Paris about the middle of next month. By that time we may begin to expect our dear Polly. It will be a circumstance of inexpressible comfort to me to have you both with me once more. The object most interesting to me for the residue of my life, will be to see you both developing daily those principles of virtue and goodness which will make you valuable to others and happy in yourselves, and acquiring those talents and that degree of science which will guard you at all times against ennui, the most dangerous poison of life. A mind always employed is always happy. This is the true secret, the grand recipe, for felicity. The idle are the only wretched. In a world which furnishes so many employments which are useful, so many which are amusing, it is our own fault if we ever know what ennui is, or if we are ever driven to the miserable resource of gaming, which corrupts our dispositions, and teaches us a habit of hostility against all mankind. We are now entering the port of Toulouse, where I quit my bark, and of course must conclude my letter. Be good and be industrious, and you will be what I shall most love in the world. Adieu, my dear child. Yours affectionately,

TH. JEFFERSON.

The following is an extract from a letter to his daughter, dated Nantes, June 1st, 1787:

I forgot, in my last letter, to desire you to learn all your old tunes over again perfectly, that I may hear them on your harpsichord, on its arrival. I have no news of it, however, since I left Paris, though I presume it will arrive immediately, as I have ordered. Learn some slow movements of simple melody for the Celestini stop, as it suits such only. I am just setting out for L'Orient, and shall have the happiness of seeing you at Paris about the 12th or 15th of this month, and assuring you in person of the sincere love of, yours affectionately, TH. JEFFERSON.

CHAPTER VII.

While Mr. Jefferson was eagerly expecting the arrival of his little daughter from Virginia, the child herself was still clinging to the hope that her father might change his plans for her and agree to her remaining with her Aunt Eppes, from whom she obstinately refused to be separated. Towards the close of the month of March, 1787, we find this kind lady writing to Mr. Jefferson as follows:

Mrs. Eppes to Jefferson.

I never was more anxious to hear from you than at present, in hopes of your countermanding your orders with regard to dear Polly. We have made use of every stratagem to prevail on her to consent to visit you without effect. She is more averse to it than I could have supposed; either of my children would with pleasure take her place for the number of good things she is promised. However, Mr. Eppes has two or three different prospects of conveying her, to your satisfaction, I hope, if we do not hear from you.

On the eve of the child's departure her anxious aunt again writes:

This will, I hope, be handed you by my dear Polly, who I most ardently wish may reach you in the health she is in at present. I shall be truly wretched till I hear of her being safely landed with you. The children will spend a day or two on board the ship with her, which I hope will reconcile her to it. For God's sake give us the earliest intelligence of her arrival.

As mentioned in the above extract, her young cousins went on board the ship with the little Mary, and were her playmates there until she had become somewhat at home and acquainted with those around her. Then, while the child was one day asleep, they were all taken away, and before she awoke the vessel had cut loose from her moorings, and was fairly launched on the tedious voyage before her.

The bark bearing this precious little charge, and the object of so many hopes and prayers on both sides of the Atlantic, made a prosperous voyage, and landed the young child safely in England. There, at her father's request, she was received by Mrs. Adams, who treated her with the tenderness of a mother, until he could arrange to get her across the Channel. Some of his French friends, who were at the time in England, were to have taken her to Paris, but his impatience to see her could not brook the delay of their return, and he sent a servant—Petit, his steward—for her. In the mean time he announced her safe arrival to her friends in Virginia in the following letter:

To Francis Eppes.

Paris, July 2d, 1787.

Dear Sir—The present is merely to inform you of the safe arrival of Polly in London, in good health. I have this moment dispatched a servant for her. Mr. Ammonit did not come, but she was in the best hands possible, those of Captain Ramsay. Mrs. Adams writes me she was so much attached to him that her separation from him was a terrible operation. She has now to go through the same with Mrs. Adams. I hope that in ten days she will join those from whom she is no more to be separated. As this is to pass through post-offices, I send it merely to relieve the anxieties which Mrs. Eppes and yourself are so good as to feel on her account, reserving myself to answer both your favors by the next packet. I am, with very sincere esteem, dear Sir, your affectionate friend and servant,

TH. JEFFERSON.

The loneliness of the little girl's situation on her arrival in a strange land, among strangers, her distress at having parted with her good aunt, Mrs. Eppes, her gratitude to Mrs. Adams for her kindness, her singular beauty, and the sweetness of her disposition, are touchingly and vividly described by Mrs. Adams in a letter to her sister. She writes:

From Mrs. Adams.

I have had with me for a fortnight a little daughter of Mr. Jefferson's, who arrived here, with a young negro girl, her servant, from Virginia. Mr. Jefferson wrote me some months ago that he expected them, and desired me to receive them. I did so, and was amply repaid for my trouble. A finer child of her age I never saw.* So mature an understanding, so womanly a behavior, and so much sensibility united, are rarely to be met with. I grew so fond of her, and she was so much attached to me, that, when Mr. Jefferson sent for her, they were obliged to force the little creature away. She is but eight years old. She would sit, sometimes, and describe to me the parting with her aunt, who brought her up, the obligation she was under to her, and the love she had for her little cousins, till the tears would stream down her cheeks; and how I had been her friend, and she loved me. Her papa would break her heart by making her go again. She clung round me so that I could not help shedding a tear at parting with her. She was the favorite of every one in the house. I regret that such fine spirits must be spent in the walls of a convent. She is a beautiful girl too.

The following letter written by Mr. Jefferson to Mrs. Eppes describes the arrival of his little one in Paris, and her visits to the convent.

To Mrs. Eppes.

Paris, July 28th, 1787.

Dear Madam—Your favors of March 31st and May 7th have been duly received; the last by Polly, whose arrival has given us great joy. Her disposition to attach herself

---

* She was in her ninth year.

to those who are kind to her had occasioned successive distresses on parting with Captain Ramsay first, and afterwards with Mrs. Adams. She had a very fine passage, without a storm, and was perfectly taken care of by Captain Ramsay. He offered to come to Paris with her, but this was unnecessary. I sent a trusty servant to London to attend her here. A parent may be permitted to speak of his own child when it involves an act of justice to another. The attentions which your goodness has induced you to pay her prove themselves by the fruits of them. Her reading, her writing, her manners in general, show what everlasting obligations we are all under to you. As far as her affections can be a requital, she renders you the debt, for it is impossible for a child to prove a more sincere affection to an absent person than she does to you. She will surely not be the least happy among us when the day shall come in which we may be all reunited. She is now established in the convent, perfectly happy. Her sister came and staid a week with her, leading her from time to time to the convent, until she became familiarized to it. This soon took place, as she became a universal favorite with the young ladies and the mistresses. She writes you a long letter, giving an account of her voyage and journey here. She neither knew us, nor should we have known her had we met with her unexpectedly. Patsy enjoys good health, and will write to you. She has grown much the last year or two, and will be very tall. She retains all her anxiey to get back to her country and her friends, particularly yourself. Her dispositions give me perfect satisfaction, and her progress is well; she will need, however, your instruction to render her useful in her own country. Of domestic economy she can learn nothing here, yet she must learn it somewhere, as being of more solid value than any thing else. I answer Jack's* letter by this occasion. I wish he would give me often occasion to do it; though at this distance I can be of no use to him, yet I am willing to show my disposition to be useful to him, as I shall be forever bound to be to every one connected with yourself and Mr. Eppes, had no other connection rendered the obligation dear to my heart. I shall present my affec-

---

* Mrs. Eppes's son, and little Polly's future husband.

tions to Mr. and Mrs. Skipwith in a letter to the former. Kiss the children for me, and be assured of the unchangeable esteem and respect of, dear Madam, your affectionate friend and servant,

TH. JEFFERSON.

When little Mary Jefferson first went to Paris, instead of " Polly," she was called by the French *Mademoiselle Polie.* In a short time, however, she was called Marie, and on her return to America, the Virginian pronunciation of that French name soon ran into Maria, by which name, strange to say, she was ever after called, even by her father and sister; and Maria, instead of Mary, is the name now inscribed on the marble slab which rests upon her grave.

The following is a letter written a short while after his return to Paris, to one of his lady friends, then on a visit to England:

To Madame de Corny.

Paris, June 30th, 1787.

On my return to Paris it was among my first attentions to go to the Rue Chaussée d'Antin, No. 17, and inquire after my friends whom I had left there. I was told they were in England. And how do you like England, Madam? I know your taste for the works of art gives you a little disposition to Anglomania. Their mechanics certainly exceed all others in some lines. But be just to your own nation. They have not patience, it is true, to sit rubbing a piece of steel from morning to night, as a lethargic Englishman will do, full-charged with porter. But do not their benevolence, their amiability, their cheerfulness, when compared with the growling temper and manners of the people among whom you are, compensate their want of patience? I am in hopes that when the splendor of their shops, which is all that is worth seeing in London, shall have lost the charm of novelty, you will turn a wishful eye to the good people of Paris, and find that you can not be so happy with any others. The Bois de Boulogne invites you earnestly to come and survey its beautiful verdure, to retire to its umbrage from the heats of the season. I was through it to-day, as I am every day. Every tree charged me with this invitation to you. Passing by La Muette, it wished for you as a mistress. You want a country-house. This is for sale; and in the Bois de Boulogne, which I have always insisted to be most worthy of your preference. Come, then, and buy it. If I had had confidence in your speedy return, I should have embarrassed you in earnest with my little daughter. But an impatience to have her with me, after her separation from her friends, added to a respect for your ease, has induced me to send a servant for her.

I tell you no news, because you have correspondents infinitely more *au fait* of the details of Paris than I am. And I offer you no services, because I hope you will come as soon as the letter could which should command them. Be assured, however, that nobody is more disposed to render them, nor entertains for you a more sincere and respectful attachment, than him who, after charging you with his compliments to Monsieur de Corny, has the honor of offering you the homage of those sentiments of distinguished esteem and regard, with which he is, dear Madam, your most obedient and most humble servant,

TH. JEFFERSON.

In a letter to J. Bannister, Jr., he thus speaks of the ill-fated traveller Ledyard, and of the pleasures of his own recent tour through the southern part of France:

To J. Bannister.

I had a letter from Ledyard lately, dated at St. Petersburg. He had but two shirts, and yet, more shirts than shillings. Still he was determined to obtain the palm of being the first circumambulator of the earth. He says that, having no money, they kick him from place to place, and thus he expects to be kicked around the globe. Are you become a great walker? You know I preach up that kind of exercise. Shall I send you a conte-pas? It will cost you a dozen louis, but be a great stimulus to walking, as it will record your steps. I finished my tour a week or ten days ago. I went as far as Turin, Milan, Genoa; and never passed three months and a half more delightfully. I returned through the Canal of Languedoc, by Bourdeaux, Nantes,

I

L'Orient, and Rennes; then returned to Nantes and came up the Loire to Orléans. I was alone through the whole, and think one travels more usefully when alone, because he reflects more.

To Mrs. Bolling.

Paris, July 23d, 1787.

Dear Sister—I received with real pleasure your letter of May 3d, informing me of your health and of that of your family. Be assured it is, and ever has been, the most interesting thing to me. Letters of business claiming their rights before those of affection, we often write seldomest to those whom we love most. The distance to which I am removed has given a new value to all I valued before in my own country, and the day of my return to it will be the happiest I expect to see in this life. When it will come is not yet decided, as far as depends on myself. My dear Polly is safely arrived here, and in good health. She had got so attached to Captain Ramsay that they were obliged to decoy her from him. She staid three weeks in London with Mrs. Adams, and had got up such an attachment to her, that she refused to come with the person I sent for her. After some days she was prevailed on to come. She did not know either her sister or myself, but soon renewed her acquaintance and attachment. She is now in the same convent with her sister, and will come to see me once or twice a week. It is a house of education altogether, the best in France, and at which the best masters attend. There are in it as many Protestants as Catholics, and not a word is ever spoken to them on the subject of religion. Patsy enjoys good health, and longs much to return to her friends. We shall doubtless find much change when we do get back; many of our older friends withdrawn from the stage, and our younger ones grown out of our knowledge. I suppose you are now fixed for life at Chestnut Grove. I take a part of the misfortune to myself, as it will prevent my seeing you as often as would be practicable at Lickinghole. It is still a greater loss to my sister Carr. We must look to Jack for indemnification, as I think it was the plan that he should live at Lickinghole. I suppose he is now become the father of a family, and that we may hail you as grandmother. As we approach that term it becomes less fearful. You mention Mr. Bolling's being unwell, so as not to write to me. He has just been sick enough all his life to prevent his writing to any body. My prayer is, therefore, only that he may never be any worse; were he to be so, nobody would feel it more sensibly than myself, as nobody has a more sincere esteem for him than myself. I find as I grow older, that I love those most whom I loved first. Present me to him in the most friendly terms; to Jack also, and my other nephews and nieces of your fireside, and be assured of the sincere love with' which I am, dear sister, your affectionate brother,

TH. JEFFERSON.

In the autumn of this year (1787) the Count de Moustier was sent by the Court of St. Germains as minister plenipotentiary to the United States. In a letter to Mr. Jay, Jefferson recommends the Count and his sister-in-law, Madame de Brehan, to the kind attentions of Mr. Jay and his family in the following terms:

To John Jay.

The connection of your offices will necessarily connect you in acquaintance; but I beg leave to present him to you on account of his personal as well as his public character. You will find him open, communicative, candid, simple in his manners, and a declared enemy to ostentation and luxury. He goes with a resolution to add no aliment to it by his example, unless he finds that the dispositions of our countrymen require it indispensably. Permit me, at the same time, to solicit your friendly notice, and through you, that also of Mrs. Jay, to Madame la Marquise de Brehan, sister-in-law to Monsieur de Moustier. She accompanies him, in hopes that a change of climate may assist her feeble health, and also that she may procure a more valuable education for her son, and safer from seduction, in America than in France. I think it impossible to find a better woman, more amiable, more modest, more simple in her manners, dress, and way of thinking. She will deserve the friendship of Mrs. Jay, and the way to obtain hers is to receive her and treat her without the shadow of etiquette.

On the eve of her departure for America, Jefferson wrote the following graceful note of adieu:

To Madame de Brehan.

Paris, October 9th, 1787.

Persuaded, Madam, that visits at this moment must be troublesome, I beg you to accept my adieus in this form. Be assured that no one mingles with them more regret at separating from you. I will ask your permission to inquire of you by letter sometimes how our country agrees with your health and your expectations, and will hope to hear it from yourself. The imitation of European manners, which you will find in our towns, will, I fear, be little pleasing. I beseech you to practice still your own, which will furnish them a model of what is perfect. Should you be singular, it will be by excellence, and after a while you will see the effect of your example.

Heaven bless you, Madam, and guard you under all circumstances—give you smooth waters, gentle breezes, and clear skies, hushing all its elements into peace, and leading with its own hand the favored bark, till it shall have safely landed its precious charge on the shores of our new world.

TH. JEFFERSON.

The following pleasant letter is to another of his lady friends:

To Madame de Corny.

Paris, October 18th, 1787.

I now have the honor, Madam, to send you the Memoir of M. de Calonnes. Do not injure yourself by hurrying its perusal. Only when you shall have read it at your leisure, be so good as to send it back, that it may be returned to the Duke of Dorset. You will read it with pleasure. It has carried comfort to my heart, because it must do the same to the King and the nation. Though it does not prove M. de Calonnes to be more innocent than his predecessors, it shows him not to have been that exaggerated scoundrel which the calculations and the clamors of the public have supposed. It shows that the public treasures have not been so inconceivably squandered as the Parliaments of Grenoble, Toulouse, etc., had affirmed. In fine, it shows him less wicked, and France less badly governed, than I had feared. In examining my little collection of books, to see what it could furnish you on the subject of Poland, I find a small piece which may serve as a supplement to the history I had sent you. It contains a mixture of history and politics, which I think you will like.

How do you do this morning? I have feared you exerted and exposed ,yourself too much yesterday. I ask you the question, though I shall not await its answer. The sky is clearing, and I shall away to my hermitage. God bless you, my dear Madam, now and always. Adieu.

TH. JEFFERSON.

In a letter written to Mr. Donald in the year 1788, his weariness of public life shows itself in the following lines:

To Mr. Donald.

Your letter has kindled all the fond recollections of ancient times—recollections much dearer to me than any thing I have known since. There are minds which can be pleased with honors and preferments; but I see nothing in them but envy and enmity. It is only necessary to possess them to know how little they contribute to happiness, or rather how hostile they are to it. No attachments soothe the mind so much as those contracted in early life; nor do I recollect any societies which have given me more pleasure than those of which you have partaken with me. I had rather be shut up in a very modest cottage with my books, my family, and a few old friends, dining on simple bacon, and letting the world roll on as it liked, than to occupy the most splendid post that any human power can give. I shall be glad to hear from you often. Give me the small news as well as the great.

Early in March, Mr. Jefferson was called by business to meet Mr. Adams in Amsterdam. After an absence of some weeks he returned to Paris. About this time we find him very delicately writing to Mr. Jay on the subject of an outfit, which, it seems, Congress had not at that time allowed to its ministers abroad, and the want of which was painfully felt by them.

To John Jay.

It is the usage here (and I suppose at all courts), that a minister resident shall establish his house in the first instant. If this is to be done out of his salary, he will be a twelvemonth, at least, without a copper to live on. It is the universal practice, therefore, of all nations to allow the outfit as a separate article from the salary. I have inquired here into the usual amount of it. I find that sometimes the sovereign pays the actual cost. This is particularly the case of the Sardinian ambassador now coming here, who is to provide a service of plate and every article of furniture and other matters of first expense, to be paid for by his court. In other instances, they give a service of plate, and a fixed sum for all other articles, which fixed sum is in no case lower than a year's salary.

I desire no service of plate, having no ambition for splendor. My furniture, carriage, and apparel are all plain; yet they have cost me more than a year's salary. I suppose that in every country and every condition of life, a year's expense would be found a moderate measure for the furniture of a man's house. It is not more certain to me that the sun will rise to-morrow, than that our Government must allow the outfit, on their future appointment of foreign ministers; and it would be hard on me so to stand between the discontinuance of a former rule and the institution of a future one as to have the benefit of neither.

In writing to Mr. Izard, who wrote to make some inquiries about a school for his son in France, he makes the following remarks about the education of boys:

To Mr. Izard.

I have never thought a boy should undertake abstruse or difficult sciences, such as mathematics in general, till fifteen years of age at soonest. Before that time they are best employed in learning the languages, which is merely a matter of memory. The languages are badly taught here. If you propose he should learn the Latin, perhaps you will prefer the having him taught it in America, and, of course, to retain him there two or three years more.

One of the most beautiful traits in Jefferson's character was the tenderness of his love for a sister—Ann Scott Jefferson—who was deficient in intellect, and who, on that account, was more particularly the object of his brotherly love and attentions. The two following letters addressed to her husband and herself on the event of their marriage, while handsome and graceful letters in themselves, are more interesting and greater proofs of the goodness of his heart and the sincere warmth of his affections, from the simple character and nature of those to whom they were addressed.

To Mrs. Anna Scott Marks.

Paris, July 12th, 1788.

My dear Sister—My last letters from Virginia inform me of your marriage with Mr. Hastings Marks. I sincerely wish you joy and happiness in the new state into which you have entered. Though Mr. Marks was long my neighbor, eternal occupations in business prevented my having a particular acquaintance with him, as it prevented me from knowing more of my other neighbors, as I would have wished to have done. I saw enough, however, of Mr. Marks to form a very good opinion of him, and to believe that he will endeavor to render you happy. I am sure you will not be wanting on your part. You have seen enough of the different conditions of life to know that it is neither wealth nor splendor, but tranquillity and occupation, which give happiness. This truth I can confirm to you from longer observation and a greater scope of experience. I should wish to know where Mr. Marks proposes to settle and what line of life he will follow. In every situation I should wish to render him and you every service in my power, as you may be assured I shall ever feel myself warmly interested in your happiness, and preserve for you that sincere love I have always borne you. My daughters remember you with equal affection, and will, one of these days, tender it to you in person. They join me in wishing you all earthly felicity, and a continuance of your love to them. Accept assurances of the sincere attachment with which I am, my dear sister, your affectionate brother,

TH. JEFFERSON.

To Hastings Marks.

Paris, July 12th, 1788.

Dear Sir—My letters from Virginia informing me of your intermarriage with my sister, I take the earliest opportunity of presenting you my sincere congratulations on that occasion. Though the occupations in which I was engaged prevented my forming with you that particular acquaintance which our neighborhood might have admitted, it did not prevent my entertaining a due sense of your merit. I am particularly pleased that Mr. Lewis has taken the precise measures which I had intended to recommend to him in order to put you into immediate possession of my sister's fortune in my hands. I should be happy to know where you mean to settle and what occupation you propose to follow—whether any other than that of a farmer, as I shall ever feel myself interested in your success, and wish to promote it by any means in my power, should any fall in my way. The happiness of a sister whom I very tenderly love being committed to your hands, I can not but offer prayers to Heaven for your prosperity and mutual satisfaction. A thorough knowledge of her merit and good dispositions encourages me to hope you will both find your happiness in this union, and this hope is encouraged by my knowledge of yourself. I beg you to be assured of the sentiments of sincere esteem and regard with which I shall be on all occasions, dear Sir, your friend and servant,

TH. JEFFERSON.

The following is to his only brother:

To Randolph Jefferson.

Paris, January 11th, 1789.

Dear Brother—The occurrences of this part of the globe are of a nature to interest you so little that I have never made them the subject of a letter to you. Another discouragement has been the distance and time a letter would be on its way. I have not the less continued to entertain for you the same sincere affection, the same wishes for your health and that of your family, and almost an envy of your quiet and retirement. The very short period of my life which I have passed unconnected with public business suffices to convince me it is the happiest of all situations, and that no society is so precious as that of one's own family. I hope to have the pleasure of seeing you for a while the next summer. I have asked of Congress a leave of absence for six months, and if I obtain it in time I expect to sail from hence in April, and to return in the fall. This will enable me to pass two months at Monticello, during which I hope I shall see you and my sister there. You will there meet an old acquaintance, very small when you knew her, but now of good stature.* Polly you hardly remember, and she scarcely recollects you. Both will be happy to see you and my sister, and to be once more placed among their friends they well remember in Virginia....... Nothing in this country can make amends for what one loses by quitting their own. I suppose you are by this time the father of a numerous family, and that my namesake is big enough to begin the thraldom of education. Remember me affectionately to my sister, joining my daughters therein, who present their affectionate duty to you also ; and accept yourself assurances of the sincere attachment and esteem of, dear brother,

Yours affectionately,

TH. JEFFERSON.

Six months before writing the above he wrote the following :

To Mrs. Eppes.

Paris, July 12th, 1788.

Dear Madam—Your kind favor of January 6th has come duly to hand. These marks of your remembrance are always dear to me, and recall to my mind the happiest portion of my life. It is among my greatest pleasures to receive news of your welfare and that of your family. You improve in your trade, I see, and I heartily congratulate you on the double blessings of which Heaven has just begun to open her stores to you. Polly is infinitely flattered to find a namesake in one of them. She promises in return to

---

* Martha Jefferson.

teach them both French. This she begins to speak easily enough, and to read as well as English. She will begin Spanish in a few days, and has lately begun the harpsichord and drawing. She and her sister will be with me to-morrow, and if she has any tolerable scrap of her pencil ready I will inclose it herein for your diversion. I will propose to her, at the same time, to write to you. I know she will undertake it at once, as she has done a dozen times. She gets all the apparatus, places herself very formally with pen in hand, and it is not till after all this and rummaging her head thoroughly that she calls out, "Indeed, papa, I do not know what to say; you must help me," and, as I obstinately refuse this, her good resolutions have always proved abortive, and her letters ended before they were begun. Her face kindles with love whenever she hears your name, and I assure you Patsy is not behind her in this. She remembers you with warm affection, recollects that she was bequeathed to you, and looks to you as her best future guide and guardian. She will have to learn from you things which she can not learn here, and which after all are among the most valuable parts of education for an American. Nor is the moment so distant as you imagine; on this I will enter into explanations in my next letter. I will only engage, from her dispositions, that you will always find in her the most passive compliance. You say nothing to us of Betsy, whom we all remember too well not to remember her affectionately. Jack, too, has failed to write to me since his first letter. I should be much pleased if he would himself give me the details of his occupations and progress. I would write to Mrs. Skipwith,* but I could only repeat to her what I say to you, that we love you both sincerely, and pass one day in every week together, and talk of nothing but Eppington, Hors-du-monde, and Monticello, and were we to pass the whole seven, the theme would still be the same. God bless you both, Madam, your husbands, your children, and every thing near and dear to you, and be assured of the constant affection of your sincere friend and humble servant,

TH. JEFFERSON.

---

* His sister-in-law, Mrs. Eppes's sister.

CHAPTER VIII.

In November, 1788, Mr. Jefferson wrote to Mr. Jay to petition Congress for a leave of absence of five or six months.
He earnestly desired this leave, that he might return to
America to look after his own private affairs, which sadly
needed his personal attention, and that he might carry his
daughters back to Virginia and leave them with their relations there, as he thought they were now at an age when
they should be associating with those among whom they
were to live.

During the months which elapsed before he received leave
to return home, his correspondence with his friends in America continued to be interesting. In a letter written to Mr.
Jay early in January, 1789, we find the following sketch of a
character then notorious in Europe:

To John Jay.

As the character of the Prince of Wales is becoming interesting, I have endeavored to learn what it truly is. This is
less difficult in his case than it is in other persons of his rank,
because he has taken no pains to hide himself from the world.
The information I most rely on is from a person here, with
whom I am intimate, who divides his time between Paris
and London—an Englishman by birth, of truth, sagacity, and
science. He is of a circle, when in London, which has had

good opportunities of knowing the Prince; but he has also, himself, had special occasions of verifying their information by his own personal observations. He happened, when last in London, to be invited to a dinner of three persons. The Prince came by chance, and made the fourth. He ate half a leg of mutton; did not taste of small dishes, because small; drank Champagne and Burgundy as small beer during dinner, and Bourdeaux after dinner, as the rest of the company. Upon the whole, he ate as much as the other three, and drank about two bottles of wine without seeming to feel it.

My informant sat next him, and being until then unknown to the Prince personally (though not by character), and lately from France, the Prince confined his conversation to him almost entirely. Observing to the Prince that he spoke French without the slightest foreign accent, the Prince told him that, when very young, his father had put only French servants about him, and that it was to that circumstance he owed his pronunciation. He led him from this to give an account of his education, the total of which was the learning a little Latin. He has not a single element of mathematics, of natural or moral philosophy, or of any other science on earth, nor has the society he has kept been such as to supply the void of education. It has been that of the lowest, the most illiterate and profligate persons of the kingdom, without choice of rank or mind, and with whom the subjects of conversation are only horses, drinking-matches, bawdy-houses, and in terms the most vulgar. The young nobility who begin by associating with him soon leave him disgusted by the insupportable profligacy of his society; and Mr. Fox, who has been supposed his favorite, and not over-nice in the choice of company, would never keep his company habitually. In fact, he never associated with a man of sense. He has not a single idea of justice, morality, religion, or of the rights of men, or any anxiety for the opinion of the world. He carries that indifference for fame so far, that he probably would not be hurt if he were to lose his throne, provided he could be assured of having always meat, horses, and women. In the article of women, nevertheless, he has become more correct since his connection with Mrs. Fitzherbert, who is an honest and worthy woman; he is even less crapulous than he was.

He had a fine person, but it is becoming coarse. He possesses good native common sense, is affable, polite, and very good-humored—saying to my informant, on another occasion, "Your friend such a one dined with me yesterday, and I made him damned drunk;" he replied, "I am sorry for it. I had heard that your royal highness had left off drinking." The Prince laughed, tapped him on the shoulder very good-naturedly, without saying a word, or ever after showing any displeasure.

The Duke of York, who was for some time cried up as the prodigy of the family, is as profligate and of less understanding. To these particular traits, from a man of sense and truth, it would be superfluous to add the general terms of praise or blame in which he is spoken of by other persons, in whose impartiality and penetration I have less confidence. A sample is better than a description. For the peace of Europe, it is best that the King should give such gleamings of recovery as would prevent the Regent or his ministry from thinking themselves firm, and yet that he should not recover.

The following letters were written by Jefferson to his friend Madame de Brehan, who was still in America. The first is a note of introduction given to one of his lady friends, and the second contains an interesting account of the severity of the winter of 1788–'89 and of the sufferings of the poor in Paris.

To Madame de Brehan.

Paris, Feb. 15th, 1789.

It is an office of great pleasure to me, my dear Madam, to bring good people together. I therefore present to you Mrs. Church, who makes a short visit to her native country. I will not tell you her amiable qualities, but leave you the pleasure of seeing them yourself. You will see many *au premier abord*, and you would see more every day of your lives, were every day of your lives to bring you together. In truth, I envy you the very gift I make you, and would willingly, if I could, take myself the moments of her society which I am procuring you. I need not pray you to load her with civilities. Both her character and yours will insure this. I will thank you for them in person, however, very soon after you shall receive this. Adieu, ma chère Madame. Agreez toutes les hommages de respect et d'attachement avec lesquelles j'ai l'honneur d'être, Madame, votre très humble et très obeissant serviteur,

TH. JEFFERSON.

To Madame de Brehan.

Paris, March 14th, 1789.

Dear Madam—I had the honor of writing to you on the 15th of February, soon after which I had that of receiving your favor of December the 29th. I have a thousand questions to ask you about your journey to the Indian treaty, how you like their persons, their manners, their costumes, *cuisine*, etc. But this I must defer until I can do it personally in New York, where I hope to see you for a moment in the summer, and to take your commands for France. I have little to communicate to you from this place. It is deserted; every body being gone into the country to choose or be chosen deputies to the States General. I hope to see that great meeting before my departure. It is to be on the 27th of next month. A great political revolution will take place in your country, and that without bloodshed. A king, with two hundred thousand men at his orders, is disarmed by the force of public opinion and the want of money. Among the economies becoming necessary, perhaps one may be the Opera. They say it has cost the public treasury a hundred thousand crowns in the last year. A new theatre is established since your departure—that of the Opera Buffons, where Italian operas are given, and good music. Paris is every day enlarging and beautifying. I do not count among its beauties, however, the wall with which they have inclosed us. They have made some amends for this by making fine Boulevards within and without the walls. These are in considerable forwardness, and will afford beautiful rides around the city of between fifteen and twenty miles in circuit. We have had such a winter, Madame, as makes me shiver yet whenever I think of it. All communications, almost, were cut off. Dinners and suppers were suppressed, and the money laid out in feeding and warming the poor, whose labors were suspended by the rigors of the season. Loaded carriages passed the Seine on the ice, and it was covered with

thousands of people from morning to night, skating and slid-
ing. Such sights were never seen before, and they continued
two months. We have nothing new and excellent in your
charming art of painting. In fact, I do not feel an interest
in any pencil but that of David. But I must not hazard
details on a subject wherein I am so ignorant and you are
such a connoisseur. Adieu, my dear Madam; permit me always the honor of esteeming and being esteemed by you,
and of tendering you the homage of that respectful attachment, with which I am and shall ever be, dear Madam, your
most obedient, humble servant,

TH. JEFFERSON.

Jefferson's devotion to the study of Natural History is
well known, and the accuracy of his knowledge in it is most
strikingly illustrated in the following anecdote, which we
quote from his biography by Randall:

An amusing anecdote is preserved of the subject of his
correspondence with the celebrated Buffon. The story used
to be so well told by Daniel Webster—who probably heard
it from the lips of the New Hampshire party to it—that we
will give it in his words, as we find it recorded by an intelligent writer, and one evidently very familiar with Mr. Webster, in an article in Harper's Magazine, entitled "Social
Hours of Daniel Webster:"

"Mr. Webster, in the course of his remarks, narrated a story of Jefferson's
overcoming Buffon on a question of Natural History. It was a dispute in relation to the moose—the moose-deer, as it is called in New Hampshire—and
in one of the circles of *beaux-esprits* in Paris. Mr. Jefferson contended for
certain characteristics in the formation of the animal which Buffon stoutly
denied. Whereupon Mr. Jefferson, without giving any one notice of his intention, wrote from Paris to General John Sullivan, then residing in Dur-
ham, New Hampshire, to procure and send him the whole frame of a moose.
The General was no little astonished at a request he deemed so extraordinary; but, well acquainted with Mr. Jefferson, he knew he must have sufficient
motive for it; so he made a hunting-party of his neighbors, and took the
field. They captured a moose of unusual proportions, stripped it to the bone,
and sent the skeleton to Mr. Jefferson, at a cost of fifty pounds sterling. On
its arrival Mr. Jefferson invited Buffon and some other *savants* to a supper at
his house, and exhibited his dear-bought specimen. Buffon immediately acknowledged his error, and expressed his great admiration for Mr. Jefferson's

energetic determination to establish the truth. 'I should have consulted you, Monsieur,' he said, with usual French civility, 'before publishing my book on Natural History, and then I should have been sure of my facts.'"

This has the advantage of most such anecdotes of eminent men, of being accurate nearly to the letter, as far as it goes. The box of President Sullivan (he was President of New Hampshire), containing the bones, horns, and skin of a moose, and horns of the caribou elk, deer, spiked horned buck, etc., reached Mr. Jefferson on the 2d of October. They were the next day forwarded to Buffon—who, however, proved to be out of town. On his return, he took advantage of a supper at Jefferson's, to make the handsome admissions mentioned by Mr. Webster.*

In a letter written early in the summer of the year 1788 to the Rev. Mr. Madison, of William and Mary College, we find Jefferson again right and Buffon wrong on a scientific subject. The student of chemistry will smile at Buffon's opinion, while he can not but admire Jefferson's wonderful foresight in predicting the discoveries to be made in that science, even though he should have erred in his opinion of Lavoisier's chemical nomenclature. We quote the following from the above-mentioned letter:

To Rev. Mr. Madison.

Speaking one day with Monsieur de Buffon on the present ardor of chemical inquiry, he affected to consider chemistry but as cookery, and to place the toils of the laboratory on a footing with those of the kitchen. I think it, on the contrary, among the most useful of sciences, and big with future discoveries for the utility and safety of the human race. It is yet, indeed, a mere embryon. Its principles are contested; experiments seem contradictory, their subjects are so minute as to escape our senses; and their results too fallacious to satisfy the mind. It is probably an age too soon to propose the establishment of a system. The attempts, therefore, of Lavoisier to reform the chemical nomenclature is premature.

---

* See Randall's Life of Jefferson, vol. i., p. 490.

One single experiment may destroy the whole filiation of his terms, and his string of sulphates, sulphites, and sulphures may have served no other end than to have retarded the progress of the science, by a jargon, from the confusion of which time will be requisite to extricate us. Accordingly, it is not likely to be admitted generally.

The letter of which we now give the conclusion shows how closely and how minutely Jefferson watched and studied the improvements and progress made in the arts and sciences during his stay in Europe. This letter—to be found in both editions of his correspondence—was written in the spring of the year 1789, and addressed to Doctor Willard, professor in the University of Harvard, which University had just conferred on Jefferson a diploma as Doctor of Laws. After mentioning and criticising all the late publications bearing on the different branches of science and letters, he makes the following eloquent conclusion :

To Dr. Willard.

What a field have we at our doors to signalize ourselves in ! The Botany of America is far from being exhausted, its mineralogy is untouched, and its Natural History or Zoology totally mistaken and misrepresented. As far as I have seen, there is not one single species of terrestrial birds common to Europe and America, and I question if there be a single species of quadrupeds. (Domestic animals are to be excepted.) It is for such institutions as that over which you preside so worthily, Sir, to do justice to our country, its productions, and its genius. It is the work to which the young men you are forming should lay their hands. We have spent the prime of our lives in procuring them the precious blessing of liberty. Let them spend theirs in showing that it is the great parent of *science* and of virtue, and that a nation will be great in both always in proportion as it is free. Nobody wishes more warmly for the success of your good exhortations on this subject than he who has the honor to be, with sentiments of great esteem and respect, Sir, your most obedient humble servant, etc.

K

Mr. Jefferson, as I have elsewhere noticed, placed his daughters at school in a convent, and they were there educated during his stay in Paris. His daughter Martha was now in her sixteenth year. She had not failed to take advantage of the fine opportunities of being an accomplished and well-informed woman which had been secured to her by the most thoughtful and devoted of fathers. She was a good linguist, an accomplished musician, and well read for her years; and we doubt whether any of her Virginian or even American female contemporaries could boast so thorough an education as could the modest, yet highly-gifted, Martha Jefferson. The gentle and loving kindness lavished on her by the inmates of the convent won for them her warmest affection, while the sweet amiability of her disposition, the charming simplicity of her manner, and the unusual powers of her mind endeared her to them. Thus her school-days flowed peacefully and gently by. But while their father had so carefully secured for his daughters a good mental and moral training by the situation in which he had placed them, he had overlooked the danger of their becoming too fond of it. He was startled, therefore, by receiving a note from Martha requesting permission to enter the convent and spend the rest of her days in the discharge of the duties of a religious life. He acted on this occasion with his usual tact. He did not reply to the note, but after a day or two drove to the Abbaye, had a private interview with the Abbess, and then asked for his daughters. He received them with more than usual affectionate warmth of manner, and, without making the least allusion to Martha's note or its contents, told his daughters that he had called to take them from school, and accordingly he drove back home accompanied by them. Martha was soon introduced into society at the brilliant court of Louis the Sixteenth, and soon forgot her girlish desire to enter a convent. No word in allusion to the subject ever passed between the father and daughter, and it was not referred to by either of them until years afterwards, when she spoke of it to her children.

Getting more and more impatient for leave to return home for a few months, we find Jefferson writing to Washington, in the spring of 1789, as follows:

To George Washington.

In a letter of November 19th to Mr. Jay, I asked a leave of absence to carry my children back to their own country, and to settle various matters of a private nature, which were left unsettled, because I had no idea of being absent so long. I expected that letter would have been received in time to be acted upon by the Government then existing. I know now that it would arrive when there was no Congress, and consequently that it must have awaited your arrival in New York. I hope you found the request not an unreasonable one. I am excessively anxious to receive the permission without delay, that I may be able to get back before the winter sets in. Nothing can be so dreadful to me as to be shivering at sea for two or three months in a winter passage. Besides, there has never been a moment at which the presence of a minister here could be so well dispensed with, from certainty of no war this summer, and that the Government will be so totally absorbed in domestic arrangements as to attend to nothing exterior.

In the same letter we find him congratulating Washington on his election as President, and seizing that occasion to pay a graceful tribute to him of praise and admiration, and also of affection. He says:

Though we have not heard of the actual opening of the new Congress, and consequently have not official information of your election as President of the United States, yet, as there never could be a doubt entertained of it, permit me to express here my felicitations, not to yourself, but to my country. Nobody who has tried both public and private life can doubt but that you were much happier on the banks of the Potomac than you will be at New York. But there was nobody so well qualified as yourself to put our new machine into a regular course of action—nobody, the authority of whose name could have so effectually crushed opposition at home and produced respect abroad. I am sensible of the immensity of the sacrifice on your part. Your measure of fame was full to the brim; and therefore you have nothing to gain. But there are cases wherein it is a duty to risk all against nothing, and I believe this was exactly the case. We may presume, too, according to every rule of probability, that, after doing a great deal of good, you will be found to have lost nothing but private repose.

How anxiously Jefferson awaited the arrival of his leave of absence will be seen from the letter below, written by him to his sister-in-law :

To Mrs. Eppes.

Paris, Dec. 15th, 1788.

Dear Madam—In my last, of July 12th, I told you that in my next I would enter into explanations about the time my daughters would have the happiness to see you. Their future welfare requires that this should be no longer postponed. It would have taken place a year sooner, but that I wished Polly to perfect herself in her French. I have asked leave of absence of Congress for five or six months of the next year, and if I obtain it in time I shall endeavor to sail about the middle of April. As my time must be passed principally at Monticello during the two months I destine for Virginia, I shall hope that you will come and encamp there with us a while. He who feedeth the sparrow must feed us also. Feasting we shall not expect, but this will not be our object. The society of our friends will sweeten all. Patsy has just recovered from an indisposition of some days. Polly has the same; it is a slight but continual fever, not sufficient, however, to confine her to her bed. This prevents me from being able to tell you that they are absolutely well. I inclose a letter which Polly wrote a month ago to her aunt Skipwith, and her sickness will apologize for her not writing to you or her cousins; she makes it up in love to you all, and Patsy equally, but this she will tell you herself, as she is writing to you. I hope you will find her an estimable friend as well as a dutiful niece. She inherits stature from her father, and that, you know, is inheriting no trifle. Polly grows fast. I should write to Mrs. Skipwith also, but that I rely on your friendship to repeat to her the assurance of my affection for her and Mr. Skipwith. We look forward with impatience to the moment when we may be all reunited, though but for a little time. Kiss your dear children for us, the little and the big, and tender them my warmest affections, accepting yourself assurances of the sincere esteem and attachment, with which I am, my dear Madam, your affectionate and humble servant,

TH. JEFFERSON.

The long-expected leave of absence came at last, and was received by Jefferson during the last days of August (1789). October being deemed the best month in which to be at sea, he postponed his voyage until that time. He left Paris on the 26th of September, as he thought, to be absent only a few months, but, as the event proved, never to return again. We find in his Memoir the following affectionate farewell to the kind people and the fair land of France:

I can not leave this great and good country without expressing my sense of its pre-eminence of character among the nations of the earth. A more benevolent people I have never known, nor greater warmth and devotedness in their select friendships. Their kindness and accommodation to strangers is unparalleled, and the hospitality of Paris is beyond any thing I had conceived to be practicable in a large city. Their eminence, too, in science, the communicative dispositions of their scientific men, the politeness of their general manners, the ease and vivacity of their conversation, give a charm to their society to be found nowhere else. In a comparison of this with other countries, we have the proof of primacy which was given to Themistocles after the battle of Salamis. Every general voted to himself the first reward of valor, and the second to Themistocles. So, ask the travelled inhabitant of any nation, on what country on earth would you rather live?—Certainly in my own, where are all my friends, my relations, and the earliest and sweetest affections and recollections of my life. Which would be your second choice? France.

Of Jefferson's discharge of his duties as minister at the Court of St. Germains, Mr. Webster spoke thus:

Mr. Jefferson's discharge of his diplomatic duties was marked by great ability, diligence, and patriotism; and while he resided at Paris, in one of the most interesting periods, his character for intelligence, his love of knowledge and of the society of learned men, distinguished him in the highest circles of the French capital. No court in Europe had at that time a representative in Paris commanding or enjoying higher regard, for political knowledge or for general attainments, than the minister of this then infant republic.

So, too, the Edinburgh Review, though no admirer of Jefferson's political creed, says of his ambassadorial career:

His watchfulness on every subject which might bear on the most favorable arrangement of their new commercial treaties, his perseverance in seeking to negotiate a general alliance against Algiers, the skill and knowledge with which he argued the different questions of national interest that arose during his residence, will not suffer even in comparison with Franklin's diplomatic talents. Every thing he sees seems to suggest to him the question whether it can be made useful in America. Could we compare a twelvemonth's letters from our ambassadors' bags at Paris, Florence, or elsewhere, we should see whether our enormous diplomatic salaries are any thing else than very successful measures for securing our business being ill and idly done.

Jefferson, as I have just mentioned, left Paris the last of September. The account given below, of his journey home and reception there, is from the narrative of Martha Jefferson, before quoted:

In returning, he was detained ten days at Havre de Grace, and, after crossing the Channel, ten more at Cowes, in the Isle of Wight, which were spent in visiting different parts of the island, when the weather permitted: among others, Carisbrook Castle, remarkable for the confinement of Charles the

First, and also for a well of uncommon depth. We sailed on the 23d of October, 1789, in company with upwards of thirty vessels who had collected there and been detained, as we were, by contrary winds. Colonel Trumbull, who chartered the ship for my father in London, applied to Mr. Pitt to give orders to prevent his baggage from being searched on his arrival, informing Mr. Pitt at the same time that the application was made without his knowledge. The orders to such an effect were accordingly issued, I presume, as he was spared the usual vexation of such a search. The voyage was quick and not unpleasant. When we arrived on the coast there was so thick a mist as to render it impossible to see a pilot, had any of them been out. After beating about three days, the captain, a bold as well as an experienced seaman, determined to run in at a venture, without having seen the Capes. The ship came near running upon what was conjectured to be the Middle Ground, when anchor was cast at ten o'clock P.M. The wind rose, and the vessel drifted down, dragging her anchor, one or more miles. But she had got within the Capes, while a number which had been less bold were blown off the coast, some of them lost, and all kept out three or four weeks longer. We had to beat up against a strong head-wind, which carried away our topsails; and we were very near being run down by a brig coming out of port, which, having the wind in her favor, was almost upon us before we could get out of the way. We escaped, however, with only the loss of a part of our rigging. My father had been so anxious about his public accounts, that he would not trust them to go until he went with them. We arrived at Norfolk in the forenoon, and in two hours after landing, before an article of our baggage was brought ashore, the vessel took fire, and seemed on the point of being reduced to a mere hull. They were in the act of scuttling her, when some abatement in the flames was discovered, and she was finally saved. So great had been the activity of her crew, and of those belonging to other ships in the harbor who came to their aid, that every thing in her was saved. Our trunks, and perhaps also the papers, had been put in our state-rooms, and the doors incidentally closed by the captain. They were so close that the flames did not penetrate; but the powder in a musket in one of them was silently consumed, and the thickness of the travelling-trunks alone saved their contents from the excessive heat. I understood at the time that the state-rooms alone, of all the internal partitions, escaped burning. Norfolk had not recovered from the effects of the war, and we should have found it difficult to obtain rooms but for the politeness of the gentlemen at the hotel (Lindsay's), who were kind enough to give up their own rooms for our accommodation.

There were no stages in those days. We were indebted to the kindness of our friends for horses; and visiting all on the way homeward, and spending more or less time with them all in turn, we reached Monticello on the 23d of December. The negroes discovered the approach of the carriage as soon as it reached Shadwell,* and such a scene I never witnessed in my life. They collected in crowds around it, and almost drew it up the mountain by hand. The shouting, etc., had been sufficiently obstreperous before, but the moment it arrived at the top it reached the climax. When the door of the carriage was opened, they received him in their arms and bore him to the house, crowding around and kissing his hands and feet—some blubbering and crying—others laughing. It seemed impossible to satisfy their anxiety to touch and kiss the very earth which bore him. These were the first ebullitions of joy for his return, after a long absence, which they would of course feel; but perhaps it is not out of place here to add that they were at all times very devoted in their attachment to him.

A letter written by Mr. Jefferson to his overseer had been the means of the negroes getting information of their master's return home some days before he arrived. They were wild with joy, and requested to have holiday on the day on which he was expected to reach home. Their request was, of course, granted, and they accordingly assembled at Monticello from Mr. Jefferson's different farms. The old and the young came—women and children—and, growing impatient, they sauntered down the mountain-side and down the road until they met the carriage-and-four at Shadwell, when the

* Shadwell is four miles distant from Monticello.

welkin rang with their shouts of welcome. Martha Jefferson speaks of their "almost" drawing the carriage by hand up the mountain: her memory in this instance may have failed her, for I have had it from the lips of old family servants who were present as children on the occasion, that the horses were actually "unhitched," and the vehicle drawn by the strong black arms up to the foot of the lawn in front of the door at Monticello. The appearance of the young ladies, before whom they fell back and left the way clear for them to reach the house, filled them with admiration. They had left them when scarcely more than children in the arms, and now returned—Martha a tall and stately-looking girl of seventeen years, and the little Maria, now in her eleventh year, more beautiful and, if possible, more lovable than when, two years before, her beauty and her loveliness had warmed into enthusiasm the reserved but kind-hearted Mrs. Adams.

The father and his two daughters were then at last once more domiciled within the walls of their loved Monticello. How grateful it would have been for him never again to have been called away from home to occupy a public post, the following extract from a letter written by him before leaving Paris will show. He writes to Madison:

You ask me if I would accept any appointment on that side of the water? You know the circumstances which led me from retirement, step by step, and from one nomination to another, up to the present. My object is to return to the same retirement. Whenever, therefore, I quit the present, it will not be to engage in any other office, and most especially any one which would require a constant residence from home.

CHAPTER IX.

Letters on the French Revolution.

I HAVE thought it best to throw into one chapter the extracts from Mr. Jefferson's Letters and Memoir which relate to the scenes that he witnessed at the beginning of the Revolution. These are so interesting as almost to make us regret, with himself, that he should have been recalled from France at that most fearfully interesting period of her history. What pictures his pen would have preserved to us of scenes, of many of which he would have been an eye-witness, and how the student of history would revel in his dispatches home, which, like those he has left us, must have abounded in interesting details and sketches of character!

In giving these extracts, I shall merely indicate the date of the letters, and the persons to whom they were addressed:

To John Jay, February 23d, 1787.

The Assemblée des Notables being an event in the history of this country which excites notice, I have supposed it would not be disagreeable to you to learn its immediate objects, though no way connected with our interests. The Assembly met yesterday; the King, in a short but affectionate speech, informed them of his wish to consult with them on the plans he had digested, and on the general good of his people, and his desire to imitate the head of his family, Henry IV., whose memory is so dear to the nation. The Garde des Sceaux then spoke about twenty minutes, chiefly in compliment to the orders present. The Comptroller-general, in a speech of about an hour, opened the budjet, and enlarged on the several subjects which will be under their deliberation.

To James Madison, June 20th, 1787.

The King loves business, economy, order, and justice, and wishes sincerely the good of his people; but he is irascible, rude, very limited in his understanding, and religious bordering on bigotry. He has no mistress, loves his queen, and is too much governed by her. She is capricious, like her brother, and governed by him; devoted to pleasure and expense, and not remarkable for any other vices or virtues. Unhappily, the King shows a propensity for the pleasures of the table. That for drink has increased lately, or, at least, it has become more known.

To John Jay, August 7th, 1787.

The Parliament were received yesterday very harshly by the King. He obliged them to register the two edicts for the impôt, territorial, and stamp-tax. When speaking in my letter of the reiterated orders and refusals to register, which passed between the King and Parliament, I omitted to insert the King's answer to a deputation of Parliament, which attended him at Versailles. It may serve to show the spirit which exists between them. It was in these words, and these only: "Je vous ferai savoir mes intentions. Allez-vous-en. Qu'on ferme la porte !"

To John Adams, August 30th, 1787.

. It is urged principally against the King, that his revenue is one hundred and thirty millions more than that of his predecessor was, and yet he demands one hundred and twenty millions further...... In the mean time, all tongues in Paris (and in France, as it is said) have been let loose, and never was a license of speaking against the Government exercised in London more freely or more universally. Caricatures, placards, bons-mots, have been indulged in by all ranks of people, and I know of no well-attested instance of a single punishment. For some time mobs of ten, twenty, and thirty thousand people collected daily, surrounded the Parliament-house, huzzaed the members, even entered the doors and examined into their conduct, took the horses out of the carriages of those who did well, and drew them home. The Government thought it prudent to prevent these, drew some regiments into the neighborhood, multiplied the guards, had the streets constantly patrolled by strong parties, suspended privileged places, forbade all clubs, etc. The mobs have ceased : perhaps this may be partly owing to the absence of Parliament. The Count d'Artois, sent to hold a bed of justice in the Cour des Aides, was hissed and hooted without reserve by the populace ; the carriage of Madame de (I forget the name), in the Queen's livery, was stopped by the populace, under the belief that it was Madame de Polignac, whom they would have insulted; the Queen going to the theatre at Versailles with Madame de Polignac, was received with a general hiss. The King, long in the habit of drowning his cares in wine, plunges deeper and deeper. The Queen cries, but sins on. The Count d'Artois is detested, and Monsieur the general favorite. The Archbishop of Toulouse is made minister principal—a virtuous, patriotic, and able character. The Marechal de Castries retired yesterday, notwithstanding strong solicitations to remain in office. The Marechal de Segur retired at the same time, prompted to it by the court.

To John Jay, October 8th, 1787.

There has long been a division in the Council here on the question of war and peace. Monsieur de Montmorin and Monsieur de Breteuil have been constantly for war. They are supported in this by the Queen. The King goes for nothing. He hunts one-half the day, is drunk the other, and signs whatever he is bid. The Archbishop of Toulouse desires peace. Though brought in by the Queen, he is opposed to her in this capital object, which would produce an alliance with her brother. Whether the Archbishop will yield or not, I know not. But an intrigue is already begun for ousting him from his place, and it is rather probable it will succeed. He is a good and patriotic minister for peace, and very capable in the department of finance. At least, he is so in theory. I have heard his talents for execution censured.

To John Jay, November 3d, 1787.

It may not be uninstructive to give you the origin and nature of his (the Archbishop of Toulouse) influence with the Queen. When the Duke de Choiseul proposed the marriage of the Dauphin with this lady, he thought it proper to send a person to Vienna to perfect her in the language. He asked his friend, the Archbishop of Toulouse, to recommend to him a proper person. He recommended a certain Abbé. The Abbé, from his first arrival at Vienna, either tutored by his patron or prompted by gratitude, impressed on the Queen's mind the exalted talents and merit of the Archbishop, and continually represented him as the only man fit to be placed at the helm of affairs. On his return to Paris, being retained near the person of the Queen, he kept him constantly in her view. The Archbishop was named of the Assemblée des Notables, had occasion enough there to prove his talents, and Count de Vergennes, his great enemy, dying opportunely, the Queen got him into place.

Writing to Mr. Jay on September 3d, 1788, Mr. Jefferson, after alluding to the public bankruptcy and the moneyless condition of the treasury, goes on to say:

To John Jay, September 3d, 1788.

The Archbishop was hereupon removed, with Monsieur Lambert, the Comptroller-general; and M. Necker was called in as Director-general of the finance. To soften the Archbishop's dismission, a cardinal's hat is asked for him from Rome, and his nephew promised the succession to the Archbishopric of Sens. The public joy on this change of administration was very great indeed. The people of Paris were amusing themselves with trying and burning the Archbishop in effigy, and rejoicing in the appointment of M. Necker. The commanding officer of the City Guards undertook to forbid this, and, not being obeyed, he charged the mob with fixed bayonets, killed two or three, and wounded many. This stopped their rejoicings for that day; but, enraged at being thus obstructed in amusements wherein they had committed no disorder whatever, they collected in great numbers the next day, attacked the Guards in various places, burnt ten or twelve guard-houses, killed two or three of the guards, and had about six or eight of their own number killed. The city was hereupon put under martial law, and after a while the tumult subsided, and peace was restored.

To George Washington, December 21st, 1788.

In my opinion, a kind of influence which none of their plans of reform take into account, will elude them all—I mean the influence of women in the Government. The manners of the nation allow them to visit, alone, all persons in office, to solicit the affairs of the husband, family, or friends, and their solicitations bid defiance to laws and regulations. This obstacle may seem less to those who, like our countrymen, are in the precious habit of considering right as a barrier against all solicitation. Nor can such an one, without the evidence of his own eyes, believe in the desperate state to which things are reduced in this country, from the omnipotence of an influence which, fortunately for the happiness of the sex itself, does not endeavor to extend itself, in our country, beyond the domestic line.

To Colonel Humphreys, March 18th, 1789.

The change in this country, since you left it, is such as you can form no idea of. The frivolities of conversation have given way entirely to politics. Men, women, and children talk nothing else; and all, you know, talk a great deal. The press groans with daily productions which, in point of boldness, make an Englishman stare, who hitherto has thought himself the boldest of men. A complete revolution in this Government has, within the space of two years (for it began with the Notables of 1787), been effected merely by the force of public opinion, aided, indeed, by the want of money, which the dissipations of the court had brought on. And this revolution has not cost a single life, unless we charge to it a little riot lately in Bretagne, which began about the price of bread, became afterwards political, and ended in the loss of four or five lives. The Assembly of the States General begins the 27th of April. The representation of the people will be perfect; but they will be alloyed by an equal number of the nobility and clergy. The first great question they will have to decide will be, whether they shall vote by orders or persons. And I have hopes that the majority of the nobles are already disposed to join the Tiers Etat in deciding that the vote shall be by persons. This is the opinion *à la mode* at present, and mode has acted a wonderful part in the present instance. All the handsome young women, for example, are for the Tiers Etat, and this is an army more powerful in France than the two hundred thousand men of the King.

To William Carmichael, May 8th, 1789.

The States General were opened day before yesterday. Viewing it as an opera, it was imposing; as a scene of business, the King's speech was exactly what it should have been, and very well delivered; not a word of the Chancellor's was heard by any body, so that, as yet, I have never heard a single guess at what it was about. M. Necker's was as good as such a number of details would permit it to be. The picture of their resources was consoling, and generally plausible. I could have wished him to have dwelt more on those great constitutional reformations, which his " Rapport au Roi " had prepared us to expect. But they observe that these points were proper for the speech of the Chancellor.

To John Jay, May 9th, 1789.

The revolution of this country has advanced thus far without encountering any thing which deserves to be called a difficulty. There have been riots in a few instances, in three or four different places, in which there may have been a dozen or twenty lives lost. The exact truth is not to be got at. A few days ago a much more serious riot took place in this city, in which it became necessary for the troops to engage in regular action with the mob, and probably about one hundred of the latter were killed. Accounts vary from twenty to two hundred. They were the most abandoned banditti of Paris, and never was a riot more unprovoked and unpitied. They began, under a pretense that a paper manufacturer had proposed, in an assembly, to reduce their wages to fifteen sous a day. They rifled his house, destroyed every thing in his magazines and shops, and were only stopped in their career of mischief by the carnage above mentioned. Neither this nor any other of the riots have had a professed connection with the great national reformation going on. They are such as have happened every year since

I have been here, and as will continue to be produced by common incidents.

In the same letter, in speaking of the King, he says:

Happy that he is an honest, unambitious man, who desires neither money nor power for himself; and that his most operative minister, though he has appeared to trim a little, is still, in the main, a friend to public liberty.

In a letter to Mr. Jay, June 17, 1789, after alluding to the continued disagreement between the orders composing the States General, as to whether they should vote by persons or orders, he says:

To John Jay, June 17th, 1789.

The Noblesse adhered to their former resolutions, and even the minority, well disposed to the Commons, thought they could do more good in their own chamber, by endeavoring to increase their numbers and fettering the measures of the majority, than by joining the Commons. An intrigue was set on foot between the leaders of the majority in that House, the Queen and Princes. They persuaded the King to go for some time to Marly; he went. On the same day the leaders moved, in the Chamber of Nobles, that they should address the King to declare his own sentiments on the great question between the orders. It was intended that this address should be delivered to him at Marly, where, separated from his ministers, and surrounded by the Queen and Princes, he might be surprised into a declaration for the Nobles. The motion was lost, however, by a very great majority, that Chamber being not yet quite ripe for throwing themselves into the arms of despotism. Necker and Monmorin, who had discovered this intrigue, had warned some of the minority to defeat it, or they could not answer for what would happen...... The Commons (Tiers Etat) having verified their powers, a motion was made, the day before yesterday, to declare themselves constituted, and to proceed to business. I left them at two o'clock yesterday; the debates not then finished......

It is a tremendous cloud, indeed, which hovers over this nation, and he (Necker) at the helm has neither the courage nor the skill necessary to weather it. Eloquence in a high degree, knowledge in matters of account, and order, are distinguishing traits in his character. Ambition is his first passion, virtue his second. He has not discovered that sublime truth, that a bold, unequivòcal virtue is the best handmaid even to ambition, and would carry him farther, in the end, than the temporizing, wavering policy he pursues. His judgment is not of the first order, scarcely even of the second; his resolution frail; and, upon the whole, it is rare to meet an instance of a person so much below the reputation he has obtained.

To John Jay, June 24th, 1789.

My letter of the 17th and 18th instant gave you the progress of the States General to the 17th, when the Tiers had declared the illegality of all the existing taxes, and their discontinuance from the end of their present session. The next day being a jour de fête, could furnish no indication of the impression that vote was likely to make on the Government. On the 19th, a Council was held at Marly, in the afternoon. It was there proposed that the King should interpose by a declaration of his sentiments in a *seance royale.* The declaration prepared by M. Necker, while it censured, in general, the proceedings both of the Nobles and Commons, announced the King's views, such as substantially to coincide with the Commons. It was agreed to in Council, as also that the *seance royale* should be held on the 22d, 'and the meetings till then be suspended. While the Council was engaged in this deliberation at Marly, the Chamber of the Clergy was in debate, whether they should accept the invitation of the Tiers to unite with them in the common chamber. On the first question, to unite simply and unconditionally, it was decided in the negative by a very small majority. As it was known, however, that some members who had voted in the negative would be for the affirmative, with some modifications, the question was put with these modifications, and it was determined, by a majority of eleven members, that their body should join the Tiers.

L

These proceedings of the Clergy were unknown to the Council at Marly, and those of the Council were kept secret from every body. The next morning (the 20th) the members repaired to the House, as usual, found the doors shut and guarded, and a proclamation posted up for holding a *seance royale* on the 22d, and a suspension of their meetings till then. They presumed, in the first moment, that their dissolution was decided, and repaired to another place, where they proceeded to business. They there bound themselves to each other by an oath never to separate of their own accord till they had settled a Constitution for the nation on a solid basis, and, if separated by force, that they would reassemble in some other place. It was intimated to them, however, that day, privately, that the proceedings of the *seance royale* would be favorable to them. The next day they met in a church, and were joined by a majority of the Clergy. The heads of the aristocracy saw that all was lost without some violent exertion. The King was still at Marly. Nobody was permitted to approach him but their friends. He was assailed by lies in all shapes. He was made to believe that the Commons were going to absolve the army from their oath of fidelity to him, and to raise their pay....... They procured a committee to be held, consisting of the King and his ministers, to which Monsieur and the Count d'Artois should be admitted. At this committee the latter attacked M. Necker personally, arraigned his plans, and proposed one which some of his engines had put into his hands. M. Necker, whose characteristic is the want of firmness, was browbeaten and intimidated, and the King shaken.

He determined that the two plans should be deliberated on the next day, and the *seance royale* put off a day longer. This encouraged a fiercer attack on M. Necker the next day; his plan was totally dislocated, and that of the Count d'Artois inserted into it. Himself and Monsieur de Montmorin offered their resignation, which was refused; the Count d'Artois saying to M. Necker, "No, Sir, you must be kept as the hostage; we hold you responsible for all the ill which shall happen." This change of plan was immediately whispered without doors. The nobility were in triumph, the people in consternation. When the King passed, the next day, through the lane they formed from the Château to the Hôtel des Etats (about half a mile), there was a dead silence. He was about an hour in the House delivering his speech and declaration, copies of which I inclose you. On his coming out, a feeble cry of "Vive le Roi" was raised by some children, but the people remained silent and sullen. When the Duke of Orleans followed, however, their applauses were excessive. This must have been sensible to the King. He had ordered, in the close of his speech, that the members should follow him, and resume their deliberations the next day. The Noblesse followed him, and so did the Clergy, except about thirty, who, with the Tiers, remained in the room and entered into deliberation. They protested against what the King had done, adhered to all their former proceedings, and resolved the inviolability of their own persons. An officer came twice to order them out of the room, in the King's name, but they refused to obey.

In the afternoon, the people, uneasy, began to assemble in great numbers in the courts and vicinities of the palace. The Queen was alarmed, and sent for M. Necker. He was conducted amidst the shouts and acclamations of the multitude, who filled all the apartments of the palace. He was a few minutes only with the Queen, and about three-quarters of an hour with the King. Not a word has transpired of what passed at these interviews. The King was just going to ride out. He passed through the crowd to his carriage, and into it, without being in the least noticed. As M. Necker followed him, universal acclamations were raised of "Vive Monsieur Necker, vive le sauveur de la France opprimée." He was conducted back to his house with the same demonstrations of affection and anxiety....... These circumstances must wound the heart of the King, desirous as he is to possess the affections of his subjects......

June 25th.—Just returned from Versailles, I am enabled to continue my narration. On the 24th nothing remarkable passed, except an attack by the mob of Versailles on the Archbishop of Paris, who had been one of the instigators of the court to the proceedings of the *seance royale.* They threw mud and stones at his carriage, broke the windows of it, and he in a fright promised to join the Tiers.

To John Jay, June 29th, 1789.

I have before mentioned to you the ferment into which the proceedings at the *seance royale* of the 23d had thrown the people. The soldiery also were affected by it. It began in the French Guards, extended to those of every other denomination (except the Swiss), and even to the body-guards of the King. They began to quit their barracks, to assemble in squads, to declare they would defend the life of the King, but would not cut the throats of their fellow-citizens. They were treated and caressed by the people, carried in triumph through the streets, called themselves the soldiers of the nation, and left no doubt on which side they would be in case of a rupture.

In his Memoir Jefferson writes, in allusion to the spirit among the soldiery above noticed:

Extract from Memoir.

The operation of this medicine at Versailles was as sudden as it was powerful. The alarm there was so complete, that in the afternoon of the 27th the King wrote, with his own hand, letters to the Presidents of the Clergy and Nobles, engaging them immediately to join the Tiers. These two bodies were debating and hesitating, when notes from the Count d'Artois decided their compliance. They went in a body, and took their seats with the Tiers, and thus rendered the union of the orders in one Chamber complete...... But the quiet of their march was soon disturbed by information that troops, and particularly the foreign troops, were advancing on Paris from various quarters. The King had probably been advised to this, on the pretext of preserving peace in Paris. But his advisers were believed to have other things in contemplation. The Marshal de Broglio was appointed to their command—a high-flying aristocrat, cool, and capable of every thing. Some of the French Guards were soon arrested under other pretexts, but really on account of their dispositions in favor of the national cause. The people of Paris forced their prison, liberated them, and sent a deputation to the Assembly to solicit a pardon. The Assembly recommended peace and order to the people of

Paris, the prisoners to the King, and asked from him the removal of the troops. His answer was negative and dry, saying they might remove themselves, if they pleased, to Noyons or Soissons. In the mean time, these troops, to the number of twenty or thirty thousand, had arrived, and were posted in and between Paris and Versailles. The bridges and passes were guarded. At three o'clock in the afternoon of the 11th of July, the Count de la Luzerne was sent to notify M. Necker of his dismission, and to enjoin him to retire instantly, without saying a word of it to any body. He went home, dined, and proposed to his wife a visit to a friend, but went in fact to his country-house at St. Ouen, and at midnight set out for Brussels. This was not known till the next day (the 12th), when the whole ministry was changed, except Villederril, of the domestic department, and Barenton, Garde des Sceaux.......

The news of this change began to be known at Paris about one or two o'clock. In the afternoon a body of about one hundred German cavalry were advanced and drawn up in the Place Louis XV., and about two hundred Swiss posted at a little distance in their rear. This drew people to the spot, who thus accidentally found themselves in front of the troops, merely at first as spectators; but, as their numbers increased, their indignation rose. They retired a few steps, and posted themselves on and behind large piles of stones, large and small, collected in that place for a bridge, which was to be built adjacent to it. In this position, happening to be in my carriage on a visit, I passed through the lane they had formed without interruption. But the moment after I had passed the people attacked the cavalry with stones. They charged, but the advantageous position of the people, and the showers of stones, obliged the horses to retire and quit the field altogether, leaving one of their number on the ground, and the Swiss in their rear not moving to their aid. This was the signal for universal insurrection, and this body of cavalry, to avoid being massacred, retired towards Versailles.

After describing the events of the 13th and 14th, and of the imperfect report of them which reached the King, he says:

But at night the Duke de Liancourt forced his way into the King's bed-chamber, and obliged him to hear a full and animated detail of the disasters of the day in Paris. He went to bed fearfully impressed.

After alluding to the demolition of the Bastile, he says:

The alarm at Versailles increased. The foreign troops were ordered off instantly. Every minister resigned. The King confirmed Bailly as Prévôt des Marchands, wrote to M. Necker to recall him, sent his letter open to the Assembly, to be forwarded by them, and invited them to go with him to Paris the next day, to satisfy the city of his dispositions. [Then comes a list of the Court favorites who fled that night.] The King came to Paris, leaving the Queen in consternation for his return. Omitting the less important figures of the procession, the King's carriage was in the centre; on each side of it, the Assembly, in two ranks, afoot; at their head the Marquis de Lafayette, as commander-in-chief, on horseback, and Bourgeois guards before and behind. About sixty thousand citizens, of all forms and conditions, armed with the conquests of the Bastile and Invalides, as far as they would go, the rest with pistols, swords, pikes, pruning-hooks, scythes, etc., lined all the streets through which the procession passed, and with the crowds of the people in the streets, doors, and windows, saluted them everywhere with the cries of "Vive la nation," but not a single "Vive le roi" was heard. The King stopped at the Hôtel de Ville. There M. Bailly presented, and put into his hat, the popular cockade, and addressed him. The King being unprepared, and unable to answer, Bailly went to him, gathered some scraps of sentences, and made out an answer, which he delivered to the audience as from the King. On their return, the popular cries were, "Vive le roi et la nation!" He was conducted by a garde Bourgeoise to his palace at Versailles, and thus concluded such an "amende honorable" as no sovereign ever made, and no people ever received.

After speaking of the precious occasion that was here lost, of sparing to France the crimes and cruelties through which she afterwards passed, and of the good disposition of the young King, he says:

But he had a queen of absolute sway over his weak mind and timid virtue, and of a character the reverse of his in all points. This angel, so gaudily painted in the rhapsodies of Burke, with some smartness of fancy but no sound sense, was proud, disdainful of restraint, indignant at all obstacles to her will, eager in the pursuit of pleasure, and firm enough to hold to her desires, or perish in their wreck. Her inordinate gambling and dissipations, with those of the Count d'Artois and others of her *clique*, had been a sensible item in the exhaustion of the treasury, which called into action the reforming hand of the nation; and her opposition to it, her inflexible perverseness, and dauntless spirit, led herself to the guillotine, drew the King on with her, and plunged the world into crimes and calamities which will forever stain the pages of modern history. I have ever believed that, had there been no queen, there would have been no revolution. No force would have been provoked nor exercised. The King would have gone hand in hand with the wisdom of his sounder counsellors, who, guided by the increased lights of the age, wished only with the same pace to advance the principles of their social constitution. The deed which closed the mortal course of these sovereigns I shall neither approve nor condemn. I am not prepared to say that the first magistrate of a nation can not commit treason against his country, or is unamenable to its punishment; nor yet that, where there is no written law, no regulated tribunal, there is not a law in our hearts and a power in our hands, given for righteous employment in maintaining right and redressing wrong......

I should have shut up the Queen in a convent, putting harm out of her power, and placed the King in his station, investing him with limited powers, which, I verily believe, he would have honestly exercised, according to the measure of his understanding.

After giving further details, he goes on to say:

In this uneasy state of things, I received one day a note from the Marquis de Lafayette, informing me that he should bring a party of six or eight friends to ask a dinner of me the next day. I assured him of their welcome. When they arrived they were Lafayette himself, Duport, Barnave,

Alexander la Meth, Blacon, Mounier, Maubourg, and Dagout. These were leading patriots of honest but differing opinions, sensible of the necessity of effecting a coalition by mutual sacrifices, knowing each other, and not afraid, therefore, to unbosom themselves mutually. This last was a material principle in the selection. With this view the Marquis had invited the conference, and had fixed the time and place inadvertently, as to the embarrassment under which it might place me. The cloth being removed, and wine set on the table, after the American manner, the Marquis introduced the objects of the conference...... The discussions began at the hour of four, and were continued till ten o'clock in the evening; during which time I was a silent witness to a coolness and candor of argument unusual in the conflicts of political opinion—to a logical reasoning and chaste eloquence disfigured by no gaudy tinsel of rhetoric or declamation, and truly worthy of being placed in parallel with the finest dialogues of antiquity, as handed to us by Xenophon, by Plato, and Cicero.......

But duties of exculpation were now incumbent on me. I waited on Count Montmorin the next morning, and explained to him, with truth and candor, how it had happened that my house had been made the scene of conferences of such a character. He told me he already knew every thing which had passed; that, so far from taking umbrage at the use made of my house on that occasion, he earnestly wished I would habitually assist at such conferences, being sure I should be useful in moderating the warmer spirits, and promoting a wholesome and practicable reformation.

Nothing of further interest as regards the French Revolution appears in Jefferson's Memoir.

CHAPTER X.

Washington nominates Jefferson as Secretary of State.—Jefferson's Regret.—Devotion of Southern Statesmen to Country Life.—Letter to Washington.—Jefferson accepts the Appointment.—Marriage of his Daughter.—He leaves for New York.—Last Interview with Franklin.—Letters to Son-in-law.—Letters of Adieu to Friends in Paris.—Family Letters.

The calls of his country would not allow Jefferson to withdraw from public life, and, living in that retirement for which he so longed, abandon himself to the delights of rural pursuits. On his way from Norfolk to Monticello he stopped to pay a visit, in Chesterfield County, to his sister-in-law, Mrs. Eppes. There he received letters from General Washington telling him that he had nominated him as Secretary of State, and urging him so earnestly and so affectionately to accept the appointment as to put a refusal on his part out of the question. He tells us in his Memoir that he received the proffered appointment with "real regret;" and we can not doubt his sincerity. In reading the lives of the Fathers of the Republic, we can but be struck with their weariness of public life, and their longings for the calm enjoyment of the sweets of domestic life in the retirement of their quiet homes. This was eminently the case with our great men from the South. Being for the most part large land-owners, their presence being needed on their estates, and agricultural pursuits seeming to have an indescribable fascination for them, all engagements grew irksome which prevented the enjoyment of that manly and independent life which they found at the head of a Southern plantation. The pomps and splendor of office had no charms for them, and we find Washington turning with regret from the banks of the Potomac to go and fill the highest post in the gift of his countrymen;

Jefferson sighing after the sublime beauties of his distant Monticello, and longing to rejoin his children and grandchildren there, though winning golden opinions in the discharge of his duties as Premier; while Henry chafed in the Congressional halls, and was eager to return to his woods in Charlotte, though gifted with that wonderful power of speech whose fiery eloquence could at any moment startle his audience to their feet. But Jefferson, in this instance, had peculiar reasons for wishing a reprieve from public duties. His constant devotion to them had involved his private affairs in sad confusion, and there was danger of the ample fortune which his professional success and the skillful management of his property had secured to him being lost, merely from want of time and opportunity to look after it. He dreaded, then, to enter upon a public career whose close he could not foresee; and there is a sad tone of resignation in his letter of acceptance to General Washington, which seems to show that he felt he was sacrificing his private repose to his duty to his country; yet he did not know how entirely he was sacrificing his own for his country's good. I give the whole letter:

To George Washington.

Chesterfield, December 15th, 1789.

Sir—I have received at this place the honor of your letters of October 13th and November the 30th, and am truly flattered by your nomination of me to the very dignified office of Secretary of State, for which permit me here to return you my very humble thanks. Could any circumstance induce me to overlook the disproportion between its duties and my talents, it would be the encouragement of your choice. But when I contemplate the extent of that office, embracing as it does the principal mass of domestic administration, together with the foreign, I can not be insensible to my inequality to it; and I should enter on it with gloomy forebodings from the criticisms and censures of a public, just indeed in their intentions, but sometimes misinformed and misled, and always too respectable to be neglected. I can not but foresee the possibility that this may end disagreeably for me, who, having no motive to public service but the public satisfaction, would certainly retire the moment that satisfaction should appear to languish. On the other hand, I feel a degree of familiarity with the duties of my present office, as far, at least, as I am capable of understanding its duties. The ground I have already passed over enables me to see my way into that which is before me. The change of government, too, taking place in the country where it is exercised, seems to open a possibility of procuring from the new rulers some new advantages in commerce, which may be agreeable to our countrymen. So that as far as my fears, my hopes, or my inclination might enter into this question, I confess they would not lead me to prefer a change.

But it is not for an individual to choose his post. You are to marshal us as may be best for the public good; and it is only in the case of its being indifferent to you, that I would avail myself of the option you have so kindly offered in your letter. If you think it better to transfer me to another post, my inclination must be no obstacle; nor shall it be, if there is any desire to suppress the office I now hold or to reduce its grade. In either of these cases, be so good as only to signify to me by another line your ultimate wish, and I will conform to it cordially. If it should be to remain at New York, my chief comfort will be to work under your eye, my only shelter the authority of your name, and the wisdom of measures to be dictated by you and implicitly executed by me. Whatever you may be pleased to decide, I do not see that the matters which have called me hither will permit me to shorten the stay I originally asked; that is to say, to set out on my journey northward till the month of March. As early as possible in that month, I shall have the honor of paying my respects to you in New York. In the mean time, I have that of tendering you the homage of those sentiments of respectful attachment with which I am, Sir, your most obedient and most humble servant,

TH. JEFFERSON.

After some further correspondence with General Washington on the subject, Mr. Jefferson finally accepted the appointment of Secretary of State, though with what reluctance the reader can well judge from the preceding letter.

Before setting out for New York, the seat of government, Jefferson gave away in marriage his eldest daughter, Martha. The wedding took place at Monticello on the 23d of February (1790), and the fortunate bridegroom was young Thomas Mann Randolph, of Tuckahoe, the son of Colonel Thomas Mann Randolph, of Tuckahoe, who had been Colonel Peter Jefferson's ward. Young Randolph had visited Paris in 1788, and spent a portion of the summer there after the completion of his education at the University of Edinburgh, and we may suppose that the first love-passages which resulted in their marriage took place between the young people at that time. They were second-cousins, and had known each other from their earliest childhood.

The marriage ceremony was performed by the Rev. Mr. Maury of the Episcopal Church, and two people were rarely ever united in marriage whose future seemed to promise a happier life. I have elsewhere noticed the noble qualities both of head and heart which were possessed by Martha Jefferson. It was the growth and development of these which years afterwards made John Randolph, of Roanoke— though he had quarrelled with her father—pronounce her the "noblest woman in Virginia."* Thomas Mann Randolph was intellectually not less highly gifted. He was a constant student, and for his genius and acquirements ranked among the first students at the University of Edinburgh. In that city he received the same attentions and held the same position in society which his rank, his wealth, and his brilliant attainments commanded for him at home. The bravest of the brave, chivalric in his devotion to his friends and in his admiration and reverence for the gentler sex; tall and graceful in person, renowned in his day as an athlete and for his splendid horsemanship, with a head and face of unusual intellectual beauty, bearing a distinguished name, and pos-

---

* It was on the occasion of a dinner-party, when some one proposing to drink the health of Mrs. Randolph, John Randolph rose and said, "Yes, gentlemen, let us drink the health of the noblest woman in Virginia."

sessing an ample fortune, any woman might have been deemed happy who was led by him to the hymeneal altar.

A few days after his daughter's marriage, Mr. Jefferson set out for New York, going by the way of Richmond. At Alexandria the Mayor and citizens gave him a public reception. He had intended travelling in his own carriage, which met him at that point, but a heavy fall of snow taking place, he sent it around by water, and took a seat in the stage, having his horses led. In consequence of the bad condition of the roads, his journey was a tedious one, it taking a fortnight for him to travel from Richmond to New York. He occasionally left the stage floundering in the mud, and, mounting one of his led horses, accomplished parts of his journey on horseback. On the 17th of March he arrived in Philadelphia, and hearing of the illness of his aged friend, Dr. Franklin, went at once to visit him, and in his Memoir speaks thus of his interview with him:

At Philadelphia I called on the venerable and beloved Franklin. He was then on the bed of sickness, from which he never rose. My recent return from a country in which he had left so many friends, and the perilous convulsions to which they had been exposed, revived all his anxieties to know what part they had taken, what had been their course, and what their fate. He went over all in succession with a rapidity and animation almost too much for his strength. When all his inquiries were satisfied and a pause took place, I told him I had learned with pleasure that, since his return to America, he had been occupied in preparing for the world the history of his own life. "I can not say much of that," said he; "but I will give you a sample of what I shall leave," and he directed his little grandson (William Bache), who was standing by the bedside, to hand him a paper from the table to which he pointed. He did so; and the Doctor, putting it into my hands, desired me to take it and read it at my leisure. It was about a quire of folio paper, written in a large and running hand, very like his own. I looked into it slightly, then shut it, and said I would accept his permission to read it, and would carefully return it. He said "No, keep it." Not certain of his meaning, I again looked into it, folded it for my pocket, and said again, I would certainly return it. "No," said he; "keep it." I put it into my pocket, and shortly after took leave of him.

He died on the 17th of the ensuing month of April; and as I understood he had bequeathed all his papers to his grandson, William Temple Franklin, I immediately wrote to Mr. Franklin, to inform him I possessed this paper, which I should consider as his property, and would deliver it to his order. He came on immediately to New York; called on me for it, and I delivered it to him. As he put it into his pocket, he said, carelessly, he had either the original, or another copy of it, I do not recollect which. This last expression struck my attention forcibly, and for the first time suggested to me the thought that Dr. Franklin had meant it as a confidential deposit in my hands, and that I had done wrong in parting from it.

I have not yet seen the collection of Dr. Franklin's works that he published, and therefore know not if this is among them. I have been told it is not. It contained a narrative of the negotiations between Dr. Franklin and the British Ministry, when he was endeavoring to prevent the contest of arms that followed. The negotiation was brought about by the intervention of Lord Howe and his sister, who, I believe, was called Lady Howe, but I may misremember her title.

Lord Howe seems to have been friendly to America, and exceedingly anxious to prevent a rupture. His intimacy with Dr. Franklin, and his position with the Ministry, induced him to undertake a mediation between them, in which his sister seems to have been associated. They carried from one to the other, backward and forward, the several propositions and answers which passed, and seconded with their own intercessions the importance of mutual sacrifices, to preserve the peace and connection of the two countries. I remember that Lord North's answers were dry, unyielding, in the spirit of unconditional submission, and betrayed an absolute indifference to the occurrence of a rupture; and he said to the mediators, distinctly, at last, that "a rebellion was not to be deprecated on the part of Great Britain; that the confiscations it would produce would provide for many of their friends." This expression was reported by the mediators to Dr. Franklin, and indicated so cool and calculated a purpose in the Ministry as to render compromise impossible, and the negotiation was discontinued.

If this is not among the papers published, we ask what has become of it? I delivered it with my own hands into those of Temple Franklin. It certainly established views so atrocious in the British Government, that its suppression would be to them worth a great price. But could the grandson of Dr. Franklin be in such a degree an accomplice in the parricide of the memory of his immortal grandfather? The suspension for more than twenty years of the general publication, bequeathed and confided to him, produced for a while hard suspicion against him; and if at last all are not published, a part of these suspicions may remain with some.

I arrived at New York on the 21st of March, where Congress was in session.

Jefferson's first letter from New York was to his son-in-law, Mr. Randolph, and is dated New York, March 28th. He gives him an account of the journey, which speaks much for the tedium of travelling in those days.

Jefferson to Thomas Mann Randolph.

I arrived here on the 21st instant, after as laborious a journey of a fortnight from Richmond as I ever went through, resting only one day at Alexandria and another at Baltimore. I found my carriage and horses at Alexandria, but a snow of eighteen inches falling the same night, I saw the impossibility of getting on in my carriage, so left it there, to be sent to me by water, and had my horses led on to this place, taking my passage in the stage, though relieving myself a little sometimes by mounting my horse. The roads through the whole way were so bad that we could never go more than three miles an hour, sometimes not more than two, and in the night not more than one. My first object was to look out a house in the Broadway, if possible, as being the centre of my business. Finding none there vacant for the present, I have taken a small one in Maiden Lane, which may give me time to look about me. Much business had been put by for my arrival, so that I found myself all at once involved under an accumulation of it. When this shall be got through, I will be able to judge whether the ordinary business of my department will leave me any leisure. I fear there will be little.

The reader, I feel sure, will not find out of place here the following very graceful letters of adieu, written by Jefferson to his kind friends in France:

To the Marquis de Lafayette.

New York, April 2d, 1790.

Behold me, my dear friend, elected Secretary of State, instead of returning to the far more agreeable position which placed me in the daily participation of your friendship. I found the appointment in the newspapers the day of my arrival in Virginia. I had, indeed, been asked, while in France, whether I would accept of any appointment at home, and I had answered that, not meaning to remain long where I was, I meant it to be the last office I should ever act in. Unfortunately this letter had not arrived at the time of fixing the new Government. I expressed freely to the President my desire to return. He left me free, but still showing his own desire. This and the concern of others, more general than I had any right to expect, induced me, after three months' parleying, to sacrifice my own inclinations.

I have been here these ten days harnessed in my new gear. Wherever I am, or ever shall be, I shall be sincere in my friendship to you and your nation. I think, with others, that nations are to be governed with regard to their own interests, but I am convinced that it is their interest, in the long run, to be grateful, faithful to their engagements, even in the worst of circumstances, and honorable and generous always. If I had not known that the Head of our Government was in these sentiments, and his national and private ethics were the same, I would never have been where I am. I am sorry to tell you his health is less firm than it used to be. However, there is nothing in it to give alarm......

Our last news from Paris is of the eighth of January. So far it seemed that your revolution had got along with a steady pace — meeting, indeed, occasional difficulties and dangers; but we are not translated from depotism to liberty on a feather-bed. I have never feared for the ultimate result, though I have feared for you personally. Indeed, I hope you will never see such another 5th or 6th of October. Take care of yourself, my dear friend, for though I think your nation would in any event work out her own salvation, I am persuaded, were she to lose you, it would cost her oceans of blood, and years of confusion and anarchy. Kiss and bless your dear children for me. Learn them to be as you are, a cement between our two nations. I write to Madame de Lafayette, so have only to add assurances of the respect of your affectionate friend and humble servant.

To Madame de Corny.

New York, April 2d, 1790.

I had the happiness, my dear friend, to arrive in Virginia, after a voyage of twenty-six days only of the finest autumn weather it was possible, the wind having never blown harder than we would have desired it. On my arrival I found my name announced in the papers as Secretary of State. I made light of it, supposing I had only to say " No," and there would be an end of it. It turned out, however, otherwise. For though I was left free to return to France, if I insisted on it, yet I found it better in the end to sacrifice my own inclinations to those of others.

After holding off, therefore, near three months, I acquiesced. I did not write you while this question was in suspense, because I was in constant hope to say to you certainly I should return. Instead of that, I am now to say certainly the contrary, and instead of greeting you personally in Paris, I am to write you a letter of adieu. Accept, then, my dear Madam, my cordial adieu, and my grateful thanks for all the civilities and kindnesses I have received from you. They have been greatly more than I had a right to expect, and they have excited in me a warmth of esteem which it was imprudent in me to have given way to for a person whom I was one day to be separated from. Since it is so, continue towards me those friendly sentiments that I always flattered myself you entertained; let me hear from you sometimes, assured that I shall always feel a warm interest in your happiness.

Your letter of November 25th afflicts me; but I hope that

M

a revolution so pregnant with the general happiness of the nation will not in the end injure the interests of persons who are so friendly to the general good of mankind as yourself and M. de Corny. Present to him my most affectionate esteem, and ask a place in his recollection...... Your affectionate friend and humble servant,

TH. JEFFERSON.

To the Comtesse d'Houdetôt.

New York, April 2d, 1790.

Being called by our Government to assist in the domestic administration, instead of paying my respects to you in person as I hoped, I am to write you a letter of adieu. Accept, I pray you, Madame, my grateful acknowledgments for the manifold kindnesses by which you added so much to the happiness of my life in Paris. I have found here a philosophic revolution, philosophically effected. Yours, though a little more turbulent, has, I hope, by this time issued in success and peace. Nobody prays for it more sincerely than I do, and nobody will do more to cherish a union with a nation dear to us through many ties, and now more approximated by the change in its Government.

I found our friend Dr. Franklin in his bed—cheerful and free from pain, but still in his bed. He took a lively interest in the details I gave him of your revolution. I observed his face often flushed in the course of it. He is much emaciated. M. de Crevecœur is well, but a little apprehensive that the spirit of reforming and economizing may reach his office. A good man will suffer if it does. Permit me, Madame la Comtesse, to present here my sincere respects to Monsieur le Comte d'Houdetôt and to Monsieur de Sainte Lambert. The philosophy of the latter will have been greatly gratified to see a regeneration of the condition of man in Europe so happily begun in his own country. Repeating to you, Madame, my sincere sense of your goodness to me, and my wishes to prove it on every occasion, adding my sincere prayer that Heaven may bless you with many years of life and health, I pray you to accept here the homage of those sentiments of respect and attachment with which I have the honor to be, Madame la Comtesse, your most obedient and humble servant,

TH. JEFFERSON.

We find the following interesting passage in a letter from Jefferson to M. Grand, written on the 23d of April:

The good old Dr. Franklin, so long the ornament of our country, and I may say of the world, has at length closed his eminent career. He died on the 17th instant, of an imposthume of his lungs, which having suppurated and burst, he had not strength to throw off the matter, and was suffocated by it. His illness from this imposthume was of sixteen days. Congress wear mourning for him, by a resolve of their body.

Nearly a year later we find him writing to the President of the National Assembly of France as follows:

I have it in charge from the President of the United States of America, to communicate to the National Assembly of France the peculiar sensibility of Congress to the tribute paid to the memory of Benjamin Franklin by the enlightened and free representatives of a great nation, in their decree of the 11th of June, 1790.

That the loss of such a citizen should be lamented by us among whom he lived, whom he so long and eminently served, and who feel their country advanced and honored by his birth, life, and labors, was to be expected. But it remained for the National Assembly of France to set the first example of the representatives of one nation doing homage, by a public act, to the private citizen of another, and, by withdrawing arbitrary lines of separation, to reduce into one fraternity the good and the great, wherever they have lived or died.

Jefferson's health was not good during the spring of the year 1790, and although he remained at his post he was incapacitated for business during the whole of the month of May. He was frequently prostrated from the effects of severe headaches, which sometimes lasted for two or three days. His health was not re-established before July.

I give now his letters home, which were written to his daughters. Mrs. Randolph was living at Monticello, and

Maria, or "little Poll," now not quite twelve years old, was at Eppington on a visit to her good Aunt Eppes. These letters give an admirable picture of Jefferson as the father, and betray an almost motherly tenderness of love for, and watchfulness over, his daughters. Martha, though a married woman, is warned of the difficulties and little cares of her new situation in life, and receives timely advice as to how to steer clear of them; while little Maria is urged to prosecute her studies, to be good and industrious, in terms so full of love as to make his fatherly advice almost irresistible. The letters show, too, his longing for home, and how eagerly he craved the small news, as well as the great, of the loved ones he had left behind in Virginia. I give sometimes an extract, instead of the whole letter.

To Martha Jefferson Randolph.—[Extract.]

New York, April 4th, 1790.

I am anxious to hear from you of your health, your occupations, where you are, etc. Do not neglect your music. It will be a companion which will sweeten many hours of life to you. I assure you mine here is triste enough. Having had yourself and dear Poll to live with me so long, to exercise my affections and cheer me in the intervals of business, I feel heavily the separation from you. It is a circumstance of consolation to know that you are happier, and to see a prospect of its continuance in the prudence and even temper of Mr. Randolph and yourself. Your new condition will call for abundance of little sacrifices. But they will be greatly overpaid by the measure of affection they secure to you. The happiness of your life now depends on the continuing to please a single person. To this all other objects must be secondary, even your love for me, were it possible that could ever be an obstacle. But this it never can be. Neither of you can ever have a more faithful friend than myself, nor one on whom you can count for more sacrifices. My own is become a secondary object to the happiness of you both. Cherish, then, for me, my dear child, the affection of your husband, and continue to love me as you have done, and to render my life a blessing by the prospect it may hold up to me of seeing you happy. Kiss Maria for me if she is with you, and present me cordially to Mr. Randolph; assuring yourself of the constant and unchangeable love of yours, affectionately,

TH. JEFFERSON.

His daughter Maria, to whom the following letter is addressed, was at the time, as I have said, not quite twelve years old.

To Mary Jefferson.

New York, April 11th, 1790.

Where are you, my dear Maria? how are you occupied? Write me a letter by the first post, and answer me all these questions. Tell me whether you see the sun rise every day? how many pages you read every day in Don Quixote? how far you are advanced in him? whether you repeat a grammar lesson every day; what else you read? how many hours a day you sew? whether you have an opportunity of continuing your music? whether you know how to make a pudding yet, to cut out a beefsteak, to sow spinach? or to set a hen? Be good, my dear, as I have always found you; never be angry with any body, nor speak harm of them; try to let every body's faults be forgotten, as you would wish yours to be; take more pleasure in giving what is best to another than in having it yourself, and then all the world will love you, and I more than all the world. If your sister is with you, kiss her, and tell her how much I love her also, and present my affections to Mr. Randolph. Love your aunt and uncle, and be dutiful and obliging to them for all their kindness to you. What would you do without them, and with such a vagrant for a father? Say to both of them a thousand affectionate things for me; and adieu, my dear Maria.

TH. JEFFERSON.

To Martha Jefferson Randolph.

New York, April 26th, 1791.

I write regularly once a week to Mr. Randolph, yourself, or Polly, in hopes it may induce a letter from one of you every week also. If each would answer by the first post my letter to them, I should receive it within the three weeks, so as to keep a regular correspondence with each.......

I long to hear how you pass your time. I think both Mr. Randolph and yourself will suffer with ennui at Richmond. Interesting occupations are essential to happiness. Indeed the whole art of being happy consists in the art of finding employment. I know none so interesting, and which crowd upon us so much as those of a domestic nature. I look forward, therefore, to your commencing housekeepers in your own farm, with some anxiety. Till then you will not know how to fill up your time, and your weariness of the things around you will assume the form of a weariness of one another. I hope Mr. Randolph's idea of settling near Monticello will gain strength, and that no other settlement will, in the mean time, be fixed on. I wish some expedient may be devised for settling him at Edgehill. No circumstance ever made me feel so strongly the thralldom of Mr. Wayles's debt. Were I liberated from that, I should not fear but that Colonel Randolph and myself, by making it a joint contribution, could effect the fixing you there, without interfering with what he otherwise proposes to give Mr. Randolph. I shall hope, when I return to Virginia in the fall, that some means may be found of effecting all our wishes.

From Mary Jefferson.

Richmond, April 25th, 1790.

My dear Papa—I am afraid you will be displeased in knowing where I am, but I hope you will not, as Mr. Randolph certainly had some good reason, though I do not know it.* I have not been able to read in Don Quixote every day, as I have been travelling ever since I saw you last, and the dictionary is too large to go in the pocket of the chariot, nor have I yet had an opportunity of continuing my music. I am now reading Robertson's America. I thank you for the advice you were so good as to give me, and will try to follow it. Adieu, my dear papa. I am your affectionate daughter,

MARIA JEFFERSON.

To Mary Jefferson.

New York, May 2d, 1790.

My dear Maria—I wrote to you three weeks ago, and have not yet received an answer. I hope, however, that one is on

---

* Mr. Randolph took her to Richmond.

the way, and that I shall receive it by the first post. I think it very long to have been absent from Virginia two months, and not to have received a line from yourself, your sister, or Mr. Randolph, and I am very uneasy at it. As I write once a week to one or the other of you in turn, if you would answer my letter the day, or the day after you receive it, it would always come to hand before I write the next to you. We had two days of snow the beginning of last week. Let me know if it snowed where you are. I send you some prints of a new kind for your amusement. I send several to enable you to be generous to your friends. I want much to hear how you employ yourself. Present my best affections to your uncle, aunt, and cousins, if you are with them, or to Mr. Randolph and your sister, if with them. Be assured of my tender love to you, and continue yours to your affectionate,

TH. JEFFERSON.

From Mary Jefferson.

Eppington, May 23d, 1790.

Dear Papa—I received your affectionate letter when I was at Presqu'il, but was not able to answer it before I came here, as the next day we went to Aunt Bolling's and then came here. I thank you for the pictures you were so kind as to send me, and will try that your advice shall not be thrown away. I read in Don Quixote every day to my aunt, and say my grammar in Spanish and English, and write, and read in Robertson's America. After I am done that, I work till dinner, and a little more after. It did not snow at all last month. My cousin Bolling and myself made a pudding the other day. My aunt has given us a hen and chickens. Adieu, my dear papa. Believe me to be your dutiful and affectionate daughter,

MARIA JEFFERSON.

To Mary Jefferson.

New York, May 23d, 1790.

My dear Maria—I was glad to receive your letter of April 25th, because I had been near two months without hearing from any of you. Your last told me what you were not doing; that you were not reading Don Quixote, not applying to your music. I hope your next will tell me what you are doing. Tell your uncle that the President, after having been so ill as at one time to be thought dying, is now quite recovered.* I have been these three weeks confined by a periodical headache. It has been the most moderate I ever had, but it has not yet left me. Present my best affections to your uncle and aunt. Tell the latter I shall never have thanks enough for her kindness to you, and that you will repay her in love and duty. Adieu, my dear Maria.

Yours affectionately,

TH. JEFFERSON.

To Mrs. Eppes.

New York, June 13th, 1790.

Dear Madam—I have received your favor of May 23, and with great pleasure, as I do every thing which comes from you. I have had a long attack of my periodical headache, which was severe for a few days, and since that has been very moderate. Still, however, it hangs upon me a little, though for about ten days past I have been able to resume business. I am sensible of your goodness and attention to my dear Poll, and really jealous of you; for I have always found that you disputed with me the first place in her affections. It would give me infinite pleasure to have her with me, but there is no good position here, and indeed we are in too unsettled a state; the House of Representatives voted the day before yesterday, by a majority of 53 against 6, to remove to Baltimore; but it is very doubtful whether the Senate will concur. However, it may, very possibly, end in a removal either to that place or Philadelphia. In either case, I shall be nearer home, and in a milder climate, for as yet we have had not more than five or six summer days. Spring and fall they never have, as far as I can learn; they have ten months of winter, two of summer, with some winter days interspersed. Does Mr. Eppes sleep any better since the 6th of March. Remember me to him in the most friendly terms, and be assured of the cordial and eternal affection of yours sincerely,

TH. JEFFERSON.

---

* In a letter to his daughter, Mrs. Randolph, after mentioning the President's illness and convalescence, he says, "He continues mending to-day, and from total despair we are now in good hopes of him."

To Mary Jefferson.

New York, June 13th, 1790.

My dear Maria—I have received your letter of May 23d, which was in answer to mine of May 2d, but I wrote you also on the 23d of May, so that you still owe me an answer to that, which I hope is now on the road. In matters of correspondence as well as of money, you must never be in debt. I am much pleased with the account you give me of your occupations, and the making the pudding is as good an article of them as any. When I come to Virginia I shall insist on eating a pudding of your own making, as well as on trying other specimens of your skill. You must make the most of your time while you are with so good an aunt, who can learn you every thing. We had not peas nor strawberries here till the 8th day of this month. On the same day I heard the first whip-poor-will whistle. Swallows and martins appeared here on the 21st of April. When did they appear with you? and when had you peas, strawberries, and whip-poor-wills in Virginia? Take notice hereafter whether the whip-poor-wills always come with the strawberries and peas. Send me a copy of the maxims I gave you, also a list of the books I promised you. I have had a long touch of my periodical headache, but a very moderate one. It has not quite left me yet. Adieu, my dear; love your uncle, aunt, and cousins, and me more than all.

Yours affectionately,

TH. JEFFERSON.

To Mary Jefferson.

New York, July 4th, 1790.

I have written you, my dear Maria, four letters since I have been here, and I have received from you only two. You owe me two, then, and the present will make three. This is a kind of debt I will not give up. You may ask how I will help myself. By petitioning your aunt, as soon as you receive a letter, to make you go without your dinner till you have answered it. How goes on the Spanish? How many chickens have you raised this summer? Send me a list of the books I have promised you at different times.

Tell me what sort of weather you have had, what sort of crops are likely to be made, how your uncle and aunt and the family do, and how you do yourself. I shall see you in September for a short time. Adieu, my dear Poll.

Yours affectionately,

TH. JEFFERSON.

From Mary Jefferson.

Eppington, July 20th, 1790.

Dear Papa—I hope you will excuse my not writing to you before, though I have none for myself. I am very sorry to hear that you have been sick, but flatter myself that it is over. My aunt Skipwith has been very sick, but she is better now; we have been to see her two or three times. You tell me in your last letter that you will see me in September, but I have received a letter from my brother that says you will not be here before February; as his is later than yours, I am afraid you have changed your mind. The books that you have promised me are Anacharsis and Gibbon's Roman Empire. If you are coming in September, I hope you will not forget your promise of buying new jacks for the piano-forte that is at Monticello. Adieu, my dear papa.

I am your affectionate daughter,

MARY JEFFERSON.

From Mary Jefferson.

Eppington, ——, 1790.

Dear Papa—I have just received your last favor, of July 25th, and am determined to write to you every day till I have discharged my debt. When we were in Cumberland we went to church, and heard some singing-masters that sang very well. They are to come here to learn my sister to sing; and as I know you have no objection to my learning any thing, I am to be a scholar, and hope to give you the pleasure of hearing an anthem. We had peas the 10th of May, and strawberries the 17th of the same month, though not in that abundance we are accustomed to, in consequence of a frost this spring. As for the martins, swallows, and whip-poor-wills, I was so taken up with my chickens that I never attended to them, and therefore can not tell you when they came, though I was so unfortunate as to lose half of them (the chickens), for my cousin Bolling and myself have raised but thirteen between us. Adieu, my dear papa.

Believe me to be your affectionate daughter,

MARIA JEFFERSON.

The following beautiful letter to Mrs. Randolph was called forth by the marriage of her father-in-law to a lady of a distinguished name in Virginia. At the time of his second marriage, Colonel Randolph was advanced in years, and his bride still in her teens. The marriage settlement alluded to in the letter secured to her a handsome fortune.

To Martha Jefferson Randolph.

New York, July 17th, 1790.

My dear Patsy—I received two days ago yours of July 2d, with Mr. Randolph's of July 3d. Mine of the 11th to Mr. Randolph will have informed you that I expect to set out from hence for Monticello about the 1st of September. As this depends on the adjournment of Congress, and they begin to be impatient, it is more probable that I may set out sooner than later. However, my letters will keep you better informed as the time approaches.

Col. Randolph's marriage was to be expected. All his amusements depending on society, he can not live alone. The settlement spoken of may be liable to objections in point of prudence and justice. However, I hope it will not be the cause of any diminution of affection between him and Mr. Randolph, and yourself. That can not remedy the evil, and may make it a great deal worse. Besides your interests, which might be injured by a misunderstanding, be assured that your happiness would be infinitely affected. It would be a canker-worm corroding eternally on your minds. Therefore, my dear child, redouble your assiduities to keep the affections of Col. Randolph and his lady (if he is to have one), in proportion as the difficulties increase. He is an excellent, good man, to whose temper nothing can be objected, but too much facility, too much milk. Avail yourself of this softness, then, to obtain his attachment.

If the lady has any thing difficult in her disposition, avoid what is rough, and attach her good qualities to you. Consider what are otherwise as a bad stop in your harpsichord, and do not touch on it, but make yourself happy with the good ones. Every human being, my dear, must thus be viewed, according to what it is good for; for none of us, no not one, is perfect; and were we to love none who had imperfections, this world would be a desert for our love. All we can do is to make the best of our friends, love and cherish what is good in them, and keep out of the way of what is bad; but no more think of rejecting them for it, than of throwing away a piece of music for a flat passage or two. Your situation will require peculiar attentions and respects to both parties. Let no proof be too much for either your patience or acquiescence. Be you, my dear, the link of love, union, and peace for the whole family. The world will give you the more credit for it, in proportion to the difficulty of the task, and your own happiness will be the greater as you perceive that you promote that of others. Former acquaintance and equality of age will render it the easier for you to cultivate and gain the love of the lady. The mother, too, becomes a very necessary object of attentions.

This marriage renders it doubtful with me whether it will be better to direct our overtures to Col. R. or Mr. H. for a farm for Mr. Randolph. Mr. H. has a good tract of land on the other side of Edgehill, and it may not be unadvisable to begin by buying out a dangerous neighbor. I wish Mr. Randolph could have him sounded to see if he will sell, and at what price; but sounded through such a channel as would excite no suspicion that it comes from Mr. Randolph or myself. Col. Monroe would be a good and unsuspected hand, as he once thought of buying the same lands. Adieu, my dear child. Present my warm attachment to Mr. Randolph.

Yours affectionately,

TH. JEFFERSON.

CHAPTER XI.

Jefferson goes with the President to Rhode Island.—Visits Monticello.—
Letter to Mrs. Eppes.—Goes to Philadelphia.—Family Letters.—Letter
to Washington.—Goes to Monticello.—Letters to his Daughter.—His
Ana.—Letters to his Daughter.—To General Washington.—To Lafayette.—To his Daughter.

In the month of August (1790) Jefferson went with the
President on a visit to Rhode Island. In his recent tour
through New England, the President had not visited Rhode
Island, because that State had not then adopted the new Constitution ; now, however, wishing to recruit a little after his
late illness, he bent his steps thither. On the 1st of September Jefferson set out for Virginia. He offered Mr. Madison a seat in his carriage, and the two friends journeyed home
together, stopping at Mount Vernon to pay a visit of two
days to the President. He arrived at Monticello on the 19th,
and found his whole family assembled there to welcome him
back after his six months' absence.

On the eve of his return to the seat of government he
wrote a letter to Mrs. Eppes, from which I give the following extract :

The solitude she (Mrs. Randolph) will be in induces me to
leave Polly with her this winter. In the spring I shall have
her at Philadelphia, if I can find a good situation for her
there. I would not choose to have her there after fourteen
years of age. As soon as I am fixed in Philadelphia, I shall
be in hopes of receiving Jack. Load him, on his departure,
with charges not to give his heart to any object he will find
there. I know no such useless bauble in a house as a girl
of mere city education. She would finish by fixing him
there and ruining him. I will enforce on him your charges,
and all others which shall be for his good.

After enjoying the society of his children and the sweets of domestic life for not quite two months, Jefferson reluctantly turned his back upon home once more, and set out for the seat of government on the 8th of November. Mr. Madison again took a seat in his carriage on returning, and they once more stopped at Mount Vernon, where Washington still lingered, enjoying the repose of home life on the peaceful banks of the Potomac.

After having established himself in his new abode in Philadelphia, Mr. Jefferson began his regular weekly correspondence with his family in Virginia ; and I give the following letters to tell the tale of his life during his absence from home on this occasion, which continued from the 8th of November, 1790, to the 12th of September, 1791.

To Martha Jefferson Randolph.

Philadelphia, Dec. 1st, 1790.

My dear Daughter—In my letter of last week to Mr. Randolph, I mentioned that I should write every Wednesday to him, yourself, and Polly alternately ; and that my letters arriving at Monticello the Saturday, and the answer being sent off on Sunday, I should receive it the day before I should have to write again to the same person, so as that the correspondence with each would be exactly kept up. I hope you will do it, on your part. I delivered the fan and note to your friend Mrs. Waters (Miss Rittenhouse that was), she being now married to a Dr. Waters. They live in the house with her father. She complained of the *petit format* of your letter, and Mrs. Trist of no letter. I inclose you the "Magasin des Modes" of July. My furniture is arrived from Paris; but it will be long before I can open the packages, as my house will not be ready to receive them for some weeks. As soon as they are opened, the mattresses, etc., shall be sent on. News for Mr. Randolph—the letters from Paris inform that as yet all is safe there. They are emitting great sums of paper money. They rather believe there will be no war between Spain and England ; but the letters from London count on a war, and it seems rather probable. A general peace is established in the north of Europe, except between

Russia and Turkey. It is expected between them also. Wheat here is a French crown the bushel.

Kiss dear Poll for me. Remember me to Mr. Randolph. I do not know yet how the Edgehill negotiation has terminated. Adieu, my dear. Yours affectionately,

TH. JEFFERSON.

To Mary Jefferson.

Philadelphia, Dec. 7th, 1790.

My dear Poll—This week I write to you, and if you answer my letter as soon as you receive it, and send it to Colonel Bell at Charlottesville, I shall receive it the day before I write to you again—that will be three weeks hence, and this I shall expect you to do always, so that by the correspondence of Mr. Randolph, your sister, and yourself, I may hear from home once a week. Mr. Randolph's letter from Richmond came to me about five days ago. How do you all do? Tell me that in your letter; also what is going forward with you, how you employ yourself, what weather you have had. We have already had two or three snows here. The workmen are so slow in finishing the house I have rented here, that I know not when I shall have it ready, except one room, which they promise me this week, and which will be my bed-room, study, dining-room, and parlor. I am not able to give any later news about peace or war than of October 16th, which I mentioned in my last to your sister. Wheat has fallen a few pence, and will, I think, continue to fall, slowly at first, and rapidly after a while. Adieu, my dear Maria; kiss your sister for me, and assure Mr. Randolph of my affection. I will not tell you how much I love you, lest, by rendering you vain, it might render you less worthy of my love. Encore adieu.

TH. J.

To Martha Jefferson Randolph.

Philadelphia, Dec. 23d, 1790.

My dear Daughter—This is a scolding letter for you all. I have not received a scrip of a pen from home since I left it. I think it so easy for you to write me one letter every week, which will be but once in the three weeks for each of you, when I write one every week, who have not one moment's repose from business, from the first to the last moment of the week.

Perhaps you think you have nothing to say to me. It is a great deal to say you are all well; or that one has a cold, another a fever, etc.: besides that, there is not a sprig of grass that shoots uninteresting to me; nor any thing that moves, from yourself down to Bergère or Grizzle. Write, then, my dear daughter, punctually on your day, and Mr. Randolph and Polly on theirs. I suspect you may have news to tell me of yourself of the most tender interest to me. Why silent, then?

To Mary Jefferson.

Philadelphia, Jan. 5th, 1791.

I did not write to you, my dear Poll, the last week, because I was really angry at receiving no letter. I have now been near nine weeks from home, and have never had a scrip of a pen, when by the regularity of the post I might receive your letters as frequently and as exactly as if I were at Charlottesville. I ascribed it at first to indolence, but the affection must be weak which is so long overruled by that. Adieu. TH. J.

To Martha Jefferson Randolph.

Philadelphia, Feb. 9th, 1791.

My dear Martha—Your two last letters are those which have given me the greatest pleasure of any I ever received from you. The one announced that you were become a notable housewife; the other, a mother. The last is undoubtedly the key-stone of the arch of matrimonial happiness, as the first is its daily aliment. Accept my sincere congratulations for yourself and Mr. Randolph.

I hope you are getting well; towards which great care of yourself is necessary; for however advisable it is for those in health to expose themselves freely, it is not so for the sick. You will be out in time to begin your garden, and that will tempt you to be out a great deal, than which nothing will tend more to give you health and strength. Remember me affectionately to Mr. Randolph and Polly, as well as to Miss Jenny. Yours sincerely,

TH. JEFFERSON.

From Mary Jefferson.

Monticello, January 22d, 1791.

Dear Papa—I received your letter of December the 7th about a fortnight ago, and would have answered it directly, but my sister had to answer hers last week and I this. We are all well at present. Jenny Randolph and myself keep house—she one week, and I the other. I owe sister thirty-five pages in Don Quixote, and am now paying them as fast as I can. Last Christmas I gave sister the "Tales of the Castle," and she made me a present of the "Observer," a little ivory box, and one of her drawings; and to Jenny she gave "Paradise Lost," and some other things. Adieu, dear Papa. I am your affectionate daughter,

MARIA JEFFERSON.

To Mary Jefferson.

Philadelphia, February 16th, 1791.

My dear Poll—At length I have received a letter from you. As the spell is now broken, I hope you will continue to write every three weeks. Observe, I do not admit the excuse you make of not writing because your sister had not written the week before; let each write their own week without regard to what others do, or do not do. I congratulate you, my dear aunt, on your new title. I hope you pay a great deal of attention to your niece, and that you have begun to give her lessons on the harpsichord, in Spanish, etc. Tell your sister I make her a present of Gregory's "Comparative View," inclosed herewith, and that she will find in it a great deal of useful advice for a young mother. I hope herself and the child are well. Kiss them both for me. Present me affectionately to Mr. Randolph and Miss Jenny. Mind your Spanish and your harpsichord well, and think often and always of, yours affectionately,

TH. JEFFERSON.

P.S.—Letter inclosed, with the book for your sister.

From Mary Jefferson.

Monticello, February 13th, 1791.

Dear Papa—I am very sorry that my not having written to you before made you doubt my affection towards

N

you, and hope that after having read my last letter you were not so displeased as at first. In my last I said that my sister was very well, but she was not; she had been sick all day without my knowing any thing of it, as I staid up stairs the whole day; however, she is very well now, and the little one also. She is very pretty, has beautiful deep-blue eyes, and is a very fine child. Adieu, my dear papa. Believe me to be your affectionate daughter,

MARIA JEFFERSON.

To Mary Jefferson.

Philadelphia, March 9th, 1791.

My dear Maria—I am happy at length to have a letter of yours to answer, for that which you wrote to me February 13th came to hand February 28th. I hope our correspondence will now be more regular, that you will be no more lazy, and I no more in the pouts on that account. On the 27th of February I saw blackbirds and robin-redbreasts, and on the 7th of this month I heard frogs for the first time this year. Have you noted the first appearance of these things at Monticello? I hope you have, and will continue to note every appearance, animal and vegetable, which indicates the approach of spring, and will communicate them to me. By these means we shall be able to compare the climates of Philadelphia and Monticello. Tell me when you shall have peas, etc., up; when every thing comes to table; when you shall have the first chickens hatched; when every kind of tree blossoms, or puts forth leaves; when each kind of flower blooms. Kiss your sister and niece for me, and present me affectionately to Mr. Randolph and Miss Jenny.

Yours tenderly, my dear Maria,

TH. J.

To Martha Jefferson Randolph.

Philadelphia, March 24th, 1791.

My dear Daughter—The badness of the roads retards the post, so that I have received no letter this week from Monticello. I shall hope soon to have one from yourself; to know from that that you are perfectly re-established, that the little Anne is becoming a big one, that you have received Dr. Gregory's book and are daily profiting from it. This will hardly reach you in time to put you on the watch for the annular eclipse of the sun, which is to happen on Sunday se'nnight, to begin about sunrise. It will be such a one as is rarely to be seen twice in one life. I have lately received a letter from Fulwar Skipwith, who is Consul for us in Martinique and Guadaloupe. He fixed himself first in thè former, but has removed to the latter. Are any of your acquaintances in either of those islands? If they are, I wish you would write to them and recommend him to their acquaintance. He will be a sure medium through which you may exchange souvenirs with your friends of a more useful kind than those of the convent. He sent me half a dozen pots of very fine sweetmeats. Apples and cider are the greatest presents which can be sent to those islands. I can make those presents for you whenever you choose to write a letter to accompany them, only observing the season for apples. They had better deliver their letters for you to F. S. Skipwith. Things are going on well in France, the Revolution being past all danger. The National Assembly being to separate soon, that event will seal the whole with security. Their islands, but more particularly St. Domingo and Martinique, are involved in a horrid civil war. Nothing can be more distressing than the situation of their inhabitants, as their slaves have been called into action, and are a terrible engine, absolutely ungovernable. It is worse in Martinique, which was the reason Mr. Skipwith left it. An army and fleet from France are expected every hour to quell the disorders. I suppose you are busily engaged in your garden. I expect full details on that subject as well as from Poll, that I may judge what sort of a gardener you make. Present me affectionately to all around you, and be assured of the tender and unalterable love of, yours,

TH. JEFFERSON.

From Mary Jefferson.

Monticello, March 6th, 1791.

According to my dear papa's request I now sit down to write. We were very uneasy for not having had a letter from you since six weeks, till yesterday I received yours, which I now answer. The marble pedestal and a dressing-table are come. Jenny is gone down with Mrs. Fleming, who came here to see sister when she was sick. I suppose you have not received the letter in which Mr. Randolph desires you to name the child. We hope you will come to see us this summer, therefore you must not disappoint us, and I expect you want to see my little niece as much as you do any of us. We are all well, and hope you are so too. Adieu, dear papa. I am your affectionate daughter,

MARIA JEFFERSON.

P.S. My sister says I must tell you the child grows very fast.

To Mary Jefferson.

Philadelphia, March 31st, 1791.

My dear Maria—I am happy to have a letter of yours to answer. That of March 6th came to my hands on the 24th. By-the-by, you never acknowledged the receipt of my letters, nor tell me on what day they came to hand. I presume that by this time you have received the two dressing-tables with marble tops. I give one of them to your sister, and the other to you : mine is here with the top broken in two. Mr. Randolph's letter, referring to me the name of your niece, was very long on the road. I answered it as soon as I received it, and hope the answer got duly to hand. Lest it should have been delayed, I repeated last week to your sister the name of Anne, which I had recommended as belonging to both families. I wrote you in my last that the frogs had begun their songs on the 7th; since that the blue-birds saluted us on the 17th; the weeping-willow began to leaf on the 18th ; the lilac and gooseberry on the 25th; and the golden-willow on the 26th. I inclose for your sister three kinds of flowering beans, very beautiful and very rare. She must plant and nourish them with her own hand this year, in order to save enough seeds for herself and me. Tell Mr. Randolph I have sold my tobacco for five dollars per c., and the rise between this and September. Warehouse and shipping expenses in Virginia, freight and storage here, come to 2*s.* 9*d.* a hundred, so that it is as if I had sold it in Richmond for 27*s.* 3*d.* credit till September, or half per cent. per month discount for the ready money. If he chooses it, his Bedford tobacco may be included in the sale. Kiss every body for me. Yours affectionately,

TH. JEFFERSON.

To Martha Jefferson Randolph.

Philadelphia, April 17th, 1791.

My dear Daughter—Since I wrote last to you, which was on the 24th of March, I have received yours of March 22. I am indeed sorry to hear of the situation of Walter Gilmer, and shall hope the letters from Monticello will continue to inform me how he does. I know how much his parents will suffer, and how much he merited all their affection. Mrs. Trist has been so kind as to have your calash made, but either by mistake of the maker or myself it is not lined with green. I have, therefore, desired a green lining to be got, which you can put in yourself if you prefer it. Mrs. Trist has observed that there is a kind of veil lately introduced here, and much approved. It fastens over the brim of the hat, and then draws round the neck as close or open as you please. I desire a couple to be made, to go with the calash and other things. Mr. Lewis not liking to write letters, I do not hear from him; but I hope you are readily furnished with all the supplies and conveniences the estate affords. I shall not be able to see you till September, by which time the young grand-daughter will begin to look bold and knowing. I inclose you a letter to a woman who lives, I believe, on Buck Island. It is from her sister in Paris, which I would wish you to send *express*. I hope your garden is flourishing. Present me affectionately to Mr. Randolph and Polly.

Yours sincerely, my dear,

TH. JEFFERSON.

I find among his letters for this month (March) the following friendly note to Mr. Madison:

Jefferson to Madison.

What say you to taking a wade into the country at noon? It will be pleasant above head at least, and the party will finish by dining here. Information that Colonel Beckwith is coming to be an inmate with you, and I presume not a desirable one, encourages me to make a proposition, which I did not venture as long as you had your agreeable Congressional society about you; that is, to come and take a bed and plate with me. I have four rooms, of which any one is at your service. Three of them are up two pair of stairs, the other on the ground-floor, and can be in readiness to receive you in twenty-four hours. Let me entreat you, my dear Sir, to do it, if it be not disagreeable to you. To me it will be a relief from a solitude of which I have too much; and it will lessen your repugnance to be assured it will not increase my expenses an atom. When I get my library open, you will often find a convenience in being close at hand to it. The approaching season will render this situation more agreeable than Fifth Street, and even in the winter you will not find it disagreeable. Let me, I beseech you, have a favorable answer to both propositions.

March 13th, 1791.

To Mary Jefferson.

Philadelphia, April 24th, 1791.

I have received, my dear Maria, your letter of March 26th. I find I have counted too much on you as a botanical and zoological correspondent, for I undertook to affirm here that the fruit was not killed in Virginia, because I had a young daughter there who was in that kind of correspondence with me, and who, I was sure, would have mentioned it if it had been so. However, I shall go on communicating to you whatever may contribute to a comparative estimate of the two climates, in hopes it will induce you to do the same to me. Instead of waiting to send the two veils for your sister and yourself round with the other things, I inclose them with this letter. Observe that one of the strings is to be drawn tight round the root of the crown of the hat, and the veil then falling over the brim of the hat, is drawn by the lower string as tight or loose as you please round the neck. When the veil is not chosen to be down, the lower string is also tied round the root of the crown, so as to give the appearance of a puffed bandage for the hat. I send also inclosed the green lining for the calash. J. Eppes is arrived here. Present my affections to Mr. R., your sister, and niece.

Yours with tender love,

TH. JEFFERSON.

April 5. Apricots in bloom,
         Cherry leafing.
"   9. Peach in bloom,
         Apple leafing.
" 11. Cherry in blossom.

From Mary Jefferson.

Monticello, April 18th, 1791.

Dear Papa—I received your letter of March 31st the 14th of this month; as for that of March 9, I received it some time last month, but I do not remember the day. I have finished Don Quixote, and as I have not Desoles yet, I shall read Lazarillo de Tormes. The garden is backward, the inclosure having but lately been finished. I wish you would be so kind as to send me seven yards of cloth like the piece I send you. Adieu, my dear papa.

I am your affectionate daughter,

MARIA JEFFERSON.

To Martha Jefferson Randolph.—[Extract.]

Philadelphia, May 8th, 1791.

I thank you for all the small news of your letter, which it is very grateful for me to receive. I am happy to find you are on good terms with your neighbors. It is almost the most important circumstance in life, since nothing is so corroding as frequently to meet persons with whom one has any difference. The ill-will of a single neighbor is an immense drawback on the happiness of life, and therefore their good-will can not be bought too dear.

To Mary Jefferson.

Philadelphia, May 8th, 1791.

My dear Maria—Your letter of April 18th came to hand on the 30th; that of May 1st I received last night. By the stage which carries this letter I send you twelve yards of striped nankeen of the pattern inclosed. It is addressed to the care of Mr. Brown, merchant in Richmond, and will arrive there with this letter. There are no stuffs here of the kind you sent. April 30th the lilac blossomed. May 4th the gelder-rose, dogwood, redbud, azalea were in blossom. We have still pretty constant fires here. I shall answer Mr. Randolph's letter a week hence. It will be the last I shall write to Monticello for some weeks, because about this day se'nnight I set out to join Mr. Madison at New York, from whence we shall go up to Albany and Lake George, then cross over to Bennington, and so through Vermont to the

Connecticut River, down Connecticut River, by Hartford, to New Haven, then to New York and Philadelphia. Take a map and trace this route. I expect to be back in Philadelphia about the middle of June. I am glad you are to learn to ride, but hope that your horse is very gentle, and that you will never be venturesome. A lady should never ride a horse which she might not safely ride without a bridle. I long to be with you all. Kiss the little one every morning for me, and learn her to run about before I come. Adieu, my dear. Yours affectionately,

TH. JEFFERSON.

The following letter from Jefferson to his brother-in-law, Mr. Eppes, gives us a glimpse of young Jack Eppes, his future son-in-law:

To Francis Eppes.

Philadelphia, May 15th, 1791.

Dear Sir—Jack's letters will have informed you of his arrival here safe and in health....... Your favors of April 5th and 27th are received. I had just answered a letter of Mr. Skipwith's on the subject of the Guineaman, and therefore send you a copy of that by way of answer to your last. I shall be in Virginia in October, but can not yet say whether I shall be able to go to Richmond.

Jack is now set in to work regularly. He passes from two to four hours a day at the College, completing his courses of sciences, and four hours at the law. Besides this, he will write an hour or two to learn the style of business and acquire a habit of writing, and will read something in history and government. The course I propose for him will employ him a couple of years. I shall not fail to impress upon him a due sense of the advantage of qualifying himself to get a living independently of other resources. As yet I discover nothing but a disposition to apply closely. I set out to-morrow on a journey of a month to Lakes George, Champlain, etc., and having yet a thousand things to do, I can only add assurances of the sincere esteem with which I am, dear sir, your affectionate friend and servant,

TH. JEFFERSON.

FRANCIS EPPES, Esq., Eppington.

In a letter of the same date to Mrs. Eppes, he writes:

To Mrs. Eppes.

I received your favor of April 6th by Jack, and my letter of this date to Mr. Eppes will inform you that he is well under way. If we can keep him out of love, he will be able to go straight forward and to make good progress. I receive with real pleasure your congratulations on my advancement to the venerable corps of grandfathers, and can assure you with truth that I expect from it more felicity than any other advancement ever gave me. I only wish for the hour when I may go and enjoy it entire. It was my intention to have troubled you with Maria when I left Virginia in November, satisfied it would be better *for her* to be with you; but the solitude of her sister, and the desire of keeping them united in that affection for each other which is to be the best future food of their lives, induced me to leave her at Monticello.

To Martha Jefferson Randolph.

Lake Champlain, May 31st, 1791.

My dear Martha—I wrote to Maria yesterday while sailing on Lake George, and the same kind of leisure is afforded me to-day to write to you. Lake George is, without comparison, the most beautiful water I ever saw; formed by a contour of mountains into a basin thirty-five miles long, and from two to four miles broad, finely interspersed with islands, its water limpid as crystal, and the mountain sides covered with rich groves of thuja, silver fir, white pine, aspen, and paper birch down to the water-edge; here and there precipices of rock to checker the scene and save it from monotony. An abundance of speckled trout, salmon trout, bass, and other fish, with which it is stored, have added, to our other amusements, the sport of taking them. Lake Champlain, though much larger, is a far less pleasant water. It is muddy, turbulent, and yields little game. After penetrating into it about twenty-five miles, we have been obliged, by a head wind and high sea, to return, having spent a day and a half in sailing on it. We shall take our route again through Lake George, pass through Vermont, down Connecti-

cut River, and through Long Island to New York and Philadelphia. Our journey has hitherto been prosperous and
pleasant, except as to the weather, which has been as sultry
and hot through the whole as could be found in Carolina or
Georgia. I suspect, indeed, that the heats of Northern climates may be more powerful than those of Southern ones in
proportion as they are shorter. Perhaps vegetation requires
this. There is as much fever and ague, too, and other bilious
complaints on Lake Champlain as on the swamps of Carolina. Strawberries here are in the blossom, or just formed.
With you, I suppose, the season is over. On the whole, I
find nothing anywhere else, in point of climate, which Virginia need envy to any part of the world. Here they are
locked up in ice and snow for six months. Spring and autumn, which make a paradise of our country, are rigorous
winter with them; and a tropical summer breaks on them
all at once. When we consider how much climate contrib-
utes to the happiness of our condition, by the fine sensations
it excites, and the productions it is the parent of, we have
reason to value highly the accident of birth in such a one as
that of Virginia.

From this distance I can have little domestic to write to
you about. I must always repeat how much I love you.
Kiss the little Anne for me. I hope she grows lustily, enjoys
good health, and will make us all, and long, happy as the
centre of our common love. Adieu, my dear.

Yours affectionately,

TH. JEFFERSON.*

The allusion in the following letter to the Duke of Dorset,
and to his niece, the charming Lady Caroline Tufton, deserves a word of explanation. The Duke was British Minister in France during Mr. Jefferson's stay there. The two
became acquainted and warm personal friends, and an intimate friendship sprang up between Martha Jefferson and
Lady Caroline. On her return to America, Martha requested
her father to call one of his farms by her friend's name,

---

* This letter, as a matter of curiosity probably, was written in a book of
the bark of the paper birch, having leaves seven inches long by four wide.
(Note from Randall's Jefferson.)

which he did, and a fine farm lying at the foot of Monticello bears at this day the name of Tufton.

To Martha Jefferson Randolph.—[Extract.]

Philadelphia, June 23d, 1791.

I wrote to each of you once during my journey, from which I returned four days ago, having enjoyed through the whole of it very perfect health. I am in hopes the relaxation it gave me from business has freed me from the almost constant headache with which I had been persecuted during the whole winter and spring. Having been entirely clear of it while travelling, proves it to have been occasioned by the drudgery of business. I found here, on my return, your letter of May 23d, with the pleasing information that you were all in good health. I wish I could say when I shall be able to join you; but that will depend on the motions of the President, who is not yet returned to this place.

In a letter written to me by young Mr. Franklin, who is in London, is the following paragraph: "I meet here with many who ask kindly after you. Among these the Duke of Dorset, who is very particular in his inquiries. He has mentioned to me that his niece has wrote once or twice to your daughter since her return to America; but not receiving an answer, had supposed she meant to drop her acquaintance, which his niece much regretted. I ventured to assure him that was not likely, and that possibly the letters might have miscarried. You will take what notice of this you may think proper." Fulwar Skipwith is on his return to the United States. Mrs. Trist and Mrs. Waters often ask after you. Mr. Lewis being very averse to writing, I must trouble Mr. Randolph to inquire of him relative to my tobacco, and to inform me about it. I sold the whole of what was good here. Seventeen hogsheads only are yet come; and by a letter of May 29, from Mr. Hylton, there were then but two hogsheads more arrived at the warehouse. I am uneasy at the delay, because it not only embarrasses me with guessing at excuses to the purchaser, but is likely to make me fail in my payments to Hanson, which ought to be made in Richmond on the 19th of next month. I wish much to know when the rest may be expected.

In your last you observed you had not received a letter

from me in five weeks. My letters to you have been of Jan. 20, Feb. 9, March 2, 24, April 17, May 8, which you will observe to be pretty regularly once in three weeks. Matters in France are still going on safely. Mirabeau is dead; also the Duke de Richelieu; so that the Duke de Fronsac has now succeeded to the head of the family, though not to the title, these being all abolished. Present me affectionately to Mr. Randolph and Polly, and kiss the little one for me.

To Mary Jefferson.

Philadelphia, June 26th, 1791.

My dear Maria—I hope you have received the letter I wrote you from Lake George, and that you have well fixed in your own mind the geography of that lake, and of the whole of my tour, so as to be able to give me a good account of it when I shall see you. On my return here I found your letter of May 29th, giving me the information it is always so pleasing to me to receive—that you are all well. Would to God I could be with you to partake of your felicities, and to tell you in person how much I love you all, and how necessary it is to my happiness to be with you. In my letter to your sister, written to her two or three days ago, I expressed my uneasiness at hearing nothing more of my tobacco, and asked some inquiries to be made of Mr. Lewis on the subject. But I received yesterday a letter from Mr. Lewis with full explanations, and another from Mr. Hylton, informing me the tobacco was on its way to this place. Therefore desire your sister to suppress that part of my letter and say nothing about it. Tell her from me how much I love her. Kiss her and the little one for me, and present my best affections to Mr. Randolph, assured of them also yourself, from yours,

TH. J.

To Mary Jefferson.

Philadelphia, July 31st, 1791.

The last letter I have from you, my dear Maria, was of the 29th of May, which is nine weeks ago. Those which you ought to have written the 19th of June and 10th of July would have reached me before this if they had been written. I mentioned in my letter of the last week to your sister that

I had sent off some stores to Richmond, which I should be glad to have carried to Monticello in the course of the ensuing month of August. They are addressed to the care of Mr. Brown. You mentioned formerly that the two commodes were arrived at Monticello. Were my two sets of ivory chessmen in the drawers? They have not been found in any of the packages which came here, and Petit seems quite sure they were packed up. How goes on the music, both with your sister and yourself? Adieu, my dear Maria. Kiss and bless all the family for me.

Yours affectionately,

TH. JEFFERSON.

From Mary Jefferson.

Monticello, July 10th, 1791.

My dear Papa—I have received both your letters, that from Lake George and of June the 26th. I am very much obliged to you for them, and think the bark that you wrote on prettier than paper. Mrs. Monroe and Aunt Bolling are here. My aunt would have written to you, but she was unwell. She intends to go to the North Garden. Mr. Monroe is gone to Williamsburg to stay two or three weeks, and has left his lady here. She is a charming woman. My sweet Anne grows prettier every day. I thank you for the pictures and nankeen that you sent me, which I think very pretty. Adieu, dear papa.

I am your affectionate daughter,

MARIA JEFFERSON.

To Mary Jefferson.

Philadelphia, August 21st, 1791.

My dear Maria—Your letter of July 10th is the last news I have from Monticello. The time of my setting out for that place is now fixed to some time in the first week of September, so that I hope to be there between the 10th and 15th. My horse is still in such a condition as to give little hope of his living: so that I expect to be under the necessity of buying one when I come to Virginia, as I informed Mr. Randolph in my last letter to him. I am in hopes, therefore, he will have fixed his eye on some one for me, if I should be obliged to buy. In the mean time, as Mr. Madison comes with me, he has a horse which will help us on to Virginia. Kiss little Anne for me, and tell her to be putting on her best looks. My best affections to Mr. Randolph, your sister, and yourself. Adieu, my dear Maria,

TH. JEFFERSON.

In a letter written to Mrs. Randolph in July he announced the arrival of his French steward, Petit,* who he said accosted him " with the assurance that he had come pour rester toujours avec moi," he goes on, as follows :

The principal small news he brings is that Panthemont is one of the convents to be kept up for education; that the old Abbess is living, but Madame de Taubenheim dead; that some of the nuns have chosen to rejoin the world, others to stay ; that there are no English prisoners there now ; Botidorer remains there, etc., etc.   Mr. Short lives in the Hôtel d'Orleans, where I lived when you first went to Panthemont.

The following extract from a letter of Jefferson to Washington, written early in the spring of this year (1791), shows the warmth of his affection for him, and betrays a touching anxiety for his welfare :

I shall be happy to hear that no accident has happened to you in the bad roads you have passed, and that you are better prepared for those to come by lowering the hang of your carriage, and exchanging the coachman for two postilions, circumstances which I confess to you appeared to me essential for your safety ; for which no one on earth more sincerely prays, both from public and private regard, than he who has the honor to be, with sentiments of the most profound respect, Sir, your most obedient and most humble servant.

Mr. Jefferson left Philadelphia for Virginia on the 2d of September, and arrived at Monticello on the 12th. He re-

---

* This servant had made himself invaluable to Mr. Jefferson ; and in a previous letter he wrote to Mrs. Randolph, " I have been made happy by Petit's determination to come to me. I did not look out for another, because I still hoped he would come. In fact, he retired to Champaigne to live with his mother, and after a short time wrote to Mr. Short 'qu'il mourait d'ennui,' and was willing to come."

mained there just one month, leaving for the seat of government on the 12th of October. His regrets at leaving home were on this occasion lessened by the pleasure of being accompanied on his return to Philadelphia by his beautiful young daughter, Maria. His establishment in Philadelphia was one suitable to his rank and position. He kept five horses, and besides his French steward, Petit, who presided over the ménage of his house, he had four or five hired male servants and his daughter's maid.

In a letter to Mr. Randolph written on the 25th of October, he writes thus of his journey:

The first part of our journey was pleasant, except some hair-breadth escapes which our new horse occasioned us in going down hills the first day or two, after which he behaved better, and came through the journey preserving the fierceness of his spirit to the last. I believe he will make me a valuable horse. Mrs. Washington took possession of Maria at Mount Vernon, and only restored her to me here (Philadelphia). It was fortunate enough, as we had to travel through five days of north-east storm, having learned at Mount Vernon that Congress was to meet on the 24th instead of the 31st, as I had thought. We got here only on the 22d. The sales at Georgetown were few, but good. They averaged $2400 the acre. Maria is immersed in new acquaintances; but particularly happy with Nelly Custis, and particularly attended to by Mrs. Washington. She will be with Mrs. Pine a few days hence.

In a later letter to Mrs. Randolph, he says:

Maria is fixed at Mrs. Pine's, and perfectly at home. She has made young friends enough to keep herself in a bustle, and has been honored with the visits of Mrs. Adams, Mrs. Randolph, Mrs. Rittenhouse, etc., etc.

Towards the close of this year Jefferson began to keep his "Ana," or notes on the passing transactions of the day.

The tale of his life will be found pleasantly carried on in the following letters to his daughter:

To Martha Jefferson Randolph.

Philadelphia, January 15th, 1792.

My dear Martha—Having no particular subject for a letter, I find none more soothing to my mind than to indulge itself in expressions of the love I bear you, and the delight with which I recall the various scenes through which we have passed together in our wanderings over the world. These reveries alleviate the toils and inquietudes of my present situation, and leave me always impressed with the desire of being at home once more, and of exchanging labor, envy, and malice for ease, domestic occupation, and domestic love and society; where I may once more be happy with you, with Mr. Randolph, and dear little Anne, with whom even Socrates might ride on a stick without being ridiculous. Indeed it is with difficulty that my resolution will bear me through what yet lies between the present day and that which, on mature consideration of all circumstances respecting myself and others, my mind has determined to be the proper one for relinquishing my office. Though not very distant, it is not near enough for my wishes. The ardor of these, however, would be abated if I thought that, on coming home, I should be left alone. On the contrary, I hope that Mr. Randolph will find a convenience in making only leisurely preparations for a settlement, and that I shall be able to make you both happier than you have been at Monticello, and relieve you of désagrémens to which I have been sensible you were exposed, without the power in myself to prevent it, but by my own presence. Remember me affectionately to Mr. Randolph, and be assured of the tender love of, yours,

TH. JEFFERSON.

To Martha Jefferson Randolph.

Philadelphia, February 26th, 1792.

My dear Martha—We are in daily expectation of hearing of your safe return to Monticello, and all in good health. The season is now coming on when I shall envy you your occupations in the fields and garden, while I am shut up drudging within four walls. Maria is well and lazy, therefore does not write. Your friends, Mrs. Trist and Mrs. Waters, are well also, and often inquire after you. We have nothing new and interesting from Europe for Mr. Randolph. He will perceive by the papers that the English are beaten off the ground by Tippoo Saib. The Leyden Gazette assures that they were only saved by the unexpected arrival of the Mahrattas, who were suing to Tippoo Saib for peace for Lord Cornwallis. My best esteem to Mr. Randolph, and am, my dear Martha, yours affectionately,

TH. JEFFERSON.

To Martha Jefferson Randolph.

Philadelphia, March 22d, 1792.

My dear Martha—Yours of February 20th came to me with that welcome which every thing brings from you. It is a relief to be withdrawn from the torment of the scenes amidst which we are. Spectators of the heats and tumults of conflicting parties, we can not help participating of their feelings. I should envy you the tranquil occupations of your situation, were it not that I value your happiness more than my own, but I too shall have my turn. The ensuing year will be the longest of my life, and the last of such hateful labors; the next we will sow our cabbages together. Maria is well. Having changed my day of writing from Sunday to Thursday or Friday, she will oftener miss writing, as not being with me at the time. I believe you knew Otchakitz, the Indian who lived with the Marquis de Lafayette. He came here lately with some deputies from his nation, and died here of a pleurisy. I was at his funeral yesterday; he was buried standing up, according to their manner. I think it will still be a month before your neighbor, Mrs. Monroe, will leave us. She will probably do it with more pleasure than heretofore, as I think she begins to tire of the town and feel a relish for scenes of more tranquillity. Kiss dear Anne for her aunt, and twice for her grandpapa. Give my best affections to Mr. Randolph, and accept yourself all my tenderness.

TH. JEFFERSON.

In the following extract from a letter to General Washington, written on the 23d of May (1792), Jefferson makes an eloquent appeal to him to remain for another term at the head of the Government. After speaking of the evil of a dissolution of the Union, he goes on to say:

O

To George Washington.

Yet, when we consider the mass which opposed the original coalescence; when we consider that it lay chiefly in the Southern quarter; that the Legislature have availed themselves of no occasion of allaying it, but, on the contrary, whenever Northern and Southern prejudices have come into conflict, the latter have been sacrificed and the former soothed; that the owners of the debt are in the Southern, and the holders of it in the Northern division; ...... who can be sure that these things may not proselyte the small number that was wanting to place the majority on the other side? And this is the event at which I tremble, and to prevent which I consider your continuing at the head of affairs as of the last importance. The confidence of the whole Union is centred in you. Your being at the helm will be more than an answer to every argument which can be used to alarm and lead the people in any quarter into violence and secession. North and South will hang together if they have you to hang on; and if the first correction of a numerous representation should fail in its effect, your presence will give time for trying others not inconsistent with the union and peace of the State.

I am perfectly aware of the oppression under which your present office lays your mind, and of the ardor with which you pant for domestic life. But there is sometimes an eminence of character on which society have such peculiar claims as to control the predilections of the individual for a particular walk of happiness, and restrain him to that alone arising from the present and future benedictions of mankind. This seems to be your condition, and the law imposed on you by Providence in forming your character, and fashioning the events on which it was to operate; and it is to motives like these, and not to personal anxieties of mine or others, who have no right to call on you for sacrifices, that I appeal, and urge a revisal of it, on the ground of change in the aspect of things....... One or two sessions will determine the crisis, and I can not but hope that you can resolve to add more to the many years you have already sacrificed to the good of mankind.

The fear of suspicion that any selfish motive of continuance in office may enter into this solicitation on my part, obliges me to declare that no such motive exists. It is a thing of mere indifference to the public whether I retain or relinquish my purpose of closing my tour with the first periodical renovation of the Government. I know my own measure too well to suppose that my services contribute any thing to the public confidence or the public utility. Multitudes can fill the office in which you have been pleased to place me, as much to their advantage and satisfaction. I have, therefore, no motive to consult but my own inclination, which is bent irresistibly on the tranquil enjoyment of my family, my farm, and my books. I should repose among them, it is true, in far greater security if I were to know that you remained at the watch; and I hope it will be so.

The following extract is taken from an affectionate letter written by Jefferson to Lafayette on the 16th of June, in which he congratulates him on his promotion to the command of the French armies:

Behold you, then, my dear friend, at the head of a great army establishing the liberties of your country against a foreign enemy. May Heaven favor your cause, and make you the channel through which it may pour its favors. While you are extirpating the monster aristocracy, and pulling out the teeth and fangs of its associate monarchy, a contrary tendency is discovered in some here. A sect has shown itself among us, who declare they espoused our new Constitution not as a good and sufficient thing in itself, but only as a step to an English Constitution, the only thing good and sufficient in itself, in their eye. It is happy for us that these are preachers without followers, and that our people are firm and constant in their republican purity. You will wonder to be told that it is from the eastward chiefly that these champions for a King, Lords, and Commons come.

On the 22d of the same month he writes from Philadelphia to Mrs. Randolph as follows:

To Martha Jefferson Randolph.

My dear Martha—Yours of May 27th came to hand on the very day of my last to you, but after it was gone off. That of June 11th was received yesterday. Both made us happy in informing us you were all well. The rebuke to Maria produced the inclosed letter. The time of my departure for Monticello is not yet known. I shall, within a week from this time, send off my stores as usual, that they may arrive before me. So that, should any wagons be going down from the neighborhood, it would be well to desire them to call on Mr. Brown in order to take up the stores should they be arrived. I suspect, by the account you give me of your garden, that you mean a surprise, as good singers always preface their performances by complaints of cold, hoarseness, etc. Maria is still with me. I am endeavoring to find a good lady to put her with, if possible. If not, I shall send her to Mrs. Brodeaux, as the last shift. Old Mrs. Hopkinson is living in town, but does not keep house. I am in hopes you have visited young Mrs. Lewis, and borne with the old one, so as to keep on visiting terms. Sacrifices and suppression of feeling in this way cost much less pain than open separation. The former are soon over; the latter haunt the peace of every day of one's life, be that ever so long. Adieu, my dear, with my best affections to Mr. Randolph. Anne enjoys them without valuing them.

TH. JEFFERSON.

CHAPTER XII.

Anonymous Attacks on Jefferson.—Washington's Letter to him.—His Reply.—Letter to Edmund Randolph.—Returns to Philadelphia.—Washington urges him to remain in his Cabinet.—Letters to his Daughter.—To his Son-in-law.—To his Brother-in-law.—Sends his Resignation to the President.—Fever in Philadelphia.—Weariness of Public Life.—Letters to his Daughters.—To Mrs. Church.—To his Daughter.—Visits Monticello.—Returns to Philadelphia.—Letter to Madison.—To Mrs. Church.—To his Daughters.—Interview with Genet.—Letter to Washington.—His Reply.—Jefferson returns to Monticello.—State of his Affairs, and Extent of his Possessions.—Letter to Washington.—To Mr. Adams.—Washington attempts to get Jefferson back in his Cabinet.—Letter to Edmund Randolph, declining.—Pleasures of his Life at Monticello.—Letter to Madison.—To Giles.—To Rutledge.—To young Lafayette.

In a letter which Jefferson wrote to Edmund Randolph (September 17th, 1792) while on a visit to Monticello, he thus alludes to an anonymous newspaper attack on himself:

To Edmund Randolph.

Every fact alleged under the signature of "An American" as to myself is false, and can be proved so, and perhaps will be one day. But for the present lying and scribbling must be free to those mean enough to deal in them, and in the dark. I should have been setting out for Philadelphia within a day or two; but the addition of a grandson and indisposition of my daughter will probably detain me here a week longer.

The grandson whose birth is announced in this letter received the name of his distinguished grandsire, and grew up to bear in after life the relations and fulfill the duties of a son to him.

On his way back to Philadelphia, after a stay of some months at Monticello, Jefferson stopped at Mount Vernon, and was there earnestly entreated by the President to reconsider his determination to resign his office as Secretary of State.

Washington having consented to be elected President for a second term, was more and more persistent in his efforts to retain Jefferson in his cabinet, and his wishes, added to the entreaties of his friends, shook his resolution to retire, and finally succeeded in making him agree to remain in office at least for a short time longer. How reluctantly he yielded, and with what sacrifice of his own feelings and interests, the reader may judge from the following letter written by him to his daughter before his mind was finally made up on the subject:

To Martha Jefferson Randolph.

Philadelphia, January 26th, 1793.

My dear Martha—I received two days ago yours of the 16th. You were never more mistaken than in supposing you were too long on the prattle, etc., of little Anne. I read it with quite as much pleasure as you write it. I sincerely wish I could hear of her perfect re-establishment. I have for some time past been under an agitation of mind which I scarcely ever experienced before, produced by a check on my purpose of returning home at the close of this session of Congress. My operations at Monticello had all been made to bear upon that point of time; my mind was fixed on it with a fondness which was extreme, the purpose firmly declared to the President, when I became assailed from all quarters with a variety of objections. Among these it was urged that my retiring just when I had been attacked in the public papers would injure me in the eyes of the public, who would suppose I either withdrew from investigation, or because I had not tone of mind sufficient to meet slander. The only reward I ever wished on my retirement was to carry with me nothing like a disapprobation of the public. These representations have for some weeks past shaken a determination which I have thought the whole world could not have shaken. I have not yet finally made up my mind on the subject, nor changed my declaration to the President. But having perfect reliance in the disinterested friendship of some of those who have counselled and urged it strongly; believing they can see and judge better a question between the public and myself than I can, I feel a possibility that I may be detained here into the summer. A few days will decide. In the mean time I have permitted my house to be rented after the middle of March, have sold such of my furniture as would not suit Monticello, and am packing up the rest and storing it ready to be shipped off to Richmond as soon as the season of good sea-weather comes on. A circumstance which weighs on me next to the weightiest is the trouble which, I foresee, I shall be constrained to ask Mr. Randolph to undertake. Having taken from other pursuits a number of hands to execute several purposes which I had in view this year, I can not abandon those purposes and lose their labor altogether. I must, therefore, select the most important and least troublesome of them, the execution of my canal, and (without embarrassing him with any details which Clarkson and George are equal to) get him to tell them always what is to be done and how, and to attend to the levelling the bottom; but on this I shall write him particularly if I defer my departure. I have not received the letter which Mr. Carr wrote me from Richmond, nor any other from him since I left Monticello. My best affections to him, Mr. Randolph, and your fireside, and am, with sincere love, my dear Martha, yours,

TH. JEFFERSON.

To Thomas Mann Randolph.—[Extract.]

Philadelphia, Feb. 3d, 1793.

In my letter to my daughter, of the last week, I suggested to her that a possibility had arisen that I might not return home as early as I had determined. It happened unfortunately that the attack made on me in the newspapers came out soon after I began to speak freely and publicly of my purpose to retire this spring, and, from the modes of publication, the public were possessed of the former sooner than of the latter; and I find that as well those who are my friends as those who are not, putting the two things together as cause and effect, conceived I was driven from my office either from want of firmness or perhaps fear of investigation. Desirous that my retirement may be clouded by no imputations of this kind, I see not only a possibility, but rather a probability, that I shall postpone it for some time. Whether for weeks or months, I can not now say. This must depend in some degree on the will of those who troubled the waters before. When they suffer them to be calm I will go into port. My inclinations never before suffered such violence, and my interests also are materially affected.

The following extracts from letters to his daughter show the tenderness of his feelings for his young grandchildren:

To Martha Jefferson Randolph.

The last letter received from Mr. Randolph or yourself is of Oct. 7, which is near seven weeks ago. I ascribe this to your supposed absence from Monticello, but it makes me uneasy when I recollect the frail state of your two little ones. I hope some letter is on the way to me. I have no news for you except the marriage of your friend, Lady Elizabeth Tufton, to some very rich person.

I have this day received yours of the 18th November, and sincerely sympathize with you on the state of dear Anne, if that can be called sympathy which proceeds from affection at first-hand; for my affections had fastened on her for her own sake, and not merely for yours. Still, however, experience (and that in your own case) has taught me that an infant is never desperate. Let me beseech you not to destroy the powers of her stomach with medicine. Nature alone can re-establish infant organs; only taking care that her efforts be not thwarted by any imprudences of diet. I rejoice in the health of your other hope.

The following will be found of interest:

To Francis Eppes.

Philadelphia, Jan. 4th, 1793.

Dear Sir—The greatest council of Indians which has been or will be held in our day, is to be at the River Glaise, about the southwest corner of Lake Erie, early in the spring. Three commissioners will be appointed to go there on our part. Jack is desirous of accompanying them; and though I do not know who they will be, I presume I can get him un-

der their wing...... He will never have another chance
for seeing so great a collection of Indian (probably 3000)
nations from beyond the lakes and the Mississippi. It is
really important that those who come into public life should
know more of these people than we generally do...... I
know no reason against his going, but that Mrs. Eppes will
be thinking of his scalp. However, he may safely trust his
where the commissioners will trust theirs......

      Your affectionate friend and servant,

                      TH. JEFFERSON.

The address to the following letter from Jefferson is lost:

                      Philadelphia, March 18th, 1793.

Dear Sir—I received your kind favor of the 26th ult., and
thank you for its contents as sincerely as if I could engage
in what they propose. When I first entered on the stage of
public life (now twenty-four years ago), I came to a resolution never to engage, while in public office, in any kind of en-
terprise for the improvement of my fortune, nor to wear any
other character than that of a farmer. I have never departed from it in a single instance; and I have in multiplied instances found myself happy in being able to decide and to
act as a public servant, clear of all interest, in the multiform
questions that have arisen, wherein I have seen others embarrassed and biased by having got themselves in a more
interested situation. Thus I have thought myself richer in
contentment than I should have been with any increase of
fortune. Certainly, I should have been much wealthier had
I remained in that private condition which renders it lawful,
and even laudable, to use proper efforts to better it. However, my public career is now closing, and I will go through
on the principle on which I have hitherto acted. But I feel
myself under obligations to repeat my thanks for this mark
of your attention and friendship.

After quoting this letter, Jefferson's biographer well says:
"If Mr. Jefferson would have consented to adopt a different
rule, the saddest page in his personal history would not be
for us to write."

On the last day of July, Jefferson, still longing for the

quiet of home-life, wrote to the President, tendering his resignation. After stating his reasons for so doing, he says:

To George Washington.

At the close, therefore, of the ensuing month of September, I shall beg leave to retire to scenes of greater tranquillity from those which I am every day more and more convinced that neither my talents, tone of mind, nor time of life fit me. I have thought it my duty to mention the matter thus early, that there may be time for the arrival of a successor from any part of the Union from which you may think proper to call one. That you may find one more able to lighten the burthen of your labors, I most sincerely wish; for no man living more sincerely wishes that your administration could be rendered as pleasant to yourself as it is useful and necessary to our country, nor feels for you a more rational or cordial attachment and respect than, dear Sir, your most obedient and most humble servant.

Early in August the President visited Jefferson at his house in the country, and urged that he would allow him to defer the acceptance of his resignation until the 1st of January. This Jefferson finally, though reluctantly, agreed to do. The following extract from a letter written by him to Madison in June will show how irksome public life was to him:

To James Madison.

If the public, then, has no claim on me, and my friends nothing to justify, the decision will rest on my own feelings alone. There has been a time when these were very different from what they are now; when, perhaps, the esteem of the world was of higher value in my eye than every thing in it. But age, experience, and reflection, preserving to that only its due value, have set a higher on tranquillity. The motion of my blood no longer keeps time with the tumult of the world. It leads me to seek for happiness in the lap and love of my family, in the society of my neighbors and my books, in the wholesome occupations of my farms and my affairs, in an interest or affection in every bud that opens, in every breath that blows around me, in an entire freedom of rest, of motion, of thought—owing account to myself alone of my hours and actions. What must be the principle of that calculation which would balance against these the circumstances of my present existence—worn down with labors from morning to night, and day to day; knowing them as fruitless to others as they are vexatious to myself, committed singly in desperate and eternal contest against a host who are systematically undermining the public liberty and prosperity, even the rare hours of relaxation sacrificed to the society of persons in the same intentions, of whose hatred I am conscious, even in those moments of conviviality when the heart wishes most to open itself to the effusions of friendship and confidence; cut off from my family and friends, my affairs abandoned to chaos and derangement; in short, giving every thing I love in exchange for every thing I hate, and all this without a single gratification in possession or prospect, in present enjoyment or future wish. Indeed, my dear friend, duty being out of the question, inclination cuts off all argument, and so never let there be more between you and me on this subject.

To Mr. Morris he wrote, on September the 11th:

An infectious and mortal fever is broke out in this place. The deaths under it, the week before last, were about forty; the last week about fifty; this week they will probably be about two hundred, and it is increasing. Every one is getting out of the city who can. Colonel Hamilton is ill of the fever, but is on the recovery. The President, according to an arrangement of some time ago, set out for Mount Vernon on yesterday. The Secretary of War is setting out on a visit to Massachusetts. I shall go in a few days to Virginia. When we shall reassemble again may, perhaps, depend on the course of this malady, and on that may depend the date of my next letter.

I shall now carry the reader back to the beginning of this year (1793), and give extracts from Jefferson's letters to his daughter, Mrs. Randolph, giving them in their chronological order:

To Martha Jefferson Randolph.

Philadelphia, January 14th, 1793.

Though his letter informed me of the re-establishment of Anne, yet I wish to learn that time confirms our hopes. We were entertained here lately with the ascent of Mr. Blanchard in a balloon. The security of the thing appeared so great, that every body is wishing for a balloon to travel in. I wish for one sincerely, as, instead of ten days, I should be within five hours of home.

Philadelphia, February 24th, 1793.

Kiss dear Anne, and ask her if she remembers me and will write to me. Health to the little one, and happiness to you all.

Philadelphia, March 10th, 1793.

When I shall see you I can not say; but my heart and thoughts are all with you till I do. I have given up my house here, and taken a small one in the country, on the banks of the Schuylkill, to serve me while I stay. We are packing all our superfluous furniture, and shall be sending it by water to Richmond when the season becomes favorable. My books, too, except a very few, will be packed and go with the other things; so that I shall put it out of my own power to return to the city again to keep house, and it would be impossible to carry on business in the winter at a country residence. Though this points out an ultimate term of stay here, yet my mind is looking to a much shorter one, if the circumstances will permit it which broke in on my first resolution. Indeed, I have it much at heart to be at home in time to run up the part of the house, the latter part of the summer and fall, which I had proposed to do in the spring.

The following was written to an old friend:

To Mrs. Church.

Philadelphia, June 7th, 1793.

Dear Madam—Monsieur de Noailles has been so kind as to deliver me your letter. It fills up the measure of his titles to any service I can render him. It has served to recall to my mind remembrances which are very dear to it, and which often furnish a delicious resort from the dry and oppressive scenes of business. Never was any mortal more tired of these than I am. I thought to have been clear of them some months ago, but shall be detained a little longer, and then I hope to get back to those scenes for which alone my heart was made. I had understood we were shortly to have the happiness of seeing you in America. It is now, I think, the only country of tranquillity, and should be the asylum of all those who wish to avoid the scenes which have crushed our friends in Paris. What is become of Madame de Corny? I have never heard of her since I returned to America. Where is Mrs. Cosway? I have heard she was become a mother; but is the new object to absorb all her affections? I think, if you do not return to America soon, you will be fixed in England by new family connections; for I am sure my dear Kitty is too handsome and too good not to be sought, and sought till, for peace' sake, she must make somebody happy. Her friend Maria writes to her now, and I greet her with sincere attachment. Accept yourself assurances of the same from, dear Madam, your affectionate and humble servant,

TH. JEFFERSON.

I continue his letters to his daughter, Mrs. Randolph.

To Martha Jefferson Randolph.

Philadelphia, June 10th, 1793.

I sincerely congratulate you on the arrival of the mocking-bird. Learn all the children to venerate it as a superior being in the form of a bird, or as a being which will haunt them if any harm is done to itself or its eggs. I shall hope that the multiplication of the cedar in the neighborhood, and of trees and shrubs round the house, will attract more of them; for they like to be in the neighborhood of our habitations if they furnish cover.

Philadelphia, July 7th, 1793.

My head has been so full of farming since I have found it necessary to prepare a place for my manager, that I could not resist the addressing my last weekly letters to Mr. Randolph and boring him with my plans. Maria writes to you to-day. She is getting into tolerable health, though not good. She passes two or three days in the week with me under the trees, for I never go into the house but at the hour of bed. I never before knew the full value of trees. My house is entirely embosomed in high plane-trees, with good grass below; and under them I breakfast, dine, write, read, and receive my company. What would I not give that the trees planted nearest round the house at Monticello were full-grown.

Philadelphia, July 21st, 1793.

We had peaches and Indian corn the 12th inst. When do they begin with you this year? Can you lay up a good stock of seed-peas for the ensuing summer? We will try this winter to cover our garden with a heavy coating of manure. When earth is rich it bids defiance to droughts, yields in abundance, and of the best quality. I suspect that the insects which have harassed you have been encouraged by the feebleness of your plants; and that has been produced by the lean state of the soil. We will attack them another year with joint efforts.

Philadelphia, Aug. 4th, 1793.

I inclose you two of Petit's recipes. The orthography will amuse you, while the matter may be useful. The last of the two is really valuable, as the beans preserved in that manner are as firm, fresh, and green as when gathered.

The orthography alluded to in this letter was that of the word pancakes — the French cook spelling it thus: *pannequaiques.*

On August 18th, Jefferson writes to Mrs. Randolph:

Maria and I are scoring off the weeks which separate us from you. They wear off slowly; but time is sure, though slow....... My blessings to your little ones; love to you all, and friendly howd'ye's to my neighbors. Adieu.

Jefferson visited Monticello in the autumn, and left his daughter Maria there on his return to Philadelphia, or rather to Germantown, from which place the following letter was written. The address of this is lost, but it was probably written to Madison. I give only extracts:

Germantown, November 2d, 1793.

I overtook the President at Baltimore, and we arrived here yesterday, myself fleeced of seventy odd dollars to get from Fredericksburg here, the stages running no further than Baltimore. I mention this to put yourself and Monroe on your guard. The fever in Philadelpha has so much abated as to have almost disappeared. The inhabitants are about returning. It has been determined that the President shall not interfere with the meeting of Congress....... According to present appearances, this place can not lodge a single person more. As a great favor, I have got a bed in the corner of the public room of a tavern; and must continue till some of the Philadelphians make a vacancy by removing into the city. Then we must give him from four to six or eight dollars a week for cuddies without a bed, and sometimes without a chair or table. There is not a single lodging-house in the place. Ross and Willing are alive. Hancock is dead.

To James Madison.

Germantown, November 17th, 1793.

Dear Sir—I have got good lodgings for Monroe and yourself—that is to say, a good room with a fire-place and two beds, in a pleasant and convenient position, with a quiet family. They will breakfast you, but you must mess in a tavern; there is a good one across the street. This is the way in which all must do, and all, I think, will not be able to get even half beds. The President will remain here, I believe, till the meeting of Congress, merely to form a point of union for them before they can have acquired information and courage. For at present there does not exist a single subject in the disorder, no new infection having taken place since the great rains of the 1st of the month, and those before infected being dead or recovered...... Accept, both of you, my sincere affection.

Though bearing a later date than some which follow, we give the following letter here:

To Mrs. Church.

Germantown, Nov. 27th, 1793.

I have received, my very good friend, your kind letter of August 19th, with the extract from that of Lafayette, for whom my heart has been constantly bleeding. The influence of the United States has been put into action, as far as it could be either with decency or effect. But I fear that distance and difference of principle give little hold to General Washington on the jailers of Lafayette. However, his friends may be assured that our zeal has not been inactive. Your letter gives me the first information that our dear friend Madame de Corny has been, as to her fortune, among the victims of the times. Sad times, indeed! and much-lamented victim! I know no country where the remains of a fortune could place her so much at her ease as this, and where public esteem is so attached to worth, regardless of wealth; but our manners, and the state of our society here, are so different from those to which her habits have been formed, that she would lose more, perhaps, in that scale. And Madam Cosway in a convent! I knew that to much goodness of heart she joined enthusiasm and religion; but I thought that very enthusiasm would have prevented her from shutting up her adoration of the God of the universe within the walls of a cloister; that she would rather have sought the *mountain-top*. How happy should I be that it were *mine* that you, she, and Madame de Corny would seek. You say, indeed, that you are coming to America, but I know that means New York. In the mean time, I am going to Virginia. I have at length been able to fix that to the beginning of the new year. I am then to be liberated from the hated occupations of politics, and to remain in the bosom of my family, my farm, and my books. I have my house to build, my fields to farm, and to watch for the happiness of those who labor for mine. I have one daughter married to a man of science, sense, virtue, and competence; in whom indeed I have nothing more to wish. They live with me. If the other shall be as fortunate, in due process of time I shall imagine myself as blessed as the most blessed of the patriarchs. Nothing could then withdraw my thoughts a moment from home but a recollection of my friends abroad. I often put the question, whether yourself and Kitty will ever come to see your friends at Monticello ? but it is my affection, and not my experience of things, which has leave to answer, and I am determined to believe the answer, because in that belief I find I sleep sounder, and wake more cheerful. *En attendant,* God bless you.

Accept the homage of my sincere and constant affection,

TH. JEFFERSON.

The following letters and extracts will be found interesting by the reader :

To Mary Jefferson.

Germantown, Nov. 17th, 1793.

No letter yet from my dear Maria, who is so fond of writing, so punctual in her correspondence. I enjoin as a penalty that the next be written in French....... I have not yet been in [to Philadelphia], not because there is a shadow of danger, but because I am afoot. Thomas is returned into my service. His wife and child went into town the day we left them. They then had the infection of the yellow fever, were taken two or three days after, and both died. Had we staid those two or three days longer, they would have been taken at our house. Mrs. Fullarton left Philadelphia. Mr. and Mrs. Rittenhouse remained here, but have escaped the fever. Follow closely your music, reading, sewing, housekeeping, and love me, as I do you, most affectionately.

TH. JEFFERSON.

P.S.—Tell Mr. Randolph that Gen. Wayne has had a convoy of twenty-two wagons of provisions and seventy men cut off in his rear by the Indians.

To Mary Jefferson.

Philadelphia, Dec. 15th, 1793.

My dear Maria—I should have written to you last Sunday in turn, but business required my allotting your turn to Mr. Randolph, and putting off writing to you till this day. I have now received your and your sister's letters of November 27 and 28. I agree that Watson shall make the writing-desk for you. I called the other day on Mrs. Fullarton, and there saw your friend Sally Cropper. She went up to Trenton the morning after she left us, and staid there till lately. The maid-servant who waited on her and you at our house caught the fever, on her return to town, and died. In my letter of last week, I desired Mr. Randolph to send horses for me, to be at Fredericksburg on the 12th of January. Lest that letter should miscarry, I repeat it here, and wish you to mention it to him. I also informed him that a person of the name of Eli Alexander would set out this day from Elktown to take charge of the plantations under Byrd Rogers, and praying him to have his accommodations at the place got ready as far as should be necessary before my arrival. I hope to be with you all by the 15th of January, no more to leave you. My blessings to your dear sister and little ones; affections to Mr. Randolph and your friends with you. Adieu, my dear. Yours tenderly,

TH. JEFFERSON.

To Martha Jefferson Randolph.—[Extract.]

Philadelphia, Dec. 22d, 1793.

In my letter of this day fortnight to Mr. Randolph, and that of this day week to Maria, I mentioned my wish that my horses might meet me at Fredericksburg on the 12th of January. I now repeat it, lest those letters should miscarry. The President made yesterday what I hope will be the last set at me to continue; but in this I am now immovable by any considerations whatever. My books and remains of furniture embark to-morrow for Richmond...... I hope that by the next post I shall be able to send Mr. Randolph a printed copy of our correspondence with Mr. Genet and Mr. Hammond, as communicated to Congress. Our affairs with England and Spain have a turbid appearance. The letting loose the Algerines on us, which has been contrived by England, has produced peculiar irritation. I think Congress will indemnify themselves by high duties on all articles of British importation. If this should produce war, though not wished for, it seems not to be feared.

The well-informed reader is familiar with the controversy alluded to in the preceding letter, between the United States Government and the French and English ministers, Messrs.

Genet and Hammond. I can not refrain from giving the following extract from Jefferson's report of an interview between Mr. Genet and himself:

He (Genet) asked if they (Congress) were not the Sovereign. I told him no, they were sovereign in making laws only; the Executive was sovereign in executing them; and the Judiciary in construing them when they related to their department. "But," said he, "at least Congress are bound to see that the treaties are observed!" I told him no; there were very few cases, indeed, arising out of treaties, which they could take notice of; that the President is to see that treaties are observed. "If he decides against the treaty, to whom is a nation to appeal?" I told him the Constitution had made the President the last appeal. He made me a bow, and said that indeed he would not make me his compliments on such a Constitution, expressed the utmost astonishment at it, and seemed never before to have had such an idea.

The following letter explains itself:

To George Washington.

Philadelphia, December 31st, 1793.

Dear Sir—Having had the honor of communicating to you in my letter of the last of July my purpose of retiring from the office of Secretary of State at the end of the month of September, you were pleased, for particular reasons, to wish its postponement to the close of the year. That term being now arrived, and my propensities to retirement becoming daily more and more irresistible, I now take the liberty of resigning the office into your hands. Be pleased to accept with it my sincere thanks for all the indulgences which you have been so good as to exercise towards me in the discharge of its duties. Conscious that my need of them has been great, I have still ever found them greater, without any other claim on my part than a firm pursuit of what has appeared to me to be right, and a thorough disdain of all means which were not as open and honorable as their object was pure. I carry into my retirement a lively sense of your goodness, and shall continue gratefully to remember it. With very sincere prayers for your life, health, and tranquillity, I pray you to accept the homage of the great and constant respect and attachment with which I have the honor to be, dear Sir, your most obedient and most humble servant,

TH. JEFFERSON.

This called forth from Washington the following handsome and affectionate letter:

From George Washington.

Philadelphia, Jan. 1st, 1794.

Dear Sir—I yesterday received with sincere regret your resignation of the office of Secretary of State. Since it has been impossible to prevail upon you to forego any longer the indulgence of your desire for private life, the event, however anxious I am to avert it, must be submitted to.

But I can not suffer you to leave your station without assuring you that the opinion which I had formed of your integrity and talents, and which dictated your original nomination, has been confirmed by the fullest experience, and that both have been eminently displayed in the discharge of your duty. Let a conviction of my most earnest prayers for your happiness accompany you in your retirement; and while I accept with the warmest thanks your solicitude for my welfare, I beg you to believe that I am, dear Sir, etc.

Perhaps no man ever received a higher compliment for the able discharge of his official duties than that paid to Jefferson by his adversaries, who, in opposing his nomination as President, urged as an objection—"that Nature had made him only for a Secretary of State."

Jefferson set out on the 5th of January for his loved home, Monticello—fondly imagining that he would never again leave the peaceful shelter of its roof to enter upon the turmoils of public life, but in reality destined to have only a short respite from them in the far sweeter enjoyments of domestic life, surrounded by his children and grandchildren.

His private affairs were in sad need of his constant presence at home after such long absences in the public service. He now owned in his native State over ten thousand acres of land, which for ten long years had been subject to the bad cultivation, mismanagement, and ravages of hired overseers. Of these large landed estates, between five and six thousand acres, comprising the farms of Monticello, Montalto, Tufton, Shadwell, Lego, Pantops, Pouncey's, and Limestone, were in the county of Albemarle; while another fine and favorite estate, called Poplar Forest, lay in Bedford County, and contained over four thousand acres. Of his land in Albemarle only twelve hundred acres were in cultivation, and in Bedford eight hundred—the two together making two thousand acres of arable land. The number of slaves owned by Jefferson was one hundred and fifty-four—a very small number in proportion to his landed estate. Some idea may be formed of the way things were managed on these farms, from the fact that out of the thirty-four horses on them eight were saddle-horses. The rest of the stock on them consisted of five mules, two hundred and forty-nine cattle, three hundred and ninety hogs, and three sheep.

The few months' continuous stay at home which Jefferson had been able to make during the past ten years had not been sufficient for him to set things to rights. How greatly his farms needed a new system of management may be seen from the following letter to General Washington, written by him in the spring of 1794. He says:

To George Washington.

I find, on a more minute examination of my lands than the short visits heretofore made to them permitted, that a ten years' abandonment of them to the ravages of overseers has brought on them a degree of degradation far beyond what I had expected. As this obliges me to adopt a milder course of cropping, so I find that they have enabled me to do it, by having opened a great deal of lands during my absence. I have therefore determined on a division of my farms into six fields, to be put under this rotation: First year, wheat; second, corn, potatoes, peas; third, rye or wheat, according to circumstances; fourth and fifth, clover, where the fields will bring it, and buckwheat-dressings where they will not; sixth, folding and buckwheat-dressing. But it will take me from three to six years to get this plan under way. I am not yet satisfied that my acquisition of overseers from the head of Elk has been a happy one, or that much will be done this year towards rescuing my plantations from their wretched condition. Time, patience, and perseverance must be the remedy; and the maxim of your letter, " slow and sure," is not less a good one in agriculture than in politics....... But I cherish tranquillity too much to suffer political things to enter my mind at all. I do not forget that I owe you a letter for Mr. Young; but I am waiting to get full information. With every wish for your health and happiness, and my most friendly respects to Mrs. Washington, I have the honor to be, dear Sir, your most obedient and most humble servant.

Notwithstanding this disordered and disheartening state of his affairs (due to no fault of his), we still find him luxuriating in the quiet and repose of private life. On this subject he writes to Mr. Adams, on April 25th, as follows:

To John Adams.

Dear Sir—I am to thank you for the work you were so kind as to transmit me, as well as the letter covering it, and your felicitations on my present quiet. The difference of my present and past situation is such as to leave me nothing to regret but that my retirement has been postponed four years too long. The principles on which I calculated the value of life are entirely in favor of my present course. I return to farming with an ardor which I scarcely knew in my youth, and which has got the better entirely of my love of study. Instead of writing ten or twelve letters a day, which I have been in the habit of doing as a thing in course, I put off answering my letters now, farmer-like, till a rainy day, and then find them sometimes postponed by other necessary occupations....... With wishes of every degree of happiness to you, both public and private, and with my best respects to Mrs. Adams, I am your affectionate and humble servant.

The land not having been prepared for cultivation during the preceding fall, Jefferson's farming operations during the summer of 1794 amounted to nothing. Unfortunately, when the next season came around for the proper preparation to be made for the coming year, it found him in such a state of health as to prevent his giving his personal direction to his farms, and thus he was cut off from any profit from them for another twelvemonth. Just about this time General Washington made another attempt, through his Secretary of State, Edmund Randolph, to get Jefferson back into his cabinet. Though at the time ill, Jefferson at once sent the following reply to Randolph:

To Edmund Randolph.

Monticello, September 7th, 1794.

Dear Sir—Your favor of August the 28th finds me in bed under a paroxysm of the rheumatism, which has now kept me for ten days in constant torment, and presents no hope of abatement. But the express and the nature of the case requiring immediate answer, I write you in this situation. No circumstances, my dear Sir, will ever more tempt me to engage in any thing public. I thought myself perfectly fixed in this determination when I left Philadelphia, but every day and hour since has added to its inflexibility. It is a great pleasure to me to retain the esteem and approbation of the President, and this forms the only ground of any reluctance at being unable to comply with every wish of his. Pray convey these sentiments, and a thousand more to him, which my situation does not permit me to go into.......

I find nothing worthy of notice in Jefferson's life during the year 1795. He continued tranquilly and happily enjoying the society of his children and grandchildren in his beautiful mountain home. Mrs. Randolph was now the mother of three children. We have seen from his letters to her how devotedly she was loved by her father. From the time of her mother's death she had been his constant companion until her own marriage; Maria Jefferson, now seventeen years old, was as beautiful and loving as a girl as she had been as a child. The brilliancy of her beauty is spoken of with enthusiasm by those still living who remember her.

In a letter to Mr. Madison written in the spring of this year (1795), Mr. Jefferson writes thus of himself:

To James Madison.

If these general considerations were sufficient to ground a firm resolution never to permit myself to think of the office, or be thought of for it, the special ones which have supervened on my retirement still more insuperably bar the door to it. My health is entirely broken down within the last eight months; my age requires that I should place my affairs in a clear state; these are sound if taken care of, but capable of considerable dangers if longer neglected; and above all things, the delights I feel in the society of my family, and in the agricultural pursuits in which I am so eagerly engaged. The little spice of ambition which I had in my younger days has long since evaporated, and I set still less store by a posthumous than present name....... I long to see you....... May we hope for a visit from you? If we may, let it be after the middle of May, by which time I hope to be returned from Bedford.

In writing on the same day to his friend, Mr. Giles, he says:

I shall be rendered very happy by the visit you promise me. The only thing wanting to make me completely so is the more frequent society of my friends. It is the more wanting, as I am become more firmly fixed to the glebe. If you visit me as a farmer, it must be as a con-disciple; for I am but a learner—an eager one indeed, but yet desperate, being too old now to learn a new art. However, I am as much delighted and occupied with it as if I were the greatest adept. I shall talk with you about it from morning till night, and put you on very short allowance as to political aliment. Now and then a pious ejaculation for the French and Dutch republicans, returning with due dispatch to clover, potatoes, wheat, etc.

To Edward Rutledge he wrote, on November 30th, 1795:

I received your favor of October the 12th by your son, who has been kind enough to visit me here, and from whose visit I have received all that pleasure which I do from whatever comes from you, and especially from a subject so deservedly dear to you. He found me in a retirement I doat on, living like an antediluvian patriarch among my children and grandchildren, and tilling my soil. As he had lately come from Philadelphia, Boston, etc., he was able to give me a great deal of information of what is passing in the world; and I pestered him with questions, pretty much as our friends Lynch, Nelson, etc., will us when we step across the Styx, for they will wish to know what has been passing above ground since they left us. You hope I have not abandoned entirely the service of our country. After five-and-twenty years' continual employment in it, I trust it will be thought I have fulfilled my tour, like a punctual soldier, and may claim my discharge. But I am glad of the sentiment from you, my friend, because it gives a hope you will practice what you preach, and come forward in aid of the public vessel. I will not admit your old excuse, that you are in public service, though at home. The campaigns which are fought in a man's own house are not to be counted. The present situation of the President, unable to get the offices filled, really calls with uncommon obligation on those whom nature has fitted for them.

Early in the spring of 1796, in a letter to his friend Giles, he gives us the following glimpse of his domestic operations:

We have had a fine winter. Wheat looks well. Corn is scarce and dear: twenty-two shillings here, thirty shillings in Amherst. Our blossoms are but just opening. I have begun the demolition of my house, and hope to get through its re-edification in the course of the summer. We shall have the eye of a brick-kiln to poke you into, or an octagon to air you in.

To another friend he wrote, a few weeks later:

I begin to feel the effects of age. My health has suddenly broken down, with symptoms which give me to believe I shall not have much to encounter of the *tedium vitæ.*

The reader will read with interest the following kind and affectionate letter to young Lafayette—son of the Marquis de Lafayette:

To Lafayette, Junior.

Monticello, June 19th, 1796.

Dear Sir—The inquiries of Congress were the first intimation which reached my retirement of your being in this country; and from M. Volney, now with me, I first learned where you are. I avail myself of the earliest moments of this information to express to you the satisfaction with which I learn that you are in a land of safety, where you will meet in every person the friend of your worthy father and family. Among these, I beg leave to mingle my own assurances of sincere attachment to him, and my desire to prove it by every service I can render you. I know, indeed, that you are already under too good a patronage to need any other, and that my distance and retirement render my affections unavailing to you. They exist, nevertheless, in all their warmth and purity towards your father and every one embraced by his love; and no one has wished with more anxiety to see him once more in the bosom of a nation who, knowing his works and his worth, desire to make him and his family forever their own. You were, perhaps, too young to remember me personally when in Paris. But I pray you to remember that, should any occasion offer wherein I can be useful to you, there is no one on whose friendship and zeal you may more confidently count. You will some day, perhaps, take a tour through these States. Should any thing in this part of them attract your curiosity, it would be a circumstance of great gratification to me to receive you here, and to assure you in person of those sentiments of esteem and attachment, with which I am, dear Sir, your friend and humble servant,

TH. JEFFERSON.

CHAPTER XIII.

Description of Monticello and Jefferson by the Duc de la Rochefoucauld-Li-
ancourt.—Nominated Vice-President.—Letter to Madison.—To Adams.
—Preference for the Office of Vice-President.—Sets out for Philadelphia.
—Reception there.—Returns to Monticello.—Letters to his Daughter.—
Goes to Philadelphia. — Letter to Rutledge. — Family Letters. — To Miss
Church.—To Mrs. Church.

I HAVE elsewhere given a charming picture of Monticello
and its inmates in 1782, from the pen of an accomplished
Frenchman—the Marquis de Chastellux. A countryman of
his—equally as accomplished and distinguished, the Duc de
la Rochefoucauld-Liancourt—has left us a similar one of a
later date. This patriotic French nobleman, who had been
Lieutenant-general of France and President of the National
Assembly, while in exile spent some days at Monticello, in
the month of June, 1796—a month when the mountains of
Albemarle are clothed in all the brilliancy of their summer
beauty. The lovely landscapes around Monticello were well
calculated to charm the eye of a foreigner; and I give the
Duc's detailed but agreeable description of the place, its
owner, and its surroundings. There are one or two trifling
mistakes in it as regards geographical names; the rest is
accurate :

Monticello is situated three miles from Milton, in that
chain of mountains which stretches from James River to the
Rappahannock, twenty-eight miles in front of the Blue Ridge,
and in a direction parallel to those mountains. This chain,
which runs uninterrupted in its small extent, assumes suc-
cessively the names of the West, South, and Green Mountains.
It is in the part known by the name of the South Mountains that Monticello is situated. The house stands on the

summit of the mountain, and the taste and arts of Europe
have been consulted in the formation of its plan.   Mr. Jefferson had commenced its construction before the American
Revolution; since that epocha his life has been constantly
engaged in public affairs, and he has not been able to complete the execution of the whole extent of the project which
it seems he had at first conceived.   That part of the building
which was finished has suffered from the suspension of the
work, and Mr. Jefferson, who two years since resumed the
habits and leisure of private life, is now employed in repairing
the damage occasioned by this interruption, and still more
by his absence; he continues his original plan, and even
improves on it by giving to his buildings more elevation
and extent.   He intends that they shall consist only of one
story, crowned with balustrades; and a dome is to be con-
structed in the centre of the structure.   The apartments will
be large and convenient; the decoration, both outside and
inside, simple, yet regular and elegant.   Monticello, according to its first plan, was infinitely superior to all other houses
in America, in point of taste and convenience; but at that
time Mr. Jefferson had studied taste and the fine arts in
books only.   His travels in Europe have supplied him with
models; he has appropriated them to his design; and his
new plan, the execution of which is already much advanced,
will be accomplished before the end of next year, and then
his house will certainly deserve to be ranked with the most
pleasant mansions in France and England.

Mr. Jefferson's house commands one of the most extensive
prospects you can meet with.   On the east side, the front of
the building, the eye is not checked by any object, since the
mountain on which the house is seated commands all the
neighboring heights as far as the Chesapeake.   The Atlantic
might be seen, were it not for the greatness of the distance,
which renders that prospect impossible.   On the right and
left the eye commands the extensive valley that separates
the Green, South, and West Mountains from the Blue Ridge,
and has no other bounds but these high mountains, of which,
on a clear day, you discern the chain on the right upward
of a hundred miles, far beyond James River; and on the
left as far as Maryland, on the other side of the Potomac.
Through some intervals formed by the irregular summits of

the Blue Mountains, you discover the Peaked Ridge, a chain
of mountains placed between the Blue and North Mountains,
another more distant ridge. But in the back part the prospect is soon interrupted by a mountain more elevated than
that on which the house is seated. The bounds of the view
on this point, at so small a distance, form a pleasant resting-
place, as the immensity of prospect it enjoys is perhaps already too vast. A considerable number of cultivated fields,
houses, and barns, enliven and variegate the extensive landscape, still more embellished by the beautiful and diversified
forms of mountains, in the whole chain of which not one
resembles another. The aid of fancy is, however, required
to complete the enjoyment of this magnificent view; and
she must picture to us those plains and mountains such as
population and culture will render them in a greater or
smaller number of years. The disproportion existing between the cultivated lands and those which are still covered
with forests as ancient as the globe, is at present much too
great; and even when that shall have been done away, the
eye may perhaps further wish to discover a broad river, a
great mass of water—destitute of which, the grandest and
most extensive prospect is ever destitute of an embellish-
ment requisite to render it completely beautiful.

On this mountain, and in the surrounding valleys on both
banks of the Rivanna, are situated the five thousand acres
of land which Mr. Jefferson possesses in this part of Virginia.
Eleven hundred and twenty only are cultivated. The land,
left to the care of stewards, has suffered as well as the
buildings from the long absence of the master; according to
the custom of the country, it has been exhausted by successive culture. Its situation on the declivities of hills and
mountains renders a careful cultivation more necessary than
is requisite in lands situated in a flat and even country; the
common routine is more pernicious, and more judgment and
mature thought are required, than in a different soil. This
forms at present the chief employment of Mr. Jefferson. But
little accustomed to agricultural pursuits, he has drawn the
principles of culture either from works which treat on this
subject or from conversation. Knowledge thus acquired oft-
en misleads, and is at all times insufficient in a country where
agriculture is well understood; yet it is preferable to mere

practical knowledge, and a country where a bad practice prevails, and where it is dangerous to follow the routine, from which it is so difficult to depart. Above all, much good may be expected, if a contemplative mind like that of Mr. Jefferson, which takes the theory for its guide, watches its application with discernment, and rectifies it according to the peculiar circumstances and nature of the country, climate, and soil, and conformably to the experience which he daily acquires.......

In private life Mr. Jefferson displays a mild, easy, and obliging temper, though he is somewhat cold and reserved. His conversation is of the most agreeable kind, and he possesses a stock of information not inferior to that of any other man. In Europe he would hold a distinguished rank among men of letters, and as such he has already appeared there. At present he is employed with activity and perseverance in the management of his farms and buildings; and he orders, directs, and pursues in the minutest details every branch of business relative to them. I found him in the midst of the harvest, from which the scorching heat of the sun does not prevent his attendance. His negroes are nourished, clothed, and treated as well as white servants could be. As he can not expect any assistance from the two small neighboring towns, every article is made on his farm: his negroes are cabinet-makers, carpenters, masons, bricklayers, smiths, etc. The children he employs in a nail factory, which yields already a considerable profit. The young and old negresses spin for the clothing of the rest. He animates them by rewards and distinctions; in fine, his superior mind directs the management of his domestic concerns with the same abilities, activity, and regularity which he evinced in the conduct of public affairs, and which he is calculated to display in every situation of life. In the superintendence of his household he is assisted by his two daughters, Mrs. Randolph and Miss Maria, who are handsome, modest, and amiable women. They have been educated in France.......

Mr. Randolph is proprietor of a considerable plantation, contiguous to that of Mr. Jefferson's. He constantly spends the summer with him, and, from the affection he bears him, he seems to be his son rather than his son-in-law. Miss Maria constantly resides with her father; but as she is

seventeen years old, and is remarkably handsome, she will, doubtless, soon find that there are duties which it is still sweeter to perform than those of a daughter. Mr. Jefferson's philosophic turn of mind, his love of study, his excellent library, which supplies him with the means of satisfying it, and his friends, will undoubtedly help him to endure this loss, which, moreover, is not likely to become an absolute privation; as the second son-in-law of Mr. Jefferson may, like Mr. Randolph, reside in the vicinity of Monticello, and, if he be worthy of Miss Maria, will not be able to find any company more desirable than that of Mr. Jefferson.......
Left Monticello on the 29th of June.

All through this summer Mr. Jefferson was much occupied with the rebuilding of his house, which he hoped to finish before the winter set in; but just as the walls were nearly ready to be roofed in, a stiff freeze arrested, in November, all work on it for the winter.

General Washington having declared his determination to retire from public life at the expiration of his second term, new candidates had to be run for the Presidential chair. The Federalists chose John Adams as their candidate; while the Republicans, having no thought of running as theirs any man but Jefferson, placed his name at the head of their ticket. How little interest Jefferson took in the elections, so far as his own success was concerned, may be inferred from the fact that he did not leave home during the whole campaign, and in that time wrote only one political letter.

As the constitution then stood, the candidate who received the highest number of votes was elected President, and the one who received the next highest—whether he was run for President or Vice-president—was elected to fill the latter office. The elections were over, but the result still unknown, when Jefferson wrote, on December 17th, to Mr. Madison, as follows·

To James Madison.

Your favor of the 5th came to hand last night. The first wish of my heart was that you should have been proposed

for the administration of the Government. On your declining it, I wish any body rather than myself; and there is
nothing I so anxiously hope, as that my name may come out
either second or third. These would be indifferent to me;
as the last would leave me at home the whole year, and the
other two-thirds of it.

After the result of the elections was no longer doubtful,
and it was known that Adams had been chosen as President
and Jefferson Vice-president, the latter wrote the following
.feeling and handsome letter to the former:

To John Adams.

Monticello, Dec. 28th, 1796.

Dear Sir—The public and the public papers have been
much occupied lately in placing us in a point of opposition
to each other. I trust with confidence that less of it has
been felt by ourselves personally. In the retired canton
where I am, I learn little of what is passing; pamphlets I
see never; papers but a few, and the fewer the happier.
Our latest intelligence from Philadelphia at present is of the
16th inst. But though at that date your election to the first
magistracy seems not to have been known as a fact, yet with
me it has never been doubted. I knew it impossible you
should lose a vote north of the Delaware, and even if that of
Pennsylvania should be against you in the mass, yet that you
would get enough south of that to place your succession out
of danger. I have never one single moment expected a different issue; and though I know I shall not be believed, yet it
is not the less true that I have never wished it. My neighbors, as my compurgators, could aver that fact, because they
see my occupations and my attachment to them.......
I leave to others the sublime delight of riding in the
storm, better pleased with sound sleep and a warm berth
below, with the society of neighbors, friends, and fellow-laborers of the earth, than of spies and sycophants. No one,
then, will congratulate you with purer disinterestedness than
myself. The share, indeed, which I may have had in the late
vote I shall still value highly, as an evidence of the share I
have in the esteem of my fellow-citizens. But still, in this
point of view, a few votes less would be little sensible; the

difference in the effect of a few more would be very sensible and oppressive to me. I have no ambition to govern men. It is a painful and thankless office. Since the day, too, on which you signed the treaty of Paris, our horizon was never so overcast. I devoutly wish you may be able to shun for us this war, by which our agriculture, commerce, and credit will be destroyed. If you are, the glory will be all your own; and that your adminstration may be filled with glory and happiness to yourself and advantage to us, is the sincere wish of one who, though, in the course of our voyage through life, various little incidents have happened or been contrived to separate us, retains still for you the solid esteem of the moments when we were working for our independence, and sentiments of respect and attachment.

TH. JEFFERSON.

Of the office of Vice-president, we find Jefferson, in a letter to Madison written on January 1st, 1797, saying:

To James Madison.

It is the only office in the world about which I am unable to decide in my own mind whether I had rather have it or not have it. Pride does not enter into the estimate; for I think, with the Romans, that the general of to-day should be a soldier to-morrow, if necessary. I can particularly have no feelings which could revolt at a secondary position to Mr. Adams. I am his junior in life, was his junior in Congress, his junior in the diplomatic line, his junior lately in our civil government.

He always spoke of this office as being of all others the most desirable, from the fact that it gave the incumbent a high position, good salary, and ample leisure. To him this last advantage was its greatest recommendation, and made him accept it with less reluctance than he would have done any other which his countrymen could have forced upon him.

Jefferson set out on the 20th of February for Philadelphia, there to be installed in his new office. He drove his phaeton and pair as far as Alexandria, when he sent his servant Jupi-

Q

ter back home with his horses, while he continued his journey in the stage-coach. He arrived in Philadelphia on the 2d of March.

With his usual modesty and dislike of display, he had written in January to his friend Mr. Tazewell, who was in Congress, begging that he might be notified of his election by the common channel of the ordinary post, and not by a deputation of men of position, as had been the case when the Government was first inaugurated. So, too, from the same feeling of diffidence he sought to enter the national capital as a private citizen, and without being the recipient of any popular demonstrations. It was, however, in vain for him to attempt to do so. A body of troops were on the look-out for him and signalled his approach by a discharge of artillery, and, marching before him into the city, bore a banner aloft on which were inscribed the words: " Jefferson, the Friend of the People."

An incident characteristic of Jefferson occurred on the day of the inauguration. After the oaths of office had been administered, the President (Mr. Adams) resumed his seat for a moment, then rose and, bowing to the assembly, left the hall. Jefferson rose to follow, but seeing General Washington also rise to leave, he at once fell back to let him pass out first. The General, perceiving this, declined to go before, and forced the new Vice-president to precede him. The doors of the hall closed upon them both amid the tumultuous cheering of the assembly.

Jefferson set out for home on the 12th of March and arrived there on the 20th, having performed the last stages of his journey in his sulky. His two daughters were not at Monticello, being absent on a long visit to an estate of Colonel Randolph's on James River. A few days after his return home he wrote to Mrs. Randolph.

To Martha Jefferson Randolph.—[*Extract.*]

Monticello, March 27th, '97.

I arrived in good health at home this day se'nnight. The

mountain had then been in bloom ten days. I find that the
natural productions of the spring are about a fortnight earlier here than at Fredericksburg; but where art and attention can do any thing, some one in a large collection of inhabitants, as in a town, will be before ordinary individuals,
whether of town or country. I have heard of you but once
since I left home, and am impatient to know that you are all
well. I have, however, so much confidence in the dose of
health with which Monticello charges you in summer and
autumn, that I count on its carrying you well through the
winter. The difference between the health enjoyed at Varina and Presqu'isle* is merely the effect of this. Therefore
do not ascribe it to Varina and stay there too long. The
bloom of Monticello is chilled by my solitude. It makes me
wish the more that yourself and sister were here to enjoy it.
I value the enjoyments of this life only in proportion as you
participate them with me. All other attachments are weak-
ening, and I approach the state of mind when nothing will
hold me here but my love for yourself and sister, and the
tender connections you have added to me. I hope you will
write to me; as nothing is so pleasing during your absence
as these proofs of your love. Be assured, my dear daughter,
that you possess mine in its utmost limits. Kiss the dear
little ones for me. I wish we had one of them here. Adieu
affectionately,

TH. JEFFERSON.

Again, on April 9th, he writes:

My love to Maria. Tell her I have made a new law;
which is, only to *answer* letters. It would have been her
turn to have received a letter had she not lost it by not
writing. Adieu most affectionately, both of you.

An extra session of Congress recalled Jefferson to Philadelphia during the spring; and the following extract from
a letter written to Edward Rutledge while there gives an
animated picture of the bitterness of party feeling at that
time.

---

* A former residence of Mr. and Mrs. Randolph.

To Edward Rutledge.

You and I have seen warm debates and high political passions. But gentlemen of different politics would then speak to each other, and separate the business of the Senate from that of society. It is not so now. Men who have been intimate all their lives, cross the streets to avoid meeting, and turn their heads another way, lest they should be obliged to touch their hats. This may do for young men with whom passion is enjoyment, but it is afflicting to peaceable minds.

The following charming family letters will be read with pleasure, I feel sure:

To Mary Jefferson.

Philadelphia, May 25th, 1797.

My dear Maria—I wrote to your sister the last week, since which I have been very slowly getting the better of my rheumatism, though very slowly indeed; being only able to walk a little stronger. I see by the newspapers that Mr. and Mrs. Church and their family are arrived at New York. I have not heard from them, and therefore am unable to say any thing about your friend Kitty, or whether she be still Miss Kitty. The condition of England is so unsafe that every prudent person who can quit it, is right in doing so. James is returned to this place, and is not given up to drink as I had before been informed. He tells me his next trip will be to Spain. I am afraid his journeys will end in the moon. I have endeavored to persuade him to stay where he is, and lay up money. We are not able yet to judge when Congress will rise. Opinions differ from two to six weeks. A few days will probably enable us to judge. I am anxious to hear that Mr. Randolph and the children have got home in good health; I wish also to hear that your sister and yourself continue in health; it is a circumstance on which the happiness of my life depends. I feel the desire of never separating from you grow daily stronger, for nothing can compensate with me the want of your society. My warmest affections to you both. Adieu, and continue to love me as I do you. Yours affectionately,

TH. JEFFERSON.

The letter which comes next was written to Mrs. Randolph in reply to one from her announcing to her father the engagement of his daughter Maria, to her cousin John Wayles Eppes.

To Martha Jefferson Randolph.

Philadelphia, June 8th, 1797.

I receive with inexpressible pleasure the information your letter contained. After your happy establishment, which has given me an inestimable friend, to whom I can leave the care of every thing I love, the only anxiety I had remaining was to see Maria also so associated as to insure her happiness. She could not have been more so to my wishes if I had had the whole earth free to have chosen a partner for her.

I now see our fireside formed into a group, no one member of which has a fibre in their composition which can ever produce any jarring or jealousies among us. No irregular passions, no dangerous bias, which may render problematical the future fortunes and happiness of our descendants. We are quieted as to their condition for at least one generation more.

In order to keep us all together, instead of a present position in Bedford, as in your case, I think to open and resettle the plantation of Pantops for them. When I look to the ineffable pleasure of my family society, I become more and more disgusted with the jealousies, the hatred, and the rancorous and malignant passions of this scene, and lament my having ever again been drawn into public view. Tranquillity is now my object. I have seen enough of political honors to know that they are but splendid torments; and however one might be disposed to render services on which any of their fellow-citizens should set a value, yet, when as many would depreciate them as a public calamity, one may well entertain a modest doubt of their real importance, and feel the impulse of duty to be very weak. The real difficulty is, that being once delivered into the hands of others whose feelings are friendly to the individual and warm to the public cause, how to withdraw from them without leaving a dissatisfaction in their mind, and an impression of pusillanimity with the public.

Maria Jefferson was married on the 13th of October, 1797, to John Wayles Eppes, who was in every respect worthy of the high opinion which we have found Jefferson expressing for him in the preceding letters. His manners were frank and engaging, while his high talents and fine education placed him among the first men of the country. The young couple spent the early days of their married life at Eppington, where the little "Polly," so beautiful and so timid, had received such motherly care and affection from her good Aunt Eppes when heart-broken at the death of her own mother.

I continue Mr. Jefferson's family letters.

To Mary Jefferson Eppes.

Philadelphia, January 7th, '98.

I acknowledged, my dear Maria, the receipt of yours in a letter I wrote to Mr. Eppes. It gave me the welcome news that your sprain was well. But you are not to suppose it entirely so. The joint will remain weak for a considerable time, and give you occasional pains much longer. The state of things at —— is truly distressing. Mr. ——'s habitual intoxication will destroy himself, his fortune, and family. Of all calamities this is the greatest. I wish my sister could bear his misconduct with more patience. It would lessen his attachment to the bottle, and at any rate would make her own time more tolerable. When we see ourselves in a situation which must be endured and gone through, it is best to make up our minds to it, meet it with firmness, and accommodate every thing to it in the best way practicable. This lessens the evil, while fretting and fuming only serves to increase our own torments. The errors and misfortunes of others should be a school for our own instruction. Harmony in the married state is the very first object to be aimed at. Nothing can preserve affections uninterrupted but a firm resolution never to differ in will, and a determination in each to consider the love of the other as of more value than any object whatever on which a wish had been fixed. How light, in fact, is the sacrifice of any other wish when weighed against the affections of one with whom we are to pass our whole life! And though opposition in a single instance will hardly of itself produce alienation, yet every one has their pouch into which all these little oppositions are put; while that is filling the alienation is insensibly going on, and when filled it is complete. It would puzzle either to say why; because no one difference of opinion has been marked enough to produce a serious effect by itself. But he finds his affections wearied out by a constant stream of little checks and obstacles. Other sources of discontent, very common indeed, are the little cross-purposes of husband and wife, in common conversation, a disposition in either to criticise and question whatever the other says, a desire always to demonstrate and make him feel himself in the wrong, and especially in company. Nothing is so goading. Much better, therefore, if our companion views a thing in a light different from what we do, to leave him in quiet possession of his view. What is the use of rectifying him if the thing be unimportant; and if important, let it pass for the present, and wait a softer moment and more conciliatory occasion of revising the subject together. It is wonderful how many persons are rendered unhappy by inattention to these little rules of prudence.

I have been insensibly led, by the particular case you mention, to sermonize you on the subject generally; however, if it be the means of saving you from a single heartache, it will have contributed a great deal to my happiness; but before I finish the sermon, I must add a word on economy. The unprofitable condition of Virginia estates in general leaves it now next to impossible for the holder of one to avoid ruin. And this condition will continue until some change takes place in the mode of working them. In the mean time, nothing can save us and our children from beggary but a determination to get a year beforehand, and restrain ourselves vigorously this year to the clear profits of the last. If a debt is once contracted by a farmer, it is never paid but by a sale.

The article of dress is perhaps that in which economy is the least to be recommended. It is so important to each to continue to please the other, that the happiness of both requires the most pointed attention to whatever may contribute to it—and the more as time makes greater inroads on our person. Yet, generally, we become slovenly in proportion as personal decay requires the contrary. I have great

comfort in believing that your understanding and dispositions will engage your attention to these considerations;
and that you are connected with a person and family, who
of all within the circle of my acquaintance are most in the dispositions which will make you happy. Cultivate their affections, my dear, with assiduity. Think every sacrifice a gain
which shall tend to attach them to you. My only object in
life is to see yourself and your sister, and those deservedly
dear to you, not only happy, but in no danger of becoming
unhappy.

I have lately received a letter from your friend Kitty
Church. I inclose it to you, and think the affectionate expressions relative to yourself, and the advance she has made,
will require a letter from you to her. It will be impossible
to get a crystal here to fit your watch without the watch
itself. If you should know of any one coming to Philadelphia, send it to me, and I will get you a stock of crystals.
The river being frozen up, I shall not be able to send you
things till it opens, which will probably be some time in February. I inclose to Mr. Eppes some pamphlets. Present
me affectionately to all the family, and be assured of my
tenderest love to yourself. Adieu.

TH. JEFFERSON.

To Martha Jefferson Randolph.

Philadelphia, Feb. 8th, '98.

I ought oftener, my dear Martha, to receive your letters,
for the very great pleasure they give me, and especially when
they express your affections for me; for, though I can not
doubt them, yet they are among those truths which, though
not doubted, we love to hear repeated. Here, too, they serve,
like gleams of light, to cheer a dreary scene; where envy,
hatred, malice, revenge, and all the worst passions of men,
are marshalled to make one another as miserable as possible.
I turn from this with pleasure, to contrast it with your fireside, where the single evening I passed at it was worth more
than ages here. Indeed, I find myself detaching very fast,
perhaps too fast, from every thing but yourself, your sister,
and those who are identified with you. These form the last
hold the world will have on me, the cords which will be cut
only when I am loosened from this state of being. I am look-

ing forward to the spring with all the fondness of desire to meet you all once more, and with the change of season to enjoy also a change of scene and society. Yet the time of our leaving this is not yet talked of.

I am much concerned to hear of the state of health of Mr. Randolph and family, mentioned in your letters of Jan. 22d and 28th. Surely, my dear, it would be better for you to remove to Monticello. The south pavilion, the parlor, and study will accommodate your family ; and I should think Mr. Randolph would find less inconvenience in the riding it would occasion him than in the loss of his own and his family's health. Let me beseech you, then, to go there, and to use every thing and every body as if I were there.......

All your commissions shall be executed, not forgetting the Game of the Goose, if we can find out what it is, for there is some difficulty in that. Kiss all the little ones for me. Present me affectionately to Mr. Randolph, and my warmest love to yourself. Adieu.

TH. JEFFERSON.

To Martha Jefferson Randolph.—[*Extract.*]

Philadelphia, May 17th, '98.

Having nothing of business to write on to Mr. Randolph this week, I with pleasure take up my pen to express all my love to you, and my wishes once more to find myself in the only scene where, for me, the sweeter affections of life have any exercise. But when I shall be with you seems still uncertain. We have been looking forward from three weeks to three weeks, and always with disappointment, so that I know not what to expect. I shall immediately write to Maria, and recommend to Mr. Eppes and her to go up to Monticello......

For you to feel all the happiness of your quiet situation, you should know the rancorous passions which tear every breast here, even of the sex which should be a stranger to them. Politics and party hatreds destroy the happiness of every being here. They seem, like salamanders, to consider fire as their element. The children, I am afraid, will have forgotten me. However, my memory may perhaps be hung on the Game of the Goose which I am to carry them. Kiss them for me....... And to yourself, my tenderest love, and adieu.

To Martha Jefferson Randolph.—[Extract.]

Philadelphia, May 31st, '98.

Yours of the 12th did not get to hand till the 29th; so it must have laid by a post somewhere. The receipt of it, by kindling up all my recollections, increases my impatience to leave this place, and every thing which can be disgusting, for Monticello and my dear family, comprising every thing which is pleasurable to me in this world. It has been proposed in Congress to adjourn on the 14th of June. I have little expectation of it; but, whatever be their determination, I am determined myself; and my letter of next week will probably carry orders for my horses. Jupiter should, therefore, be in readiness to depart at a night's warning.......

I am sorry to hear of Jefferson's indisposition, but glad you do not physic him. This leaves nature free and unembarrassed in her own tendencies to repair what is wrong. I hope to hear or find that he is recovered. Kiss them all for me.

To Mary Jefferson Eppes.

Monticello, July 13th, '98.

My dear Maria—I arrived here on the 3d instant, expecting to have found you here, and we have been ever since imagining that every sound we heard was that of the carriage which was once more to bring us together. It was not till yesterday I learnt, by the receipt of Mr. Eppes's letter of June 30th, that you had been sick, and were only on the recovery at that date. A preceding letter of his, referred to in that of the 30th, must have miscarried. We are now infinitely more anxious, not so much for your arrival here, as your firm establishment in health, and that you may not be thrown back by your journey. Much, therefore, my dear, as I wish to see you, I beg you not to attempt the journey till you are quite strong enough, and then only by short days' journeys. A relapse will only keep us the longer asunder, and is much more formidable than a first attack. Your sister and family are with me. I would have gone to you instantly on the receipt of Mr. Eppes's letter, had not that assured me you were well enough to take the bark. It would also have stopped my workmen here, who can not proceed an hour without me, and I am anxious to provide a cover which may enable me to have my family and friends about me. Nurse yourself, therefore, with all possible care for your own sake, for mine, and that of all those who love you, and do not attempt to move sooner or quicker than your health admits. Present me affectionately to Mr. Eppes, father and son, to Mrs. Eppes and all the family, and be assured that my impatience to see you can only be moderated by the stronger desire that your health may be safely and firmly re-established. Adieu, affectionately.

TH. J.

To Martha Jefferson Randolph.

Ellen appeared to be feverish the evening you went away; but visiting her, a little before I went to bed, I found her quite clear of fever, and was convinced the quickness of pulse which had alarmed me had proceeded from her having been in uncommon spirits and constantly running about the house through the day, and especially in the afternoon. Since that she has had no symptom of fever, and is otherwise better than when you left her. The girls, indeed, suppose she had a little fever last night; but I am sure she had not, as she was well at 8 o'clock in the evening, and very well in the morning, and they say she slept soundly through the night. They judged only from her breathing. Every body else is well, and only wishing to see you. I am persecuted with questions "When I think you will come?"...... If you set out after dinner, be sure to get off between four and five. Adieu, my dear.

Wednesday, Aug. 15th, '98.

The following letter, without date, was written to the daughter of his friend Mrs. Church:

To Catherine Church.

I received, my dear Catherine, from the hands of your brother, the letter you have done me the favor to write me. I see in that letter the excellent disposition which I knew in you in an earlier period of life. These have led you to mistake, to your own prejudice, the character of our attentions to you. They were not favors, but gratifications of our own affections to an object who had every quality which might endear her to us. Be assured we have all continued to love you as if still of our fireside, and to make you the very frequent theme of our family conversations. Your friend Maria has, as you supposed, changed her condition; she is now Mrs. Eppes. She and her sister, Mrs. Randolph, retain all their affection for you, and never fail in their friendly inquiries after you whenever an opportunity occurs. During my winter's absence, Maria is with the family with which she has become allied; but on my return they will also return to reside with me. My daughter Randolph has hitherto done the same, but lately has removed with Mr. Randolph to live and build on a farm of their own, adjoining me; but I still count on their passing the greater part of their time at Monticello. Why should we forbid ourselves to believe that some day or other some circumstance may bring you also to our little society, and renew the recollections of former scenes very dear to our memory. Hope is so much more charming than disappointments and forebodings, that we will not set it down among impossible things. We will calculate on the circumstance that you have already crossed the ocean which laid between us, and that in comparison with that the space which remains is as nothing. Who knows but you may travel to see our springs and our curiosities—not, I hope, for your health, but to vary your summer scenes, and enlarge your knowledge of your own country. In that case we are on your road, and will endeavor to relieve the fatigues of it by all the offices of friendship and hospitality. I thank you for making me acquainted with your brother. The relations he bears to the best of people are sufficient vouchers to me of his worth. He must be of your party when you come to Monticello. Adieu, my dear Catherine. I consign in a separate letter my respects to your good mother. I have here, therefore, only to claim your acceptance of the sincere attachment of yours affectionately,

TH. JEFFERSON.

The following gives some glimpses of the French friends of Jefferson:

To Mrs. Church.

Dear Madam—Your favor of July 6th was to have found me here, but I had departed before it arrived. It followed me here, and of necessity the inquiries after our friend Madame de Corny were obliged to await Mrs. M.'s arrival at her own house. This was delayed longer than was expected, so that by the time I could make the inquiries I was looking again to my return to Philadelphia. This must apologize for the delay which has taken place. Mrs. M. tells me that Madame Corny was at one time in extreme distress, her revenue being in rents, and these paid in assignats worth nothing. Since their abolition, however, she receives her rents in cash, and is now entirely at her ease. She lives in hired lodgings furnished by herself, and every thing about her as nice as you know she always had. She visited Mrs. M. freely and familiarly in a family way, but would never dine when she had company, nor remain if company came. She speaks seriously sometimes of a purpose to come to America, but she surely mistakes a wish for a purpose; you and I know her constitution too well, and her horror of the sea, to believe she could pass or attempt the Atlantic. Mrs. M. could not give me her address. In all events, it is a great consolation that her situation is easy. We have here a Mr. Niemcewitz, a Polish gentleman who was with us in Paris while Mrs. Cosway was there, and who was of her society in London last summer. He mentions the loss of her daughter, the gloom into which that and other circumstances have thrown her, and that it has taken the form of religion. Also that she is solely devoted to religious exercises and the superintendence of a school for Catholic children, which she has instituted, but she still speaks of her friends with tenderness. Our letters have been rare, but they have let me see that her gayety was gone, and her mind entirely fixed on a world to come. I have received from my young friend Catherine a letter, which gratifies me much, as it proves that our friendly impressions have not grown out of her memory..... Be so good as to present my respects to Mr. C., and accept assurances of the unalterable attachment of your affectionate friend and servant,

TH. JEFFERSON.

CHAPTER XIV.

Jefferson goes to Philadelphia.—Letters to his Daughters.—Returns to Monticello.—Letters to his Daughter.—Goes back to Philadelphia.—Family Letters.—Letters to Mrs. and Miss Church.—Bonaparte.—Letters to his Daughters.—Is nominated as President.—Seat of Government moved to Washington.—Spends the Summer at Monticello.—Letters to his Daughter.—Jefferson denounced by the New England Pulpit.—Letter to Uriah Gregory.—Goes to Washington.

THE third session of the Fifth Congress compelling Mr. Jefferson to be in Philadelphia again, he left Monticello for that city the latter part of December, 1798, and arrived there on Christmas-day. During his stay in the capital he wrote the following charming and interesting letters to his daughters:

To Mary Jefferson Eppes.

Philadelphia, Jan. 1st, '99.

My dear Maria—I left Monticello on the 18th of December, and arrived here to breakfast on the 25th, having experienced no accident or inconvenience except a slight cold, which brought back the inflammation of my eyes, and still continues it, though so far mended as to give hopes of its going off soon. I took my place in Senate before a single bill was brought in or other act of business done, except the Address, which is exactly what I ought to have nothing to do with; and, indeed, I might have staid at home a week longer without missing any business for the last eleven days. The Senate have met only on five, and then little or nothing to do. However, when I am to write on politics I shall address my letter to Mr. Eppes. To you I had rather indulge the effusions of a heart which tenderly loves you, which builds its happiness on yours, and feels in every other object but little interest. Without an object here which is not alien to me, and barren of every delight, I turn to your situation with pleasure, in the midst of a good family which loves you, and merits all your love. Go on, my dear, in cultivating the invaluable possession of their affections. The circle of our nearest connections is the only one in which a faithful and lasting affection can be found, one which will adhere to us under all changes and chances. It is, therefore, the only soil on which it is worth while to bestow much culture. Of this truth you will become more convinced every day you advance into life. I imagine you are by this time about removing to Mont Blanco. The novelty of setting up housekeeping will, with all its difficulties, make you very happy for a while. Its delights, however, pass away in time, and I am in hopes that by the spring of the year there will be no obstacle to your joining us at Monticello. I hope I shall, on my return, find such preparation made as will enable me rapidly to get one room after another prepared for the accommodation of our friends, and particularly of any who may be willing to accompany or visit you there. Present me affectionately to Mrs. and Mr. Eppes, father and son, and all the family. Remember how pleasing your letters will be to me, and be assured of my constant and tender love. Adieu, my ever dear Maria.

Yours affectionately,

TH. JEFFERSON.

The following are extracts from two letters to Mrs. Randolph:

To Martha Jefferson Randolph.

Philadelphia, Jan. 23d, '99.

The object of this letter, my very dear Martha, is merely to inform you I am well, and convey to you the expressions of my love. It will not be new to tell you your letters do not come as often as I could wish. This deprives me of the gleams of pleasure wanting to relieve the dreariness of this scene, where not one single occurrence is calculated to produce pleasing sensations. I hope you are all well, and that the little ones, even Ellen, talk of me sometimes...... Kiss all the little ones, and receive the tender and unmingled effusions of my love to yourself. Adieu.

Philadelphia, Feb. 5th, '99.

Jupiter, with my horses, must be at Fredericksburg on

Tuesday evening, the 5th of March. I shall leave this place on the 1st or 2d. You will receive this the 14th instant. I am already light-hearted at the approach of my departure. Kiss my dear children for me. Inexpressible love to yourself, and the sincerest affection to Mr. Randolph. Adieu.

To Mary Jefferson Eppes.

Philadelphia, Feb. 7th, '99.

Your letter, my dear Maria, of January 21st, was received two days ago. It was, as Ossian says, or would say, like the bright beams of the moon on the desolate heath. Environed here in scenes of constant torment, malice, and obloquy, worn down in a station where no effort to render service can avail any thing, I feel not that existence is a blessing, but when something recalls my mind to my family or farm. This was the effect of your letter; and its affectionate expressions kindled up all those feelings of love for you and our dear connections which now constitute the only real happiness of my life. I am now feeding on the idea of my departure for Monticello, which is but three weeks distant. The roads will then be so dreadful, that, as to visit you even by the direct route of Fredericksburg and Richmond would add one hundred miles to the length of my journey, I must defer it, in the hope that about the last of March, or first of April, I may be able to take a trip express to see you. The roads will then be fine; perhaps your sister may join in a flying trip, as it can only be for a few days. In the mean time, let me hear from you. Letters which leave Richmond after the 21st instant should be directed to me at Monticello. I suppose you to be now at Mont Blanco, and therefore do not charge you with the delivery of those sentiments of esteem which I always feel for the family at Eppington. I write to Mr. Eppes. Continue always to love me, and be assured that there is no object on earth so dear to my heart as your health and happiness, and that my tenderest affections always hang on you. Adieu, my ever dear Maria.

TH. JEFFERSON.

Mr. Jefferson left the Seat of Government on the first of March; and the following letters, written immediately on his arrival at Monticello, will show how much his affairs at home suffered during his absence. Indeed he seemed to be able only to get the workmen fairly under way on his house, when a call to Philadelphia would again suspend operations on it almost entirely until his return.

*To Mary Jefferson Eppes.**

Monticello, March 8th, '99.

My dear Maria—I am this moment arrived here, and the post being about to depart, I sit down to inform you of it. Your sister came over with me from Belmont, where we left all well. The family will move over the day after to-morrow. They give up the house there about a week hence. We want nothing now to fill up our happiness but to have you and Mr. Eppes here. Scarcely a stroke has been done towards covering the house since I went away, so that it has remained open at the north end another winter. It seems as if I should never get it inhabitable. I have proposed to your sister a flying trip, when the roads get fine, to see you. She comes into it with pleasure ; but whether I shall be able to leave this for a few days is a question which I have not yet seen enough of the state of things to determine. I think it very doubtful. It is to your return, therefore, that I look with impatience, and shall expect as soon as Mr. Eppes's affairs will permit. We are not without hopes he will take a trip up soon to see about his affairs here, of which I yet know nothing. I hope you are enjoying good health, and that it will not be long before we are again united in some way or other. Continue to love me, my dear, as I do you most tenderly. Present me affectionately to Mr. Eppes, and be assured of my constant and warmest love. Adieu, my ever dear Maria.

Mrs. Eppes reached Monticello at last, and Jefferson was made happy by having all of his children and grandchildren once more assembled under his roof, where they spent the summer happily together. Jefferson returned to Philadelphia the last days of December; and we find the same weariness of the life he led there, and the same longing for home,

---

* At Mont Blanco, a place near Petersburg.

R

in the following letters, as we have seen in the preceding. In these we find, however, a stronger spice of politics than in the former.

To Mary Jefferson Eppes.

Philadelphia, Jan. 17th, 1800.

My dear Maria—I received at Monticello two letters from you, and meant to have answered them a little before my departure for this place; but business so crowded upon me at that moment that it was not in my power. I left home on the 21st, and arrived here on the 28th of December, after a pleasant journey of fine weather and good roads, and without having experienced any inconvenience. The Senate had not yet entered into business, and I may say they have not yet entered into it; for we have not occupation for half an hour a day. Indeed, it is so apparent that we have nothing to do but to raise money to fill the deficit of five millions of dollars, that it is proposed we shall rise about the middle of March; and as the proposition comes from the Eastern members, who have always been for sitting permanently, while the Southern are constantly for early adjournment, I presume we shall rise then. In the mean while, they are about to renew the bill suspending intercourse with France, which is in fact a bill to prohibit the exportation of tobacco, and to reduce the tobacco States to passive obedience by poverty.

J. Randolph has entered into debate with great splendor and approbation. He used an unguarded word in his first speech, applying the word "ragamuffin" to the common soldiery. He took it back of his own accord, and very handsomely, the next day, when he had occasion to reply. Still, in the evening of the second day, he was jostled, and his coat pulled at the theatre by two officers of the Navy, who repeated the word "ragamuffin." His friends present supported him spiritedly, so that nothing further followed. Conceiving, and, as I think, justly, that the House of Representatives (not having passed a law on the subject) could not punish the offenders, he wrote a letter to the President, who laid it before the House, where it is still depending. He has conducted himself with great propriety, and I have no doubt will come out with increase of reputation, being determined himself to oppose the interposition of the House when they have no law for it.

M. du Pont, his wife and family, are arrived at New York, after a voyage of three months and five days. I suppose after he is a little recruited from his voyage we shall see him here. His son is with him, as is also his son-in-law, Bureau Pusy, the companion and fellow-sufferer of Lafayette. I have a letter from Lafayette of April; he then expected to sail for America in July, but I suspect he awaits the effect of the mission of our ministers. I presume that Madame de Lafayette is to come with him, and that they mean to settle in America.

The prospect of returning early to Monticello is to me a most charming one. I hope the fishery will not prevent your joining us early in the spring. However, on this subject we can speak together, as I will endeavor, if possible, to take Mont Blanco and Eppington in my way.

A letter from Dr. Carr, of December 27, informed me he had just left you well. I become daily more anxious to hear from you, and to know that you continue well, your present state being one which is most interesting to a parent; and its issue, I hope, will be such as to give you experience what a parent's anxiety may be. I employ my leisure moments in repassing often in my mind our happy domestic society when together at Monticello, and looking forward to the renewal of it. No other society gives me now any satisfaction, as no other is founded in sincere affection. Take care of yourself, my dear Maria, for my sake, and cherish your affections for me, as my happiness rests solely on yours, and on that of your sister's and your dear connections. Present me affectionately to Mr. Eppes, to whom I inclosed some pamphlets some time ago without any letter; as I shall write no letters the ensuing year, for political reasons which I explained to him. Present my affections also to Mrs. and Mr. Eppes, Senior, and all the family, for whom I feel every interest that I do for my own. Be assured yourself, my dear, of my most tender and constant love. Adieu.

Yours affectionately and forever,

TH. JEFFERSON.

To Martha Jefferson Randolph.

Philadelphia, Jan. 21st, 1800.

I am made happy by a letter from Mr. Eppes, informing me that Maria was become a mother, and was well. It was written the day after the event. These circumstances are balm to the painful sensations of this place. I look forward with hope to the moment when we are all to be reunited again. I inclose a little tale for Anne. To Ellen you must make big promises, which I know a bit of gingerbread will pay off. Kiss them all for me. My affectionate salutations to Mr. Randolph, and tender and increasing love to yourself. Adieu, my dear Martha. Affectionately yours, etc.

To Mrs. Church.

Philadelphia, Jan. 21st, 1800.

I am honored, my dear Madam, with your letter of the 16th inst., and made happy by the information of your health. It was matter of sincere regret on my arrival here to learn that you had left it but a little before, after passing some time here. I should have been happy to have renewed to you in person the assurances of my affectionate regards, to have again enjoyed a society which brings to me the most pleasant recollections, and to have past in review together the history of those friends who made an interesting part of our circle, and for many of whom I have felt the deepest affliction. My friend Catherine I could have entertained with details of her living friends, whom you are so good as to recollect, and for whom I am to return you thankful acknowledgments.

I shall forward your letter to my daughter Eppes, who, I am sure, will make you her own acknowledgments. It will find her " in the straw ;" having lately presented me with the first honors of a grandfather on her part. Mrs. Randolph has made them cease to be novelties—she has four children. We shall teach them all to grow up in esteem for yourself and Catherine. Whether they or we may have opportunities of testifying it personally must depend on the chapter of events. I am in the habit of turning over its next leaf with hope, and though it often fails me, there is still another and another behind. In the mean time, I cherish with fondness those affectionate sentiments of esteem and respect with which I am, my dear Madam, your sincere and humble servant,

TH. JEFFERSON.

To Catherine Church.

Philadelphia, Jan. 22d, 1800.

I wrote to your mamma yesterday, my dear Catherine, intending to have written by the same post to yourself. An interruption, however, put it out of my power. It was the more necessary to have done it, as I had inadvertently made an acknowledgment in my letter to her instead of yourself, of yours of the 16th. I receive with sincere pleasure this evidence of your recollection, and assure you I reflect with great pleasure on the scenes which your letter recalls. You are often the subject of our conversation, not indeed at our fireside, for that is the season of our dispersion, but in our summer walks when the family reassembles at Monticello. You are tenderly remembered by both Mrs. Randolph and Mrs. Eppes, and I have this day notified Maria that I have promised you a letter from her. She was not much addicted to letter-writing before; and I fear her new character of mother may furnish new excuses for her remissness. Should this, however, be the occasion of my becoming the channel of your mutual love, it may lessen the zeal with which I press her pen upon her. But in whatever way I hear from you, be assured it will always be with that sincere pleasure which is inspired by the sentiments of esteem and attachment with which I am, my dear Catherine, your affectionate friend and humble servant,

TH. JEFFERSON.

In a letter to Mr. Randolph, written early in February, Mr. Jefferson makes the following remarks about Bonaparte:

To Thomas Mann Randolph.

Should it be really true that Bonaparte has usurped the Government with an intention of making it a free one, whatever his talents may be for war, we have no proofs that he is skilled in forming governments friendly to the people. Wherever he has meddled, we have seen nothing but fragments of the old Roman governments stuck into materials with which they can form no cohesion: we see the bigotry of an Italian to the ancient splendor of his country, but nothing which bespeaks a luminous view of the organization of rational government. Perhaps, however, this may end better than we augur; and it certainly will if his head is equal to true and solid calculations of glory.

And again, in a letter of a few days' later date, to Samuel Adams:

To Samuel Adams.

I fear our friends on the other side of the water, laboring in the same cause, have yet a great deal of crime and misery to wade through. My confidence has been placed in the head, not in the heart of Bonaparte. I hoped he would calculate truly the difference between the fame of a Washington and a Cromwell. Whatever his views may be, he has at least transferred the destinies of the Republic from the civil to the military arm. Some will use this as a lesson against the practicability of republican government. I read it as a lesson against the danger of standing armies.

We continue his family letters.

To Martha Jefferson Randolph.

Philadelphia, Feb. 11th, 1800.

A person here has invented the prettiest improvement in the forte-piano I have ever seen. It has tempted me to engage one for Monticello; partly for its excellence and convenience, partly to assist a very ingenious, modest, and poor young man, who ought to make a fortune by his invention....... There is really no business which ought to keep us one fortnight. I am therefore looking forward with anticipation of the joy of seeing you again ere long, and tasting true happiness in the midst of my family. My absence from you teaches me how essential your society is to my happiness. Politics are such a torment that I would advise every one I love not to mix with them. I have changed my circle here according to my wish, abandoning the rich and declining their dinners and parties, and associating entirely with the class of science, of whom there is a valuable society here. Still, my wish is to be in the midst of our own families at home....... Kiss all the dear little ones for me; do not let Ellen forget me; and continue to me your love in return for the constant and tender attachment of yours affectionately.

To Mary Jefferson Eppes.

Philadelphia, Feb. 12th, 1800.

My dear Maria—Mr. Eppes's letter of January 17th had filled me with anxiety for your little one, and that of the 25th announced what I had feared. How deeply I feel it in all its bearings I shall not say—nor attempt consolation when I know that time and silence are the only medicines. I shall only observe, as a source of hope to us all, that you are young, and will not fail to possess enough of these dear pledges which bind us to one another and to life itself. I am almost hopeless in writing to you, from observing that, at the date of Mr. Eppes's letter of January 25th, three which I had written to him and one to you had not been received. That to you was January 17th, and to him December 21, January 22, and one which only covered some pamphlets. That of December 21st was on the subject of Powell, and would of course give occasion for an answer. I have always directed to Petersburg; perhaps Mr. Eppes does not have inquiries made at the post-office there....... I will inclose this to the care of Mr. Jefferson.......

I fully propose, if nothing intervenes to prevent it, to take Chesterfield in my way home. I am not without hopes you will be ready to go on with me; but at any rate that you will soon follow. I know no happiness but when we are all together. You have, perhaps, heard of the loss of Jupiter. With all his defects, he leaves a void in my domestic arrangements which can not be filled. Mr. Eppes's last letter informed me how much you had suffered from your breasts; but that they had then suppurated, and the inflammation and consequent fever abated. I am anxious to hear again from you, and hope the next letter will announce your re-establishment. It is necessary for my tranquillity that I should hear from you often; for I feel inexpressibly whatever affects your health or happiness. My attachments to the world, and whatever it can offer, are daily wearing off; but you are one of the links which hold to my existence, and can only break off with that. You have never, by a word or deed, given me one moment's uneasiness; on the contrary, I have felt perpetual gratitude to Heaven for having given me in you a source of so much pure and unmixed happiness; go on then, my dear, as you have done, in deserving the love of every body; you will reap the rich reward of their esteem, and will find that we are working for ourselves while we do good to others.

I had a letter from your sister yesterday. They were all well. One from Mr. Randolph had before informed me they had got to Edgehill, and were in the midst of mud, smoke, and the uncomfortableness of a cold house. Mr. Trist is here alone, and will return soon.

Present me affectionately to Mr. Eppes, and tell him when you can not write he must; as also to the good family at Eppington, to whom I wish every earthly good. To yourself, my dear Maria, I can not find expressions for my love. You must measure it by the feelings of a warm heart. Adieu.

TH. JEFFERSON.

To Mary Jefferson Eppes.

Philadelphia, April 6th, 1800.

I have at length, my ever dear Maria, received by Mr. Eppes's letter of March 24 the welcome news of your recovery—welcome, indeed, to me, who have passed a long season of inexpressible anxiety for you; and the more so as written accounts can hardly give one an exact idea of the situation of a sick person.

I wish I were able to leave this place and join you; but we do not count on rising till the first or second week of May. I shall certainly see you as soon after that as possible, at Mont Blanco or Eppington, at whichever you may be, and shall expect you to go up with me, according to the promise in Mr. Eppes's letter. I shall send orders for my horses to be with you, and wait for me if they arrive before me. I must ask Mr. Eppes to write me a line immediately by post, to inform me at which place you will be during the first and second weeks of May, and what is the nearest point on the road from Richmond where I can quit the stage and borrow a horse to go on to you. If written immediately I may receive it here before my departure.

Mr. Eppes's letter informs me your sister was with you at that date; but from Mr. Randolph I learn she was to go up this month. The uncertainty where she was, prevented my writing to her for a long time. If she is still with you, express to her all my love and tenderness for her. Your tables have been ready some time, and will go in a vessel which sails for Richmond this week. They are packed in a box marked J. W. E., and will be delivered to Mr. Jefferson, probably about the latter part of this month.

I write no news for Mr. Eppes, because my letters are so slow in getting to you that he will see every thing first in the newspapers. Assure him of my sincere affections, and present the same to the family of Eppington, if you are together. Cherish your own health for the sake of so many to whom you are so dear, and especially for one who loves you with unspeakable tenderness. Adieu, my dearest Maria.

TH. JEFFERSON.

To Martha Jefferson Randolph.

Philadelphia, April 22d, 1800.

Mr. Eppes informs me that Maria was so near well that they expected in a few days to go to Mont Blanco. Your departure gives me a hope her cure was at length established. A long and painful case it has been, and not the most so to herself or those about her; my anxieties have been excessive. I shall go by Mont Blanco to take her home with me.......

I long once more to get all together again; and still hope, notwithstanding your present establishment, you will pass a great deal of the summer with us. I wish to urge it just so far as not to break in on your and 'Mr. Randolph's desires and convenience. Our scenes here can never be pleasant; but they have been less stormy, less painful than during the X Y Z paroxysms.

During the session of Congress the Republicans nominated as candidates for the coming Presidential election Mr. Jefferson for President and Aaron Burr for Vice-President. The opposite party chose as their nominees, Mr. Adams and Mr. Pinckney.

The Seat of Government was moved to Washington in June, 1800. We can well understand how disagreeable the change from the comfortable city of Philadelphia to a rough, unfinished town must have been. Mrs. Adams seems to have felt it sensibly, and in the following letter to her daughter has left us an admirable and amusing picture of it:

From Mrs. Adams.

I arrived here on Sunday last, and without meeting with any accident worth noticing, except losing ourselves when we left Baltimore, and going eight or nine miles on the Frederick road, by which means we were obliged to go the other eight through woods, where we wandered two hours without finding a guide or the path. Fortunately a straggling black came up with us, and we engaged him as a guide to extricate us out of our difficulty ; but woods are all you see from Baltimore until you reach the city, which is only so in name. Here and there is a small cot, without a glass window, interpersed among the forests, through which you travel miles without seeing any human being. In the city there are buildings enough, if they were compact and finished, to accommodate Congress and those attached to it ; but as they are, and scattered as they are, I see no great comfort for them. The river which runs up to Alexandria is in full view of my window, and I see the vessels as they pass and repass. The house is upon a grand and superb scale, requiring about thirty servants to attend and keep the apartments in proper order, and perform the ordinary business of the house and stables ; an establishment very well proportioned to the President's salary ! The lighting the apartments from the kitchen to parlors and chambers is a tax indeed, and the fires we are obliged to keep to secure us from daily agues is another very cheering comfort. To assist us in this great castle, and render less attendance necessary, bells are wholly wanting, not one single one being hung through the whole house, and promises are all you can obtain. This is so great an inconvenience, that I know not what to do, or how to do. The ladies from Georgetown and in the city have many

of them visited me. Yesterday I returned fifteen visits—
but such a place as Georgetown appears—why, our Milton is
beautiful. But no comparisons ;—if they will put me up
some bells, and let me have wood enough to keep fires, I
design to be pleased. I could content myself almost anywhere three months ; but, surrounded with forests, can you
believe that wood is not to be had, because people can not
be found to cut and cart it? Briesler entered into a contract with a man to supply him with wood. A small part,
a few cords only, has he been able to get. Most of that
was expended to dry the walls of the house before we came
in, and yesterday the man told him it was impossible for
him to procure it to be cut and carted. He has had recourse to coals ; but we can not get grates made and set.
We have, indeed, come into a new country.

You must keep all this to yourself, and when asked how I
like it, say that I write you the situation is beautiful, which
is true. The house is made habitable, but there is not a
single apartment finished, and all within side, except the
plastering, has been done since Briesler came. We have not
the least fence, yard, or other conveniences without, and the
great unfinished audience-room I make a drying-room of to
hang up the clothes in. The principal stairs are not up, and
will not be this winter. Six chambers are made comfortable ; two are occupied by the President and Mr. Shaw ; two
lower rooms, one for a common parlor, and one for a levee-
room. Up stairs there is the oval-room, which is designed
for the drawing-room, and has the crimson furniture in it.
It is a very handsome room now ; but when completed it
will be beautiful.

If the twelve years, in which this place has been considered as the future Seat of Government, had been improved, as
they would have been if in New England, very many of the
present inconveniences would have been removed. It is a
beautiful spot, capable of every improvement, and the more
I view it the more I am delighted with it.*

The whole summer of 1800 was spent by Jefferson quietly
at home. He only left Monticello once, and that was to pay

---

* Mrs. Adams's letters, vol. ii., p. 239.

a short visit to Bedford. He was unusually busy on his farms and with his house. He took no part whatever in the political campaign, and held himself entirely aloof from it.

In the following letter we find betrayed all the tender anxieties of a fond and loving father:

To Mary Jefferson Eppes.

Monticello, July 4th, 1800.

My dear Maria—We have heard not a word of you since the moment you left us. I hope you had a safe and pleasant journey. The rains which began to fall here the next day gave me uneasiness lest they should have overtaken you also. Dr. and Mrs. Bache have been with us till the day before yesterday. Mrs. Monroe is now in our neighborhood, to continue during the sickly months. Our forte-piano arrived a day or two after you left us. It has been exposed to a great deal of rain, but being well covered was only much untuned. I have given it a poor tuning. It is the delight of the family, and all pronounce what your choice will be. Your sister does not hesitate to prefer it to any harpsichord she ever saw except her own; and it is easy to see it is only the celestini which retains that preference. It is as easily tuned as a spinette and will not need it half as often. Our harvest has been a very fine one. I finish to-day. It is the heaviest crop of wheat I ever had.

A murder in our neighborhood is the theme of its present conversation. George Carter shot Birch, of Charlottesville, in his own door and on very slight provocation. He died in a few minutes. The examining court meets to-morrow.

As your harvest must be over as soon as ours, we hope to see Mr. Eppes and yourself. All are well here except Ellen, who is rather drooping than sick; and all are impatient to see you—no one so much as he whose happiness is wrapped up in yours. My affections to Mr. Eppes and tenderest love to yourself. Hasten to us. Adieu.

TH. JEFFERSON.

During the political campaign of the summer of 1800, Jefferson was denounced by many divines—who thought it their duty to preach politics instead of Christian charity—as an atheist and a French infidel. These attacks were made upon him by half the clergy of New England, and by a few in other Northern States; in the former section, however, they were most virulent. The common people of the country were told that should he be elected their Bibles would be taken from them. In New York the Reverend Doctor John M. Mason published a pamphlet attacking Jefferson, which was entitled, "The voice of Warning to Christians on the ensuing Election." In New England sermons preached against Jefferson were printed and scattered through the land; among them one in which a parallel is drawn between him and the wicked Rehoboam. In another his integrity was impeached. This last drew from Jefferson the following notice, in a letter written to Uriah McGregory, of Connecticut, on the 13th of August, 1800:

To Mr. McGregory.

From the moment that a portion of my fellow-citizens looked towards me with a view to one of their highest offices, the floodgates of calumny have been opened upon me; not where I am personally known, where their slanders would be instantly judged and suppressed, from a general sense of their falsehood; but in the remote parts of the Union, where the means of detection are not at hand, and the trouble of an inquiry is greater than would suit the hearers to undertake. I know that I might have filled the courts of the United States with actions for these slanders, and have ruined, perhaps, many persons who are not innocent. But this would be no equivalent to the loss of character. I leave them, therefore, to the reproof of their own consciences. If these do not condemn them, there will yet come a day when the false witness will meet a Judge who has not slept over his slanders.

If the reverend Cotton Mather Smith, of Shena, believed this as firmly as I do, he would surely never have affirmed that I had obtained my property by fraud and robbery; that in one instance I had defrauded and robbed a widow and fatherless children of an estate, to which I was executor, of ten thousand pounds sterling, by keeping the property, and paying them in money at the nominal rate, when it was worth no more than forty for one ; and that all this could be proved.   Every tittle of it is fable—there not having existed a single circumstance of my life to which any part of it can hang.   I never was executor but in two instances, both of which having taken place about the beginning of the Revolution, which withdrew me immediately from all private pursuits, I never meddled in either executorship.   In one of the cases only were there a widow and children.   She was my sister.   She retained and managed the estate in her own hands, and no part of it was ever in mine.   In the other I was a co-partner, and only received, on a division, the equal portion allotted me.   To neither of these executorships, therefore, could Mr. Smith refer.

Again, my property is all patrimonial, except about seven or eight hundred pounds' worth of lands, purchased by myself and paid for, not to widows and orphans, but to the very gentlemen from whom I purchased.   If Mr. Smith, therefore, thinks the precepts of the Gospel intended for those who preach them as well as for others, he will doubtless some day feel the duties of repentance, and of acknowledgment in such forms as to correct the wrong he has done.   Perhaps he will have to wait till the passions of the moment have passed away.   All this is left to his own conscience.

These, Sir, are facts well known to every person in this quarter, which I have committed to paper for your own satisfaction, and that of those to whom you may choose to mention them.   I only pray that my letter may not go out of your own hands, lest it should get into the newspapers, a bear-garden scene into which I have made it a point to enter on no provocation.

Jefferson went to Washington the last of November, the length and tedium of the journey to the new capital being nothing in comparison to what it had been to the old.

CHAPTER XV.

Results of Presidential Election.—Letter to his Daughter.—Balloting for
President.—Letter to his Daughter.—Is inaugurated.—Returns to Monti-
cello.—Letters to his Daughter.—Goes back to Washington.—Inaugu-
rates the Custom of sending a written Message to Congress.—Abolishes
Levees.—Letter to Story.—To Dickinson.—Letter from Mrs. Cosway.—
Family Letters.—Makes a short Visit to Monticello.

THE result of the Presidential Election of 1800 was the
success of the Republican candidates—both Jefferson and
Burr receiving the same number (73) of electoral votes.
The chance of any two candidates receiving a tie vote was a
circumstance which had not been provided for, and though
all knew that Jefferson had been run to fill the office of President, and Burr that of Vice-president, the tie vote gave the
latter a chance—which the Federalists urged him to seize,
and which he did not neglect—to be made President.

The following letter gives the first sign of the coming
storm, which for a week convulsed the country with excitement, and shook the young Government to its centre.

To Mary Jefferson Eppes, Bermuda Hundred.

Washington, Jan. 4th, 1801.

Your letter, my dear Maria, of Dec. 28, is just now received, and shall be immediately answered, as shall all others
received from yourself or Mr. Eppes. This will keep our accounts even, and show, by the comparative promptness of reply, which is most anxious to hear from the other. I wrote
to Mr. Eppes, December 23d, but directed it to Petersburg;
hereafter it shall be to City Point. I went yesterday to
Mount Vernon, where Mrs. Washington and Mrs. Lewis asked very kindly after you. Mrs. Lewis looks thin, and thinks
herself not healthy; but it seems to be more in opinion than
any thing else. She has a child of very uncertain health.

The election is understood to stand 73, 73, 65, 64. The

Federalists were confident, at first, they could debauch Col. B. [Burr] from his good faith by offering him their vote to be President, and have seriously proposed it to him. His conduct has been honorable and decisive, and greatly embarrasses them. Time seems to familiarize them more and more to acquiescence, and to render it daily more probable they will yield to the known will of the people, and that some one State will join the eight already decided as to their vote. The victory of the Republicans in New Jersey, lately obtained by carrying their whole Congressional members on an election by general ticket, has had weight on their spirits.

Should I be destined to remain here, I shall count on meeting you and Mr. Eppes at Monticello the first week in April, where I shall not have above three weeks to stay. We shall then be able to consider how far it will be practicable to prevent this new destination from shortening the time of our being together, for be assured that no considerations in this world would compensate to me a separation from yourself and your sister. But the distance is so moderate that I should hope a journey to this place would be scarcely more inconvenient than one to Monticello. But of this we will talk when we meet there, which will be to me a joyful moment. Remember me affectionately to Mr. Eppes, and accept yourself the effusion of my tenderest love. Adieu, my dearest Maria.

TH. JEFFERSON.

The balloting for President in the House of Representatives began on the 11th of February. A snow-storm raged without, while the bitterest partisan feeling was at work within the Congressional halls. A member who was too ill to leave his bed was borne on a litter to the Capitol; his wife accompanied him, and, remaining at his side, administered his medicines to him. The ballot-boxes were carried to his couch, so that he did not miss a single ballot. Had he failed to vote, the Republicans would have lost a vote. The people throughout the country were kept in a ferment by the wild reports which came to them of the state of affairs in Washington. The Governor of Virginia established a line of express riders between Washington and Richmond during the whole of this eventful week, that he might learn as speedily as possible the result of each ballot. The best picture of the exciting scene is found in the following dispatches sent by John Randolph to his step-father, St. George Tucker, while the balloting was going on :

*Dispatches from John Randolph.**

Chamber of the House of Representatives,
Wednesday, February 11th, 1801.

Seven times we have balloted—eight States for J. ; six for B. ; two, Maryland and Vermont, divided. Voted to postpone for an hour the process ; now half-past four—resumed —result the same. The order against adjourning, made with a view to Mr. Nicholson, who was ill, has not operated. He left his sick-bed, came through a snow-storm, brought his bed, and has prevented the vote of Maryland from being given to Burr. Mail closing. Yours with perfect love and esteem,

J. R., JR.

Thursday Morning, February 12th.

We have just taken the nineteenth ballot (the balloting continued through the night). The result has invariably been eight States for J., six for B., two divided. We continue to ballot with the interval of an hour. The rule for making the sittings permanent seems now to be not so agreeable to our Federal gentlemen. No election will, in my opinion, take place. By special permission, the mail will remain open until four o'clock. I will not close my letter till three. If there be a change, I shall notify it ; if not, I shall add no more to the assurance of my entire affection.

JOHN RANDOLPH, JR.

Chamber of the House of Representatives,
February 14th, 1801.

After endeavoring to make the question before us depend upon our physical construction, our opponents have begged for a dispensation from their own regulation, and without adjourning, we have postponed (like able casuists) from day to day the balloting. In half an hour we shall recommence the operation. The result is marked below. We have bal-

---

* See Appendix to Tucker's Life of Jefferson.

S

loted thirty-one hours.   Twelve o'clock, Saturday noon, eight for J., six for B., two divided.   Again at one, not yet decided. Same result.   Postponed till Monday, twelve o'clock.

JOHN RANDOLPH, Jr.

In the midst of these scenes Jefferson wrote the following letter to Mrs. Eppes, in which we find strangely blended politics and fatherly love—a longing for retirement and a lurking desire to leave to his children the honor of his having filled the highest office in his country's gift:

To Mary Jefferson Eppes, Bermuda Hundred.

Washington, Feb. 15th, 1801.

Your letter, my dear Maria, of the 2d instant came to hand on the 8th.   I should have answered it immediately, according to our arrangement, but that I thought by waiting to the 11th I might possibly be able to communicate something on the subject of the election.   However, after four days of balloting, they are exactly where they were on the first.   There is a strong expectation in some that they will coalesce to-morrow; but I know no foundation for it.   Whatever event happens, I think I shall be at Monticello earlier than I formerly mentioned to you.   I think it more likely I may be able to leave this place by the middle of March.   I hope I shall find you at Monticello.   The scene passing here makes me pant to be away from it—to fly from the circle of cabal, intrigue, and hatred, to one where all is love and peace.

Though I never doubted of your affections, my dear, yet the expressions of them in your letter give me ineffable pleasure.   No, never imagine that there can be a difference with me between yourself and your sister.   You have both such dispositions as engross my whole love, and each so entirely that there can be no greater degree of it than each possesses.   Whatever absences I may be led into for a while, I look for happiness to the moment when we can all be settled together, no more to separate.   I feel no impulse from personal ambition to the office now proposed to me, but on account of yourself and your sister and those dear to you. I feel a sincere wish, indeed, to see our Government brought back to its republican principles, to see that kind of government firmly fixed to which my whole life has been devoted. I hope we shall now see it so established, as that when I retire it may be under full security that we are to continue free and happy. As soon as the fate of election is over, I will drop a line to Mr. Eppes. I hope one of you will always write the moment you receive a letter from me. Continue to love me, my dear, as you ever have done, and ever have been and will be by yours, affectionately,

TH. JEFFERSON.

I give John Randolph's last dispatch :

Chamber of the House of Representatives,
February 17th.

On the thirty-sixth ballot there appeared this day ten States for Thomas Jefferson, four (New England) for A. Burr, and two blank ballots (Delaware and South Carolina). This was the second time we balloted to-day. The four Burrites of Maryland put blanks into the box of that State. The vote was therefore unanimous. Mr. Morris, of Vermont, left his seat, and the result was therefore Jeffersonian. Adieu. Tuesday, 2 o'clock P.M.

J. R., JR.

I need not add that Mr. J. was declared duly elected.

In a letter written to his son-in-law, Mr. Randolph, Mr. Jefferson says:

To Thomas Mann Randolph.

A letter from Mr. Eppes informs me that Maria is in a situation which induces them not to risk a journey to Monticello, so we shall not have the pleasure of meeting them there. I begin to hope I may be able to leave this place by the middle of March. My tenderest love to my ever dear Martha, and kisses to the little one. Accept yourself sincere and affectionate salutation. Adieu.

Mr. Jefferson thought it becoming a Republican that his inauguration should be as unostentatious and free from display as possible—and such it was. An English traveller, who was in Washington at the time, thus describes him : "His dress was of plain cloth, and he rode on horseback to the Capitol without a single guard or even servant in his train, dismounted without assistance, and hitched the bridle of his horse to the palisades." He was accompanied to the Senate Chamber by a number of his friends, when, before taking the oath of office, he delivered his Inaugural Address, whose chaste and simple beauty is so familiar to the student of American History. I can not, however, refrain from giving here the eloquent close of this admirable State paper:

Extract from Inaugural Address.

I repair, then, fellow-citizens, to the post you have assigned me. With experience enough in subordinate offices to have seen the difficulties of this, the greatest of all, I have learned to expect that it will rarely fall to the lot of imperfect man to retire from this station with the reputation and favor which bring him into it. Without pretensions to that high confidence reposed in our first and great Revolutionary character, whose pre-eminent services had entitled him to the first place in his country's love, and destined for him the fairest page in the volume of faithful history, I ask so much confidence only as may give firmness and effect to the legal administration of your affairs. I shall often go wrong through defect of judgment. When right, I shall often be thought wrong by those whose positions will not command a view of the whole ground. I ask your indulgence for my own errors, which will never be intentional; and your support against the errors of others, who may condemn what they would not if seen in all its parts. The approbation implied by your suffrage is a consolation to me for the past; and my future solicitude will be to retain the good opinion of those who have bestowed it in advance, to conciliate that of others by doing them all the good in my power, and to be instrumental to the happiness and freedom of all.

Relying, then, on the patronage of your good-will, I advance with obedience to the work, ready to retire from it whenever you become sensible how much better choice it is in your power to make. And may that Infinite Power which rules the destinies of the universe lead our councils to what is best, and give them a favorable issue for your peace and prosperity.

The house at Monticello was still unfinished when Mr. Jefferson returned there on a visit early in April. A few days before he left he wrote the following letter to his kinsman, Mr. George Jefferson, which, in an age when nepotism is so rife, may, from its principles, seem now rather out of date:

To George Jefferson.

Dear Sir—I have to acknowledge the receipt of yours of March 4th, and to express to you the delight with which I found the just, disinterested, and honorable point of view in which you saw the proposition it covered. The resolution you so properly approved had long been formed in my mind. The public will never be made to believe that an appointment of a relative is made on the ground of merit alone, uninfluenced by family views; nor can they ever see with approbation offices, the disposal of which they intrust to their Presidents for public purposes, divided out as family property. Mr. Adams degraded himself infinitely by his conduct on this subject, as General Washington had done himself the greatest honor. With two such examples to proceed by, I should be doubly inexcusable to err. It is true that this places the relations of the President in a worse situation than if he were a stranger, but the public good, which can not be effected if its confidence be lost, requires this sacrifice. Perhaps, too, it is compensated by sharing in the public esteem. I could not be satisfied till I assured you of the increased esteem with which this transaction fills me for you. Accept my affectionate expressions of it.

The following letters to Mrs. Eppes will carry on pleasantly the tale of Mr. Jefferson's private life:

To Mary Jefferson Eppes, Bermuda Hundred.

Monticello, April 11th, 1801.

My dear Maria—I wrote to Mr. Eppes on the 8th inst. by post, to inform him I should on the 12th send off a messenger to the Hundred for the horses he may have bought for me. Davy Bowles will accordingly set out to-morrow, and will be the bearer of this. He leaves us all well, and wanting nothing but your and Mr. Eppes's company to make us completely happy.   Let me know by his return when you expect to be here, that I may accommodate to that my orders as to executing the interior work of the different parts of the house.   John being at work under Lilly, Goliath is our gardener, and with his veteran aids will be directed to make what preparation he can for you.   It is probable I shall come home myself about the last week of July or first of August, to stay two months during the sickly season in autumn every year.   These terms I shall hope to pass with you here, and that either in spring or fall you will be able to pass some time with me in Washington.   Had it been possible, I would have made a tour now, on my return, to see you.   But I am tied to a day for my return to Washington, to assemble our New Administration and begin our work systematically.   I hope, when you come up, you will make very short stages, drive slow and safely, which may well be done if you do not permit yourself to be hurried.   Surely, the sooner you come the better.   The servants will be here under your commands, and such supplies as the house affords. Before that time our bacon will be here from Bedford.   Continue to love me, my dear Maria, as affectionately as I do you.   I have no object so near my heart as yours and your sister's happiness.   Present me affectionately to Mr. Eppes, and be assured yourself of my unchangeable and tenderest attachment to you.

TH. JEFFERSON.

The horses alluded to in the above letter were four full-blooded bays, which the President wished to purchase for the use of his carriage in Washington.   Mr. Eppes succeeded in making the purchase for him, and his choice was such as to suit even such a connoisseur in horse-flesh as Jefferson was, to say nothing of his faithful coachman, Joseph Dougherty, who was never so happy as when seated on the box behind this spirited and showy team.   Their cost was sixteen hundred dollars.

To Mary Jefferson Eppes, Bermuda Hundred.

Washington, June 24th, 1801.

My dear Maria—According to contract, immediately on the receipt of Mr. Eppes's letter of the 12th, I wrote him mine of the 17th; and having this moment received yours of June 18th, I hasten to reply to that also. I am very anxious you should hasten your departure for Monticello, but go a snail's pace when you set out. I shall certainly be with you the last week of July or first week of August. I have a letter from your sister this morning. All are well. They have had all their windows, almost, broken by a hail-storm, and are unable to procure glass, so that they are living almost out-of-doors. The whole neighborhood suffered equally. Two sky-lights at Monticello, which had been left uncovered, were entirely broken up. No other windows there were broke. I give reason to expect that both yourself and your sister will come here in the fall. I hope it myself, and our society here is anxious for it. I promise them that one of you will hereafter pass the spring here, and the other the fall, saving your consent to it. All this must be arranged when we meet. I am here interrupted; so, with my affectionate regards to the family at Eppington, and Mr. Eppes, and tenderest love to yourself, I must bid you adieu.

TH. JEFFERSON.

To Mary Jefferson Eppes.

Washington, July 16th, 1801.

My dear Maria—I received yesterday Mr. Eppes's letter of the 12th, informing me that you had got safely to Eppington, and would set out to-morrow at furthest for Monticello. This letter, therefore, will, I hope, find you there. I now write to Mr. Craven to furnish you all the supplies of the table which his farm affords. Mr. Lilly had before received orders to do the same. Liquors have been forwarded, and have arrived with some loss. I insist that you command and use every thing as if I were with you, and shall be very uneasy if you do not. A supply of groceries has been lying here some time waiting for a conveyance. It will probably be three weeks from this time before they can be at Monticello. In the mean time, take what is wanting from any of the stores with which I deal, on my account. I have recommended to your sister to send at once for Mrs. Marks. Remus and my chair, with Phill as usual, can go for her. I shall join you between the second and seventh—more probably not till the seventh. Mr. and Mrs. Madison leave this about a week hence. I am looking forward with great impatience to the moment when we can all be joined at Monticello, and hope we shall never again know so long a separation. I recommend to your sister to go over at once to Monticello, which I hope she will do. It will be safer for her, and more comfortable for both. Present me affectionately to Mr. Eppes, and be assured of my constant and tenderest love.

TH. JEFFERSON.

The Mrs. Marks alluded to in this last letter was Mr. Jefferson's sister. Her husband lived in Lower Virginia, and, his means being very limited, he could not afford to send his family from home during the sickly season. For a period of thirty years Mr. Jefferson never failed to send his carriage and horses for her, and kept her for three or four months at Monticello, which after her husband's death became her permanent home. Mr. Jefferson left in his will the following touching recommendation of her to his daughter: "I recommend to my daughter, Martha Randolph, the maintenance and care of my well-beloved sister, Anne Scott, and trust confidently that from affection to her, as well as for my sake, she will never let her want a comfort." It is needless to add that this trust was faithfully fulfilled, and when Mrs. Randolph had no home save her eldest son's house, the same roof sheltered Mrs. Marks as well as herself.

Mr. Jefferson paid his usual visit to Monticello this summer, and was there surrounded by his children and grandchildren. On his return to Washington, he wrote the following letters to Mrs. Eppes, in which the anxiety that he shows about her is what might have been expected from the tender love of a mother.

To Mary Jefferson Eppes, Monticello.

Washington, Oct. 26th, 1801.

My ever dear Maria—I have heard nothing of you since Mr. Eppes's letter, dated the day se'nnight after I left home. The Milton* mail will be here to-morrow morning, when I

---

* Milton was a thriving little town four miles from Monticello.

shall hope to receive something. In the mean time, this letter must go hence this evening. I trust it will still find you at Monticello, and that possibly Mr. Eppes may have concluded to take a journey to Bedford, and still further prolonged your stay. I am anxious to hear from you, lest you should have suffered in the same way now as on a former similar occasion. Should any thing of that kind take place, and the remedy which succeeded before fail now, I know nobody to whom I would so soon apply as Mrs. Suddarth. A little experience is worth a great deal of reading, and she has had great experience and a sound judgment to observe on it. I shall be glad to hear, at the same time, that the little boy is well.

If Mr. Eppes undertakes what I have proposed to him at Pantops and Poplar Forest the next year, I should think it indispensable that he should make Monticello his head-quarters. You can be furnished with all plantation articles for the family from Mr. Craven, who will be glad to pay his rent in that way. It would be a great satisfaction to me to find you fixed there in April. Perhaps it might induce me to take flying trips by stealth, to have the enjoyment of family society for a few days undisturbed. Nothing can repay me the loss of that society, the only one founded in affection and bosom confidence. I have here company enough, part of which is very friendly, part well enough disposed, part secretly hostile, and a constant succession of strangers. But this only serves to get rid of life, not to enjoy it; it is in the love of one's family only that heartfelt happiness is known, I feel it when we are all together, and, when alone, beyond what can be imagined. Present me affectionately to Mr. Eppes, Mr. Randolph, and my dear Martha, and be assured yourself of my tenderest love.

TH. JEFFERSON.

To Mary Jefferson Eppes.—[Extract.]

I perceive that it will be merely accidental when I can steal a moment to write to you; however, that is of no consequence, my health being always so firm as to leave you without doubt on that subject. But it is not so with yourself and little one. I shall not be easy, therefore, if either yourself or Mr. Eppes do not once a week or fortnight write the three words "All are well." That you may be so now, and so continue, is the subject of my perpetual anxiety, as my affections are constantly brooding over you. Heaven bless you, my dear daughter.

Congress met on the 7th of December. It had been the custom for the session to be opened pretty much as the English Parliament is by the Queen's speech. The President, accompanied by a cavalcade, proceeded in state to the Capitol, took his seat in the Senate Chamber, and, the House of Representatives being summoned, read his address. Mr. Jefferson, on the opening of this session of Congress (1801), swept away all these inconvenient forms and ceremonies by introducing the custom of the President sending a written message to Congress. Soon after his inauguration he did away with levees, and established only two public days for the reception of company, the first of January and the Fourth of July, when his doors were thrown open to the public. He received private calls, whether of courtesy or on business, at all other times.

We have preserved to us an amusing anecdote of the effect of his abolishing levees. Many of the ladies at Washington, indignant at being cut off from the pleasure of attending them, and thinking that their discontinuance was an innovation on former customs, determined to force the President to hold them. Accordingly, on the usual levee-day they resorted in full force to the White House. The President was out taking his habitual ride on horseback. On his return, being told that the public rooms were filled with ladies, he at once divined their true motives for coming on that day. Without being at all disconcerted, all booted and spurred, and still covered with the dust of his ride, he went in to receive his fair guests. Never had his reception been more graceful or courteous. The ladies, charmed with the ease and grace of his manners and address, forgot their indignation with him, and went away feeling that, of the two parties, they had shown most impoliteness in visiting his house when not expected. The result of their plot was for a long time a subject of mirth among them, and they never again attempted to infringe upon the rules of his household.

The Reverend Isaac Story having sent him some speculations on the subject of the transmigration of souls, he sent him, on the 5th of December, a reply, from which we take the following interesting extract:

To Rev. Isaac Story.

The laws of nature have withheld from us the meaning of physical knowledge of the country of spirits, and revelation has, for reasons unknown to us, chosen to leave us in darkness as we were. When I was young, I was fond of speculations which seemed to promise some insight into that hidden country; but observing at length that they left me in the same ignorance in which they had found me, I have for many years ceased to read or think concerning them, and have reposed my head on that pillow of ignorance which a benevolent Creator has made so soft for us, knowing how much we should be forced to use it. I have thought it better, by nourishing the good passions and controlling the bad, to merit an inheritance in a state of being of which I can know so little, and to trust for the future to Him who has been so good for the past.

A week or two later he wrote to John Dickinson: "The approbation of my ancient friends is, above all things, the most grateful to my heart. They know for what objects we relinquished the delights of domestic society, tranquillity, and science, and committed ourselves to the ocean of revolution, to wear out the only life God has given us here in scenes the benefits of which will accrue only to those who follow us."

Early in the ensuing year he received a letter from his old friend Mrs. Cosway, who writes:

From Mrs. Cosway.

Have we no hopes of ever seeing you in Paris? Would it not be a rest to you after your laborious situation? I often see the only friend remaining of our set, Madame de Corny, the same in her own amiable qualities, but very different in her situation, but she supports it very well.

I am come to this place in its best time, for the profusion of fine things is beyond description, and not possible to conceive. It is so changed in every respect that you would not think it the same country or people. Shall this letter be fortunate enough to get to your hands? Will it be still more fortunate in procuring me an answer? I leave you to reflect on the happiness you will afford your ever affectionate and sincere friend.

To Mary Jefferson Eppes.

Washington, Mar. 3d, 1802.

My very dear Maria—I observed to you some time ago that, during the session of Congress, I should be able to write to you but seldom; and so it has turned out. Yours of Jan. 24 I received in due time, after which Mr. Eppes's letter of Feb. 1 and 2 confirmed to me the news, always welcome, of yours and Francis's health. Since this I have no news of you. I see with great concern that I am not to have the pleasure of meeting you in Albemarle in the spring. I had entertained the hope Mr. Eppes and yourself would have passed the summer there, and, being there, that the two families should have come together on a visit here. I observe your reluctance at the idea of that visit, but for your own happiness must advise you to get the better of it. I think I discover in you a willingness to withdraw from society more than is prudent. I am convinced our own happiness requires that we should continue to mix with the world, and to keep pace with it as it goes; and that every person who retires from free communication with it is severely punished afterwards by the state of mind into which he gets, and which can only be prevented by feeding our sociable principles. I can speak from experience on this subject. From 1793 to 1797 I remained closely at home, saw none but those who came there, and at length became very sensible of the ill effect it had on my own mind, and of its direct and irresistible tendency to render me unfit for society and uneasy when necessarily engaged in it. I felt enough of the effect of withdrawing from the world then to see that it led to an anti-social and misanthropic state of mind, which severely punishes him who gives in to it; and it will be a lesson I never shall forget as to my-self. I am certain you would be pleased with the state of society here, and that after the first moments you would feel happy in having made the experiment. I take for granted your sister will come immediately after my spring visit to Monticello, and I should have thought it agreeable to both that your first visit should be made together.......

TH. JEFFERSON.

Mr. Jefferson made his spring visit to Monticello, and re-turned to Washington before the first of June. The follow-ing chatty and affectionate letters to his daughter, Mrs. Eppes, were written after this visit home. The frequent and touch-ing expressions of anxiety about her health found in them show its delicate condition.

To Mary Jefferson Eppes.—[Extract.]

Washington, July 1st, 1802.

It will be infinitely joyful to me to be with you there [Monticello] after the longest separation we have had for years. I count from one meeting to another as we do be-tween port and port at sea; and I long for the moment with the same earnestness. Present me affectionately to Mr. Eppes, and let me hear from you immediately. Be as-sured yourself of my tender and unchangeable affections.

TH. JEFFERSON.

To Mary Jefferson Eppes.

Washington, July 2d, 1802.

My dear Maria—My letter of yesterday had hardly got out of my hand when yours of June 21st and Mr. Eppes's of the 25th were delivered. I learn with extreme concern the state of your health and that of the child, and am happy to hear you have got from the Hundred to Eppington, the air of which will aid your convalescence, and will enable you to delay your journey to Monticello till you have recovered your strength to make the journey safe.

With respect to the measles, they began in Mr. Randolph's family about the middle of June, and will probably be a month getting through the family; so you had better, when you go, pass on direct to Monticello, not calling at Edgehill.

I will immediately write to your sister, and inform her I advised you to this. I have not heard yet of the disease having got to Monticello, but the intercourse with Edgehill being hourly, it can not have failed to have gone there immediately; and as there are no young children there but Bet's and Sally's, and the disease is communicable before a person knows they have it, I have no doubt those children have passed through it. The children of the plantation, being a mile and a half off, can easily be guarded against. I will write to Monticello, and direct that, should the nail-boys or any others have it, they be removed to the plantation instantly on your arrival. Indeed, none of them but Bet's sons stay on the mountain; and they will be doubtless through it. I think, therefore, you may be there in perfect security. It had gone through the neighborhood chiefly when I was there in May; so that it has probably disappeared. You should make inquiry on the road before you go into any house, as the disease is now universal throughout the State, and all the States.

Present my most friendly attachment to Mr. and Mrs. Eppes. Tell the latter I have had her spectacles these six months, waiting for a direct conveyance. My best affections to Mr. Eppes, if with you, and the family, and tender and constant love to yourself.

TH. JEFFERSON.

P.S.—I have always forgotten to answer your apologies about Critta, which were very unnecessary. I am happy she has been with you and useful to you. At Monticello there could be nothing for her to do; so that her being with you is exactly as desirable to me as she can be useful to you.

On the 16th of July he wrote Mrs. Eppes:

I leave this on the 24th, and shall be in great hopes of receiving yourself and Mr. Eppes there (Monticello) immediately. I received two days ago his letter of the 8th, in which he gives me a poor account of your health, though he says you are recruiting. Make very short stages, be off always by daylight, and have your day's journey over by ten. In this way it is probable you may find the moderate exercise of the journey of service to yourself and Francis. Nothing is more frequent than to see a child re-established by a journey. Present my sincerest affections to the family at Eppington and to Mr. Eppes. Tell him the Tory newspapers are all attacking his publication, and urging it as a proof that Virginia has for object to change the Constitution of the United States, and to make it too impotent to curb the larger States. Accept yourself assurances of my constant and tender love.

He reached Monticello on the 25th of July, and was there joyfully welcomed by his children and grandchildren. He was apparently in robust health; but we find that six months before this period, to his intimate friend Dr. Rush, he had written: "My health has always been so uniformly firm, that I have for some years dreaded nothing so much as the living too long. I think, however, that a flaw has appeared which insures me against that, without cutting short any of the period during which I could expect to remain capable of being useful. It will probably give me as many years as I wish, and without pain or debility. Should this be the case, my most anxious prayers will have been fulfilled by Heaven. I have said as much to no mortal breathing, and my florid health is calculated to keep my friends as well as foes quiet, as they should be."

He was at this time in his sixtieth year.

CHAPTER XVI.

JEFFERSON returned to Washington on the 5th of October, and, as will be seen from the following note, was looking eagerly for the promised visits of his daughters:

To Mary Jefferson Eppes.

Washington, Oct. 7th, 1802.

My dear Maria—I arrived here on the fourth day of my journey without accident. On the day and next day after my arrival, I was much indisposed with a general soreness all over, a ringing in the head, and deafness. It is wearing off slowly, and was probably produced by travelling very early two mornings in the fog. I have desired Mr. Jefferson to furnish you with whatever you may call for, on my account; and I insist on your calling freely. It never was my intention that a visit for my gratification should be at your expense. It will be absolutely necessary for me to send fresh horses to meet you, as no horses, after the three first days' journey, can encounter the fourth, which is hilly beyond any thing you have ever seen. I shall expect to learn from you soon the day of your departure, that I may make proper arrangements. Present me affectionately to Mr. Eppes, and accept yourself my tenderest love.

TH. JEFFERSON.

While President, Jefferson retained his habitual custom of taking regular daily exercise. He rarely, however, gave his coachman, Joseph, the pleasure of sitting behind the four fiery bays; always preferring his saddle-horse—the magnificent Wildair—being the same which he had ridden to the Capitol and "hitched to the palisades," on the day of his inauguration. On his journeys to Monticello he went most frequently in his one-horse chair or the phaeton. He never failed, as I have elsewhere remarked, no matter what his occupation, to devote the hours between one and three in the afternoon to exercise, which was most frequently taken on horseback. Being very choice in his selection of horses, and a bold and fearless rider, he never rode any but an animal of the highest mettle and best blood.

JEFFERSON'S HORSE-CHAIR.

We have from the most authentic source the account of an incident which occurred on one of his rides while President. He was riding along one of the highways leading into Washington, when he overtook a man wending his way towards the city. Jefferson, as was his habit, drew up his horse and touched his hat to the pedestrian. The man returned the salutation, and began a conversation with the President—not knowing, of course, who he was. He at once entered upon the subject of politics—as was the habit of the day—and began to abuse the President, alluding even to some of the infamous calumnies against his private life. Jefferson's first impulse was to say "good-morning" and ride on, but, amused at his own situation, he asked the man if he knew the President personally? "No," was the reply, "nor do I wish to." "But do you think it fair," asked Jefferson, "to repeat such stories about a man, and condemn one whom you dare not face?" "I will never shrink from meeting Mr. Jefferson should he ever come in my way," replied

T

the stranger, who was a country merchant in high standing from Kentucky. "Will you, then, go to his house to-morrow at — o'clock and be introduced to him, if I promise to meet you there at that hour?" asked Jefferson, eagerly. "Yes, I will," said the man, after a moment's thought. With a half-suppressed smile, and excusing himself from any further conversation, the President touched his hat and rode on.

Hardly had Jefferson disappeared from sight before a suspicion of the truth, which he soon verified, flashed through the stranger's mind. He stood fire, however, like a true man, and at the appointed hour the next day the card of Mr. ——, "Mr. Jefferson's yesterday's companion," was handed to the President. The next moment he was announced and entered. His situation was embarrassing, but with a gentlemanly bearing, though with some confusion, he began, "I have called, Mr. Jefferson, to apologize for having said to a stranger—" "Hard things of an imaginary being who is no relation of mine," said Jefferson, interrupting him, as he gave him his hand, while his countenance was radiant with a smile of mingled good-nature and amusement. The Kentuckian once more began his apologies, which Jefferson good-naturedly laughed off, and, changing the subject, had soon captivated his guest by launching forth into one of his most delightful strains of animated conversation, which so charmed Mr. ——, that the dinner-hour had arrived before he was aware how swiftly the pleasant hours had flown by. He rose to go, when Jefferson urged him to stay to dinner. Mr. —— declined, when Jefferson repeated the invitation, and, smiling, asked if he was afraid to meet Mr. ——, a Republican. "Don't mention him," said the other, "and I will stay."

It is needless to add that this Kentuckian remained ever afterwards firmly attached to Jefferson: his whole family became his staunch supporters, and the gentleman himself, in telling the story, would wind up with a jesting caution to young men against talking too freely with strangers.

The following letters were written to Mrs. Eppes, after her return to Virginia from a visit to Washington:

To Mary Jefferson Eppes.

Washington, Jan. 18th, 1803.

My dear Maria—Yours by John came safely to hand, and informed me of your ultimate arrival at Edgehill. Mr. Randolph's letter from Gordon's, received the night before, gave me the first certain intelligence I had received since your departure. A rumor had come here of your having been stopped two or three days at Ball Run, and in a miserable hovel; so that I had passed ten days in anxious uncertainty about you. Your apologies, my dear Maria, on the article of expense, are quite without necessity. You did not here indulge yourselves as much as I wished, and nothing prevented my supplying your backwardness but my total ignorance in articles which might suit you. Mr. Eppes's election [to Congress] will, I am in hopes, secure me your company next winter, and perhaps you may find it convenient to accompany your sister in the spring. Mr. Giles's aid, indeed, in Congress, in support of our Administration, considering his long knowledge of the affairs of the Union, his talents, and the high ground on which he stands through the United States, had rendered his continuance here an object of anxious desire to those who compose the Administration; but every information we receive states that prospect to be desperate from his ill health, and will relieve me from the imputation of being willing to lose to the public so strong a supporter, for the personal gratification of having yourself and Mr. Eppes with me. I inclose you Lemaire's receipts. The orthography will be puzzling and amusing; but the receipts are valuable. Present my tender love to your sister, kisses to the young ones, and my affections to Mr. Randolph and Mr. Eppes, whom I suppose you will see soon. Be assured of my unceasing and anxious love for yourself.

TH. JEFFERSON.

The following playfully-written note was sent to his young grandson:

To Thomas Jefferson Randolph.

Washington, Feb. 21st, 1803.

I have to acknowledge the receipt of your letter of the 3d, my dear Jefferson, and to congratulate you on your writing so good a hand. By the last post I sent you a French Grammar, and within three weeks I shall be able to ask you, "Parlez vous Français, monsieur?" I expect to leave this about the 9th, if unexpected business should not detain me, and then it will depend on the weather and the roads how long I shall be going—probably five days. The roads will be so deep that I can not flatter myself with catching Ellen in bed. Tell her that Mrs. Harrison Smith desires her compliments to her. Your mamma has probably heard of the death of Mrs. Burrows. Mrs. Brent is not far from it. Present my affections to your papa, mamma, and the young ones, and be assured of them yourself.

TH. JEFFERSON.

In a letter written to a friend in the winter of this year (1803) he thus alludes to his health: "I retain myself very perfect health, having not had twenty hours of fever in forty-two years past. I have sometimes had a troublesome headache and some slight rheumatic pains; but, now sixty years old nearly, I have had as little to complain of in point of health as most people."

We have in the following letter one of the very few allusions to his religion which he ever made to any of his family:

To Martha Jefferson Randolph.

Washington, April 25th, 1803.

My dear Martha—A promise made to a friend some years ago, but executed only lately, has placed my religious creed on paper. I have thought it just that my family, by possessing this, should be enabled to estimate the libels published against me on this, as on every other possible subject. I have written to Philadelphia for Dr. Priestley's history of the corruptions of Christianity, which I will send you and recommend to an attentive perusal, because it establishes the ground-work of my view of this subject.

I have not had a line from Monticello or Edgehill since I parted with you. Peter Carr and Mrs. Carr, who staid with me five or six days, told me Cornelia had got happily through her measles, and that Ellen had not taken them. But what has become of Anne?* I thought I had her promise to write once a week, at least the words "All's well."

---

* This little grand-daughter was now twelve years old.

It is now time for you to let me know when you expect to be able to set out for Washington, and whether your own carriage can bring you half-way. I think my Chickasaws; if drove moderately, will bring you well that far. Mr. Lilly knows you will want them, and can add a fourth. I think that by changing horses half-way you will come with more comfort. I have no gentleman to send for your escort. Finding here a beautiful blue cassimere, water-proof, and thinking it will be particularly *à propos* for Mr. Randolph as a travelling-coat for his journey, I have taken enough for that purpose, and will send it to Mr. Benson, postmaster at Fredericksburg, to be forwarded by Abrahams, and hope it will be received in time.

Mr. and Mrs. Madison will set out for Orange about the last day of the month. They will stay there but a week. I write to Maria to-day; but supposing her to be at the Hundred, according to what she told me of her movements, I send my letter there. I wish you to come as early as possible; because, though the members of the Government remain here to the last week in July, yet the sickly season commences, in fact, by the middle of that month, and it would not be safe for you to keep the children here longer than that, lest any one of them, being taken sick early, might detain the whole here till the season of general danger, and perhaps through it. Kiss the children for me. Present me affectionately to Mr. Randolph, and accept yourself assurances of my constant and tenderest love.

TH. JEFFERSON.

The following extract from a letter written December 1st, 1804, to John Randolph by Jefferson, shows how little of a politician the latter was in his own family, and how careful he was not to try and influence the political opinions of those connected with him:

To John Randolph.

I am aware that in parts of the Union, and even with persons to whom Mr. Eppes and Mr. Randolph are unknown, and myself little known, it will be presumed, from their connection, that what comes from them comes from me. No men on earth are more independent in their sentiments than they are, nor any one less disposed than I am to influence the opinions of others. We rarely speak of politics, or of the proceedings of the House, but merely historically, and I carefully avoid expressing an opinion on them in their presence, that we may all be at our ease. With other members, I have believed that more unreserved communications would be advantageous to the public.

I give now Jefferson's letters to Mrs. Eppes, scattered over a period of several months. They possess unusual interest, from the fact that they are the last written by this devoted father to his lovely daughter. Mrs. Eppes being in extremely delicate health, and her husband having to be in Washington as a member of Congress, she early in the fall repaired to Edgehill, there to spend the winter with her sister, Mrs. Randolph—Mr. Randolph also being a member of Congress.

To Mary Jefferson Eppes.

Washington, Nov. 27th, 1803.

It is rare, my ever dear Maria, during a session of Congress, that I can get time to write any thing but letters of business, and this, though a day of rest to others, is not all so to me. We are all well here, and hope the post of this evening will bring us information of the health of all at Edgehill, and particularly that Martha and the new bantling* are both well, and that her example gives you good spirits. When Congress will rise no mortal can tell—not from the quantity but dilatoriness of business.

Mr. Lilly having finished the mill, is now, I suppose, engaged in the road which we have been so long wanting; and that done, the next job will be the levelling of Pantops. I anxiously long to see under way the work necessary to fix you there, that we may one day be all together. Mr. Stewart is now here on his way back to his family, whom he will probably join Thursday or Friday. Will you tell your sister that the pair of stockings she sent me by Mr. Randolph are quite large enough, and also have fur enough in them. I inclose some papers for Anne; and must continue in debt to Jefferson a letter for a while longer. Take care of your-

---

* Mrs. Randolph's sixth child.

self, my dearest Maria, have good spirits, and know that courage is as essential to triumph in your case as in that of a soldier. Keep us all, therefore, in heart of being so yourself. Give my tender affections to your sister, and receive them for yourself also, with assurances that I live in your love only and in that of your sister. Adieu, my dear daughter.

TH. JEFFERSON.

To Mary Jefferson Eppes, Edgehill.

Washington, Dec. 26th, 1803.

I now return, my dearest Maria, the paper which you lent me for Mr. Page, and which he has returned some days since. I have prevailed on Dr. Priestley to undertake the work, of which this is only the syllabus or plan. He says he can accomplish it in the course of a year. But, in truth, his health is so much impaired, and his body become so feeble, that there is reason to fear he will not live out even the short term he has asked for it.

You may inform Mr. Eppes and Mr. Randolph that no mail arrived the last night from Natchez. I presume the great rains which have fallen have rendered some of the water-courses impassable. On New-year's-day, however, we shall hear of the delivery of New Orleans* to us! Till then the Legislature seem disposed to do nothing but meet and adjourn.

Mrs. Livingston, formerly the younger Miss Allen, made kind inquiries after you the other day. She said she was at school with you at Mrs. Pine's. Not knowing the time destined for your expected indisposition, I am anxious on your account. You are prepared to meet it with courage, I hope. Some female friend of your mamma's (I forget whom) used to say it was no more than a jog of the elbow. The material thing is to have scientific aid in readiness, that if any thing uncommon takes place it may be redressed on the spot, and not be made serious by delay. It is a case which least of all will wait for doctors to be sent for; therefore with this single precaution nothing is ever to be feared. I was in

---

* The reader will remember that the purchase of Louisiana was made in Jefferson's administration.

hopes to have heard from Edgehill last night, but I suppose your post has failed.

I shall expect to see the gentlemen here next Sunday night to take part in the gala of Monday. Give my tenderest love to your sister, of whom I have not heard for a fortnight, and my affectionate salutations to the gentlemen and young ones, and continue to love me yourself, and be assured of my warmest affections.

TH. JEFFERSON.

To Mary Jefferson Eppes, Edgehill.

Washington, Jan. 29th, 1804.

My dearest Maria—This evening ought to have brought in the Western mail, but it is not arrived; consequently we hear nothing from our neighborhood. I rejoice that this is the last time our Milton mail will be embarrassed with that from New Orleans, the rapidity of which occasioned our letters often to be left in the post-office. It now returns to its former establishment of twice a week, so that we may hear oftener from you; and, in communicating to us frequently of the state of things, I hope you will not be sparing, if it be only by saying that "All is well!"

I think Congress will rise the second week in March, when we shall join you; perhaps Mr. Eppes may sooner. On this I presume he writes you. It would have been the most desirable of all things could we have got away by this time. However, I hope you will let us all see that you have within yourself the resource of a courage not requiring the presence of any body.

Since proposing to Anne the undertaking to raise bantams, I have received from Algiers two pair of beautiful fowls, something larger than our common fowls, with fine aigrettes. They are not so large nor valuable as the East India fowl, but both kinds, as well as the bantams, are well worthy of being raised. We must, therefore, distribute them among us, and raise them clear of mixture of any kind. All this we will settle together in March, and soon after we will begin the levelling and establishing of your hen-house at Pantops. Give my tenderest love to your sister, to all the young ones kisses, to yourself every thing affectionate.

TH. JEFFERSON.

To Mary Jefferson Eppes, Edgehill.

Washington, Feb. 26th, 1804.

A thousand joys to you, my dear Maria, on the happy accession to your family. A letter from our dear Martha by last post gave me the happy news that your crisis was happily over, and all well. I had supposed that if you were a little later than your calculation, and the rising of Congress as early as we expected, we might have been with you at the moment when it would have been so encouraging to have had your friends around you. I rejoice, indeed, that all is so well.

Congress talk of rising the 12th of March; but they will probably be some days later. You will doubtless see Mr. Eppes and Mr. Randolph immediately on the rising of Congress. I shall hardly be able to get away till some days after them. By that time I hope you will be able to go with us to Monticello, and that we shall *all* be there together for a month; and the interval between that and the autumnal visit will not be long. Will you desire your sister to send for Mr. Lilly, and to advise him what orders to give Goliath for providing those vegetables which may come into use for the months of April, August, and September? Deliver her also my affectionate love. I will write to her the next week. Kiss all the little ones, and be assured yourself of my tender and unchangeable affection.

TH. JEFFERSON.

The relief of Mr. Jefferson's anxieties concerning his daughter's health was of but short duration. Shortly after writing the preceding letter, he received intelligence of her being dangerously ill. It is touching to see, in his letters, his increasing tenderness for her as her situation became more critical; and we find him chafing with impatience at being prevented by official duties from flying at once to her side on hearing of her illness.

To Mary Jefferson Eppes.

Washington, Mar. 3d, 1804.

The account of your illness, my dearest Maria, was known

to me only this morning.   Nothing but the impossibility of Congress proceeding a single step in my absence presents an insuperable bar. ˙ Mr. Eppes goes off, and I hope will find you in a convalescent state.   Next to the desire that it may be so, is that of being speedily informed, and of being relieved from the terrible anxiety in which˙I shall be till I hear from you.   God bless you, my ever dear daughter, and preserve you safe to the blessing of us all.

TH. JEFFERSON.

The news of Mrs. Eppes's convalescence revived her father's hopes about her health, and we find him writing, in the following letter to Mr. Eppes, about settling him at Pantops (one of his farms a few miles from Monticello), in the fond anticipation of thus fixing his daughter near him for life.

To John W. Eppes, Edgehill.

Washington, March 15th, 1804.

Dear Sir—Your letter of the 9th has at length relieved my spirits; still the debility of Maria will need attention, lest a recurrence of fever should degenerate into typhus. I should suppose the system of wine and food as effectual to prevent as to cure that fever, and think she should use both as freely as she finds she can· bear them—light food and cordial wines. The sherry at Monticello is old and genuine, and the Pedro Ximenes much older still, and stomachic. Her palate and stomach will be the best arbiters between them.

Congress have deferred their adjournment a week, to wit, to the 26th; consequently we return a week later. I presume I can be with you by the first of April. I hope Maria will by that time be well enough to go over to Monticello with us, and I hope you will thereafter take up your residence there. The house, its contents, and appendages and servants, are as freely subjected to you as to myself, and I hope you will make it your home till we can get you fixed at Pantops. I do not think Maria should be ventured below after this date. I will endeavor to forward to Mr. Benson, postmaster at Fredericksburg, a small parcel of the oats for you. The only difficulty is to find some gentleman going on in the stage who will take charge of them by the way. My tenderest love to Maria and Patsy, and all the young ones. Affectionate salutations to yourself.

TH. JEFFERSON.

Jefferson reached Monticello early in April, where his great and tender heart was to be wrung by the severest affliction which can befall a parent—the loss of a well-beloved child. Mrs. Eppes's decline was rapid; and the following line in her father's handwriting, in his family register, tells its own sad tale:

"MARY JEFFERSON, *born* Aug. 1, 1778, 1*h*. 30*m*. A.M. *Died* April 17, 1804, between 8 and 9 A.M."

The following beautiful account of the closing scenes of this domestic tragedy is from the pen of a niece of Mrs. Eppes, and was written at the request of Mr. Randall, Jefferson's worthy biographer:

Boston, 15th January, 1856.

My dear Mr. Randall—I find an old memorandum made many years ago, I know not when nor under what circumstances, but by my own hand, in the fly-leaf of a Bible. It is to this effect:

"Maria Jefferson was born in 1778, and married, in 1797, John Wayles Eppes, son of Francis Eppes and Elizabeth Wayles, second daughter of John Wayles. Maria Jefferson died April, 1804, leaving two children, Francis, born in 1801, and Maria, who died an infant."

I have no recollection of the time when I made this memorandum, but I have no doubt of its accuracy.

Mrs. Eppes was never well after the birth of her last child. She lingered a while, but never recovered. My grandfather was in Washington, and my aunt passed the winter at Edgehill, where she was confined. I remember the tender and devoted care of my mother, how she watched over her sister, and with what anxious affection she anticipated her every want. I remember, at one time, that she left her chamber and her own infant, that she might sleep in my aunt's room, to assist in taking care of her and her child. I well recollect my poor aunt's pale, faded, and feeble look. My grandfather, during his Presidency, made two visits every year to Monticello—a short one in early spring, and a longer one the latter

part of the summer. He always stopped at Edgehill, where
my mother was then living, to take her and her whole family to Monticello with him. He came this year as usual, anxious about the health of his youngest daughter, whose situation, though such as to excite the apprehensions of her friends,
was not deemed one of immediate danger. She had been
delicate, and something of an invalid, if I remember right, for
some years. She was carried to Monticello in a litter borne
by men. The distance was perhaps four miles, and she bore
the removal well. After this, however, she continued, as before, steadily to decline. She was taken out when the weather permitted, and carried around the lawn in a carriage, I
think drawn by men, and I remember following the carriage
over the smooth green turf. How long she lived I do not
recollect, but it could have been but a short time.

One morning I heard that my aunt was dying. I crept
softly from my nursery to her chamber door, and, being
alarmed by her short, hard breathing, ran away again. I
have a distinct recollection of confusion and dismay in the
household. I did not see my mother. By-and-by one of
the female servants came running in where I was, with other
persons, to say that Mrs. Eppes was dead. The day passed I
do not know how. Late in the afternoon I was taken to the
death-chamber. The body was covered with a white cloth,
over which had been strewed a profusion of flowers. A day
or two after I followed the coffin to the burying-ground on
the mountain-side, and saw it consigned to the earth, where
it has lain undisturbed for more than fifty years.

My mother has told me that on the day of her sister's
death she left her father alone for some hours. He then
sent for her, and she found him with the Bible in his hands.
He who has been so often and so harshly accused of unbe-
lief—he, in his hour of intense affliction, sought and found
consolation in the Sacred Volume. The Comforter was
there for his true heart and devout spirit, even though his
faith might not be what the world calls orthodox.

There was something very touching in the sight of this
once beautiful and still lovely young woman, fading away
just as the spring was coming on with its buds and blossoms
—nature reviving as she was sinking, and closing her eyes on
all that she loved best in life. She perished, not in autumn

with the flowers, but as they were opening to the sun and air in all the freshness of spring. I think the weather was fine, for over my own recollections of these times there is a soft dreamy sort of haze, such as wraps the earth in warm dewy spring-time.

You know enough of my aunt's early history to be aware that she did not accompany her father, as my mother did, when he first went to France. She joined him, I think, only about two years before his return, and was placed in the same convent where my mother received her education. Here she went by the name of Mademoiselle *Polie.* As a child, she was called Polly by her friends. It was on her way to Paris that she staid a while in London with Mrs. Adams, and there is a pleasing mention of her in that lady's published letters.

I think the visit (not a very long one) made by my mother and aunt to their father in Washington must have been in the winter of 1802–'3. My aunt, I believe, was never there again; but after her death, about the winter of 1805–'6, my mother, with all her children, passed some time at the President's house. I remember that both my father and uncle Eppes were *then* in Congress, but can not say whether this was the case in 1802–'3.

My aunt, Mrs. Eppes, was singularly beautiful. She was high-principled, just, and generous. Her temper, naturally mild, became, I think, saddened by ill health in the latter part of her life. In that respect she differed from my mother, whose disposition seemed to have the sunshine of heaven in it. Nothing ever wearied my mother's patience, or exhausted, what was inexhaustible, her sweetness, her kindness, indulgence, and self-devotion. She was intellectually somewhat superior to her sister, who was sensible of the difference, though she was of too noble a nature for her feelings ever to assume an ignoble character. There was between the sisters the strongest and warmest attachment, the most perfect confidence and affection.

My aunt utterly undervalued and disregarded her own beauty, remarkable as it was. She was never fond of dress or ornament, and was always careless of admiration. She was even vexed by allusions to her beauty, saying that people only praised her for that because they could not praise her for better things. If my mother inadvertently exclaimed, half sportively, "Maria, if I only had your beauty," my aunt would resent it as far as she could resent any thing said or done by her sister.

It may be said that the extraordinary value she attached to talent was mainly founded in her idea that by the possession of it she would become a more suitable companion for her father. Both daughters considered his affection as the great good of their lives, and both loved him with all the devotion of their most loving hearts. My aunt sometimes mourned over the fear that her father *must* prefer her sister's society, and *could* not take the same pleasure in hers. This very humility in one so lovely was a charm the more in her character. She was greatly loved and esteemed by all her friends. She was on a footing of the most intimate friendship with my father's sister, Mrs. T. Eston Randolph, herself a most exemplary and admirable woman, whose daughter, long years after, married Francis, Mrs. Eppes's son.

I know not, my dear Mr. Randall, whether this letter will add any thing to the knowledge you already possess of this one of my grandfather's family. Should it not, you must take the will for the deed, and as I am somewhat wearied by the rapidity with which I have written, in order to avoid delay, I will bid you adieu, with my very best wishes for your entire success in your arduous undertaking.

Very truly yours

ELLEN W. COOLIDGE.

How heart-rending the death of this "ever dear daughter" was to Jefferson, may be judged from the following touching and beautiful letter, written by him two months after the sad event, in reply to one of condolence from his old and constant friend, Governor Page:

To Governor Page.

Your letter, my dear friend, of the 25th ultimo, is a new proof of the goodness of your heart, and the part you take in my loss marks an affectionate concern for the greatness of it. It is great indeed. Others may lose of their abundance, but I, of my want, have lost even the half of all I had.

My evening prospects now hang on the slender thread of a single life. Perhaps I may be destined to see even this last cord of parental affection broken! The hope with which I had looked forward to the moment when, resigning public cares to younger hands, I was to retire to that domestic comfort from which the last great step is to be taken, is fearfully blighted.

When you and I look back on the country over which we have passed, what a field of slaughter does it exhibit! Where are all the friends who entered it with us, under all the inspiring energies of health and hope? As if pursued by the havoc of war, they are strewed by the way, some earlier, some later, and scarce a few stragglers remain to count the numbers fallen, and to mark yet, by their own fall, the last footsteps of their party. Is it a desirable thing to bear up through the heat of action, to witness the death of all our companions, and merely be the last victim? I doubt it. We have, however, the traveller's consolation. Every step shortens the distance we have to go; the end of our journey is in sight—the bed wherein we are to rest, and to rise in the midst of the friends we have lost! "We sorrow not, then, as others who have no hope;" but look forward to the day which joins us to the great majority.

But whatever is to be our destiny, wisdom, as well as duty, dictates that we should acquiesce in the will of Him whose it is to give and take away, and be contented in the enjoyment of those who are still permitted to be with us. Of those connected by blood, the number does not depend on us. But friends we have if we have merited them. Those of our earliest years stand nearest in our affections. But in this, too, you and I have been unlucky. Of our college friends (and they are the dearest) how few have stood with us in the great political questions which have agitated our country: and these were of a nature to justify agitation. I did not believe the Lilliputian fetters of that day strong enough to have bound so many.

Will not Mrs. Page, yourself, and family, think it prudent to seek a healthier region for the months of August and September? And may we not flatter ourselves that you will cast your eye on Monticello? We have not many summers to live. While fortune places us, then, within striking distance, let us avail ourselves of it, to meet and talk over the tales of other times.

He also wrote to Judge Tyler:

I lament to learn that a like misfortune has enabled you to estimate the afflictions of a father on the loss of a beloved child. However terrible the possibility of such another accident, it is still a blessing for you of inestimable value that you would not even then descend childless to the grave. Three sons, and hopeful ones too, are a rich treasure. I rejoice when I hear of young men of virtue and talents, worthy to receive, and likely to preserve, the splendid inheritance of self-government which we have acquired and shaped for them.

Among the many letters of condolence which poured in upon Mr. Jefferson from all quarters on this sad occasion, was the following very characteristic one from Mrs. Adams. It shows in the writer a strange mixture of kind feeling, goodness of heart, and a proud, unforgiving spirit.

From Mrs. Adams.

Quincy, 20th May, 1804.

Sir—Had you been no other than the private inhabitant of Monticello, I should, ere this time, have addressed you with that sympathy which a recent event has awakened in my bosom; but reasons of various kinds withheld my pen, until the powerful feelings of my heart burst through the restraint, and called upon me to shed the tear of sorrow over the departed remains of your beloved and deserving daughter—an event which I most sincerely mourn. The attachment which I formed for her when you committed her to my care upon her arrival in a foreign land, under circumstances peculiarly interesting, has remained with me to this hour; and the account of her death, which I read in a late paper, recalled to my recollection the tender scene of her separation from me, when, with the strongest sensibility, she clung around my neck, and wet my bosom with her tears, saying, " Oh, now I have learned to love you, why will they take me from you ?"

It has been some time since I conceived that any event in this life could call forth feelings of mutual sympathy. But I know how closely entwined around a parent's are those cords which bind the parental to the filial bosom, and, when snapped asunder, how agonizing the pangs. I have tasted of the bitter cup, and bow with reverence and submission before the great Dispenser of it, without whose permission and overruling providence not a sparrow falls to the ground. That you may derive comfort and consolation, in this day of your sorrow and affliction, from that only source calculated to heal the broken heart, a firm belief in the being, perfections, and attributes of God, is the sincere and ardent wish of her who once took pleasure in subscribing herself your friend.

ABIGAIL ADAMS.*

To this letter Mr. Jefferson replied as follows:

To Mrs. Adams.

Washington, June 13th, 1804.

Dear Madam—The affectionate sentiments which you have had the goodness to express, in your letter of May the 20th, towards my dear departed daughter have awakened in me sensibilities natural to the occasion, and recalled your kindnesses to her, which I shall ever remember with gratitude and friendship. I can assure you with truth, they had made an indelible impression on her mind, and that to the last, on our meetings after long separations, whether I had heard lately of you, and how you did, were among the earliest of her inquiries. In giving you this assurance, I perform a sacred duty for her, and, at the same time, am thankful for the occasion furnished me of expressing my regret that circumstances should have arisen which have seemed to draw a line of separation between us. The friendship with which you honored me has ever been valued and fully reciprocated; and although events have been passing which might be trying to some minds, I never believed yours to be of that kind, nor felt that my own was. Neither my estimate of your character, nor the esteem founded in that, has ever been lessened for a single moment, although doubts whether

---

* The original of this letter is now in the possession of Jefferson's grandson, Colonel Jefferson Randolph.

U

it would be acceptable may have forbidden manifestations of it.

Mr. Adams's friendship and mine began at an earlier date. It accompanied us through long and important scenes. The different conclusions we had drawn from our political reading and reflections were not permitted to lessen personal esteem—each party being conscious they were the result of an honest conviction in the other. Like differences of opinion among our fellow-citizens attached them to one or the other of us, and produced a rivalship in their minds which did not exist in ours. We never stood in one another's way; but if either had been withdrawn at any time, his favorers would not have gone over to the other, but would have sought for some one of homogeneous opinions. This consideration was sufficient to keep down all jealousy between us, and to guard our friendship from any disturbance by sentiments of rivalship; and I can say with truth, that one act of Mr. Adams's life, and one only, ever gave me a moment's personal displeasure. I did consider his last appointments to office as personally unkind. They were from among my most ardent political enemies, from whom no faithful co-operation could ever be expected; and laid me under the embarrassment of acting through men whose views were to defeat mine, or to encounter the odium of putting others in their places. It seems but common justice to leave a successor free to act by instruments of his own choice. If my respect for him did not permit me to ascribe the whole blame to the influence of others, it left something for friendship to forgive; and after brooding over it for some little time, and not always resisting the expression of it, I forgave it cordially, and returned to the same state of esteem and respect for him which had so long subsisted.

Having come into life a little later than Mr. Adams, his career has preceded mine, as mine is followed by some other; and it will probably be closed at the same distance after him which time originally placed between us. I maintain for him, and shall carry into private life, an uniform and high measure of respect and good-will, and for yourself a sincere attachment.

I have thus, my dear madam, opened myself to you without reserve, which I have long wished an opportunity of doing; and without knowing how it will be received, I feel relief from being unbosomed. And I have now only to entreat your forgiveness for this transition from a subject of domestic affliction to one which seems of a different aspect. But though connected with political events, it has been viewed by me most strongly in its unfortunate bearings on my private friendships. The injury these have sustained has been a heavy price for what has never given me equal pleasure. That you may both be favored with health, tranquillity, and long life, is the prayer of one who tenders you the assurance of his highest consideration and esteem.

Several other letters were exchanged by Jefferson and Mrs. Adams, and explanations followed, which did not, however, result at the time in restoring friendly intercourse between them, that not being resumed until some years later.* Mrs. Adams, it seemed, was offended with him because, in making appointments to fill certain Federal offices in Boston, her son, who held one of these offices, was not reappointed. Jefferson did not know, when he made the appointments, that young Adams held the office, and gave Mrs. Adams an assurance to that effect in one of the letters alluded to above, but she seems not to have accepted the explanation.

The history of the midnight judges referred to in Jefferson's first letter to Mrs. Adams was briefly this: Just at the close of Adams's Administration a law was hurried through Congress by the Federalists, increasing the number of United States Courts throughout the States. At that time twelve o'clock on the night of the 3d of March was the magical hour when one Administration passed out and the other came in. The law was passed at such a late hour, that, though the appointments for the new judgeships created by it had been previously selected, yet the commissions had not been issued from the Department of State. Chief-justice Marshall, who was then acting as Secretary of State, was busily engaged filling out these commissions, that the offices might be filled with Federal appointments while the outgo-

---

* See pages 352, 353.

ing Administration was still in power. The whole proceeding was known to Jefferson. He considered the law unconstitutional, and acted in the premises with his usual boldness and decision. Having chosen Levi Lincoln as his Attorney General, he gave him his watch, and ordered him to go at midnight and take possession of the State Department, and not allow a single paper to be removed from it after that hour.

Mr. Lincoln accordingly entered Judge Marshall's office at the appointed time. "I have been ordered by Mr. Jefferson," he said to the Judge, "to take possession of this office and its papers." "Why, Mr. Jefferson has not yet qualified," exclaimed the astonished Chief-justice. "Mr. Jefferson considers himself in the light of an executor, bound to take charge of the papers of the Government until he is duly qualified," was the reply. "But it is not yet twelve o'clock," said Judge Marshall, taking out his watch. Mr. Lincoln pulled out his, and, showing it to him, said, " This is the President's watch, and rules the hour."

Judge Marshall could make no appeal from this, and was forced to retire, casting a farewell look upon the commissions lying on the table before him. In after years he used to laugh, and say he had been allowed to pick up nothing but his hat. He had, however, one or two of the commissions in his pocket, and the gentlemen who received them were called thereafter " John Adams's midnight judges."

In his message to Congress some months later, Jefferson demonstrated that, so far from requiring an increased number of courts, there was not work enough for those already existing.·

To John W. Eppes.

Monticello, August 7th, 1804.

Dear Sir—Your letters of July 16th and 29th both came to me on the 2d instant. I receive with great delight the information of the perfect health of our dear infants, and hope to see yourself, the family and them, as soon as circumstances admit. With respect to Melinda, I have too many already to leave here in idleness when I go away; and at Washington I prefer white servants, who, when they misbehave, can be exchanged. John knew he was not to expect her society but when he should be at Monticello, and then subject to the casualty of her being here or not. You mention a horse to be had—of a fine bay; and again, that he is of the color of your horse. I do not well recollect the shade of yours; but if you think this one would do with 'Castor or Fitzpartner, I would take him at the price you mention, but should be glad to have as much breadth for the payment as the seller could admit, and at any rate not less than ninety days. I know no finer horse than yours, but he is much too fiery to be trusted in a carriage—the only use I have for him while Arcturus remains. He is also too small. I write this letter in the hope you will be here before you can receive it, but on the possibility that the cause which detained you at the date of yours may continue. My affectionate salutations and esteem attend the family at Eppington and yourself.

TH. JEFFERSON.

P.S.—By your mentioning that Francis will be your constant companion, I am in hopes I shall have him here with you during the session of Congress.

CHAPTER XVII.

WEARY of office, and longing for the tranquillity of private life amidst the groves of his beautiful home at Monticello, it was the first wish of Jefferson's heart to retire at the close of his first Presidential term. His friends, however, urged his continuance in office for the next four years, and persisted in renominating him as the Republican candidate in the coming elections. There were other reasons which induced him to yield his consent besides the entreaties of his friends. We find these alluded to in the following extract from a letter written to Mazzei on the 18th of July, 1804:

I should have retired at the end of the first four years, but that the immense load of Tory calumnies which have been manufactured respecting me, and have filled the European market, have obliged me to appeal once more to my country for justification. I have no fear but that I shall receive honorable testimony by their verdict on these calumnies. At the end of the next four years I shall certainly retire. Age, inclination, and principle all dictate this. My health, which at one time threatened an unfavorable turn, is now firm.

During the summer of 1804 Jefferson made his usual visit to Monticello, where his quiet enjoyment of home-life was saddened by the remembrance of the painful scenes through which he had so lately passed there.

At the time of his second inauguration, on the 5th of March, 1805, Jefferson was in his sixty-second year. His inaugural address closed with the following eloquent words:

I fear not that any motives of interest may lead me astray; I am sensible of no passion which could seduce me knowingly from the path of justice; but the weakness of human nature, and the limits of my own understanding, will produce errors of judgment sometimes injurious to your interests. I shall need, therefore, all the indulgence I have heretofore experienced—the want of it will certainly not lessen with increasing years. I shall need, too, the favor of that Being in whose hands we are, who led our forefathers, as Israel of old, from their native land, and planted them in a country flowing with all the necessaries and comforts of life; who has covered our infancy with his providence, and our riper years with his wisdom and power; and to whose goodness I ask you to join with me in supplications that He will so enlighten the minds of your servants, guide their councils, and prosper their measures, that whatsoever they do shall result in your good, and shall secure to you the peace, friendship, and approbation of all nations.

The next two years of his life possess nothing worthy of special notice in this volume. The reader will find interesting the following extract from one of his letters of 1806:

To Mr. Harris.

Washington, April 18th, 1806.

Sir—It is now some time since I received from you, through the house of Smith & Buchanan, at Baltimore, a bust of the Emperor Alexander, for which I have to return you my thanks. These are the more cordial because of the value the bust derives from the great estimation in which its original is held by the world, and by none more than by myself. It will constitute one of the most valued ornaments of the retreat I am preparing for myself at my native home. Accept, at the same time, my acknowledgments for the elegant work of Atkinson and Walker on the customs of the

Russians. I had laid down as a law for my conduct while in office, and hitherto scrupulously observed, to accept of no present beyond a book, a pamphlet, or other curiosity of minor value; as well to avoid imputation on my motives of action, as to shut out a practice susceptible of such abuse. But my particular esteem for the character of the Emperor places his image, in my mind, above the scope of law. I receive it, therefore, and shall cherish it with affection. It nourishes the contemplation of all the good placed in his power, and of his disposition to do it.

A day later he wrote to the Emperor himself:

To the Emperor Alexander.

I owe an acknowledgment to your Imperial Majesty for the great satisfaction I have received from your letter of August the 20th, 1805, and embrace the opportunity it affords of giving expression to the sincere respect and veneration I entertain for your character. It will be among the latest and most soothing comforts of my life to have seen advanced to the government of so extensive a portion of the earth, at so early a period of his life, a sovereign whose ruling passion is the advancement of the happiness and prosperity of his people; and not of his own people only, but who can extend his eye and his good-will to a distant and infant nation, unoffending in its course, unambitious in its views.

I have lying before me a letter, written in French, and over a superb signature, from the Emperor Alexander to Mr. Jefferson. It is dated "*à St. Petersbourg, ce 7 Novembre,* 1804," and at the close has this graceful paragraph:

From the Emperor Alexander.

Truly grateful for the interest which you have proved to me that you take in the well-being and prosperity of Russia, I feel that I can not better express similar feelings towards the United States, than by hoping they may long preserve at the head of their administration a chief who is as virtuous as he is enlightened.

The bust of the Emperor was placed in the hall at Monticello, facing one of Napoleon, which stood on the opposite side of the door leading into the portico.

Writing to one of his French friends—M. le Comte Diodati —on January 13, 1807, Jefferson says:

To Comte Diodati.

At the end of my present term, of which two years are yet to come, I propose to retire from public life, and to close my days on my patrimony of Monticello, in the bosom of my family. I have hitherto enjoyed uniform health; but the weight of public business begins to be too heavy for me, and I long for the enjoyments of rural life—among my books, my farms, and my family. Having performed my *quadragena stipendia*, I am entitled to my discharge, and should be sorry, indeed, that others should be sooner sensible than myself when I ought to ask it. I have, therefore, requested my fellow-citizens to think of a successor for me, to whom I shall deliver the public concerns with greater joy than I received them. I have the consolation, too, of having added nothing to my private fortune during my public service, and of retiring with hands as clean as they are empty.

Wearied with the burden of public life, Jefferson had written his old friend, John Dickinson, two months earlier:

To John Dickinson.

I have tired you, my friend, with a long letter. But your tedium will end in a few lines more. Mine has yet two years to endure. I am tired of an office where I can do no more good than many others who would be glad to be employed in it. To myself, personally, it brings nothing but unceasing drudgery and daily loss of friends.

A letter written to Mr. Eppes in July, 1807, alludes to the death of little Maria, the youngest child left by his lost daughter. He writes:

To Mr. Eppes.

Yours of the 3d is received. At that time, I presume, you had not got mine of June 19th, asking the favor of you to procure me a horse. I have lost three since you left this place [Washington]; however, I can get along with the three I have remaining, so as to give time for looking up a fourth, suitable in as many points as can be obtained. My happiness at Monticello (if I am able to go there) will be lessened by not having Francis and yourself there; but the circumstance which prevents it is one of the most painful that ever happened to me in life. Thus comfort after comfort drops off from us, till nothing is left but what is proper food for the grave. I trust, however, we shall have yourself and Francis the ensuing winter, and the one following that, and we must let the after-time provide for itself. He will ever be to me one of the dearest objects of life.

The following letter from Lafayette to Jefferson explains itself:

From the Marquis Lafayette.

Auteuil, January 11th, 1808.

My dear friend—The constant mourning of your heart will be deepened by the grief I am doomed to impart to it. Who better than you can sympathize for the loss of a beloved wife? The angel who for thirty-four years has blessed my life, was to you an affectionate, grateful friend. Pity me, my dear Jefferson, and believe me, forever, with all my heart, yours,

LAFAYETTE.

M. and Madame de Telli, at whose house we have attended her last moments, are tolerably well. We now are, my children and myself, in the Tracy family, and shall return to La Grange as soon as we can.

We find in Jefferson's correspondence of this year a letter written to his friend Dr. Wistar, of Philadelphia, in which he bespeaks his kind offices for his young grandson, Thomas Jefferson Randolph, then in his fifteenth year, and whom Mr. Jefferson wished to send to Philadelphia, that he might there prosecute his studies in the sciences. The devotion of this grandson and grandfather for each other was constant and touching. When the former went to Philadelphia, he left Monticello with his grandfather, and went with him as far as Washington, where he spent some days. Nothing could have exceeded his grandfather's kindness and thoughtfulness for him on this occasion. He looked over, with him, his wardrobe, and examined the contents of his trunk with as much care as if he had been his mother, and then, taking out a pencil and paper, made a list of purchases to be made for him, saying, "You will need such and such things when you get to Philadelphia." Nor would he let another make the purchases, but, going out with his grandson, got for him himself what he thought was suitable for him, though kindly consulting his taste. I give this incident only as a proof of Jefferson's thoughtful devotion for his grandchildren and of the perfect confidence which existed between himself and them.

In a letter, full of good feeling and good advice, written to Mr. Monroe in February, 1808, he cautions him against the danger of politics raising a rivalship between Mr. Madison and himself, and then, alluding to his own personal feelings, closes thus affectionately:

To James Monroe.

My longings for retirement are so strong, that I with difficulty encounter the daily drudgeries of my duty. But my wish for retirement itself is not stronger than that of carrying into it the affections of all my friends. I have ever viewed Mr. Madison and yourself as two principal pillars of my happiness. Were either to be withdrawn, I should consider it as among the greatest calamities which could assail my future peace of mind. I have great confidence that the candor and high understanding of both will guard me against this misfortune, the bare possibility of which has so far weighed on my mind, that I could not be easy without unburdening it. Accept my respectful salutations for yourself and Mrs. Monroe, and be assured of my constant and sincere friendship.

The following letters to two of his grandchildren give a pleasant picture of his attachment to and intimate intercourse with them:

To Cornelia Randolph.*

Washington, April 3d, '08.

My dear Cornelia—I have owed you a letter two months, but have had nothing to write about, till last night I found in a newspaper the four lines which I now inclose you ; and as you are learning to write, they will be a good lesson to convince you of the importance of minding your stops in writing. I allow you a day to find out yourself how to read these lines, so as to make them true. If you can not do it in that time, you may call in assistance. At the same time, I will give you four other lines, which I learnt when I was but a little older than you, and I still remember.

> "I've seen the sea all in a blaze of fire
> I've seen a house high as the moon and higher
> I've seen the sun at twelve o'clock at night
> I've seen the man who saw this wondrous sight."

All this is true, whatever you may think of it at first reading. I mentioned in my letter of last week to Ellen that I was under an attack of periodical headache. This is the 10th day. It has been very moderate, and yesterday did not last more than three hours. Tell your mamma that I fear I shall not get away as soon as I expected. Congress has spent the last five days without employing a single hour in the business necessary to be finished. Kiss her for me, and all the sisterhood.† To Jefferson I give my hand, to your papa my affectionate salutations. You have always my love.

TH. JEFFERSON.

P.S.—*April 5.*—I have kept my letter open till to-day, and am able to say now that my headache for the last two days has been scarcely sensible.

To Thomas Jefferson Randolph.

Washington, Oct. 24th, 1808.

Dear Jefferson—I inclose you a letter from Ellen, which, I presume, will inform you that all are well at Edgehill. I

---

* She was just ten years old.

† Mrs. Randolph's five daughters — Anne, Ellen, Cornelia, Virginia, and Mary. She had at this time only two sons—Jefferson, her second child, and James Madison.

received yours without date of either time or place, but written, I presume, on your arrival at Philadelphia. As the commencement of your lectures is now approaching, and you will hear two lectures a day, I would recommend to you to set out from the beginning with the rule to commit to writing every evening the substance of the lectures of the day. It will be attended with many advantages. It will oblige you to attend closely to what is delivered to recall it to your memory, to understand, and to digest it in the evening; it will fix it in your memory, and enable you to refresh it at any future time. It will be much better to you than even a better digest by another hand, because it will better recall to your mind the ideas which you originally entertained and meant to abridge. Then, if once a week you will, in a letter to me, state a synopsis or summary view of the heads of the lectures of the preceding week, it will give me great satisfaction to attend to your progress, and it will further aid you by obliging you still more to generalize and to see analytically the fields of science over which you are travelling. I wish to hear of the commissions I gave you for Rigden, Voight, and Ronaldson, of the delivery of the letters I gave you to my friends there, and how you like your situation. This will give you matter for a long letter, which will give you as useful an exercise in writing as a pleasing one to me in reading.

God bless you, and prosper your pursuits.

TH. JEFFERSON.

To Thomas Jefferson Randolph.

Washington, November 24th, 1808.

My dear Jefferson—...... I have mentioned good-humor as one of the preservatives of our peace and tranquillity. It is among the most effectual, and its effect is so well imitated, and aided, artificially, by politeness, that this also becomes an acquisition of first-rate value. In truth, politeness is artificial good-humor; it covers the natural want of it, and ends by rendering habitual a substitute nearly equivalent to the real virtue. It is the practice of sacrificing to those whom we meet in society all the little conveniences and preferences which will gratify them, and deprive us of nothing worth a moment's consideration; it is the giving a pleasing and flattering turn to our expressions, which will conciliate others, and make them pleased with us as well as themselves. How cheap a price for the good-will of another! When this is in return for a rude thing said by another, it brings him to his senses, it mortifies and corrects him in the most salutary way, and places him at the feet of your good-nature in the eyes of the company. But in stating prudential rules for our government in society, I must not omit the important one of never entering into dispute or argument with another. I never yet saw an instance of one of two disputants convincing the other by argument. I have seen many of their getting warm, becoming rude, and shooting one another. Conviction is the effect of our own dispassionate reasoning, either in solitude, or weighing within ourselves, dispassionately, what we hear from others, standing uncommitted in argument ourselves.

It was one of the rules which, above all others, made Doctor Franklin the most amiable of men in society, never to contradict any body. If he was urged to announce an opinion, he did it rather by asking questions, as if for information, or by suggesting doubts. When I hear another express an opinion which is not mine, I say to myself, He has a right to his opinion, as I to mine; why should I question it? His error does me no injury, and shall I become a Don Quixote, to bring all men by force of argument to one opinion? If a fact be misstated, it is probable he is gratified by a belief of it, and I have no right to deprive him of the gratification. If he wants information, he will ask it, and then I will give it in measured terms; but if he still believes his own story, and shows a desire to dispute the fact with me, I hear him and say nothing. It is his affair, not mine, if he prefers error.

There are two classes of disputants most frequently to be met with among us. The first is of young students, just entered the threshold of science, with a first view of its outlines, not yet filled up with the details and modifications which a further progress would bring to their knowledge. The other consists of the ill-tempered and rude men in society who have taken up a passion for politics. (Good-humor and politeness never introduce into mixed society a question on which they foresee there will be a difference of opinion.)

From both of these classes of disputants, my dear Jefferson, keep aloof, as you would from the infected subjects of yellow fever or pestilence. Consider yourself, when with them, as among the patients of Bedlam, needing medical more than moral counsel. Be a listener only, keep within yourself, and endeavor to establish with yourself the habit of silence, especially in politics. In the fevered state of our country, no good can ever result from any attempt to set one of these fiery zealots to rights, either in fact or principle. They are determined as to the facts they will believe, and the opinions on which they will act. Get by them, therefore, as you would by an angry bull; it is not for a man of sense to dispute the road with such an animal. You will be more exposed than others to have these animals shaking their horns at you because of the relation in which you stand with me......

My character is not within their power. It is in the hands of my fellow-citizens at large, and will be consigned to honor or infamy by the verdict of the republican mass of our country, according to what themselves will have seen, not what their enemies and mine shall have said. Never, therefore, consider these puppies in politics as requiring any notice from you, and always show that you are not afraid to leave my character to the umpirage of public opinion. Look steadily to the pursuits which have carried you to Philadelphia, be very select in the society you attach yourself to; avoid taverns, drinkers, smokers, idlers, and dissipated persons generally; for it is with such that broils and contentions arise; and you will find your path more easy and tranquil. The limits of my paper warn me that it is time for me to close, with my affectionate adieu.

TH. JEFFERSON.

P.S.—Present me affectionately to Mr. Ogilvie; and in doing the same to Mr. Peale, tell him I am writing with his polygraph, and shall send him mine the first moment I have leisure enough to pack it.　　　　　　　　　　T. J.

To Cornelia Randolph.

Washington, Dec. 26th, '08.

I congratulate you, my dear Cornelia, on having acquired the valuable art of writing. How delightful to be enabled by it to converse with an absent friend as if present! To this we are indebted for all our reading; because it must be written before we can read it. To this we are indebted for the Iliad, the Æneid, the Columbiad, Henriad, Dunciad, and now, for the most glorious poem of all, the Terrapiniad, which I now inclose you. This sublime poem consigns to everlasting fame the greatest achievement in war ever known to ancient or modern times: in the battle of David and Goliath, the disparity between the combatants was nothing in comparison to our case. I rejoice that you have learnt to write, for another reason; for as that is done with a goose-quill, you now know the value of a goose, and of course you will assist Ellen in taking care of the half-dozen very fine gray geese which I shall send by Davy. But as to this, I must refer to your mamma to decide whether they will be safest at Edgehill or at Monticello till I return home, and to give orders accordingly. I received letters a few days ago from Mr. Bankhead and Anne. They are well. I had expected a visit from Jefferson at Christmas, had there been a sufficient intermission in his lectures; but I suppose there was not, as he is not come. Remember me affectionately to your papa and mamma, and kiss Ellen and all the children for me.

TH. JEFFERSON.

P.S.—Since writing the above, I have a letter from Mr. Peale informing me that Jefferson is well, and saying the best things of him.

The Mr. Bankhead mentioned in the preceding letter was a gentleman who had married Mrs. Randolph's eldest daughter, Anne.

The following letter I give here, though of a later date by nearly two years than others that follow:

To Cornelia Randolph.

Monticello, June 3d, '11.

My dear Cornelia—I have lately received a copy of Miss Edgeworth's Moral Tales, which, seeming better suited to your years than mine, I inclose you the first volume. The other two shall follow as soon as your mamma has read them. They are to make a part of your library. I have not looked into them, preferring to receive their character from you, after you shall have read them. Your family of silk-worms is reduced to a single individual. That is now spinning his broach. To encourage Virginia and Mary to take care of it, I tell them that, as soon as they can get wedding-gowns from this spinner, they shall be married. I propose the same to you; that, in order to hasten its work, you may hasten home; for we all wish much to see you, and to express in person, rather than by letter, the assurance of our affectionate love.

TH. JEFFERSON.

P.S.—The girls desire me to add a postscript to inform you that Mrs. Higginbotham has just given them new dolls.

The precepts inculcating good temper, good humor and amiability, which we have found Jefferson giving to his grandson in the foregoing letters were faithfully carried into practice by him. There never lived a more amiable being than himself; yet, like all men of powerful minds and strong wills, he was not incapable of being aroused in anger on occasions of strong provocation. His biographer mentions two instances of this kind. On one occasion it was with his favorite coachman, Jupiter. A boy had been ordered to take one of the carriage-horses to go on an errand. Jupiter refused to allow his horses to be used for any such purpose. The boy returned to his master with a message to that effect. Mr. Jefferson, thinking it a joke of Jupiter's played off on the boy, sent him back with a repetition of the order. He, however, returned in a short time, bearing the same refusal from the coachman. "Tell Jupiter to come to me at once," said Mr. Jefferson, in an excited tone. Jupiter came, and received the order and a rebuke from his master in tones and with a look which neither he nor the terrified bystanders ever forgot.

On another occasion he was crossing a river in a ferry-boat, accompanied by his daughter Martha. The two ferry-men were engaged in high quarrel when Mr. Jefferson and his daughter came up. They suppressed their anger for a

X

time and took in the passengers, but in the middle of the
stream it again broke forth with renewed force, and with
every prospect of their resorting to blows.   Mr. Jefferson
remonstrated with them; they did not heed him, and the
next moment, with his eyes flashing, he had snatched up an
oar, and, in a voice which rung out above the angry tones of
the men, flourished it over their heads, and cried out "Row
for your lives, or I will knock you both overboard!"   And
they did row for their lives; nor, I imagine, did they soon
forget the fiery looks and excited appearance of that tall
weird-like-looking figure brandishing the heavy oar over
their offending heads.

The following extract is taken from a letter written towards the close of the year 1808 to Doctor Logan: "As the
moment of my retirement approaches, I become more anxious for its arrival, and to begin at length to pass what yet
remains to me of life and health in the bosom of my family
and neighbors, and in communication with my friends, undisturbed by political concerns or passions."

Having heard that the good people of Albemarle wished
to meet him on the road, and give him a public reception on
his return home, with his usual dislike of being lionized, he
hastened, in a letter to his son-in-law, Mr. Randolph, to put
them off, with many thanks, by saying " the commencement
and termination " of his journey would be too uncertain for
him to fix upon a day that he might be expected.   This letter was written on Feb. 28th, 1809.   I give the following
extract:

But it is a sufficient happiness to me to know that my
fellow-citizens of the country generally entertain for me the
kind sentiments which have prompted this proposition, without giving to so many the trouble of leaving their homes to
meet a single individual.   I shall have opportunities of taking them individually by the hand at our court-house and
other public places, and of exchanging assurances of mutual
esteem.   Certainly it is the greatest consolation to me to
know that, in returning to the bosom of my native country,

I shall be again in the midst of their kind affections; and I can say with truth that my return to them will make me happier than I have been since I left them.

Two days before his release from harness he wrote to his friend Dupont de Nemours:

To Dupont de Nemours.

Within a few days I retire to my family, my books, and farms; and having gained the harbor myself, I shall look on my friends still buffeting the storm with anxiety indeed, but not with envy. Never did a prisoner, released from his chains, feel such relief as I shall on shaking off the shackles of power. Nature intended me for the tranquil pursuits of science, by rendering them my supreme delight. But the enormities of the times in which I have lived have forced me to take a part in resisting them, and to commit myself on the boisterous ocean of political passions. I thank God for the opportunity of retiring from them without censure, and carrying with me the most consoling proofs of public approbation. I leave every thing in the hands of men so able to take care of them, that, if we are destined to meet misfortunes, it will be because no human wisdom could avert them. Should you return to the United States, perhaps your curiosity may lead you to visit the hermit of Monticello. He will receive you with affection and delight; hailing you in the mean time with his affectionate salutations and assurances of constant esteem and respect.

On the day of the inauguration of his successor, Jefferson rode on horseback to the Capitol, being accompanied only by his grandson, Jefferson Randolph—then a lad in his seventeenth year. He had heard that a body of cavalry and infantry were preparing to escort him to the Capitol, and, still anxious to avoid all kinds of display, hurried off with his grandson. As they rode along Pennsylvania Avenue, Mr. Jefferson caught a glimpse of the head of the column coming down one of the cross-streets. He touched his hat to the troops, and, spurring up his horse, trotted past them. He again "hitched his horse to the palisades" around the

Capitol, and, entering the building, there witnessed the transfer of the administration of the Government from his own hands into those of the man who, above all others, was the man of his choice for that office—his long-tried and trusted friend, James Madison. Thus closed forever his public career.

The perfect harmony between himself and his cabinet is alluded to in a letter written nearly two years after his retirement from office. He writes:

The third Administration, which was of eight years, presented an example of harmony in a cabinet of six persons, to which perhaps history has furnished no parallel. There never arose, during the whole time, an instance of an unpleasant thought or word between the members. We sometimes met under differences of opinion, but scarcely ever failed, by conversing and reasoning, so to modify each other's ideas as to produce an unanimous result.

A few days before leaving Washington, he wrote to Baron Humboldt:

To Baron Humboldt.

You mention that you had before written other letters to me. Be assured I have never received a single one, or I should not have failed to make my acknowledgments of it. Indeed I have not waited for that, but for the certain information, which I had not, of the place where you might be. Your letter of May 30th first gave me that information. You have wisely located yourself in the focus of the science of Europe. I am held by the cords of love to my family and country, or I should certainly join you. Within a few days I shall now bury myself within the groves of Monticello, and become a mere spectator of the passing events. Of politics I will say nothing, because I would not implicate you by addressing to you the republican ideas of America, deemed horrible heresies by the royalism of Europe.

At the close of a letter written on the 8th of March to Mr. Short, he says: "I write this in the midst of packing and preparing for my departure, of visits of leave, and interruptions of every kind."

In February the Legislature of Virginia had passed an address of farewell to him as a public man. This address, penned by William Wirt, closes thus handsomely:

In the principles on which you have administered the Government, we see only the continuation and maturity of the same virtues and abilities which drew upon you in your youth the resentment of Dunmore. From the first brilliant and happy moment of your resistance to foreign tyranny until the present day, we mark with pleasure and with gratitude the same uniform and consistent character—the same warm and devoted attachment to liberty and the Republic— the same Roman love of your country, her rights, her peace, her honor, her prosperity. How blessed will be the retirement into which you are about to go! How deservedly blessed will it be! For you carry with you the richest of all rewards, the recollection of a life well spent in the service of your country, and proofs the most decisive of the love, the gratitude, the veneration of your countrymen. That your retirement may be as happy as your life has been virtuous and useful; that our youth may see in the blissful close of your days an additional inducement to form themselves on your model, is the devout and earnest prayer of your fellow-citizens who compose the General Assembly of Virginia.

In his reply to this address, Jefferson closes as follows:

In the desire of peace, but in full confidence of safety from our unity, our position, and our resources, I shall retire into the bosom of my native State, endeared to me by every tie which can attach the human heart. The assurances of your approbation, and that my conduct has given satisfaction to my fellow-citizens generally, will be an important ingredient in my future happiness; and that the Supreme Ruler of the universe may have our country under his special care, will be among the latest of my prayers.

The following reply to an address of welcome from the

citizens of Albemarle is one of the most beautiful, graceful, and touching productions of his pen:

To the Inhabitants of Albemarle County, in Virginia.

April 3d, 1809.

Returning to the scenes of my birth and early life, to the society of those with whom I was raised, and who have been ever dear to me, I receive, fellow-citizens and neighbors, with inexpressible pleasure, the cordial welcome you are so good as to give me.   Long absent on duties which the history of a wonderful era made incumbent on those called to them, the pomp, the turmoil, the bustle, and splendor of office have drawn but deeper sighs for the tranquil and irresponsible oc- cupations of private life, for the enjoyment of an affectionate intercourse with you, my neighbors and friends, and the en- dearments of family love, which nature has given us all, as the sweetener of every hour.   For these I gladly lay down the distressing burden of power, and seek, with my fellow- citizens, répose and safety under the watchful cares, and labors, and perplexities of younger and abler minds.   The anxieties you express to administer to my happiness, do, of themselves, confer that happiness; and the measure will be complete, if my endeavors to fulfill my duties in the several public stations to which I have been called have obtained for me the approbation of my country.   The part which I have acted on the theatre of public life has been before them, and to their sentence I submit it; but the testimony of my native county, of the individuals who have known me in private life, to my conduct in its various duties and rela- tions, is the more grateful, as proceeding from eye-witnesses and observers, from triers of the vicinage.   Of you, then, my neighbors, I may ask, in the face of the world, " Whose ox have I taken, or whom have I defrauded ?   Whom have I oppressed, or of whose hand have I received a bribe to blind mine eyes therewith ?"   On your verdict I rest with conscious security.   Your wishes for my happiness are received with just sensibility, and I offer sincere prayers for your own welfare and prosperity.

Jefferson arrived at Monticello on the 15th of March, and two days later wrote to Madison as follows:

"I had a very fatiguing journey, having found the roads excessively bad, although I have seen them worse. The last three days I found it better to be on horseback, and travelled eight hours through as disagreeable a snow-storm as I was ever in. Feeling no inconvenience from the expedition but fatigue, I have more confidence in my *vis vitæ* than I had before entertained."

He was at this time in his sixty-sixth year.

The following anecdote of Jefferson—which I have on the best authority—is too characteristic of his feeling for the suffering of another, his bold and rash spirit of reform, and the bitter feelings towards him of his political adversaries, to be omitted.

In going from Washington to Monticello, Jefferson generally left the city in the afternoon, and spent the first night of his journey with his friend Mr. William Fitzhugh, of Ravensworth, who lived nine or ten miles from Washington. It so happened that there lived near Ravensworth a Doctor Stuart, of Chantilly, who was a bitter Federalist, and consequently a violent hater of Jefferson, in whom he could not believe there was any good whatever. He was intimate, however, with Mr. Fitzhugh, and, being a great politician, generally found his way over to Ravensworth the morning after Jefferson's visit, to inquire what news he had brought from the capital.

On the occasion of one of these visits, while Mr. Fitzhugh and his distinguished guest were strolling round the beautiful lawn at Ravensworth enjoying the fresh morning air, a servant ran up to tell them that a negro man had cut himself severely with an axe. Mr. Fitzhugh immediately ordered the servant to go for a physician. Jefferson suggested that the poor negro might bleed to death before the doctor could arrive, and, saying that he himself had some little skill and experience in surgery, proposed that they should go and see what could be done for the poor fellow. Mr. Fitzhugh willingly acquiesced, and, on their reaching the patient, they found he had a severe cut in the calf of his leg. Jefferson

soon procured a needle and silk, and in a little while had
sewed up the wound and carefully bandaged the leg.

As they walked back from the negro's cabin, Jefferson remarked to his friend that, though the ways of Divine Providence were all wise and beneficent, yet it had always struck
him as being strange that the thick, fleshy coverings and
defenses of the bones in the limbs of the human frame were
placed in their rear, when the danger of their fracture generally came from the front. The remark struck Fitzhugh
as being an original and philosophical one, and served to
increase his favorable impressions of his friend's sagacity.

Jefferson had not long departed and resumed his journey,
before Dr. Stuart arrived, and greeted Mr. Fitzhugh with the
question of, "What news did your friend give you, and what
new heresy did the fiend incarnate attempt to instill into
your mind?" "Ah! Stuart," Mr. Fitzhugh began, "you do
Jefferson injustice; he is a great man, a very great man;"
and then went on to tell of the accident which had befallen
the negro, Jefferson's skill in dressing the wound, and his remark afterwards, which had made such an impression upon
him.

"Well," cried Dr. Stuart, raising his hands with horror,
"what is the world coming to! Here this fellow, Jefferson,
after turning upside down every thing on the earth, is now
quarrelling with God Almighty himself!"

CHAPTER XVIII.

His final Return home.—Wreck of his Fortunes.—Letter to Mr. Eppes.—To his Grand-daughter, Mrs. Bankhead.—To Kosciusko.—Description of the Interior of the House at Monticello.—Of the View from Monticello.—Jefferson's Grandson's Description of his Manners and Appearance.—Anecdotes.—His Habits.—Letter to Governor Langdon.—To Governor Tyler. —Life at Monticello, and Sketch of Jefferson by a Grand-daughter.— Reminiscences of him by another Grand-daughter.

FULL of years and full of honors, we behold, then, the veteran statesman attaining at last the goal of his wishes. Joyfully received into the arms of his family, Jefferson returned home, fondly hoping to pass in tranquillity the evening of an eventful and honorable life surrounded by those he loved best, and from whom he was never again to be parted except by death. His whole demeanor betokened the feelings of one who had been relieved of a heavy and wearisome burden. His family noticed the elasticity of his step while engaged in his private apartments arranging his books and papers, and not unfrequently heard him humming a favorite air, or singing snatches of old songs which had been almost forgotten since the days of his youth. But, alas! who can control his destiny? Who can foresee the suffering to be endured? It required but a brief sojourn at home, and a thorough investigation of his affairs, for Jefferson to see that his long-continued absence had told fearfully on the value of his farms; that his long enlistment in the service of his country had been his pecuniary ruin. The state of his feelings on this subject is painfully shown in the following extract from a letter written by him to Kosciusko:

To Thaddeus Kosciusko.

Instead of the unalloyed happiness of retiring unembarrassed and independent to the enjoyment of my estate, which is ample for my limited views, I have to pass such a length of time in a thraldom of mind never before known to me. Except for this, my happiness would have been perfect. That yours may never know disturbance, and that you may enjoy as many years of life, health, and ease as yourself shall wish, is the sincere prayer of your constant and affectionate friend.

Towards the close of the year 1809 we find him writing to his son-in-law, Mr. Eppes, then in Washington, as follows:

To John W. Eppes.

I should sooner have informed you of Francis's safe arrival here, but that the trip you meditated to North Carolina rendered it entirely uncertain where a letter would find you. Nor had I any expectation you could have been at the first meeting of Congress, till I saw your name in the papers brought by our last post. Disappointed in sending this by the return of the post, I avail myself of General Clarke's journey to Washington for its conveyance. Francis has enjoyed perfect and constant health, and is as happy as the day is long. He has had little success as yet with either his traps or bow and arrows. He is now engaged in a literary contest with his cousin, Virginia, both having begun to write together. As soon as he gets to *z* (being now only at *h*) he promises you a letter.

The following to his oldest grandchild shows how completely Jefferson had thrown off the cares and thoughts of public life and plunged into the sweets and little enjoyments of a quiet country life.

To Mrs. Anne C. Bankhead.

Monticello, Dec. 29th, 1809.

My dear Anne—Your mamma has given me a letter to inclose to you, but whether it contains any thing contraband I know not. Of that the responsibility must be on her; I therefore inclose it. I suppose she gives you all the small news of the place—such as the race in writing between Virginia and Francis, that the wild geese are well after a flight of a mile and a half into the river, that the plants in the green-house prosper, etc., etc. *A propos* of plants, make a thousand acknowledgments to Mrs. Bankhead for the favor proposed of the Cape jessamine. It will be cherished with all the possible attentions; and in return proffer her calycanthuses, pecans, silk-trees, Canada martagons, or any thing else we have. Mr. Bankhead, I suppose, is seeking a merry Christmas in all the wit and merriments of Coke upon Littleton. God send him a good deliverance! Such is the usual prayer for those standing at the bar. Deliver to Mary my kisses, and tell her I have a present from one of her acquaintances, Miss Thomas, for her—the minutest gourd ever seen, of which I send her a draught in the margin. What is to become of our flowers? I left them so entirely to yourself, that I never knew any thing about them, what they are, where they grow, what is to be done for them. You must really make out a book of instructions for Ellen, who has fewer cares in her head than I have. Every thing shall be furnished on my part at her call. Present my friendly respects to Dr. and Mrs. Bankhead. My affectionate attachment to Mr. Bankhead and yourself, not forgetting Mary.

TH. JEFFERSON.

We find in a letter written by Jefferson to Kosciusko (Feb. 26th, 1810) an interesting account of his habits of daily life. He writes:

To Thaddeus Kosciusko.

My mornings are devoted to correspondence. From breakfast to dinner I am in my shops, my garden, or on horseback among my farms; from dinner to dark, I give to society and recreation with my neighbors and friends; and from candle-light to early bed-time I read. My health is perfect, and my strength considerably reinforced by the activity of the course I pursue; perhaps it is as great as usually falls to the lot of near sixty-seven years of age. I talk of ploughs and harrows, of seeding and harvesting with my neighbors, and of politics too, if they choose, with as little reserve as the rest of my fellow-citizens, and feel, at length, the blessing of being free to say and do what I please without being responsible for it to any mortal. A part of my occupation, and by no means the least pleasing, is the direction of the studies of such young men as ask it. They place themselves in the neighboring village, and have the use of my library and counsel, and make a part of my society. In advising the course of their reading, I endeavor to keep their attention fixed on the main objects of all science, the freedom and happiness of man. So that, coming to bear a share in the councils and government of their country, they will keep ever in view the sole objects of all legitimate government.

I now give a description of the interior of the mansion at Monticello, which was prepared for me by a member of Mr. Jefferson's family, who lived there for many years:

The mansion, externally, is of the Doric order of Grecian architecture, with its heavy cornice and massive balustrades, its public rooms finished in the Ionic. The front hall of entrance recedes six feet within the front wall of the building, covered by a portico the width of the recess, projecting twenty-five feet, and the height of the house, with stone pillars and steps. The hall is also the height of the house. From about midway of this room, passages lead off to either extremity of the building. The rooms at the extremity of these passages terminate in octagonal projections, leaving a recess of three equal sides, into which the passages enter; piazzas the width of this recess, projecting six feet beyond, their roofs the height of the house, and resting on brick arches, cover the recesses. The northern one connects the house with the public terrace, while the southern is sashed in for a green-house. To the east of these passages, on each side of the hall, are lodging-rooms. This front is one-and-a-half stories. The west front the rooms occupy the whole height, making the house one story, except the parlor or central room, which is surmounted by an octagonal story, with a dome or spherical roof. This was designed for a billiard-room; but, before completion, a law was passed prohibiting public and private billiard-tables in the State. It was to have been approached by stairways connected with a gallery at the inner extremity of the hall, which itself forms the communication between the lodging-rooms on either side above. The use designed for the room being prohibited, these stairways were never erected, leaving in this respect a great deficiency in the house.

MONTICELLO:—PLAN OF THE FIRST FLOOR.

1. Mr. Madison's room.
2. Abbé Correa's room.
3. Turning Buffet.
4. Niche in tea-room, intended for a statue.
5. Jefferson's chair and candle-stand.
6. Mrs. Randolph's harpsichord.
7. Globes.
8. Work-bench.
9. Couch on which Jefferson reclined while studying.
10. Jefferson's dressing-table and mirror.
11. A convenient contrivance on which to hang clothes.
12. Jefferson's chair, with a small book-case near it.
13. Great clock over the hall-door.

14. Reclining statue of Ariadne.
15. Gallery connecting the upper stories of the house.

PORTRAITS.

4. Americus Vespucius.
b. Columbus.
c. Locke.
d. Bacon.
e. Washington.
f. Adams.
g. Franklin.
h. Madison.
16. Bust of Napoleon.
17. Ceracchi's Bust of Jefferson.
18. Bust of Hamilton.
19. Bust of Voltaire.
20. Bust of Turgot.
21. Bust of Alexander, Emperor of Russia.

The parlor projects twenty feet beyond the body of the house, covered by a portico one story, and surmounted by the billiard-room. The original plan of the projection was square; but when the cellar was built up to the floor above, the room was projected beyond the square by three sides of an octagon, leaving a place beyond the cellar-wall not excavated, and it was in this space that the faithful Cæsar and Martin concealed their master's plate when the British visited Monticello.* The floor of this room is in squares, the squares being ten inches, of the wild cherry, very hard, susceptible of a high polish, and the color of mahogany. The border of each square, four inches wide, is of beech, light-colored, hard, and bearing a high polish. Its original cost was two hundred dollars. After nearly seventy years of use and abuse, a half-hour's dusting and brushing will make it compare favorably with the handsomest tessellated floor.

From the same pen are the following graphic descriptions of the views seen from Monticello:

Monticello is five hundred and eighty feet high. It slopes eastward one-and-a-half miles by a gentle declivity to the Rivanna River. Half a mile beyond is Shadwell, the birthplace of Jefferson, a beautiful spot overlooking the river. The northeastern side of the mountain and slope is precipitous, having dashed aside the countless floods of the Rivanna through all the tide of time.

On the southwest, it is separated from the next mountain of the range, rising three hundred feet above it, by a road-pass two hundred and twenty feet below. This obstructs the view to the southwest. From the southwest to the northeast is a horizon unbroken, save by one solitary, pyramid-shaped mountain, its peak under the true meridian, and distant by air-line forty-seven miles. Northeast the range pointing to the west terminates two miles off, its lateral spurs descending by gentle slopes to the Rivanna at your feet, covered with farms and green wheat-fields. This view of farms extends northeast and east six or seven miles. You trace the Rivanna by its cultivated valley as it passes east, apparently through an unbroken forest; an inclined plane

---

* See page 56.

descends from your feet to the ocean two hundred miles distant. All the western and northwestern slopes being poor, and the eastern and southeastern fertile, as the former are presented to the spectator, and are for the most part in wood, it presents the appearance of unbroken forest, bounded by an ocean-like horizon.

Turn now and look from the north to the west. You stand at the apex of a triangle, the water-shed of the Rivanna, the opposite side, at the base of the Blue Ridge, forty miles in length; its perpendicular twenty, descending five hundred feet to the base of your position, where the Rivanna concentrates its muddy waters over an artificial cascade, marked by its white line of foam.

West and southwest, the space between the Southwest Mountains and the Blue Ridge is filled by irregular mountains, the nearer known as the Ragged Mountains. At the northeast base of these, distant two and three miles, are Charlottesville and the University of Virginia, forming nuclei connected by a scattered village. From west to northeast no mountain interposes between your position and the base of the Blue Ridge, which sinks below the horizon eighty or one hundred miles distant. Two mountains only are seen northeast—one ten, the other forty miles off. The country, ascending from your position, and presenting to you its fertile slopes, gives the view of one highly cultivated. The railroad train is traced ten miles. This is the view so much admired.

The top of the mountain has been levelled by art. This space is six hundred by two hundred feet, circular at each end. The mountain slopes gently on every side from this lawn; one hundred feet from the eastern end stands the mansion. Its projecting porticoes, east and west, with the width of the house, occupy one hundred feet each way. It approaches on either hand within fifty feet of the brow of the mountain, with which it is connected by covered ways ten feet wide, whose floors are level with the cellars, and whose flat roofs, forming promenades, are nearly level with the first floor of the dwelling. These, turning at right angles at the brow, and widening to twenty feet, extend one hundred feet, and terminate in one-story pavilions twenty feet square, the space beneath these terraces forming basement offices. From this northern terrace the view is sublime; and here Jefferson and his company were accustomed to sit, bare-headed, in the summer until bed-time, having neither dew nor insects to annoy them. Here, perhaps, has been assembled more love of liberty, virtue, wisdom, and learning than on any other private spot in America.

Jefferson's grandson, Colonel Jefferson Randolph, writes of his appearance and manners thus:

His manners were of that polished school of the Colonial Government, so remarkable in its day—under no circumstances violating any of those minor conventional observances which constitute the well-bred gentleman, courteous and considerate to all persons. On riding out with him when a lad, we met a negro who bowed to us; he returned his bow; I did not. Turning to me, he asked,

"Do you permit a negro to be more of a gentleman than yourself?"

Mr. Jefferson's hair, when young, was of a reddish cast; sandy as he advanced in years; his eye, hazel. Dying in his 84th year, he had not lost a tooth, nor had one defective; his skin thin, peeling from his face on exposure to the sun, and giving it a tettered appearance; the superficial veins so weak, as upon the slightest blow to cause extensive suffusions of blood—in early life, upon standing to write for any length of time, bursting beneath the skin; it, however, gave him no inconvenience. His countenance was mild and benignant, and attractive to strangers.

While President, returning on horseback from Charlottesville with company whom he had invited to dinner, and who were, all but one or two, riding ahead of him, on reaching a stream over which there was no bridge, a man asked him to take him up behind him and carry him over. The gentlemen in the rear coming up just as Mr. Jefferson had put him down and ridden on, asked the man how it happened that he had permitted the others to pass without asking them? He replied,

"From their looks, I did not like to ask them; the old gentleman looked as if he would do it, and I asked him."

He was very much surprised to hear that he had ridden behind the President of the United States.

Y

Mr. Jefferson's stature was commanding—six feet two-and-a-half inches in height, well formed, indicating strength, activity, and robust health; his carriage erect; step firm and elastic, which he preserved to his death; his temper, naturally strong, under perfect control; his courage cool and impassive. No one ever knew him exhibit trepidation. His moral courage of the highest order—his will firm and inflexible—it was remarked of him that he never abandoned a plan, a principle, or a friend.

A bold and fearless rider, you saw at a glance, from his easy and confident seat, that he was master of his horse, which was usually the fine blood-horse of Virginia. The only impatience of temper he ever exhibited was with his horse, which he subdued to his will by a fearless application of the whip on the slightest manifestation of restiveness. He retained to the last his fondness for riding on horseback; he rode within three weeks of his death, when, from disease, debility, and age, he mounted with difficulty. He rode with confidence, and never permitted a servant to accompany him; he was fond of solitary rides and musing, and said that the presence of a servant annoyed him.

He held in little esteem the education which made men ignorant and helpless as to the common necessities of life; and he exemplified it by an incident which occurred to a young gentleman returned from Europe, where he had been educated. On riding out with his companions, the strap of his girth broke at the hole for the buckle; and they, perceiving it an accident easily remedied, rode on and left him. A plain man coming up, and seeing that his horse had made a circular path in the road in his impatience to get on, asked if he could aid him.

"Oh, sir," replied the young man, "if you could only assist me to get it up to the next hole."

"Suppose you let it out a hole or two on the other side," said the man.

His habits were regular and systematic. He was a miser of his time, rose always at dawn, wrote and read until breakfast, breakfasted early, and dined from three to four......; retired at nine, and to bed from ten to eleven. He said, in his last illness, that the sun had not caught him in bed for fifty years.

He always made his own fire. He drank water but once a day, a single glass, when he returned from his ride. He ate heartily, and much vegetable food, preferring French cookery, because it made the meats more tender. He never drank ardent spirits or strong wines. Such was his aversion to ardent spirits, that when, in his last illness, his physician desired him to use brandy as an astringent, he could not induce him to take it strong enough.

In looking over his correspondence, I select the following extracts, which the reader will find most interesting:

To Governor Langdon, March 5th, 1810.

While in Europe, I often amused myself with contemplating the characters of the then reigning sovereigns of Europe. Louis the XVI. was a fool, of my own knowledge, and despite of the answers made for him at his trial. The King of Spain was a fool; and of Naples, the same. They passed their lives in hunting, and dispatched two couriers a week one thousand miles to let each know what game they had killed the preceding days. The King of Sardinia was a fool. All these were Bourbons. The Queen of Portugal, a Braganza, was an idiot by nature; and so was the King of Denmark. Their sons, as regents, exercised the powers of government. The King of Prussia, successor to the great Frederick, was a mere hog in body as well as in mind. Gustavus of Sweden, and Joseph of Austria, were really crazy; and George of England, you know, was in a strait-waistcoat. There remained, then, none but old Catherine, who had been too lately picked up to have lost her common sense. In this state Bonaparte found Europe; and it was this state of its rulers which lost it with scarce a struggle. These animals had become without mind and powerless; and so will every hereditary monarch be after a few generations. Alexander, the grandson of Catherine, is as yet an exception. He is able to hold his own. But he is only of the third generation. His race is not yet worn out. And so endeth the book of Kings, from all of whom the Lord deliver us, and have you, my friend, and all such good men and true, in his holy keeping.

To Governor Tyler, May 26th, 1810.

I have long lamented with you the depreciation of law science. The opinion seems to be that Blackstone is to us what the Alkoran is to the Mohammedans, that every thing which is necessary is in him, and what is not in him is not necessary. I still lend my counsel and books to such young students as will fix themselves in the neighborhood. Coke's Institutes and Reports are their first, and Blackstone their last book, after an intermediate course of two or three years. It is nothing more than an elegant digest of what they will then have acquired from the real fountains of the law. Now men are born scholars, lawyers, doctors; in our day this was confined to poets.

The following letters, containing such charming pictures of life at Monticello and of Jefferson's intercourse with his family, were written to Mr. Randall by one of Mr. Jefferson's grand-daughters:

My dear Mr. Randall—You seem possessed of so many facts and such minute details of Mr. Jefferson's family life, that I know not how I can add to the amount...... When he returned from Washington, in 1809, I was a child, and of that period I have childish recollections. He seemed to return to private life with great satisfaction. At last he was his own master, and could, he hoped, dispose of his time as he pleased, and indulge his love of country life. You know how greatly he preferred it to town life. You recollect, as far back as his "Notes on Virginia," he says, "Those who labor in the earth are the chosen people of God."

With regard to the tastes and wishes which he carried with him into the country, his love of reading alone would have made leisure and retirement delightful to him. Books were at all times his chosen companions, and his acquaintance with many languages gave him great power of selection. He read Homer, Virgil, Dante, Corneille, Cervantes, as he read Shakspeare and Milton. In his youth he had loved poetry, but by the time I was old enough to observe, he had lost his taste for it, except for Homer and the great Athenian tragics, which he continued to the last to enjoy.

He went over the works of Æschylus, Sophocles, and Euripides, not very long before I left him (the year before his death). Of history he was very fond, and this he studied in all languages, though always, I think, preferring the ancients. In fact, he derived more pleasure from his acquaintance with Greek and Latin than from any other resource of literature, and I have often heard him express his gratitude to his father for causing him to receive a classical education. I saw him more frequently with a volume of the classics in his hand than with any other book. Still he read new publications as they came out, never missed the new number of a review, especially of the Edinburgh, and kept himself acquainted with what was being done, said, or thought in the world from which he had retired.

He loved farming and gardening, the fields, the orchards, and his asparagus-beds. Every day he rode through his plantation and walked in his garden. In the cultivation of the last he took great pleasure. Of flowers, too, he was very fond. One of my early recollections is of the attention which he paid to his flower-beds. He kept up a correspondence with persons in the large cities, particularly, I think, in Philadelphia, for the purpose of receiving supplies of roots and seeds both for his kitchen and flower garden. I remember well, when he first returned to Monticello, how immediately he began to prepare new beds for his flowers. He had these beds laid off on the lawn, under the windows, and many a time I have run after him when he went out to direct the work, accompanied by one of his gardeners, generally Wormley, armed with spade and hoe, while he himself carried the measuring-line.

I was too young to aid him, except in a small way, but my sister, Mrs. Bankhead, then a young and beautiful woman, was his active and useful assistant. I remember the planting of the first hyacinths and tulips, and their subsequent growth. The roots arrived labelled, each one with a fancy name. There was "Marcus Aurelius" and the "King of the Gold Mine," the "Roman Empress" and the "Queen of the Amazons," "Psyche," the "God of Love," etc., etc. Eagerly, and with childish delight, I studied this brilliant nomenclature, and wondered what strange and surprisingly beautiful creations I should see arising from the ground when spring returned; and these precious roots were committed to the earth under my grandfather's own eye, with his beautiful grand-daughter Anne standing by his side, and a crowd of happy young faces, of younger grandchildren, clustering round to see the progress, and inquire anxiously the name of each separate deposit.

Then, when spring returned, how eagerly we watched the first appearance of the shoots above ground. Each root was marked with its own name written on a bit of stick by its side; and what joy it was for one of us to discover the tender green breaking through the mould, and run to grandpapa to announce that we really believed Marcus Aurelius was coming up, or the Queen of the Amazons was above ground! With how much pleasure, compounded of our pleasure and his own, on the new birth, he would immediately go out to verify the fact, and praise us for our diligent watchfulness.

Then, when the flowers were in bloom, and we were in ecstasies over the rich purple and crimson, or pure white, or delicate lilac, or pale yellow of the blossoms, how he would sympathize with our admiration, or discuss with my mother and elder sister new groupings and combinations and contrasts. Oh, these were happy moments for us and for him!

It was in the morning, immediately after our early breakfast, that he used to visit his flower-beds and his garden. As the day, in summer, grew warmer, he retired to his own apartments, which consisted of a bed-chamber and library opening into each other. Here he remained until about one o'clock, occupied in reading, writing, looking over papers, etc. My mother would sometimes send me with a message to him. A gentle knock, a call of "Come in," and I would enter, with a mixed feeling of love and reverence, and some pride in being the bearer of a communication to one whom I approached with all the affection of a child, and something of the loyalty of a subject. Our mother educated all her children to look up to her father, as she looked up to him herself—literally looked up, as to one standing on an eminence of greatness and goodness. And it is no small proof of his real elevation that, as we grew older and better able to judge for ourselves, we were more and more confirmed in the opinions we had formed of it.

About one o'clock my grandfather rode out, and was absent, perhaps, two hours; when he returned to prepare for his dinner, which was about half-past three o'clock. He sat some time at table, and after dinner returned for a while to his room, from which he emerged before sunset to walk on the terrace or the lawn, to see his grandchildren run races, or to converse with his family and friends. The evenings, after candle-light, he passed with us, till about ten o'clock. He had his own chair and his own candle a little apart from the rest, where he sat reading, if there were no guests to require his attention, but often laying his book on his little round table or his knee, while he talked with my mother, the elder members of the family, or any child old enough to make one of the family-party. I always did, for I was the most active and the most lively of the young folks, and most wont to thrust myself forward into notice.......

———, 185–.

My dear Mr. Randall—With regard to Mr. Jefferson's conduct and manners in his family, after I was old enough to form any judgment of it, I can only repeat what I have said before—and I say it calmly and advisedly, with no spirit of false enthusiasm or exaggeration—I have never known anywhere, under any circumstances, so good a domestic character as my grandfather Jefferson's. I have the testimony of his sisters and his daughter that he was, in all the relations of private life, at all times, just what he was when I knew him. My mother was ten years old when her mother died. Her impression was, that her father's conduct as a husband had been admirable in its ensemble, charming in its detail. She distinctly recalled her mother's passionate attachment to him, and her exalted opinion of him. On one occasion she heard her blaming him for some generous acts which had met with an ungrateful return. "But," she exclaimed, "it was always so with him; he is so good himself, that he can not understand how bad other people may be.".......

On one occasion my mother had been punished for some fault, not harshly nor unjustly, but in a way to make an impression. Some little time after, her mother being displeased with her for some trifle, reminded her in a slightly taunting way of this painful past. She was deeply mortified, her heart swelled, her eyes filled with tears, she turned away, but she heard her father say in a kind tone to her mother, "My dear, a fault in so young a child once punished should be forgotten." My mother told me she could never forget the warm gush of gratitude that filled her childish heart at these words, probably not intended for her ear. These are trifling details, but they show character.......

My grandfather's manners to us, his grandchildren, were *delightful;* I can characterize them by no other word. He talked with us freely, affectionately; never lost an opportunity of giving a pleasure or a good lesson. He reproved without wounding us, and commended without making us vain. He took pains to correct our errors and false ideas, checked the bold, encouraged the timid, and tried to teach us to reason soundly and feel rightly. Our smaller follies he treated with good-humored raillery, our graver ones with kind and serious admonition. He was watchful over our manners, and called our attention to every violation of propriety. He did not interfere with our education, technically so called, except by advising us what studies to pursue, what books to read, and by questioning us on the books which we did read.

I was thrown most into companionship with him. I loved him very devotedly, and sought every opportunity of being with him. As a child, I used to follow him about, and draw as near to him as I could. I remember when I was small enough to sit on his knee and play with his watch-chain. As a girl, I would join him in his walks on the terrace, sit with him over the fire during the winter twilight, or by the open windows in summer. As child, girl, and woman, I loved and honored him above all earthly beings. And well I might. From him seemed to flow all the pleasures of my life. To him I owed all the small blessings and joyful surprises of my childish and girlish years. His nature was so eminently sympathetic, that, with those he loved, he could enter into their feelings, anticipate their wishes, gratify their tastes, and surround them with an atmosphere of affection.

I was fond of riding, and was rising above that childish simplicity when, provided I was mounted on a horse, I cared nothing for my equipments, and when an old saddle or broken bridle were matters of no moment. I was beginning to be fastidious, but I had never told my wishes. I was standing one bright day in the portico, when a man rode up to the door with a beautiful lady's saddle and bridle before him. My heart bounded. These coveted articles were deposited at my feet. My grandfather came out of his room to tell me they were mine.

When about fifteen years old, I began to think of a watch, but knew the state of my father's finances promised no such indulgence. One afternoon the letter-bag was brought in. Among the letters was a small packet addressed to my grandfather. It had the Philadelphia mark upon it. I looked at it with indifferent, incurious eye. Three hours after, an elegant lady's watch, with chain and seals, was in my hand, which trembled for very joy. My Bible came from him, my Shakspeare, my first writing-table, my first handsome writing-desk, my first Leghorn hat, my first silk dress. What, in short, of all my small treasures did not come from him?......

My sisters, according to their wants and tastes, were equally thought of, equally provided for. Our grandfather seemed to read our hearts, to see our invisible wishes, to be our good genius, to wave the fairy wand, to brighten our young lives by his goodness and his gifts. But I have written enough for this time; and, indeed, what can I say hereafter but to repeat the same tale of love and kindness........

I remain, my dear Mr. Randall, very truly yours,

ELLEN W. COOLIDGE.

The following contains the reminiscences of a younger grand-daughter of Jefferson:

St. Servan, France, May 26th, 1839.

Faithful to my promise, dearest ——, I shall spend an hour every Sunday in writing all my childish recollections of my dear grandfather which are sufficiently distinct to relate to you. My memory seems crowded with them, and they have the vividness of realities; but all are trifles in themselves, such as I might talk to you by the hour, but when I have taken up my pen, they seem almost too childish to write down. But these remembrances are precious to me, because they are of *him*, and because they restore him to me as he then was, when his cheerfulness and affection were the

warm sun in which his family all basked and were invigo-
rated. Cheerfulness, love, benevolence, wisdom, seemed to
animate his whole form. His face beamed with them. You
remember how active was his step, how lively, and even
playful, were his manners.

I can not describe the feelings of veneration, admiration,
and love that existed in my heart towards him. I looked
on him as a being too great and good for my comprehen-
sion; and yet I felt no fear to approach him and be taught
by him some of the childish sports that I delighted in.
When he walked in the garden and would call the children
to go with him, we raced after and before him, and we were
made perfectly happy by this permission to accompany him.
Not one of us, in our wildest moods, ever placed a foot on
one of the garden-beds, for that would violate one of his
rules, and yet I never heard him utter a harsh word to one
of us, or speak in a raised tone of voice, or use a threat. He
simply said, " Do," or " Do not." He would gather fruit for
us, seek out the ripest figs, or bring down the cherries from
on high above our heads with a long stick, at the end of
which there was a hook and little net bag......

One of our earliest amusements was in running races on
the terrace, or around the lawn. He placed us according to
our ages, giving the youngest and smallest the start of all
the others by some yards, and so on; and then he raised his
arm high, with his white handkerchief in his hand, on which
our eager eyes were fixed, and slowly counted three, at which
number he dropped the handkerchief, and we started off to
finish the race by returning to the starting-place and receiving our reward of dried fruit—three figs, prunes, or dates to
the victor, two to the second, and one to the lagger who
came in last. These were our summer sports with him.

I was born the year he was elected President, and, except
one winter that we spent with him in Washington, I never
was with him during that season until after he had retired
from office. During his absences, all the children who could
write corresponded with him. Their letters were duly answered, and it was a sad mortification to me that I had not
learned to write before his return to live at home, and of
course had no letter from him. Whenever an opportunity
occurred, he sent us books; and he never saw a little story

or piece of poetry in a newspaper, suited to our ages and tastes, that he did not preserve it and send it to us; and from him we learnt the habit of making these miscellaneous collections, by pasting in a little paper book made for the purpose any thing of the sort that we received from him or got otherwise.

On winter evenings, when it grew too dark to read, in the half hour which passed before candles came in, as we all sat round the fire, he taught us several childish games, and would play them with us. I remember that "Cross-questions," and "I love my Love with an A," were two I learned from him; and we would teach some of ours to him.

When the candles were brought, all was quiet immediately, for he took up his book to read; and we would not speak out of a whisper, lest we should disturb him, and generally we followed his example and took a book; and I have seen him raise his eyes from his own book, and look round on the little circle of readers and smile, and make some remark to mamma about it. When the snow fell, we would go out, as soon as it stopped, to clear it off the terraces with shovels, that he might have his usual walk on them without treading in snow.

He often made us little presents. I remember his giving us "Parents' Assistant," and that we drew lots, and that she who drew the longest straw had the first reading of the book; the next longest straw entitled the drawer to the second reading; the shortest to the last reading, and ownership of the book.

Often he discovered, we knew not how, some cherished object of our desires, and the first intimation we had of his knowing the wish was its unexpected gratification. Sister Anne gave a silk dress to sister Ellen. Cornelia (then eight or ten years old), going up stairs, involuntarily expressed aloud some feelings which possessed her bosom on the occasion, by saying, "I never had a silk dress in my life." The next day a silk dress came from Charlottesville to Cornelia, and (to make the rest of us equally happy) also a pair of pretty dresses for Mary and myself. One day I was passing hastily through the glass door from the hall to the portico; there was a broken pane which caught my muslin dress and tore it sadly. Grandpapa was standing by and saw the disaster.

A few days after, he came into mamma's sitting-room with a bundle in his hand, and said to me, "I have been mending your dress for you." He had himself selected for me another beautiful dress. I had for a long time a great desire to have a guitar. A lady of our neighborhood was going to the West, and wished to part with her guitar, but she asked so high a price that I never in my dreams aspired to its possession. One morning, on going down to breakfast, I saw the guitar. It had been sent up by Mrs. —— for us to look at, and grandpapa told me that if I would promise to learn to play on it I should have it. I never shall forget my ecstasies. I was but fourteen years old, and the first wish of my heart was unexpectedly gratified......

VIRGINIA J. TRIST.

CHAPTER XIX.

THE extracts from Jefferson's letters which I give in this
chapter the reader will find to be of unusual interest.
Among his family letters I find the following touching note
to one of his grand-daughters.

To Mrs. Anne C. Bankhead.

Monticello, May 26th, 1811.

My dear Anne—I have just received a copy of the Modern
Griselda, which Ellen tells me will not be unacceptable to
you; I therefore inclose it. The heroine presents herself certainly as a perfect model of ingenious perverseness, and of
the art of making herself and others unhappy. If it can be
made of use in inculcating the virtues and felicities of life,
it must be by the rule of contraries.

Nothing new has happened in our neighborhood since you
left us; the houses and the trees stand where they did; the
flowers come forth like the belles of the day, have their short
reign of beauty and splendor, and retire, like them, to the
more interesting office of reproducing their like. The Hyacinths and Tulips are off the stage, the Irises are giving place
to the Belladonnas, as these will to the Tuberoses, etc.; as
your mamma has done to you, my dear Anne, as you will do
to the sisters of little John, and as I shall soon and cheerful-
ly do to you all in wishing you a long, long good-night.
Present me respectfully to Doctor and Mrs. Bankhead, and

accept for Mr. Bankhead and yourself the assurances of my cordial affections, not forgetting that Cornelia shares them.

TH. JEFFERSON.

In January, 1811, Dr. Rush, in a friendly letter to Mr. Jefferson, expressed regret at the suspension of intercourse between Mr. Adams and himself. Jefferson's letter in reply is one of the most charming he ever wrote.

To Benjamin Rush.—[Extract.]

I receive with sensibility your observations on the discontinuance of friendly correspondence between Mr. Adams and myself, and the concern you take in its restoration. This discontinuance has not proceeded from me, nor from the want of sincere desire and of effort on my part to renew our intercourse. You know the perfect coincidence of principle and of action, in the early part of the Revolution, which produced a high degree of mutual respect and esteem between Mr. Adams and myself. Certainly no man was ever truer than he was, in that day, to those principles of rational republicanism which, after the necessity of throwing off our monarchy, dictated all our efforts in the establishment of a new Government. And although he swerved afterwards towards the principles of the English Constitution, our friendship did not abate on that account. While he was Vicepresident, and I Secretary of State, I received a letter from President Washington, then at Mount Vernon, desiring me to call together the Heads of Department, and to invite Mr. Adams to join us (which, by-the-by, was the only instance of that being done), in order to determine on some measure which required dispatch; and he desired me to act on it, as decided, without again recurring to him. I invited them to dine with me, and after dinner, sitting at our wine, having settled our question, other conversation came on, in which a collision of opinion arose between Mr. Adams and Colonel Hamilton on the merits of the British Constitution; Mr. Adams giving it as his opinion that, if some of its defects and abuses were corrected, it would be the most perfect constitution of government ever devised by man. Hamilton, on the contrary, asserted that, with its existing vices, it was the most perfect model of government that could be formed, and that the correction of its vices would render it an impracticable government. And this, you may be assured, was the real line of difference between the political principles of these two gentlemen.

Another incident took place on the same occasion, which will further delineate Mr. Hamilton's political principles. The room being hung around with a collection of the portraits of remarkable men, among them were those of Bacon, Newton, and Locke. Hamilton asked me who they were. I told him they were my trinity of the three greatest men the world had ever produced, naming them. He paused for some time: "The greatest man," said he, "that ever lived was Julius Cæsar." Mr. Adams was honest as a politician, as well as a man; Hamilton honest as a man, but, as a politician, believing in the necessity of either force or corruption to govern men.

Writing to Colonel Duane in the same year, speaking of the state of the country and differences of opinion, he says: "These, like differences of face, are a law of our nature, and should be viewed with the same tolerance. The clouds which have appeared for some time to be gathering around us have given me anxiety, lest an enemy, always on the watch, always prompt and firm, and acting in well-disciplined phalanx, should find an opening to dissipate hopes, with the loss of which I would wish that of life itself. To myself, personally, the sufferings would be short. The powers of life have declined with me more in the last six months than in as many preceding years. A rheumatic indisposition, under which your letter found me, has caused this delay in acknowledging its receipt."

In a letter of December 5th, 1811, to Dr. Benjamin Rush, Jefferson, after alluding to letters from him, wherein he expresses a desire to bring about a reconciliation between Mr. Adams and himself, says:

To Benjamin Rush.

Two of the Mr. Coles, my neighbors and friends, took a tour to the northward during the last summer. In Boston they fell into company with Mr. Adams, and by his invitation passed a day with him at Braintree. He spoke out to them every thing which came uppermost, and as it occurred to his mind, without any reserve; and seemed most disposed to dwell on those things which happened during his own Administration. He spoke of his *masters*, as he called his Heads of Departments, as acting above his control, and often against his opinions. Among many other topics, he adverted to the unprincipled licentiousness of the press against myself, adding, "I always loved Jefferson, and still love him."

This is enough for me. I only needed this knowledge to revive towards him all the affections of the most cordial moments of our lives...... I wish, therefore, but for an apposite occasion to express to Mr. Adams my unchanged affection for him. There is an awkwardness which hangs over the resuming a correspondence so long discontinued, unless something could arise which should call for a letter. Time and chance may perhaps generate such an occasion, of which I shall not be wanting in promptitude to avail myself. From this fusion of mutual affections, Mrs. Adams is, of course, separated. It will only be necessary that I never name her.* In your letters to Mr. Adams you can perhaps

---

* It should here be shown that the coldness between Jefferson and Mrs. Adams was but a temporary interruption of a friendship which lasted for fully forty years, closed only by the death of Mrs. Adams, in 1818. The following letter from Mrs. Adams, written in 1786, will evince the friendship which then, and for years before, existed between her and Jefferson. Hereinbefore, at page 304 of this volume, will be found a letter of condolence from Mrs. Adams to Jefferson, upon the death of his daughter, Maria Jefferson Eppes (1804); and hereafter, at page 368, Jefferson's last letter to Mrs. Adams, written in 1817; followed by Jefferson's letter of condolence to John Adams (November, 1818), upon the death of Mrs. Adams.

From Mrs. Adams.

London, Grosvenor Square, Feb. 11th, 1786.

Col. Humphries talks of leaving us on Monday. It is with regret, I assure you, Sir, that we part with him. His visit here has given us an opportunity of becoming more acquainted with his real worth and merit, and our friendship for him has risen in proportion to our intimacy. The two American Secretaries of Legation would do honor to their country placed in more distinguished stations. Yet these missions abroad, circumscribed as they are in point of expenses, place the ministers of the United States in the lowest point of view of any envoy from any other Court; and in Europe every being is estimated, and every country valued, in proportion to their show and splendor. In a private station I have not a wish for expensive living, but, whatever my

suggest my continued cordiality towards him, and, knowing this, should an occasion of writing first present itself to him, he will perhaps avail himself of it, as I certainly will, should it first occur to me. No ground for jealousy now existing, he will certainly give fair play to the natural warmth of his heart. Perhaps I may open the way in some letter to my old friend Gerry, who, I know, is in habits of the greatest intimacy with him. I have thus, my friend, laid my heart open to you, because you were so kind as to take an interest in healing again Revolutionary affections, which have ceased in expression only, but not in their existence. God ever bless you, and preserve you in life and health.

To this letter Dr. Rush replied as follows:

From Benjamin Rush.—[Extract.]

Philadelphia, Dec. 17th, 1811.

My dear old Friend — Yours of December 5th came to hand yesterday. I was charmed with the subject of it. In

---

fair countrywomen may think, and I hear they envy my situation, I will most joyfully exchange Europe for America, and my public for a private life. I am really surfeited with Europe, and most heartily long for the rural cottage, the purer and honester manners of my native land, where domestic happiness reigns unrivalled, and virtue and honor go hand in hand. I hope one season more will give us an opportunity of making our escape. At present we are in the situation of Sterne's starling.

Congress have by the last dispatches informed this Court that they expect them to appoint a minister. It is said (not officially) that Mr. Temple is coldly received, that no Englishman has visited him, and the Americans are not very social with him. But as Colonel Humphries will be able to give you every intelligence, there can be no occasion for my adding any thing further than to acquaint you that I have endeavored to execute your commission agreeably to your directions. Enclosed you will find the memorandum. I purchased a small trunk, which I think you will find useful to you to put the shirts in, as they will not be liable to get rubbed on the journey. If the balance should prove in my favor, I will request you to send me 4 ells of cambric at about 14 livres per ell or 15, a pair of black lace lappets—these are what the ladies wear at court—and 12 ells of black lace at 6 or 7 livres per ell. Some gentleman coming this way will be so kind as to put them in his pocket, and Mrs. Barclay, I dare say, will take the trouble of purchasing them for me; for troubling you with such trifling matters is a little like putting Hercules to the distaff.

My love to Miss Jefferson, and compliments to Mr. Short. Mrs. Siddons is acting again upon the stage, and I hope Colonel Humphries will prevail with you to cross the Channel to see her. Be assured, dear Sir, that nothing would give more pleasure to your friends here than a visit from you, and in that number I claim the honor of subscribing myself, A. ADAMS.

[4 pair of shoes for Miss Adams, by the person who made Mrs. A.'s, 2 of satin and 2 of spring silk, without straps, and of the most fashionable colors.]

order to hasten the object you have suggested, I sat down last evening and selected such passages from your letter as contained the kindest expressions of regard for Mr. Adams, and transmitted them to him. My letter which contained them was concluded, as nearly as I can recollect, for I kept no copy of it, with the following words: "Fellow-laborers, in erecting the fabric of American liberty and independence! fellow-sufferers in the calumnies and falsehoods of party rage! fellow-heirs of the gratitude and affection of posterity! and fellow-passengers in the same stage which must soon convey you both into the presence of a Judge with whom forgiveness and love of enemies is the only condition of your acceptance, embrace—embrace each other—bedew your letter of reconciliation with tears of affection and joy. Let there be no retrospect of your past differences. Explanations may be proper between contending lovers, but they are never so between divided friends. Were I near you, I would put a pen in your hand, and guide it while it wrote the following note to Mr. Jefferson: 'My dear old friend and fellow-laborer in the cause of the liberties and independence of our common country, I salute you with the most cordial good wishes for your health and happiness.   John Adams.'"

Jefferson's hopes were realized by receiving early in the year 1812 a letter from Mr. Adams. It is pleasing to see with what eagerness he meets this advance from his old friend. In his reply he says:

To John Adams.

A letter from you calls up recollections very dear to my mind. It carries me back to the times when, beset with difficulties and dangers, we were fellow-laborers in the same cause, struggling for what is most valuable to man, his right of self-government. Laboring always at the same oar, with some wave ever ahead threatening to overwhelm us, and yet passing harmless under our bark, we knew not how, we rode through the storm with heart and hand, and made a happy port...... But whither is senile garrulity leading me? Into politics, of which I have taken final leave. I think little of them, and say less. I have given up newspapers in exchange for Tacitus and Thucydides, for Newton and Euclid, and I find myself much the happier. Sometimes, indeed, I look back to former occurrences, in remembrance of our old friends and fellow-laborers who have fallen before us. Of the signers of the Declaration of Independence, I see now living not more than half a dozen on your side of the Potomac, and, on this side, myself alone.

You and I have been wonderfully spared, and myself with remarkable health, and a considerable activity of body and mind. I am on horseback three or four hours of every day; visit three or four times a year a possession I have ninety miles distant, performing the winter journey on horseback. I walk little, however, a single mile being too much for me; and I live in the midst of my grandchildren, one of whom has lately promoted me to be a great-grandfather. I have heard with pleasure that you also retain good health, and a greater power of exercise in walking than I do. But I would rather have heard this from yourself, and that, writing a letter like mine, full of egotisms, and of details of your health, your habits, occupations, and enjoyments, I should have the pleasure of knowing that in the race of life you do not keep, in its physical decline, the same distance ahead of me which you have done in political honors and achievements. No circumstances have lessened the interest I feel in these particulars respecting yourself; none have suspended for one moment my sincere esteem for you, and I now salute you with unchanged affection and respect.

Mr. Adams having had some affliction in his household, Mr. Jefferson, at the close of a letter written to him in October, 1813, says:

To John Adams.

On the subject of the postscript of yours of August the 16th, and of Mrs. Adams's letter, I am silent. I know the depth of the affliction it has caused, and can sympathize with it the more sensibly, inasmuch as there is no degree of affliction, produced by the loss of those dear to us, which experience has not taught me to estimate. I have ever found time and silence the only medicine, and these but assuage, they never can suppress, the deep-drawn sigh which recollection forever brings up, until recollection and life are extinguished together.

In a letter written to Dr. Walter Jones on the 2d of January, 1814, we have one of the most beautiful descriptions of character to be found in the English language, and the most heartfelt tribute to General Washington which has ever flowed from the pen of any man. Jefferson writes:

Jefferson's Character of Washington.

You say that in taking General Washington on your shoulders, to bear him harmless through the Federal coalition, you encounter a perilous topic. I do not think so. You have given the genuine history of the course of his mind through the trying scenes in which it was engaged, and of the seductions by which it was deceived, but not depraved. I think I knew General Washington intimately and thoroughly; and were I called on to delineate his character, it should be in terms like these:

His mind was great and powerful without being of the very first order; his penetration strong, though not so acute as that of a Newton, Bacon, or Locke; and, as far as he saw, no judgment was ever sounder. It was slow in operation, being little aided by invention or imagination, but sure in conclusion. Hence the common remark of his officers, of the advantage he derived from councils of war, where, hearing all suggestions, he selected whatever was best; and certainly no general ever planned his battles more judiciously. But if deranged during the course of the action, if any member of his plan was dislocated by sudden circumstances, he was slow in a readjustment. The consequence was, that he often failed in the field, and rarely against an enemy in station, as at Boston and York. He was incapable of fear, meeting personal danger with the calmest unconcern.

Perhaps the strongest feature in his character was prudence, never acting until every circumstance, every consideration, was maturely weighed; refraining if he saw a doubt, but, when once decided, going through with his purpose, whatever obstacles opposed. His integrity was most pure, his justice the most inflexible I have ever known, no motives of interest or consanguinity, of friendship or hatred, being able to bias his decision. He was, indeed, in every sense of the words, a wise, a good, and a great man. His temper was

naturally irritable and high-toned; but reflection and resolution had obtained a firm and habitual ascendency over
it. If ever, however, it broke its bonds, he was most tremendous in his wrath. In his expenses he was honorable, but exact; liberal in contribution to whatever promised utility; but frowning and unyielding on all visionary
projects, and all unworthy calls on his charity. His heart
was not warm in its affections; but he exactly calculated
every man's value, and gave him a solid esteem proportioned
to it.

His person, you know, was fine, his stature exactly what
one would wish, his deportment easy, erect and noble; the
best horseman of his age, and the most graceful figure that
could be seen on horseback.

Although in the circle of his friends, where he might be
unreserved with safety, he took a free share in conversation,
his colloquial talents were not above mediocrity, possessing
neither copiousness of ideas nor fluency of words. In public,
when called on for a sudden opinion, he was unready, short,
and embarrassed. Yet he wrote readily, rather diffusely, in
an easy and correct style. This he had acquired by conversation with the world, for his education was merely reading,
writing, and common arithmetic, to which he added survey-
ing at a later day. His time was employed in action chiefly, reading little, and that only in agriculture and English
history. His correspondence became necessarily extensive,
and, with journalizing his agricultural proceedings, occupied
most of his leisure hours within-doors.

On the whole, his character was, in its mass, perfect; in
nothing bad, in few points indifferent; and it may truly be
said, that never did nature and fortune combine more perfectly to make a man great, and to place him in the same
constellation with whatever worthies have merited from
man an everlasting remembrance. For his was the singular
destiny and merit of leading the armies of his country suc-
cessfully through an arduous war, for the establishment of
its independence; of conducting its councils through the
birth of a Government new in its forms and principles, until
it had settled down into a quiet and orderly train; and of
scrupulously obeying the laws through the whole of his career, civil and military, of which the history of the world fur-

nishes no other example. How, then, can it be perilous for you to take such a man on your shoulders?......

He has often declared to me that he considered our new Constitution as an experiment on the practicability of republican government, and with what dose of liberty man could be trusted for his own good; that he was determined the experiment should have a fair trial, and would lose the last drop of his blood in support of it....... I do believe that General Washington had not a firm confidence in the durability of our Government...... I felt on his death, with my countrymen, that "Verily a great man hath fallen this day in Israel."

The following pleasing anecdote in relation to Jefferson's devotion to Washington is remembered by his family. Long years after he had retired from public life, some admirer of Jefferson's, who lived in France, sent a wreath of immortelles to a member of the family at Monticello, with the request that it might be placed round his brow on his birthday. Jefferson ordered it to be placed, instead, on Washington's bust, where it ever afterwards rested.

On another occasion, while riding after night with a member of his family, the conversation fell upon Washington. Mr. Jefferson was warm in his expressions of praise and love for him, and finally, in a burst of enthusiasm, exclaimed, "Washington's fame will go on increasing until the brightest constellation in yonder heavens shall be called by his name!"

How different was the education in which such men as Washington and Jefferson were trained from the more modern system, so happily criticised by the latter, in the following extract from a letter to John Adams, bearing date July 5, 1814:

To John Adams.

But why am I dosing you with these antediluvian topics? Because I am glad to have some one to whom they are familiar, and who will not receive them as if dropped from the moon. Our post-revolutionary youth are born under happier stars than you and I were. They acquire all learning in their mother's womb, and bring it into the world ready-made. The information of books is no longer necessary; and all knowledge which is not innate is in contempt, or neglect at least. Every folly must run its round; and so, I suppose, must that of self-learning and self-sufficiency; of rejecting the knowledge acquired in past ages, and starting on the new ground of intuition. When sobered by experience, I hope our successors will turn their attention to the advantages of education—I mean of education on the broad scale, and not that of the petty *academies*, as they call themselves, which are starting up in every neighborhood, and where one or two men, possessing Latin and sometimes Greek, a knowledge of the globes, and the first six books of Euclid, imagine and communicate this as the sum of science. They commit their pupils to the theatre of the world with just taste enough of learning to be alienated from industrious pursuits, and not enough to do service in the ranks of science.

The following to an old friend finds a place here

To Mrs. Trist.

Monticello, Dec. 26th, 1814.

My good Friend—The mail between us passes very slowly. Your letter of November 17ᵗ reached this place on the 14th inst. only. I think while you were writing it the candle must have burnt blue, and that a priest or some other conjurer should have been called in to exorcise your room. To be serious, however, your view of things is more gloomy than necessary. True, we are at war—that that war was unsuccessful by land the first year, but honorable the same year by sea, and equally by sea and land ever since. Our resources, both of men and money, are abundant, if wisely called forth and administered. I acknowledge that experience does not as yet seem to have led our Legislatures into the best course of either......

I think, however, there will be peace. The negotiators at Ghent are agreed in every thing except as to a rag of Maine, which we can not yield nor they seriously care about, but it serves them to hold by until they can hear what the Convention of Hartford will do. When they shall see, as they will see, that nothing is done there, they will let go their hold, and we shall have peace on the *status ante bellum.* You have seen that Vermont and New Hampshire refuse to join the mutineers, and Connecticut does it with a "saving of her duty to the Federal Constitution." Do you believe that Massachusetts, on the good faith and aid of little Rhode Island, will undertake a war against the rest of the Union and the half of herself? Certainly never—so much for politics.

We are all well, little and big, young and old. Mr. and Mrs. Divers enjoy very so-so health, but keep about. Mr. Randolph had the command of a select corps during summer; but that has been discharged some time. We are feeding our horses with our wheat, and looking at the taxes coming on us as an approaching wave in a storm; still I think we shall live as long, eat as much, and drink as much, as if the wave had already glided under our ship. Somehow or other these things find their way out as they come in, and so I suppose they will now. God bless you, and give you health, happiness, and hope, the real comforters of this nether world.

TH. JEFFERSON.

In a letter to Cæsar A. Rodney, inviting a visit from him, and written on March 16th, 1815, he says: "You will find me in habitual good health, great contentedness, enfeebled in body, impaired in memory, but without decay in my friendships."

In a letter written to Jean Baptiste Say a few days earlier than the one just quoted, he speaks thus of the society of the country around him: "The society is much better than is common in country situations; perhaps there is not a better *country* society in the United States. But do not imagine this a Parisian or an academical society. It consists of plain, honest, and rational neighbors, some of them well-informed, and men of reading, all superintending their farms, hospitable and friendly, and speaking nothing but English. The manners of every nation are the standard of orthodoxy within itself. But these standards being arbitrary, reasonable people in all allow free toleration for the manners, as for the religion, of others."

We get a glimpse of the state of his health and his daily habits in a letter written to a friend in the spring of 1816. He writes:

I retain good health, and am rather feeble to walk much, but ride with ease, passing two or three hours a day on horseback,* and every three or four months taking, in a carriage, a journey of ninety miles to a distant possession, where I pass a good deal of my time. My eyes need the aid of glasses by night, and, with small print, in the day also. My hearing is not quite so sensible as it used to be; no tooth shaking yet, but shivering and shrinking in body from the cold are now experienced, my thermometer having been as low as 12° this morning.

My greatest oppression is a correspondence afflictingly laborious, the extent of which I have long been endeavoring to curtail. This keeps me at the drudgery of the writing-table all the prime hours of the day, leaving for the gratification of my appetite for reading only what I can steal from the hours of sleep. Could I reduce this epistolary corvée within the limits of my friends and affairs, and give the time redeemed from it to reading and reflection, to history, ethics, mathematics, my life would be as happy as the infirmities of age would admit, and I should look on its consummation with the composure of one *"qui summum nec metuit diem nec optat."*

The cheerfulness of his bright and happy temper gleams out in the following extract from a letter written a few months later to John Adams:

To John Adams.

You ask if I would agree to live my seventy, or, rather, seventy-three, years over again? To which I say, yea. I think, with you, that it is a good world, on the whole; that it has been framed on a principle of benevolence, and more pleasure than pain dealt out to us. There are, indeed (who might say nay), gloomy and hypochondriac minds, inhabitants of diseased bodies, disgusted with the present and despairing of the future; always counting that the worst will

---

* He was at this time in his seventy-third year.

happen, because it may happen. To these I say, how much pain have cost us the evils which have never happened! My temperament is sanguine. I steer my bark with Hope in the head, leaving Fear astern. My hopes, indeed, sometimes fail; but not oftener than the forebodings of the gloomy. There are, I acknowledge, even in the happiest life, some terrible convulsions, heavy set-offs against the opposite page of the account.......

Did I know Baron Grimm while at Paris? Yes, most intimately. He was the pleasantest and most conversable member of the diplomatic corps while I was there; a man of good fancy, acuteness, irony, cunning, and egoism. No heart, not much of any science, yet enough of every one to speak its language; his forte was belles-lettres, painting, and sculpture. In these he was the oracle of the society, and, as such, was the Empress Catherine's private correspondent and factor in all things not diplomatic. It was through him I got her permission for poor Ledyard to go to Kamtschatka, and cross over thence to the western coast of America, in order to penetrate across our continent in the opposite direction to that afterwards adopted for Lewis and Clarke; which permission she withdrew after he had got within two hundred miles of Kamtschatka, had him seized, brought back, and set down in Poland.

To Mrs. Trist.

Poplar Forest, April 28th, 1816.

I am here, my dear Madam, alive and well, and, notwithstanding the murderous histories of the winter, I have not had an hour's sickness for a twelvemonth past. I feel myself indebted to the fable, however, for the friendly concern expressed in your letter, which I received in good health, by my fireside at Monticello. These stories will come true one of these days, and poor printer Davies need only reserve awhile the chapter of commiserations he had the labor to compose, and the mortification to recall, after striking off some sheets announcing to *his* readers the happy riddance. But, all joking apart, I am well, and left all well a fortnight ago at Monticello, to which I shall return in two or three days......

Jefferson is gone to Richmond to bring home my new

great-grand-daughter. Your friends, Mr. and Mrs. Divers, are habitually in poor health; well enough only to receive visits, but not to return them; and this, I think, is all our small news which can interest you.

On the general scale of nations, the greatest wonder is Napoleon at St. Helena; and yet it is where it would have been well for the lives and happiness of millions and millions, had he been deposited there twenty years ago. France would now have had a free Government, unstained by the enormities she has enabled him to commit on the rest of the world, and unprostrated by the vindictive hand, human or divine, now so heavily bearing upon her. She deserves much punishment, and her successes and reverses will be a wholesome lesson to the world hereafter; but she has now had enough, and we may lawfully pray for her resurrection, and I am confident the day is not distant. No one who knows that people, and the elasticity of their character, can believe they will long remain crouched on the earth as at present. They will rise by acclamation, and woe to their riders. What havoc are we not yet to see! But these sufferings of all Europe will not be lost. A sense of the rights of man is gone forth, and all Europe will ere long have representative governments, more or less free.......

We are better employed in establishing universities, colleges, canals, roads, maps, etc. What do you say to all this? Who could have believed the Old Dominion would have roused from her supineness, and taken such a scope at her first flight? My only fear is that an hour of repentance may come, and nip in the bud the execution of conceptions so magnanimous. With my friendly respects to Mr. and Mrs. Gilmer, accept the assurance of my constant attachment and respect.

TH. JEFFERSON.

In a letter to John Adams, written at the beginning of the next year (1817), he complains bitterly of the burden of his extensive correspondence.

To John Adams.

Monticello, Jan. 11th, 1817.

Dear Sir—Forty-three volumes read in one year, and twelve of them quarto! Dear Sir, how I envy you! Half a dozen octavos in that space of time are as much as I am allowed. I can read by candle-light only, and stealing long hours from my rest; nor would that time be indulged to me, could I by that light see to write. From sunrise to one or two o'clock, and often from dinner to dark, I am drudging at the writing-table. All this to answer letters into which neither interest nor inclination on my part enters; and often from persons whose names I have never before heard. Yet, writing civilly, it is hard to refuse them civil answers. This is the burthen of my life, a very grievous one indeed, and one which I must get rid of.

Delaplaine lately requested me to give him a line on the subject of his book; meaning, as I well knew, to publish it. This I constantly refuse; but in this instance yielded, that in saying a word for him I might say two for myself. I expressed in it freely my sufferings from this source; hoping it would have the effect of an indirect appeal to the discretion of those, strangers and others, who, in the most friendly dispositions, oppress me with their concerns, their pursuits, their projects, inventions, and speculations, political, moral, religious, mechanical, mathematical, historical, etc., etc., etc. I hope the appeal will bring me relief, and that I shall be left to exercise and enjoy correspondence with the friends I love, and on subjects which they, or my own inclinations, present. In that case your letters shall not be so long on my files unanswered, as sometimes they have been to my great mortification.

From a letter to his son-in-law, Mr. Eppes, written the previous year, I take the following extract:

To John W. Eppes.

I am indeed an unskillful manager of my farms, and sensible of this from its effects, I have now committed them to better hands, of whose care and skill I have satisfactory knowledge, and to whom I have ceded the entire direction.* This is all that is necessary to make them adequate to all my wants, and to place me at entire ease. And for whom

---

* The person here alluded to was his grandson, Thomas Jefferson Randolph.

should I spare in preference to Francis, on sentiments either of duty or affection? I consider all my grandchildren as if they were my children, and want nothing but for them. It is impossible that I could reconcile it to my feelings, that he alone of them should be a stranger to my cares and contributions.

From this extract we learn that Mr. Jefferson had found the cares of his large estates too great a burden for him to carry in his advancing years, and gladly handed them over into the hands of the young grandson, in whose skill and energy he expresses such perfect confidence. From this time until the day of Jefferson's death, we shall find this grandson interposing himself, as far as possible, between his grandfather and his financial troubles, and trying to shield him, at least during his life, from the financial ruin which the circumstances of his situation made unavoidable. With his usual sanguine temper, Jefferson did not appreciate the extent to which his property was involved.

In a letter to his young grandson, Francis Eppes, after alluding to his studies, he says:

To Francis Eppes.

But while you endeavor, by a good store of learning, to prepare yourself to become a useful and distinguished member of your country, you must remember that this never can be without uniting merit with your learning. Honesty, disinterestedness, and good-nature are indispensable to procure the esteem and confidence of those with whom we live, and on whose esteem our happiness depends. Never suffer a thought to be harbored in your mind which you would not avow openly. When tempted to do any thing in secret, ask yourself if you would do it in public; if you would not, be sure it is wrong. In little disputes with your companions, give way rather than insist on trifles, for their love and the approbation of others will be worth more to you than the trifle in dispute. Above all things and at all times, practise yourself in good humor; this, of all human qualities, is the most amiable and endearing to society. Whenever you feel a warmth of temper rising, check it at once, and suppress it, recollecting it would make you unhappy within yourself and disliked by others. Nothing gives one person so great an advantage over another under all circumstances. Think of these things, practise them, and you will be rewarded by the love and confidence of the world.

I have given, in the earlier pages of this work, the charming sketches of Monticello and its owner from the pens of two distinguished Frenchmen,* and, fortunately, the Travels of Lieutenant Hall, a British officer, enable me to give a similar sketch from the pen of an Englishman. Their national prejudices and enthusiasm might be thought to have made the French noblemen color their pictures too highly when describing Jefferson; but certainly, if ever he had a critical visitor, a British officer might be considered to have been one, and in this view the following pleasantly-written account of Mr. Hall's visit to Monticello in 1816 will be found particularly interesting:

Lieut. Hall's Visit to Jefferson.†

Having an introduction to Mr. Jefferson (Mr. Hall writes), I ascended his little mountain on a fine morning, which gave the situation its due effect. The whole of the sides and base are covered with forest, through which roads have been cut circularly, so that the winding may be shortened at pleasure; the summit is an open lawn, near to the south side of which the house is built, with its garden just descending the brow; the saloon, or central hall, is ornamented with several pieces of antique sculpture, Indian arms, mammoth bones, and other curiosities collected from various parts of the Union. I found Mr. Jefferson tall in person, but stooping and lean with old age, thus exhibiting the fortunate mode of bodily decay which strips the frame of its most cumbersome parts, leaving it still strength of muscle and activity of limb. His deportment was exactly such as the Marquis de Chastellux describes it above thirty years ago. "At first serious, nay even cold," but in a very short time relaxing

---

* Pages 58 *et seq.*, and 235 *et seq.*

† Travels in Canada and the United States, in 1816 and 1817, by Lieutenant Francis Hall.

into a most agreeable amenity, with an unabated flow of conversation on the most interesting topics discussed in the most gentlemanly and philosophical manner.

I walked with him round his grounds, to visit his pet trees and improvements of various kinds. During the walk he pointed out to my observation a conical mountain, rising singly at the edge of the southern horizon of the landscape; its distance, he said, was forty miles, and its dimensions those of the greater Egyptian pyramid; so that it actually represents the appearance of the pyramid at the same distance. There is a small cleft visible on the summit, through which the true meridian of Monticello exactly passes; its most singular property, however, is, that on different occasions it looms, or alters its appearance, becoming sometimes cylindrical, sometimes square, and sometimes assuming the form of an inverted cone. Mr. Jefferson had not been able to connect this phenomenon with any particular season or state of the atmosphere, except that it most commonly occurred in the forenoon. He observed that it was not only wholly unaccounted for by the laws of vision, but that it had not as yet engaged the attention of philosophers so far as to acquire a name; that of "looming" being, in fact, a term applied by sailors to appearances of a similar kind at sea. The Blue Mountains are also observed to loom, though not in so remarkable a degree......

I slept a night at Monticello, and left it in the morning, with such a feeling as the traveller quits the mouldering remains of a Grecian temple, or the pilgrim a fountain in the desert. It would, indeed, argue a great torpor, both of understanding and heart, to have looked without veneration or interest on the man who drew up the Declaration of American Independence, who shared in the councils by which her freedom was established; whom the unbought voice of his fellow-citizens called to the exercise of a dignity from which his own moderation impelled him, when such an example was most salutary, to withdraw; and who, while he dedicates the evening of his glorious days to the pursuits of science and literature, shuns none of the humbler duties of private life; but, having filled a seat higher than that of kings, succeeds with graceful dignity to that of the good neighbor, and becomes the friendly adviser, lawyer, physician, and even gardener of his vicinity. This is the still small voice of philosophy, deeper and holier than the lightnings and earthquakes which have preceded it. What monarch would venture thus to exhibit himself in the nakedness of his humanity? On what royal brow would the laurel replace the diadem? But they who are born and educated to be kings are not expected to be philosophers. This is a just answer, though no great compliment, either to the governors or the governed.

Early in 1817 Jefferson wrote the following delightful letter to Mrs. Adams—the last, I believe, that he ever addressed to her:

To Mrs. Adams.

Monticello, Jan. 11th, 1817.

I owe you, dear Madam, a thousand thanks for the letters communicated in your favor of December 15th, and now returned. They give me more information than I possessed before of the family of Mr. Tracy.* But what is infinitely interesting, is the scene of the exchange of Louis XVIII. for Bonaparte. What lessons of wisdom Mr. Adams must have read in that short space of time! More than fall to the lot of others in the course of a long life. Man, and the man of Paris, under those circumstances, must have been a subject of profound speculation! It would be a singular addition to that spectacle to see the same beast in the cage of St. Helena, like a lion in the tower. That is probably the closing verse of the chapter of his crimes. But not so with Louis. He has other vicissitudes to go through.

I communicated the letters, according to your permission, to my grand-daughter, Ellen Randolph, who read them with pleasure and edification. She is justly sensible of, and flattered by, your kind notice of her; and additionally so by the favorable recollections of our Northern visiting friends. If Monticello has any thing which has merited their remembrance, it gives it a value the more in our estimation; and could I, in the spirit of your wish, count backward a score of years, it would not be long before Ellen and myself would pay our homage personally to Quincy. But those twenty

---

* One of his French friends, the Comte de Tracy.

years! Alas! where are they? With those beyond the flood. Our next meeting must then be in the country to which they have flown—a country for us not now very distant. For this journey we shall need neither gold nor silver in our purse, nor scrip, nor coats, nor staves. Nor is the provision for it more easy than the preparation has been kind. Nothing proves more than this, that the Being who presides over the world is essentially benevolent—stealing from us, one by one, the faculties of enjoyment, searing our sensibilities, leading us, like the horse in his mill, round and round the same beaten circle—

> To see what we have seen,
> To taste the tasted, and at each return
> Less tasteful; o'er our palates to decant
> Another vintage—

until, satiated and fatigued with this leaden iteration, we ask our own *congé*.

I heard once a very old friend, who had troubled himself with neither poets nor philosophers, say the same thing in plain prose, that he was tired of pulling off his shoes and stockings at night, and putting them on again in the morning. The wish to stay here is thus gradually extinguished; but not so easily that of returning once in a while to see how things have gone on. Perhaps, however, one of the elements of future felicity is to be a constant and unimpassioned view of what is passing here. If so, this may well supply the wish of occasional visits. Mercier has given us a vision of the year 2440; but prophecy is one thing, and history another. On the whole, however, perhaps it is wise and well to be contented with the good things which the Master of the feast places before us, and to be thankful for what we have, rather than thoughtful about what we have not.

You and I, dear Madam, have already had more than an ordinary portion of life, and more, too, of health than the general measure. On this score I owe boundless thankfulness. Your health was some time ago not so good as it has been, and I perceive in the letters communicated some complaints still. I hope it is restored; and that life and health may be continued to you as many years as yourself shall wish, is the sincere prayer of your affectionate and respectful friend.

A A

The pleasant intercourse between Mr. Jefferson and Mrs. Adams terminated only with the death of the latter, which took place in the fall of the year 1818, and drew from Jefferson the following beautiful and touching letter to his ancient friend and colleague:

To John Adams.

Monticello, November 13th, 1818.

The public papers, my dear friend, announce the fatal event of which your letter of October the 20th had given me ominous foreboding. Tried myself in the school of affliction, by the loss of every form of connection which can rive the human heart, I know well, and feel what you have lost, what you have suffered, are suffering, and have yet to endure. The same trials have taught me that for ills so immeasurable time and silence are the only medicine. I will not, therefore, by useless condolences, open afresh the sluices of your grief, nor, although mingling sincerely my tears with yours, will I say a word more where words are vain, but that it is of some comfort to us both that the term is not very distant at which we are to deposit in the same cerement our sorrows and suffering bodies, and to ascend in essence to an ecstatic meeting with the friends we have loved and lost, and whom we shall still love and never lose again. God bless you and support you under your heavy affliction.

TH. JEFFERSON.

In the following letter we have a most interesting and minute account of Mr. Jefferson's habits and mode of life:

To Doctor Vine Utley.

Monticello, March 21st, 1819.

Sir—Your letter of February the 18th came to hand on the 1st instant; and the request of the history of my physical habits would have puzzled me not a little, had it not been for the model with which you accompanied it of Doctor Rush's answer to a similar inquiry. I live so much like other people, that I might refer to ordinary life as the history of my own. Like my friend the Doctor, I have lived temperately, eating little animal food, and that not as an aliment so much as a condiment for the vegetables, which constitute my principal diet. I double, however, the Doctor's glass-and-a-half of wine, and even treble it with a friend; but halve its effect by drinking the weak wines only. The ardent wines I can not drink, nor do I use ardent spirits in any form. Malt liquors and cider are my table drinks, and my breakfast, like that also of my friend, is of tea and coffee. I have been blest with organs of digestion which accept and concoct without ever murmuring whatever the palate chooses to consign to them, and I have not yet lost a tooth by age.

I was a hard student until I entered on the business of life, the duties of which leave no idle time to those disposed to fulfill them; and now, retired, at the age of seventy-six, I am again a hard student. Indeed, my fondness for reading and study revolts me from the drudgery of letter-writing; and a stiff wrist, the consequence of an early dislocation, makes writing both slow and painful. I am not so regular in my sleep as the Doctor says he was, devoting to it from five to eight hours, according as my company or the book I am reading interests me; and I never go to bed without an hour, or half-hour's reading of something moral whereon to ruminate in the intervals of sleep. But whether I retire to bed early or late, I rise with the sun. I use spectacles at night, but not necessarily in the day, unless in reading small print. My hearing is distinct in particular conversation, but confused when several voices cross each other, which unfits me for the society of the table.

I have been more fortunate than my friend in the article of health. So free from catarrhs, that I have not had one (in the breast, I mean) on an average of eight or ten years through life. I ascribe this exemption partly to the habit of bathing my feet in cold water every morning for sixty years past. A fever of more than twenty-four hours I have not had above two or three times in my life. A periodical headache has afflicted me occasionally, once, perhaps, in six or eight years, for two or three weeks at a time, which seems now to have left me; and, except on a late occasion of indisposition, I enjoy good health; too feeble, indeed, to walk much, but riding without fatigue six or eight miles a day, and sometimes thirty or forty.

I may end these egotisms, therefore, as I began, by saying that my life has been so much like that of other people, that I might say with Horace, to every one, " *Nomine mutato, narratur fabula de te.*" I must not end, however, without due thanks for the kind sentiments of regard you are so good as to express towards myself; and with my acknowledgments for these, be pleased to accept the assurances of my respect and esteem.

TH. JEFFERSON.

In the following month of the same year we find him receiving a letter from Mrs. Cosway, who had long been silent. I give the following quotation from this letter, Jefferson's reply, and other letters from her, which close their pleasant correspondence.

From Mrs. Cosway.—[Extract.]

London, April 7th, 1819.

My different journeys to the Continent were either caused by bad health or other particular private melancholy motives; but on any sudden information of Mr. C.'s bad health, I hastened home to see him. In my stay on the Continent, I was called to form establishments of education: one at Lyons, which met with the most flattering success; and lastly, one in Italy, equally answering every hoped-for consolation. Oh! how often have I thought of America, and wished to have exerted myself there! Who would ever have imagined that I should have taken up this line! It has afforded me satisfactions unfelt before, after having been deprived of my own child. What comfortable feelings in seeing children grow up accomplished, modest, and virtuous women! They are hardly gone home from the establishment at fifteen, but are married and become patterns to their sex.

But am I not breaking the rules of modesty myself, and boasting too much? In what better manner can I relate this? However, though seemingly settled at Lodi, I was ever ready to return home when called. At last, at the first opening of communication on the cessation of the cruel hostilities which kept us all asunder, alarmed at the indifferent accounts of Mr. C.'s health, I hastened home. He is much broken, and has had two paralytic strokes, the last of which has deprived him of the use of his right hand and arm. Forgotten by the arts, suspended from the direction of education (though it is going on vastly well in my absence), I am now discharging the occupations of a nurse, happy in the self-gratification of doing my duty with no other consolation. In your "Dialogue," your Head would tell me, "That is enough;" your Heart, perhaps, will understand I might wish for more. God's will be done!

What a loss to me not having the loved Mrs. Church! and how grieved I was when told she was no more among the living! I used to see Madame de Corny in Paris. She still lives, but in bad health. She is the only one left of the common friends we knew. Strange changes, over and over again, all over Europe—you only are proceeding on well.

Now, my dear Sir, forgive this long letter. May I flatter myself to hear from you? Give me some accounts of yourself as you used to do; instead of Challion and Paris, talk to me of Monticello.

To Mrs. Cosway.

Monticello, Dec. 27th, 1820.

"Over the length of silence I draw a curtain," is an expression, my dear friend, of your cherished letter of April 7, 1819, of which, it might seem, I have need to avail myself; but not so really. To seventy-seven heavy years add two of prostrate health, during which all correspondence has been suspended of necessity, and you have the true cause of not having heard from me. My wrist, too, dislocated in Paris while I had the pleasure of being there with you, is, by the effect of years, now so stiffened that writing is become a slow and painful operation, and scarcely ever undertaken but under the goad of imperious business. But I have never lost sight of your letter, and give it now the first place among those of my trans-Atlantic friends which have been lying unacknowledged during the same period of ill health.

I rejoice, in the first place, that you are well; for your silence on that subject encourages me to presume it. And next, that you have been so usefully and pleasingly occupied in preparing the minds of others to enjoy the blessings you yourself have derived from the same source—a cultivated mind. Of Mr. Cosway I fear to say any thing, such is the disheartening account of the state of his health given in your letter; but here or wherever, I am sure he has all the happiness which an honest life assures. Nor will I say any thing of the troubles of those among whom you live. I see they are great, and wish them happily out of them, and especially that you may be safe and happy, whatever be their issue.

I will talk about Monticello, then, and my own country, as is the wish expressed in your letter. My daughter Randolph, whom you knew in Paris a young girl, is now the mother of eleven living children, the grandmother of about half a dozen others, enjoys health and good spirits, and sees the worth of her husband attested by his being at present Governor of the State in which we live. Among these I live like a patriarch of old. Our friend Trumbull is well, and is profitably and honorably employed by his country in commemorating with his pencil some of its Revolutionary honors. Of Mrs. Conger I hear nothing, nor, for a long time, of Madame de Corny. Such is the present state of our former coterie— dead, diseased, and dispersed. But "tout ce qui est differé n'est pas perdu," says the French proverb, and the religion you so sincerely profess tells us we shall meet again......

Mine is the next turn, and I shall meet it with good-will; for after one's friends are all gone before them, and our faculties leaving us, too, one by one, why wish to linger in mere vegetation, as a solitary trunk in a desolate field, from which all its former companions have disappeared. You have many good years remaining yet to be happy yourself and to make those around you happy. May these, my dear friend, be as many as yourself may wish, and all of them filled with health and happiness, will be among the last and warmest wishes of an unchangeable friend.

TH. JEFFERSON.

The original of the following letter, now lying before me, is edged with black:

From Mrs. Cosway.

London, July 15th, 1821.

My dear and most esteemed Friend—The appearance of this letter will inform you I have been left a *widow.* Poor Mr. Cosway was suddenly taken by an apoplectic fit, and, being the third, proved his last. At the time we had hopes he would enjoy a few years, for he had never been so well and so happy. Change of air was rendered necessary for his health. I took a very charming house, and fitted it up handsomely and comfortably with those pictures and things which he liked most.

All my thoughts and actions were for him. He had neglected his affairs very much, and when I was obliged to take them into my hands I was astonished. I took every means of ameliorating them, and had succeeded, at least for his comfort, and my consolation was his constantly repeating how well and how happy he was. We had an auction of all his effects, and his house in Stratford Place, which lasted two months. My fatigue was excessive. The sale did not produce as much as we expected, but enough to make him comfortable, and prevent his being embarrassed, as he might have been had I not lived accordingly. Every body thought he was very rich, and I was astonished when put into the real knowledge of his situation. He made his will two years ago, and left me sole executrix and mistress of every thing.

After having settled every thing here, and provided for three cousins of Mr. C.'s, I shall retire from this bustling and insignificant world to my favorite college at Lodi, as I always intended, where I can employ myself so happily in doing good.

I wish Monticello was not so far—I would pay you a visit, were it ever so much out of my way; but it is impossible. I long to hear from you. The remembrance of a person I so highly esteem and venerate affords me the happiest consolations, and your patriarchal situation delights me—such as I expected from you. Notwithstanding your indifference for a world of which you make one of the most distinguished ornaments and members, I wish you may still enjoy many years, and feel the happiness of a nation which produces such characters.

I will write again before I leave this country (at this moment in so boisterous an occupation, as you must be informed of), and I will send you my direction. I shall go through Paris and talk of you with Madame de Corny. Believe me ever your most affectionate and obliged

MARIA COSWAY.

From Mrs. Cosway.—[Extract.]

Milan, June 18th, 1823.

I congratulate you on the undertaking you announce me of the fine building* which occupies your taste and knowledge, and gratifies your heart. The work is worthy of you —you are worthy of such enjoyment. Nothing, I think, is more useful to mankind than a good education. I may say I have been very fortunate to give a spring to it in this country, and see those children I have had the care of turn out good wives, excellent mothers, *et bonnes femmes de ménage,* which was not understood in these countries, and which is the principal object of society, and the only useful one.

I wish I could come and learn from you ; were it the farthest part of Europe nothing would prevent me, but that immense sea makes a great distance. I hope, however, to hear from you as often as you can favor me. I am glad you approve my choice of Lodi. It is a pretty place, and free from the bustle of the world, which is become troublesome. What a change since you were here ! I saw Madame de Corny when at Paris : she is the same, only a little older.

From Mrs. Cosway.

Florence, Sept. 24th, 1824.

My dear Sir, and good Friend—I am come to visit my native country, and am much delighted with every thing round it. The arts have made great progress, and Mr. Cosway's drawings have been very much admired, which induced me to place in the gallery a very fine portrait of his. I have found here an opportunity of sending this letter by Leghorn, which I had not at Milan.

I wish much to hear from you, and how you go on with your fine Seminary. I have had my grand saloon painted with the representation of the four parts of the world, and the most distinguished objects of them. I am at loss for America, as I found very few small prints—however, Washington town is marked, and I have left a hill bare where I would place Monticello and the Seminary : if you favor

---

* The University of Virginia.

me with some description, that I might have them introduced, you would oblige me much. I am just setting out for
my home. Pray write to me at Lodi, and, if this reaches
you safely, I will write longer by the same way. Believe me
ever, your most obliged and affectionate friend,

MARIA COSWAY.

CHAPTER XX.

In the following letter to Mr. Adams we find Mr. Jefferson not complaining of, but fully appreciating the rapidity with which old age and its debilities were advancing on him:

To John Adams.

Monticello, June 1st, 1822.

It is very long, my dear Sir, since I have written to you. My dislocated wrist is now become so stiff that I write slowly and with pain, and therefore write as little as I can. Yet it is due to mutual friendship to ask once in a while how we do. The papers tell us that General Stark is off at the age of 93. Charles Thompson still lives at about the same age —cheerful, slender as a grasshopper, and so much without memory that he scarcely recognizes the members of his household. An intimate friend of his called on him not long since; it was difficult to make him recollect who he was, and, sitting one hour, he told him the same story four times over. Is this life—

> "With lab'ring step
> To tread our former footsteps?—pace the round
> Eternal?—to beat and beat
> The beaten track?—to see what we have seen,
> To taste the tasted?—o'er our palates to decant
> Another vintage?"

It is at most but the life of a cabbage; surely not worth a wish. When all our faculties have left, or are leaving us, one by one—sight, hearing, memory—every avenue of pleasing sensation is closed, and athumy, debility, and malaise left in their places—when friends of our youth are all gone, and a generation is risen around us whom we know not, is death an evil?

> "When one by one our ties are torn,
> And friend from friend is snatched forlorn,
> When man is left alone to mourn,
> Oh! then how sweet it is to die!
> When trembling limbs refuse their weight,
> And films slow gathering dim the sight,
> When clouds obscure the mental light,
> 'Tis nature's kindest boon to die!"

I really think so. I have ever dreaded a doting old age; and my health has been generally so good, and is now so good, that I dread it still. The rapid decline of my strength during the last winter has made me hope sometimes that I see land. During summer I enjoy its temperature; but I shudder at the approach of winter, and wish I could sleep through it with the dormouse, and only wake with him in spring, if ever. They say that Stark could walk about his room. I am told you walk well and firmly. I can only reach my garden, and that with sensible fatigue. I ride, however, daily. But reading is my delight. I should wish never to put pen to paper; and the more because of the treacherous practice some people have of publishing one's letters without leave. Lord Mansfield declared it a breach of trust, and punishable at law. I think it should be a penitentiary felony; yet you will have seen that they have drawn me out into the arena of the newspapers.* Although I know it is too late for me to buckle on the armor of youth, yet my indignation would not permit me passively to receive the kick of an ass.

To turn to the news of the day, it seems that the cannibals of Europe are going to eating one another again. A war between Russia and Turkey is like the battle of the kite and snake. Whichever destroys the other leaves a destroyer the less for the world. This pugnacious humor of mankind seems to be the law of his nature, one of the obstacles to too great multiplication provided in the mechanism of the universe. The cocks of the hen-yard kill one another. Bears, bulls, rams, do the same. And the horse, in his wild state,

---

* Alluding to a reply which he made to an attack made on him by one signing himself a "Native Virginian."

kills all the young males, until, worn down with age and war, some vigorous youth kills him, and takes to himself the harem of females. I hope we shall prove how much happier for man the Quaker policy is, and that the life of the feeder is better than that of the fighter; and it is some consolation that the desolation by these maniacs of one part of the earth is the means of improving it in other parts. Let the latter be our office, and let us milk the cow, while the Russian holds her by the horns, and the Turk by the tail. God bless you, and give you health, strength, and good spirits, and as much of life as you think worth having.

In another letter to Mr. Adams he gives really a pitiable account of the tax on his strength which letter-writing had become. Mr. Adams had suggested that he should publish the letter just quoted, by way of letting the public know how much he suffered from the number of letters he had to answer. Jefferson, in reply, says:

To John Adams.

I do not know how far you may suffer, as I do, under the persecution of letters, of which every mail brings a fresh load. They are letters of inquiry, for the most part, always of good-will, sometimes from friends whom I esteem, but much oftener from persons whose names are unknown to me, but written kindly and civilly, and to which, therefore, civility requires answers. Perhaps the better-known failure of your hand in its function of writing may shield you in greater degree from this distress, and so far qualify the misfortune of its disability. I happened to turn to my letter-list some time ago, and a curiosity was excited to count those received in a single year. It was the year before the last. I found the number to be one thousand two hundred and sixty-seven, many of them requiring answers of elaborate research, and all to be answered with due attention and consideration. Take an average of this number for a week or a day, and I will repeat the question suggested by other considerations in mine of the 1st. Is this life? At best it is but the life of a mill-horse, who sees no end to his circle but in death. To such a life that of a cabbage is paradise.

It occurs, then, that my condition of existence, truly stated in that letter, if better known, might check the kind indiscretions which are so heavily depressing the departing hours of life. Such a relief would, to me, be an ineffable blessing.

The reader can form some idea of the extent of this correspondence, which, in his old age, became such a grievous burden to the veteran statesman, from the fact that the letters received by him that were preserved amounted to twenty-six thousand at the time of his death; while the copies left by him, of those which he himself had written, numbered sixteen thousand. These were but a small portion of what he wrote, as he wrote numbers of which he retained no copies.

Mr. Jefferson's estimate of Napoleon's character is found in the following interesting extract from a letter written to Mr. Adams, February 24, 1823:

To John Adams.—Character of Napoleon.

I have just finished reading O'Meara's Bonaparte. It places him in a higher scale of understanding than I had allotted him. I had thought him the greatest of all military captains, but an indifferent statesman, and misled by unworthy passions. The flashes, however, which escaped from him in these conversations with O'Meara prove a mind of great expansion, although not of distinct development and reasoning. He seizes results with rapidity and penetration, but never explains logically the process of reasoning by which he arrives at them.

This book, too, makes us forget his atrocities for a moment, in commiseration of his sufferings. I will not say that the authorities of the world, charged with the care of their country and people, had not a right to confine him for life, as a lion or tiger, on the principle of self-preservation. There was no safety to nations while he was permitted to roam at large. But the putting him to death in cold blood, by lingering tortures of mind, by vexations, insults, and deprivations, was a degree of inhumanity to which the poisonings and assassinations of the school of Borgia and den of Marat never attained. The book proves, also, that nature had denied him the moral sense, the first excellence of well-organized man. If he could seriously and repeatedly affirm that he had raised himself to power without ever having committed a crime, it proved that he wanted totally the sense of right and wrong. If he could consider the millions of human lives which he had destroyed, or caused to be destroyed, the desolations of countries by plunderings, burnings, and famine, the destitutions of lawful rulers of the world without the consent of their constituents, to place his brothers and sisters on their thrones, the cutting up of established societies of men and jumbling them discordantly together again at his caprice, the demolition of the fairest hopes of mankind for the recovery of their rights and amelioration of their condition, and all the numberless train of his other enormities—the man, I say, who could consider all these as no crimes, must have been a moral monster, against whom every hand should have been lifted to slay him.

You are so kind as to inquire after my health. The bone of my arm is well knitted, but my hand and fingers are in a discouraging condition, kept entirely useless by an œdematous swelling of slow amendment. God bless you, and continue your good health of body and mind.

The broken arm alluded to at the close of this letter was caused by an accident which Mr. Jefferson met with towards the close of the year 1822. While descending a flight of steps leading from one of the terraces at Monticello, a decayed plank gave way and threw him forward at full length on the ground. To a man in his eightieth year such a fall might have been fatal, and Jefferson was fortunate in escaping with a broken arm, though it gave him much pain at the time, and was a serious inconvenience to him during the few remaining years of his life. Though debarred from his usual daily exercise on horseback for a short time after the accident occurred, he resumed his rides while his arm was yet in a sling. His favorite riding-horse, Eagle, was brought up to the terrace, whence he mounted while in this disabled state. Eagle, though a spirited Virginia full-blood, seemed instinctively to know that his venerable master was an invalid; for, usually restless and spirited, he on these occasions stood as quietly as a lamb, and, leaning up towards the terrace, seemed to wish to aid the crippled octogenarian as he mounted into the saddle.

I make the following extracts from a letter full of interest, written to Judge Johnson, of South Carolina, early in the summer of 1823. He writes:

To Judge Johnson.

What a treasure will be found in General Washington's cabinet, when it shall pass into the hands of as candid a friend to truth as he was himself!......

With respect to his [Washington's] Farewell Address, to the authorship of which, it seems, there are conflicting claims, I can state to you some facts. He had determined to decline a re-election at the end of his first term, and so far determined, that he had requested Mr. Madison to prepare for him something valedictory, to be addressed to his constituents on his retirement. This was done: but he was finally persuaded to acquiesce in a second election, to which no one more strenuously pressed him than myself, from a conviction of the importance of strengthening, by longer habit, the respect necessary for that office, which the weight of his character only could effect. When, at the end of this second term, his Valedictory came out, Mr. Madison recognized in it several passages of his draught; several others, we were both satisfied, were from the pen of Hamilton; and others from that of the President himself. These he probably put into the hands of Hamilton to form into a whole, and hence it may all appear in Hamilton's handwriting, as if it were all of his composition......

The close of my second sheet warns me that it is time now to relieve you from this letter of unmerciful length. Indeed, I wonder how I have accomplished it, with two crippled wrists, the one scarcely able to move my pen, the other to hold my paper. But I am hurried sometimes beyond the sense of pain, when unbosoming myself to friends who harmonize with me in principle. You and I may differ occasionally in details of minor consequence, as no two minds, more than two faces, are the same in every feature. But our general objects are the same—to preserve the republican forms and principles of our Constitution, and cleave to the salutary distribution of powers which that has established. These are the two sheet-anchors of our Union. If driven from either, we shall be in danger of foundering. To my prayers for its safety and perpetuity, I add those for the continuation of your health, happiness, and usefulness to your country.

Towards the close of the year 1823 he wrote a long letter to Lafayette, the following extracts from which show how well he felt the infirmities of old age advancing upon him:

To the Marquis de Lafayette.—[*Extracts.*]

Monticello, November 4th, 1823.

My dear Friend—Two dislocated wrists and crippled fingers have rendered writing so slow and laborious, as to oblige me to withdraw from nearly all correspondence—not however, from yours, while I can make a stroke with a pen. We have gone through too many trying scenes together to forget the sympathies and affections they nourished......

After much sickness, and the accident of a broken and disabled arm, I am again in tolerable health, but extremely debilitated, so as to be scarcely able to walk into my garden. The hebetude of age, too, and extinguishment of interest in the things around me, are weaning me from them, and dispose me with cheerfulness to resign them to the existing generation, satisfied that the daily advance of science will enable them to administer the commonwealth with increased wisdom. You have still many valuable years to give to your country, and with my prayers that they may be years of health and happiness, and especially that they may see the establishment of the principles of government which you have cherished through life, accept the assurance of my constant friendship and respect.

Early in the following year, in a reply to a request of Isaac Engelbrecht that he would send him something from his own hand, he writes: "Knowing nothing more moral, more sublime, more worthy of your preservation than David's description of the good man, in his 15th Psalm, I will

THE UNIVERSITY OF VIRGINIA.

here transcribe it from Brady and Tate's version:" he then gives the Psalm in full.

In alluding to this year of his life, his biographer says, "Mr. Jefferson's absorbing topic throughout 1824 was the University." He had first interested himself in this institution in the year 1817. The plan originally was only to establish a college, to be called the "Central College of Virginia;" but in his hands it was enlarged, and consummated in the erection of the University of Virginia, whose classic dome and columns are now lit up by the morning rays of the same sun which shines on the ruin and desolation of his own once happy home.* The architectural plans and form of government and instruction for this institution afforded congenial occupation for his declining years, and made it emphatically the child of his old age. While the buildings were being erected, his visits to them were daily; and from the northeast corner of the terrace at Monticello he frequently watched the workmen engaged on them, through a telescope which is still preserved in the library of the University.

His toil and labors for this institution, and the obstacles which he had to overcome in procuring the necessary funds from the Virginia Legislature, served to distract his thoughts, in a measure, from those pecuniary embarrassments which, though resulting from his protracted services to his country, so imbittered the closing years of his honored life. None appreciated more highly than himself the importance of establishing Southern institutions for the instruction of Southern young men. We find allusions to this subject scattered through the whole of his correspondence during this period of his life.

How entirely he was absorbed in this darling project of his old age, may be seen from the following extract from a letter written by him to Mr. Adams, October 12, 1823:

---

* The accompanying illustration presents the University of Virginia, as it appeared in 1856.

To John Adams.

I do not write with the ease which your letter of September 18th supposes. Crippled wrists and fingers make writing slow and laborious. But while writing to you, I lose the sense of these things in the recollection of ancient times, when youth and health made happiness out of every thing. I forget for a while the hoary winter of age, when we can think of nothing but how to keep ourselves warm, and how to get rid of our heavy hours until the friendly hand of death shall rid us of all at once. Against this *tedium vitæ*, however, I am fortunately mounted on a hobby, which, indeed, I should have better managed some thirty or forty years ago; but whose easy amble is still sufficient to give exercise and amusement to an octogenary rider. This is the establishment of a University, on a scale more comprehensive, and in a country more healthy and central, than our old William and Mary, which these obstacles have long kept in a state of languor and inefficiency.

The following extract from a letter to a friend, inviting him to Monticello, shows what little interest he took in politics:

You must be contented with the plain and sober family and neighborly society, with the assurance that you shall hear no wrangling about the next President, although the excitement on that subject will then be at its acme. Numerous have been the attempts to entangle me in that imbroglio. But at the age of eighty, I seek quiet, and abjure contention. I read but a single newspaper, Ritchie's *Enquirer*, the best that is published or ever has been published in America.

In one of his letters to J. C. Cabell, written about the appointment of Professors for the University, we find the following passage, which sounds strangely now in an age when nepotism is so rife:

In the course of the trusts I have exercised through life with powers of appointment, I can say with truth, and with unspeakable comfort, that I never did appoint a relation to

office, and that merely because I never saw the case in which
some one did not offer, or occur, better qualified; and I have
the most unlimited confidence that in the appointment of
Professors to our nursling institution every individual of
my associates will look with a single eye to the sublimation
of its character, and adopt, as our sacred motto, "*Detur dig-
niori !*"   In this way it will honor us, and bless our country.

In August, 1824, the people of the United States were, as
Jefferson wrote to a friend, thrown into a " delirium " of joy
by the arrival in New York of Lafayette.   He had left their
shores forty years before, loaded with all the honors that an
admiring and victorious people could heap upon a generous
and gallant young defender.   Filled with all the enthusiasm
inspired by youth, genius, and patriotism, he had returned to
his beloved France with a future full of promise and hope;
and now, after having passed through the storms of two
Revolutions, after having seen his fairest hopes, both for
himself and his country, perish, he came back to America, an
impoverished and decrepit old man.   His misfortunes, in the
eyes of the Americans, gave him greater claims on their love
and sympathy, and his visit was really triumphal.   Jefferson, in describing his tour through the country, wrote: " He
is making a triumphant progress through the States, from
town to town, with acclamations of welcome, such as no
crowned head ever received."

In writing to Lafayette to hasten his visit to Monticello,
where he was impatiently expected, Jefferson says:

To Lafayette.

What a history have we to run over, from the evening that
yourself, Mousnier, Bernan, and other patriots settled, in my
house in Paris, the outlines of the constitution you wished.
And to trace it through all the disastrous chapters of Robes-
pierre, Barras, Bonaparte, and the Bourbons !   These things,
however, are for our meeting.   You mention the return of
Miss Wright to America, accompanied by her sister ; but do
not say what her stay is to be, nor what her course.   Should
it lead her to a visit of our University, which in its archi-

tecture only is as yet an object, herself and her companion will nowhere find a welcome more hearty than with Mrs. Randolph, and all the inhabitants of Monticello. This Athenæum of our country, in embryo, is as yet but promise; and not in a state to recall the recollections of Athens. But every thing has its beginning, its growth, and end; and who knows with what future delicious morsels of philosophy, and by what future Miss Wright raked from its ruins, the world may, some day, be gratified and instructed? . . . . . . But all these things *à revoir;* in the mean time we are impatient that your ceremonies at York should be over, and give you to the embraces of friendship.

To Monticello, where "the embraces of friendship" awaited him, Lafayette accordingly went, and the following description of the touching and beautiful scene witnessed by those who saw the meeting between these two old friends and veteran patriots has been furnished me by his grandson, Mr. Jefferson Randolph, who was present on that memorable occasion:

Lafayette and Jefferson in 1824.

The lawn on the eastern side of the house at Monticello contains not quite an acre. On this spot was the meeting of Jefferson and Lafayette, on the latter's visit to the United States. The barouche containing Lafayette stopped at the edge of this lawn. His escort—one hundred and twenty mounted men—formed on one side in a semicircle extending from the carriage to the house. A crowd of about two hundred men, who were drawn together by curiosity to witness the meeting of these two venerable men, formed themselves in a semicircle on the opposite side. As Lafayette descended from the carriage, Jefferson descended the steps of the portico. The scene which followed was touching. Jefferson was feeble and tottering with age—Lafayette permanently lamed and broken in health by his long confinement in the dungeon of Olmutz. As they approached each other, their uncertain. gait quickened itself into a shuffling run, and exclaiming, "Ah, Jefferson!" "Ah, Lafayette!" they burst into tears as they fell into each other's arms. Among the four hundred men witnessing the scene there was not a dry eye—no sound save an occasional suppressed sob. The two old men entered the house as the crowd dispersed in profound silence.

At a dinner given to Lafayette in Charlottesville, besides the " Nation's Guest," there were present Jefferson, Madison, and Monroe. To the toast: "*Thomas Jefferson and the Declaration of Independence—alike identified with the Cause of Liberty,*" Jefferson responded in a few written remarks, which were read by Mr. Southall. We find in the following extract from them a graceful and heartfelt tribute to his well-loved friend:

I joy, my friends, in your joy, inspired by the visit of this our ancient and distinguished leader and benefactor. His deeds in the war of independence you have heard and read. They are known to you, and embalmed in your memories and in the pages of faithful history. His deeds in the peace which followed that war, are perhaps not known to you; but I can attest them. When I was stationed in his country, for the purpose of cementing its friendship with ours and of advancing our mutual interests, this friend of both was my most powerful auxiliary and advocate. He made our cause his own, as in truth it was that of his native country also. His influence and connections there were great. All doors of all departments were open to him at all times; to me only formally and at appointed times. In truth I only held the nail, he drove it. Honor him, then, as your benefactor in peace as well as in war.

Towards the close of the year 1824 Daniel Webster visited Monticello, and spent a day or two there. He has left us an account of this visit, containing a minute description of Jefferson's personal appearance, style of dress, and habits. After giving extracts from this account, Mr. Randall, in his Life of Jefferson, says: "These descriptions appearing to us to lack some of those gradations and qualifications in expression which are essential to convey accurate impressions, we sought an opinion on them from one as familiar with Mr.

Jefferson, with his views and modes of expression, as any person ever was, and received the following reply :

——, 1857.

My dear Mr. Randall—...... First, on the subject of Mr. Jefferson's personal appearance. Mr. Webster's description of it did not please me, because, though I will not stop to quarrel with any of the details, the general impression it was calculated to produce seemed to me an unfavorable one; that is, a person who had never seen my grandfather, would, from Mr. Webster's description, have thought him rather an ill-looking man, which he certainly never was......

It would be, however, very difficult for me to give an accurate description of the appearance of one whom I so tenderly loved and deeply venerated. His person and countenance were to me associated with so many of my best affections, so much of my highest reverence, that I could not expect other persons to see them as I did. One thing I will say—that never in my life did I see his countenance distorted by a single bad passion or unworthy feeling. I have seen the expression of suffering, bodily and mental, of grief, pain, sadness, just indignation, disappointment, disagreeable surprise, and displeasure, but never of anger, impatience, peevishness, discontent, to say nothing of worse or more ignoble emotions. To the contrary, it was impossible to look on his face without being struck with its benevolent, intelligent, cheerful, and placid expression. It was at once intellectual, good, kind, and pleasant, while his tall, spare figure spoke of health, activity, and that *helpfulness*, that power and will, "never to trouble another for what he could do himself," which marked his character.

His dress was simple, and adapted to his ideas of neatness and comfort. He paid little attention to fashion, wearing whatever he liked best, and sometimes blending the fashions of several different periods. He wore long waistcoats, when the mode was for very short ; white cambric stocks fastened behind with a buckle, when cravats were universal. He adopted the pantaloon very late in life, because he found it more comfortable and convenient, and cut off his queue for the same reason. He made no change except from motives of the same kind, and did nothing to be in conformity with the fashion of the day. He considered such independence as the privilege of his age......

In like manner, I never heard him speak of Wirt's Life of Patrick Henry with the amount of severity recorded by Mr. Webster. My impression is that here too, Mr. Webster, from a very natural impulse, and without the least intention of misrepresentation, has put down only those parts of Mr. Jefferson's remarks which accorded with his own views, and left out all the extenuations—the "*circonstantes attendantes,*" as the French say. This, of course, would lead to an erroneous impression. Of Mr. Wirt's book my grandfather did not think very highly; but the unkind remark, so far as Mr. Wirt was personally concerned, unaccompanied by any thing to soften its severity, is, to say the least, very little like Mr. Jefferson.

ELLEN W. COOLIDGE.

Of Jefferson's opinion of Henry, Mr. Randall goes on to say:

His whole correspondence, and his Memoir written at the age of seventy-seven, exhibit his unbounded admiration of Henry in certain particulars, and his dislike or severe animadversion in none. Henry and he came to differ very widely in politics, and the former literally died leading a gallant political sortie against the conquering Republicans. On one occasion, at least, his keen native humor was directed personally against Jefferson. With his inimitable look and tone, he with great effect declared that he did not approve of gentlemen's "abjuring their native victuals."* This gave great diversion to Jefferson. He loved to talk about Henry, to narrate anecdotes of their early intimacy; to paint his taste for unrestrained nature in every thing; to describe his *bonhomie*, his humor, his unquestionable integrity, mixed with a certain waywardness and freakishness; to give illustrations of his shrewdness, and of his overwhelming power as an orator.

Mr. Randall's indefatigable industry in ferreting out every account and record of Jefferson has laid before the pub-

---

* The Republicans were accused of being adherents of France—the *cookery* of Monticello was French.—*Randall's Note.*

lic Dr. Dunglison's interesting and valuable memoranda concerning his intercourse with Mr. Jefferson and his last illness and death. I make the following extracts:

Dr. Dunglison's Memoranda.

Soon afterwards [the arrival at Charlottesville] the venerable ex-President presented himself, and welcomed us* with that dignity and kindness for which he was celebrated. He was then eighty-two years old, with his intellectual powers unshaken by age, and the physical man so active that he rode to and from Monticello, and took exercise on foot with all the activity of one twenty or thirty years younger. He sympathized with us on the discomforts of our long voyage, and on the disagreeable journey we must have passed over the Virginia roads; and depicted to us the great distress he had felt lest we had been lost at sea—for he had almost given us up, when my letter arrived with the joyful intelligence that we were safe......

The houses [the professors' houses, or "pavilions" of the University] were much better furnished than we had expected to find them, and would have been far more commodious had Mr. Jefferson consulted his excellent and competent daughter, Mrs. Randolph, in regard to the interior arrangements, instead of planning the architectural exterior first, and leaving the interior to shift for itself. Closets would have interfered with the symmetry of the rooms or passages, and hence there were none in most of the houses; and of the only one which was furnished with a closet, it was told as an anecdote of Mr. Jefferson, that, not suspecting it, according to his general arrangements, he opened the door and walked into it in his way out of the pavilion......

Mr. Jefferson was considered to have but little faith in physic; and has often told me that he would rather trust to the unaided, or, rather, uninterfered with, efforts of nature than to physicians in general. "It is not," he was wont to observe, "to physic that I object so much, as to physicians." Occasionally, too, he would speak jocularly, especially to the unprofessional, of medical practice, and on one occasion gave

---

* The professors of the University, who were all foreigners, and brought by Mr. Jefferson from Europe, with the exception of two only.

offense, when, most assuredly, if the same thing had been said to me, no offense would have been taken. In the presence of Dr. Everett, afterwards Private Secretary to Mr. Monroe, he remarked that whenever he saw three physicians together, he looked up to discover whether there was not a turkey-buzzard in the neighborhood. The annoyance of the doctor, I am told, was manifest. To me, when it was recounted, it seemed a harmless jest. But whatever may have been Mr. Jefferson's notions of physic and physicians, it is but justice to say that he was one of the most attentive and respectful of patients. He bore suffering inflicted upon him for remedial purposes with fortitude; and in my visits, showed me, by memoranda, the regularity with which he had taken the prescribed remedies at the appointed times......

In the summer of 1825, the monotonous life of the college was broken in upon by the arrival of General Lafayette, to take leave of his distinguished friend, Mr. Jefferson, preparatory to his return to France. A dinner was given to him in the rotunda by the professors and students, at which Mr. Madison and Mr. Monroe were present, but Mr. Jefferson's indisposition prevented him from attending. "The meeting at Monticello," says M. Levasseur, the Secretary to General Lafayette during his journey, in his *"Lafayette in America in* 1824 *and* 1825," vol. ii., p. 245, "of three men who, by their successive elevation to the supreme magistracy of the state, had given to their country twenty-four years of prosperity and glory, and who still offered it the example of private virtues, was a sufficiently strong inducement to make us wish to stay there a longer time; but indispensable duties recalled General Lafayette to Washington, and he was obliged to take leave of his friends. I shall not attempt to depict the sadness which prevailed at this cruel separation, which had none of the alleviation which is usually felt by youth; for in this instance the individuals who bade farewell had all passed through a long career, and the immensity of the ocean would still add to the difficulties of a reunion."

M. Levasseur has evidently confounded this banquet with that given by the inhabitants of Charlottesville, the year preceding, during the first visit of Lafayette to Mr. Jefferson. At that period there were neither professors nor students, as the institution was not opened until six months afterwards. "Every thing," says M. Levasseur (vol. i., p. 220), "had been prepared at Charlottesville, by the citizens and students, to give a worthy reception to Lafayette. The sight of the nation's guest seated at the patriotic banquet, between Jefferson and Madison, excited in those present an enthusiasm which expressed itself in enlivening sallies of wit and humor. Mr. Madison, who had arrived that day at Charlottesville to attend this meeting, was especially remarkable for the originality of his expressions and the delicacy of his allusions. Before leaving the table he gave a toast—' *To Liberty—with Virtue for her Guest, and Gratitude for the Feast,*' which was received with rapturous applause."

The same enthusiasm prevailed at the dinner given in the rotunda. One of the toasts proposed by an officer of the institution, I believe, was an example of forcing a metaphor to the full extent of its capability—"*The Apple of our Heart's Eye—Lafayette.*"

CHAPTER XXI.

I HAVE now to treat of that part of Jefferson's life which his biographer well calls "the saddest page in his personal history"—I allude to the pecuniary embarrassments which clouded the evening of his honored life. These were caused by his long absences from home when in the service of his country, the crowds of visitors which his reputation drew to his house, and the fluctuations and depression of the money market.

Jefferson inherited from his father nineteen hundred acres of land, and began the practice of law when he became of age, in 1764. His practice very soon became extensive, and yielded him an income of $3000, while from his estates he received about $2000, making a sum total of $5000. This was a handsome income, as property was then rated; for the very best highlands in Albemarle were valued at not more than two dollars per acre, and all other kinds of property bore a proportionate value. By the beginning of the Revolution, in 1774, he had increased his landed possessions to five thousand acres of the best lands around him; all paid for out of his income. This fact alone proves beyond contradiction how capable he was of managing his affairs and increasing his fortune, until called from direct supervision of them by the demands of his country.

On his marriage in 1772, he received, as his wife's dower, property which was valued at $40,000, but with a British debt on it of $13,000. He sold property to pay this debt, and the Virginia Legislature having passed a resolution to the effect that whoever would deposit in the State Treasury the amount of their British debt, the State would protect them, he deposited his in the Treasury. This resolution was afterwards rescinded, and the money was returned in Treasury Certificates. The depreciation of these was so great, that the value of those received by Jefferson was laid out in an overcoat; so that in after-years, when riding by the farm which he had sold to procure the $13,000 deposited in the State Treasury, he would smile and say, "I sold that farm for an overcoat." He sold other property to pay this debt, and this time was paid in paper money at as great a depreciation. Thus his impatience of debt cost him his wife's property. How just and exact he was in the payment of this, may be seen from the following extracts taken from one of his letters to his British creditors:

I am desirous of arranging with you such just and practicable conditions as will ascertain to you the terms at which you will receive my part of your debt, and give me the satisfaction of knowing that you are contented. What the laws of Virginia are, or may be, will in no wise influence my conduct. Substantial justice is my object, as decided by reason, and not by authority or compulsion.......
Subsequent events have been such, that the State can not, and ought not, to pay the same nominal sum in gold or silver which they received in paper; nor is it certain what they will do: my intention being, and having always been, that, whatever the State decides, you shall receive my debt fully. I am ready, to remove all difficulty arising from this deposit, to take back to myself the demand against the State, and to consider the deposit as originally made for myself and not for you.

The Revolution coming on, he was, as we have seen, in public life almost continuously from 1774 to 1809. He did not visit his largest estate for nineteen years, and at one time was absent from his home for seven years. In 1782, he was sent as Minister to France; he returned at the close of the year 1788, and in March, 1789, entered Washington's cabinet as Secretary of State. He resigned in February, 1794, and devoted himself for three years to his private affairs. We have seen with what reluctance he returned to public life when in 1797 he was elected Vice-president. He was inaugurated President in 1801; and not retiring till 1809, was thus, with the exception of three years, absent from home from 1774 to 1809.

Of the various offices which Jefferson was called to fill, he received pecuniary benefit from that of Vice-president alone. As a member of the Virginia Assembly and of Congress, as well as when Governor of Virginia, his salaries barely paid the expenses incident to his official position. As Minister to France his salary did not cover his expenses; as Secretary of State his expenditures slightly exceeded his salary, while they greatly surpassed it when he was President. Yet his biographer tells us that "in none of these offices was his style of living noticed either for parsimony or extravagance." The following extracts from a letter written by him to his commission merchant, a month or two before the expiration of his Presidential term, show in what a painful embarrassment he found himself at that time:

Nothing had been more fixed than my determination to keep my expenses here within the limits of my salary, and I had great confidence that I had done so. Having, however, trusted to rough estimates by my head, and not being sufficiently apprised of the outstanding accounts, I find, on a review of my affairs here, as they will stand on the 3d of March, that I shall be three or four months' salary behindhand. In ordinary cases this degree of arrearage would not be serious, but on the scale of the establishment here it amounts to seven or eight thousand dollars, which being to come out of my private funds will be felt by them sensibly.

After saying that in looking out for recourse to make good this deficit in the first instance, it is natural for him to turn to the principal bank of his own State, and asking that his commission merchant would try and arrange the matter for him with as little delay as possible, he goes on to say:

Since I have become sensible of this deficit I have been under an agony of mortification, and therefore must solicit as much urgency in the negotiation as the case will admit. My intervening nights will be almost sleepless, as nothing could be more distressing to me than to leave debts here unpaid, if indeed I should be permitted to depart with them unpaid, of which I am by no means certain.

When Jefferson resigned as Secretary of State in 1794, he hoped he had turned his back forever on public life, and proposed to devote the residue of his days to the restoration of his shattered fortunes. For a time he refused to listen to any application calling him from the peaceful enjoyments of his tranquil life at Monticello, but he was besieged by deputations of the most distinguished men of the day—old associates of the Revolution, who pressed his country's claim on him with an earnestness and pertinacity not to be resisted, and which finally recalled him to public life.

Jefferson, then, returned in 1809 to estates wasted by the rude management of the times, with hands, as he himself said, as clean as they were empty, and with a world-wide reputation which attracted crowds of company to devour what was left of a private property wasted by a life-long devotion to his country's demands upon him. No one could have been more hospitable than he was, and no one ever gave a more heartfelt or more cordial welcome to friends than he did; but the visits of those who were led by curiosity to Monticello was an annoyance which at times was almost painful to one of as retiring a disposition as he was. These visitors came at all hours and all seasons, and when unable to catch a glimpse of him in any other way, they not unfrequently begged to be allowed to sit in the hall, where, waiting until the dinner-hour arrived, they saw him as he passed through from his private apartments to his dining-room. On one occasion a female visitor, who was peering around the house, punched her parasol through a window-pane to get a better view of him.

The following letter from one of Mr. Jefferson's grand-daughters, which I take from Randall's Life of Jefferson, and the extracts which I also give from Dr. Dunglison's Memoranda, will give the reader a correct idea of the tax which such an influx of visitors must have been on an estate already groaning under debt:

—————, 1856.

My dear Mr. Randall—...... Mr. Jefferson was not an improvident man. He had habits of order and economy, was regular in keeping his accounts, knew the value of money, and was in no way disposed to waste it. He was simple in his tastes, careful, and spent very little on himself. 'Tis not true that he threw away his money in fantastic projects and theoretical experiments. He was eminently a practical man. He was, during all the years that I knew him, very liberal, but never extravagant......

To return to his visitors: they came of all nations, at all times, and paid longer or shorter visits. I have known a New England judge bring a letter of introduction to my grandfather, and stay three weeks. The learned Abbé Correa, always a welcome guest, passed some weeks of each year with us during the whole time of his stay in the country. We had persons from abroad, from all the States of the Union, from every part of the State—men, women, and children. In short, almost every day, for at least eight months of the year, brought its contingent of guests. People of wealth, fashion, men in office, professional men, military and civil, lawyers, doctors, Protestant clergymen, Catholic priests, members of Congress, foreign ministers, missionaries, Indian agents, tourists, travellers, artists, strangers, friends. Some came from affection and respect, some from curiosity, some to give or receive advice or instruction, some from idleness, some because others set the example, and very varied, amus-

C c

ing, and agreeable was the society afforded by this influx of guests.   I have listened to very remarkable conversations carried on round the table, the fireside, or in the summer drawing-room......

There were few eminent men of our country, except, perhaps, some political adversaries, who did not visit him in his retirement, to say nothing of distinguished foreigners.   Life at Monticello was on an easy and informal footing.   Mr. Jefferson always made his appearance at an early breakfast, but his mornings were most commonly devoted to his own occupations, and it was at dinner, after dinner, and in the evening, that he gave himself up to the society of his family and his guests.   Visitors were left free to employ themselves as they liked during the morning hours—to walk, read, or seek companionship with the ladies of the family and each other.   M. Correa passed his time in the fields and the woods; some gentlemen preferred the library; others the drawing-room; others the quiet of their own chambers; or they strolled down the mountain side and under the shade of the trees.   The ladies in like manner consulted their ease and inclinations, and whiled away the time as best they might.

ELLEN W. COOLIDGE.

Dr. Dunglison says in his Memoranda:

His daughter, Mrs. Randolph, or one of the grand-daughters, took the head of the table; he himself sat near the other end, and almost always some visitors were present.   The pilgrimage to Monticello was a favorite one with him who aspired to the rank of the patriot and the philanthropist; but it was too often undertaken from idle curiosity, and could not, under such circumstances, have afforded pleasure to, while it entailed unrequited expense on, its distinguished proprietor. More than once, indeed, the annoyance has been the subject of regretful animadversion.   Monticello, like Montpellier, the seat of Mr. Madison, was some miles distant from any tavern, and hence, without sufficient consideration, the traveller not only availed himself of the hospitality of the ex-Presidents, but inflicted upon them the expenses of his quadrupeds. On one occasion at Montpellier, where my wife and myself were paying a visit to Mr. and Mrs. Madison, no fewer than nine horses were entertained during the night; and in reply to some observation which the circumstances engendered, Mr. Madison remarked, that while he was delighted with the society of the owners, he confessed he had not so much feeling for the horses.

Sitting one evening in the porch of Monticello, two gigs drove up, each containing a gentleman and lady. It appeared to me to be evidently the desire of the party to be invited to stay all night. One of the gentlemen came up to the porch and saluted Mr. Jefferson, stating that they claimed the privilege of American citizens in paying their respects to the President, and inspecting Monticello. Mr. Jefferson received them with marked politeness, and told them they were at liberty to look at every thing around, but as they did not receive an invitation to spend the night, they left in the dusk and returned to Charlottesville. Mr. Jefferson, on that occasion, could hardly avoid an expression of impatience at the repeated though complimentary intrusions to which he was exposed.

In Mr. Jefferson's embarrassed circumstances in the evening of life, the immense influx of visitors could not fail to be attended with much inconvenience. I had the curiosity to ask Mrs. Randolph what was the largest number of persons for whom she had been called upon unexpectedly to prepare accommodations for the night, and she replied *fifty!*

In a country like our own there is a curiosity to know personally those who have been called to fill the highest office in the Republic, and he who has attained this eminence must have formed a number of acquaintances who are eager to visit him in his retirement, so that when his salary as the first officer of the state ceases, the duties belonging to it do not cease simultaneously; and I confess I have no sympathy with the feeling of economy, political or social, which denies to the ex-President a retiring allowance, which may enable him to pass the remainder of his days in that useful and dignified hospitality which seems to be demanded, by the citizens, of one who has presided over them......

At all times dignified, and by no means easy of approach to all, he was generally communicative to those on whom he could rely. In his own house he was occasionally free in his speech, even to imprudence, to those of whom he did not know enough to be satisfied that an improper use might not be made of his candor. As an example of this, I recollect a person from Rhode Island visiting the University, and being introduced to Mr. Jefferson by one of my colleagues. The person did not impress me favorably; and when I rode up to Monticello, I found that no better impression had been made by him on Mr. Jefferson and Mrs. Randolph. His adhesiveness was such that he had occupied the valuable time of Mr. Jefferson the whole morning, and staid to dinner; and during the conversation Mr. Jefferson was apprehensive that he had said something which might have been misunderstood and be incorrectly repeated. He therefore asked me to find the gentleman, if he had not left Charlottesville, and request him to pay another visit to Monticello. He had left, however, when I returned, but I never discovered he had abused the frankness of Mr. Jefferson. Mr. Jefferson took the occasion of saying to me how cautious his friends ought to be in regard to the persons they introduced to him. It would have been singular if, in the numerous visitors, some had not been found to narrate the private conversations held with such men as Jefferson and Madison.

The foregoing statements and extracts present a faithful picture of the circumstances beyond his control which tended to hopelessly involve Mr. Jefferson in pecuniary embarrassments. These were still further aggravated by the outbreak of the war of 1812, whose disastrous consequences to Virginia farmers are thus graphically and sadly depicted by him in a letter to Mr. Short:

These are my views of the war. They embrace a great deal of sufferance, trying privations, and no benefit but that of teaching our enemy that he is never to gain by wanton injuries on us. To me this state of things brings a sacrifice of all tranquillity and comfort through the residue of life. For although the debility of age disables me from the services and sufferings of the field, yet, by the total annihilation in value of the produce which was to give me subsistence and independence, I shall be, like Tantalus, up to the shoulders in water, yet dying with thirst. We can make, indeed, enough to eat, drink, and clothe ourselves; but nothing for our salt, iron, groceries, and taxes, which must be paid in money. For what can we raise for the market? Wheat? we can only give it to our horses, as we have been doing ever since harvest. Tobacco? it is not worth the pipe it is smoked in. Some say whisky; but all mankind must become drunkards to consume it. But although we feel, we shall not flinch. We must consider now, as in the Revolutionary war, that although the evils of resistance are great, those of submission would be greater. We must meet, therefore, the former as the casualties of tempests and earthquakes, and, like them, necessarily resulting from the constitution of the world.

There was then nothing to be made from farming; but while his income was thus cut short, his company and his debts continued to increase. In this emergency something had to be done; and the only thing which offered itself involved a sacrifice which none but his own family, who witnessed the struggle it cost him, could ever fully appreciate—I allude to the sale of his library.

The British having burnt the Congressional Library at Washington in 1814, he seized that occasion to write to a friend in Congress—Samuel H. Smith—and offer his library at whatever price Congress should decide to be just. His letter making this offer is manly and business-like, and contains not one word of repining at the stern necessity which forced him to part with his literary treasures—the books which in every change in the tide of his eventful life had ever remained to him as old friends with unchanged faces, and whose silent companionship had afforded him—next to the love of his friends—the sweetest and purest joys of life. The following extract from this letter shows how valuable his collection of books was:

You know my collection, its condition and extent. I have been fifty years making it, and have spared no pains, opportunity, or expense, to make it what it is. While residing in Paris, I devoted every afternoon I was disengaged, for a summer or two, in examining all the principal bookstores, turning over every book with my own hand, and putting by every thing which related to America, and, indeed, whatever is rare and valuable in every science. Besides this, I had standing orders during the whole time I was in Europe on its principal book-marts, particularly Amsterdam, Frankfort, Madrid, and London, for such works relating to America as could not be found in Paris. So that in that department particularly such a collection was made as probably can never again be effected, because it is hardly probable that the same opportunities, the same time, industry, perseverance, and expense, with some knowledge of the bibliography of the subject, would again happen to be in concurrence. During the same period, and after my return to America, I was led to procure, also, whatever related to the duties of those in the high concerns of the nation. So that the collection, which I suppose is of between nine and ten thousand volumes, while it includes what is chiefly valuable in science and literature generally, extends more particularly to whatever belongs to the American Statesman.

It is sad to think that such a man as Jefferson, whose fortunes had been ruined by the demands which his country had made on him, should have been forced, so late in life, to sell such a library to pay debts which he was in no wise responsible for having incurred. And yet, though it was known that the purchase of the library would be a pecuniary relief to him, the bill authorizing it was not passed in Congress without decided opposition, and the amount finally voted ($23,950) as the price to be paid for the books was probably but little over half their original cost, though they were all in a perfect state of preservation.

The money received for the books proved to be only a temporary relief. The country had not recovered from the depression of its agricultural interests when a disastrous financial crisis burst upon it. A vivid but melancholy picture of this period is found in Colonel Benton's Thirty Years' View:

The years of 1819 and 1820 were a period of gloom and agony. No money, either gold or silver: no paper convertible into specie: no measure or standard of value left remaining. The local banks (all but those of New England), after a brief resumption of specie payments, again sank into a state of suspension. The bank of the United States, created as a remedy for all those evils, now at the head of the evil, prostrate and helpless, with no power left but that of suing its debtors and selling their property, and purchasing for itself at its own nominal price. No price for property or produce; no sales but those of the sheriff and the marshal; no purchasers at the execution-sales but the creditor, or some hoarder of money; no employment for industry; no demand for labor; no sale for the product of the farm; no sound of the hammer, but that of the auctioneer, knocking down property. Stop laws, property laws, replevin laws, stay laws, loan-office laws, the intervention of the legislator between the creditor and the debtor—this was the business of legislation in three-fourths of the States of the Union—of all south and west of New England. No medium of exchange but depreciated paper; no change, even, but little bits of foul paper, marked so many cents, and signed by some tradesman, barber, or innkeeper; exchanges deranged to the extent of fifty or one hundred per cent. Distress the universal cry of the people; relief, the universal demand, thundered at the door of all legislatures, State and federal.

Happy the man who, having his house set in order, was able to withstand the blasts of this financial tornado. To Jefferson, with his estates burdened with debt, their produce a drug in the market, and his house constantly crowded with guests, this crisis was fatal. At the time he did not feel its practical effects in their full force, for, as we have seen in a previous chapter, he had placed, in the year 1816, the management of his affairs in the hands of his grandson, Thomas Jefferson Randolph. I have elsewhere alluded to the constant and peculiar devotion of this grandfather and grandson to each other. When he took charge of his grandfather's affairs young Randolph threw himself into the breach, and, from that time until Mr. Jefferson's death, made it the aim of his life as far as possible to alleviate his financial condition, and to this end devoted all the energy and ardor of his youth as well as his own private fortune. I have lying before me an account signed by Mr. Jefferson a few weeks before his death, which shows that this grandson had interposed himself between him and his creditors to the amount of $58,536. Another paper before me, signed by Mr. Jefferson's commission-merchant, shows that he, the commission-merchant, was guaranteed by Mr. Randolph against any loss from endorsation, over-draught, or other responsibility which he had incurred, or might incur, on his grandfather's account; that these responsibilities were all met by him, and that nevertheless, by his directions, Mr. Jefferson's crops were placed in the hands of his commission-merchant on Mr. Jefferson's account, and were drawn out solely to his order. When, at the winding up of Mr. Jefferson's estate after his death, it was found that his debts exceeded the value of his property by $40,000, this same grandson pledged himself to make good the deficit, which, by his untiring and unaided efforts, he succeeded in doing in the course of some years, having in that time paid all that was due to Jefferson's creditors.*

The letters written by Jefferson during the rest of his life betray much mental suffering, and present a picture most painful to contemplate; showing, as it does, that however beneficial to the public his services to his country had been, on himself they were allowed to entail bankruptcy and ruin. The editor of the Jefferson and Cabell correspondence, on reaching the letters which cover this period of Mr. Jefferson's life, puts the following appropriate note:

The few remaining letters of the series relate not solely to the great subject of Education, but in some measure to Mr.

---

* The bankruptcy of Mr. Jefferson has been attributed, but erroneously, to the failure of one of his warm personal friends, for whom he had endorsed heavily. This misfortune simply added to his embarrassment, and was doubtless the "coup-de-grâce;" but the same result must have ensued had this complication not occurred. It is gratifying to know that the friendship previously existing between the parties was not in the least disturbed, and that the injury inflicted was subsequently partially repaid by the sale of land relinquished for the purpose.

J.'s private affairs, which had now become hopelessly embarrassed—a liability from which no citizen can claim entire exemption under our peculiar institutions. The reflections to which this gives rise would be too painful, had not the facts been already given to the public through other channels. That under such pressure he should have been able to continue his efforts and counsels in behalf of the public interests with which he had been charged,* must excite our admiration; and still more when we observe the dignity with which he bore up under reverses that would have crushed the spirit of many a younger and stouter man.

The following extract from a letter written early in the year 1826 to his friend Mr. J. C. Cabell, who was then in the Legislature of Virginia, explains itself:

My grandson, Thomas J. Randolph, attends the Legislature on a subject of ultimate importance to my future happiness. ...... My application to the Legislature is for permission to dispose of property for payment in a way† which, bringing a fair price for it, may pay my debts and leave a living for myself in my old age, and leave something for my family. Their consent is necessary, it will injure no man, and few sessions pass without similar exercises of the same power in their discretion. But I refer you to my grandson for particular explanations. I think it just myself; and if it should appear so to you, I am sure your friendship as well as justice will induce you to pay to it the attention which you may think the case will justify. To me it is almost a question of life and death.

The generous-hearted Cabell in reply writes:

I assure you I was truly distressed to receive your letter of the 20th, and to hear the embarrassed state of your affairs. You may rely on my utmost exertions. Your grandson proposed that the first conference should be held at the Eagle. I prevailed on him to remove the scene to Judge Carr's, and to invite all the Judges of the Court of Appeals. Mr. Coalter and my brother were unable to attend; but all the court

---

* Alluding to his efforts in behalf of the University.   † By lottery.

is with you. Mr. Johnson agreed to draw the bill. I am co-operating as far as lies in my power. I wish complete justice could be done on this occasion; but we have to deal with men as they are. Your grandson will no doubt give you the fullest information. I will occasionally inform you how matters are progressing.

Shortly after writing to Mr. Cabell we find him drawing up a paper, to be shown to his friends in the Legislature, called "Thoughts on Lotteries," which was written to show that there could be nothing immoral in the lottery which he desired. The following quotation shows that his request was not without a precedent :

In this way the great estate of the late Colonel Byrd (in 1756) was made competent to pay his debts, which, had the whole been brought into market at once, would have over-done the demand, would have sold at half or quarter the value, and sacrificed the creditors, half or three-fourths of whom would have lost their debts. This method of selling was formerly very much resorted to, until it was thought to nourish too much a spirit of hazard. The Legislature were therefore induced, not to suppress it altogether, but to take it under their own special regulation. This they did for the first time by their act of 1769, c. 17, before which time every person exercised the right freely, and since which time it is made unlawful but when approved and authorized by a special act of the Legislature.

In this same paper he sums up as follows the years spent in the public service :

I came of age in 1764, and was soon put into the nomina-tion of justice of the county in which I live ; and at the first election following I became one of its representatives in the Legislature. I was thence sent to the old Congress. Then employed two years with Mr. Pendleton and Mr. Wythe, on the revisal and reduction to a single code of the whole body of the British statutes, the acts of our Assembly, and certain parts of the common law. Then elected Governor. Next, to the Legislature and Congress again. Sent to Europe as

Minister Plenipotentiary. Appointed Secretary of Sta[te]
the new Government. Elected Vice-President, and [Presi-]
dent. And lastly, a Visitor and Rector of the Universi[ty.]

In these different offices, with scarcely any interva[l be-]
tween them, I have been in the public service now sixty-one
years; and during the far greater part of the time in foreign countries or in other States. Every one knows how in-
evitably a Virginia estate goes to ruin when the owner is so
far distant as to be unable to pay attention to it himself;
and the more especially when the line of his employment is
of a character to abstract and alienate his mind entirely
from the knowledge necessary to good and even to saving
management.

Small and trifling as the favor was which Mr. Jefferson
asked of the Virginia Legislature, it cost him much pain and
mortification to do it, as we find from a sad and touching letter to Madison, in which he unbosoms himself to this long-
cherished friend. He writes:

You will have seen in the newspapers some proceedings
in the Legislature which have cost me much mortification.
...... Still, sales at a fair price would leave me compe-
tently provided. Had crops and prices for several years
been such as to maintain a steady competition of substantial bidders at market, all would have been safe. But the
long succession of years of stunted crops, of reduced prices,
the general prostration of the farming business, under levies
for the support of manufactures, etc., with the calamitous
fluctuations of value in our paper medium, have kept agriculture in a state of abject depression, which has peopled
the Western States by silently breaking up those on the
Atlantic, and glutted the land-market while it drew off its
bidders. In such a state of things property has lost its
character of being a resource for debts. Highland in Bedford, which, in the days of our plethory, sold readily for from
fifty to one hundred dollars the acre (and such sales were
many then), would not now sell for more than from ten to
twenty dollars, or one-quarter or one-fifth of its former price.
Reflecting on these things, the practice occurred to me of
selling on fair valuation, and by way of lottery, often re-

sorted to before the Revolution to effect large sales, and still in constant usage in every State for individual as well as corporation purposes. If it is permitted in my case, my lands here alone, with the mills, etc., will pay every thing, and will leave me Monticello and a farm free. If refused, I must sell every thing here, perhaps considerably in Bedford, move thither with my family, where I have not even a log hut to put my head into,* and where ground for burial will depend on the depredations which, under the form of sales, shall have been committed on my property.

The question then with me was *utrum horum.* But why afflict you with these details? Indeed, I can not tell, unless pains are lessened by communication with a friend. The friendship which has subsisted between us, now half a century, and the harmony of our political principles and pursuits, have been sources of constant happiness to me through that long period. And if I remove beyond the reach of attentions to the University, or beyond the bourne of life itself, as I soon must, it is a comfort to leave that institution under your care, and an assurance that it will not be wanting. It has also been a great solace to me to believe that you are engaged in vindicating to posterity the course we have pursued for preserving to them in all their purity the blessings of self-government, which we had assisted, too, in acquiring for them. If ever the earth has beheld a system of administration conducted with a single and steadfast eye to the general interest and happiness of those committed to it; one which, protected by truth, can never know reproach, it is that to which our lives have been devoted. To myself you have been a pillar of support through life. Take care of me when dead, and be assured that I shall leave with you my last affections.

On the 3d of February, 1826, Mr. Cabell wrote to Jefferson:

Your intended application to the Legislature has excited much discussion in private circles in Richmond. Your grandson will doubtless give you a full account of passing occurrences. A second conference was held at Mr. Baker's

---

* The house at Poplar Forest had passed out of his possession.

last evening, at which were four of the Judges of the Court of Appeals, and several members of the Legislature. Finding considerable opposition in some of your political friends to the lottery, and feeling mortified myself that the State should stop short at so limited a measure, I suggested the idea of a loan of $80,000, free of interest, from the State, during the remainder of your life. On consultation, our friends decided that it would be impracticable. At the conference of last evening it was unanimously decided to bring forward and support the lottery. I hear there will be considerable opposition, but I hope it is exaggerated. I do not think that delay would be injurious, as in every case I have found the first impression the worst. Would to God that I had the power to raise the mind of the Legislature to a just conception of its duties on the present occasion. Knowing so well as I do how much you have done for us, I have some idea of what we ought to do for you.

The following extract from a letter written on February 4th by Jefferson to his grandson portrays vividly and painfully the agonized state of his mind about his affairs:

Your letter of the 31st was received yesterday, and gave me a fine night's rest, which I had not had before since you left us, as the failure to hear from you by the preceding mail had filled me with fearful forebodings. I am pleased with the train you are proceeding in, and particularly with the appointment of valuers. Under all circumstances I think I may expect a liberal valuation; an exaggerated one I should negative myself. I would not be stained with the suspicions of selfishness at this time of life, and this will protect me from them. I hope the paper I gave you will justify me in the eyes of all those who have been consulted.

This gleam of hope which so cheered up the old man's sinking heart was soon to be extinguished. His friends found, on feeling the pulse of the Legislature, that his simple request to be allowed to sell his property by lottery would meet with violent opposition, if not absolute defeat, in that body. On his good friend Cabell devolved the painful duty of communicating this intelligence to him, which he did with all the feeling and delicacy of his chivalrous nature.

The shock to Jefferson was great, and we find him, not without some bitterness, replying:

I had hoped the length and character of my services might have prevented the fear in the Legislature of the indulgence asked being quoted as a precedent in future cases. But I find no fault with their strict adherence to a rule generally useful, although relaxable in some cases, under their discretion, of which they are the proper judges.

And again, in another letter to Cabell, he concludes sadly:

Whatever may be the sentence to be pronounced in my particular case, the efforts of my friends are so visible, the impressions so profoundly sunk to the bottom of my heart, that they can never be obliterated. They plant there a consolation which countervails whatever other indications might seem to import. The report of the Committee of Finance particularly is balm to my soul. Thanks to you all, and warm and affectionate acknowledgments. I count on nothing now. I am taught to know my standard, and have to meet with no further disappointment.

Well might such bitterness as this last sentence contained have been wrung from him, for the Legislature granted leave for the bill to be brought in by a bare majority of *four*. The noble and generous-hearted Cabell, on communicating this intelligence to him, adds: " I blush for my country, and am humiliated to think how we shall appear on the page of history."

Perhaps nothing more beautiful or more touching ever flowed from his pen than the following letter to his grandson ; giving, as it does, such a picture of his affections, his Christian resignation, manly courage, and willingness to bear up under adversity, for the sake of doing good to those he loved.

To Thomas J. Randolph.

Monticello, February 8th, '26.

My dear Jefferson—I duly received your affectionate letter of the 3d, and perceive there are greater doubts than I had apprehended whether the Legislature will indulge my request to them. It is a part of my mortification to perceive that I had so far overvalued myself as to have counted on it with too much confidence. I see, in the failure of this hope, a deadly blast of all my peace of mind during my remaining days. You kindly encourage me to keep up my spirits; but, oppressed with disease, debility, age, and embarrassed affairs, this is difficult. For myself I should not regard a prostration of fortune, but I am overwhelmed at the prospect of the situation in which I may leave my family. My dear and beloved daughter, the cherished companion of my early life, and nurse of my age, and her children, rendered as dear to me as if my own, from having lived with me from their cradle, left in a comfortless situation, hold up to me nothing but future gloom; and I should not care were life to end with the line I am writing, were it not that in the unhappy state of mind which your father's misfortunes have brought upon him, I may yet be of some avail to the family. Their affectionate devotion to me makes a willingness to endure life a duty, as long as it can be of any use to them. Yourself particularly, dear Jefferson, I consider as the greatest of the Godsends which heaven has granted to me. Without you what could I do under the difficulties now environing me? These have been produced, in some degree, by my own unskillful management, and devoting my time to the service of my country, but much also by the unfortunate fluctuation in the value of our money, and the long-continued depression of farming business. , But for these last I am confident my debts might be paid, leaving me Monticello and the Bedford estate; but where there are no bidders, property, however great, is no resource for the payment of debts; all may go for little or nothing. Perhaps, however, even in this case I may have no right to complain, as these misfortunes have been held back for my last days, when few remain to me. I duly acknowledge that I have gone through a long life with fewer circumstances of affliction than are the lot of most men—uninterrupted health—a competence for every reasonable want—usefulness to my fellow-citizens—a good portion of their esteem—no complaint against the world which has sufficiently honored me, and, above all, a family which has blessed me by their affections, and never by their conduct given me a moment's pain—and should this, my last request, be granted, I may yet close with a cloudless sun a long and serene day of life. Be assured, my dear Jefferson, that I have a just sense of the part you have contributed to this, and that I bear you unmeasured affection.

TH. JEFFERSON.

What a world of suffering and mental anguish this letter reveals! Three days after it was written his eldest grand-child, Mrs. Anne Bankhead, died. In alluding to his distress on this occasion, Dr. Dunglison says, in his Memoranda: " On the last day of the fatal illness of his grand-daughter, who had married Mr. Bankhead......Mr. Jefferson was present in the adjoining apartment; and when the announcement was made by me that but little hope remained, that she was, indeed, past hope, it is impossible to imagine more poignant distress than was exhibited by him. He shed tears, and abandoned himself to every evidence of intense grief."

Mr. Jefferson announced the death of this grand-daughter to her brother, then in Richmond, in the following touch-ingly-written note:

To Thomas Jefferson Randolph.

Monticello, Feb. 11th, '26.

Bad news, my dear Jefferson, as to your sister Anne. She expired about half an hour ago. I have been so ill for several days that I could not go to see her till this morning, and found her speechless and insensible. She breathed her last about 11 o'clock. Heaven seems to be overwhelming us with every form of misfortune, and I expect your next will give me the *coup de grâce.* Your own family are all well. Affectionately adieu.

TH. JEFFERSON.

I now hasten to drop the curtain on this painful period of his life. The bill for the lottery was still before the Legisla-ture when the people of Richmond held a meeting and pass-ed resolutions to approve its being adopted. Finally the Legislature passed the bill, on the 20th of February, by a vote in the Senate of ayes thirteen, nays four. During the next few months meetings indorsing the action of the Legislature were held in different parts of the State. We quote the following preamble to the Resolutions that were passed at a meeting held in Nelson County, though no action resulted from the meeting:

The undersigned citizens of Nelson County, concurring cordially in the views lately expressed by their fellow-citizens at the seat of government,* and heartily sympathizing in the sentiments of grateful respect and affectionate regard recently evinced both there and elsewhere for their countryman, Thomas Jefferson, can not disguise the sincere satisfaction which they derive from the prospect of a general co-operation to relieve this ancient and distinguished patriot. The important services for which we are indebted to Mr. Jefferson, from the days of his youth, when he drew upon himself the resentment of Dunmore, to the present time, when, at the close of a long life, he is laboring to enlighten the nation which he has contributed to make free, place him in the highest rank of national benefactors, and eminently entitle him to the character of the people's friend. Whether considered as the servant of the State or of the United States; whether regarded as an advocate or a statesman; whether as a patriot, a legislator, a philosopher, or a friend of liberty and republican government, he is the unquestioned ornament of his country, and unites in himself every title to our respect, our veneration, and gratitude. His services are written in the hearts of a grateful people; they are identified with the fundamental institutions of his country; they entitle him to " the fairest page of faithful history;" and will be remembered as long as reason and science are respected on earth. Profoundly impressed with these sentiments, the undersigned citizens of Nelson County consider it compatible with neither the national character nor with the gratitude of the Republic that this aged patriot should be deprived of his estate or abridged in his comforts at the close of a long life so ably spent in the service of his country.†

---

* Alluding to the meeting in Richmond.

† This handsome tribute to Jefferson, concluding with such a delicate appeal to the gratitude of his countrymen for his relief, was penned by his friend, J. C. Cabell.

Fair words these, but barren as the desert air. From his own State Mr. Jefferson received no aid whatever; but other States came to his relief in a manner which was both gratifying and efficient. Without effort, Philip Hone, the Mayor of New York, raised $8500, which he transmitted to Mr. Jefferson on behalf of the citizens of New York; from Philadelphia he received $5000, and from Baltimore $3000. These sums were promptly sent as soon as his embarrassed circumstances became known. He was much touched by this proof of the affection and esteem of his countrymen, and feelingly exclaimed: "No cent of this is wrung from the tax-payer— it is the pure and unsolicited offering of love."

Happily, he died unconscious that the sales of his property would fail to pay his debts, that his beautiful home would pass into the hands of strangers, and that his "dear and beloved daughter" would go forth into the world penniless, as its doors were closed upon her forever.*

The following quotation from a'French writer—one by no means friendly to Jefferson—forms a fitting conclusion for this sad chapter of his life. After alluding to the grand outburst of popular feeling displayed in the funeral orations throughout the country on the deaths of Adams and Jefferson, he says:

But the nobler emotions of democracy are of short duration: it soon forgets its most faithful servants. Six months had not elapsed when Jefferson's furniture was sold at auction to pay his debts, when Monticello and Poplar Forest were advertised for sale at the street corners, and when the daughter of him whom America had called "the father of democracy" had no longer a place to rest her head.†

---

* On learning the destitute condition in which Mrs. Randolph was left, the Legislature of South Carolina at once presented her with $10,000; and Louisiana, following her example, generously gave the same sum—acts which will ever be gratefully remembered by the descendants of Martha Jefferson.

† Thomas Jefferson, Étude Historique sur la Démocratie Américaine; par Cornelis De Witt, p. 380.

CHAPTER XXII.

A FRIEND and admirer of Jefferson's, who had named a son after him, requested that he would write a letter of advice for his young namesake. Jefferson accordingly wrote the following beautiful note to be kept for him until the young child came to years of understanding:

To Thomas Jefferson Smith.

This letter will, to you, be as one from the dead. The writer will be in the grave before you can weigh its counsels. Your affectionate and excellent father has requested that I would address to you something which might possibly have a favorable influence on the course of life you have to run; and I too, as a namesake, feel an interest in that course. Few words will be necessary, with good dispositions on your part. Adore God. Reverence and cherish your parents. Love your neighbor as yourself, and your country more than yourself. Be just. Be true. Murmur not at the ways of Providence. So shall the life into which you have entered, be the portal to one of eternal and ineffable bliss. And if to the dead it is permitted to care for the things of this world, every action of your life will be under my regard. Farewell.

Monticello, February 21st, 1825.

The Portrait of a Good Man by the most sublime of Poets, for your Imitation.

Lord, who's the happy man that may to thy blest courts repair;
Not stranger-like to visit them, but to inhabit there?

'Tis he whose every thought and deed by rules of virtue moves;
Whose generous tongue disdains to speak the thing his heart disproves.

Who never did a slander forge, his neighbor's fame to wound;
Nor hearken to a false report by malice whispered round.

Who vice in all its pomp and power, can treat with just neglect;
And piety, though clothed in rags, religiously respect.

Who to his plighted vows and trust has ever firmly stood;
And though he promise to his loss, he makes his promise good.

Whose soul in usury disdains his treasure to employ;
Whom no rewards can ever bribe the guiltless to destroy.

The man who, by this steady course, has happiness insured,
When earth's foundations shake, shall stand by Providence secured.

A Decalogue of Canons for Observation in Practical Life.

1. Never put off till to-morrow what you can do to-day.
2. Never trouble another for what you can do yourself.
3. Never spend your money before you have it.
4. Never buy what you do not want because it is cheap; it will be dear to you.
5. Pride costs us more than hunger, thirst, and cold.
6. We never repent of having eaten too little.
7. Nothing is troublesome that we do willingly.
8. How much pain have cost us the evils which have never happened.
9. Take things always by their smooth handle.
10. When angry, count ten before you speak; if very angry, an hundred.

A little more than a year after the date of this letter we find Jefferson writing his last letter to John Adams. The playful tone in which it is written gives no evidence of the suffering from the disease under which he was laboring at the time.

To John Adams.

Monticello, March 25th, 1826.

Dear Sir—My grandson, Thomas J. Randolph, the bearer of this letter, being on a visit to Boston, would think he had seen nothing were he to leave without seeing you. Although I truly sympathize with you in the trouble these interruptions give, yet I must ask for him permission to pay to to you his personal respects. Like other young people, he wishes to be able, in the winter nights of old age, to recount to those around him what he has heard and learnt of the heroic age preceding his birth, and which of the Argonauts individually he was in time to have seen.

It was the lot of our early years to witness nothing but the dull monotony of a colonial subservience, and of our riper years to breast the labors and perils of working out of it. Theirs are the halcyon calms succeeding the storms which our Argosy had so stoutly weathered. Gratify his ambition, then, by receiving his best bow, and my solicitude for your health, by enabling him to bring me a favorable account of it. Mine is but indifferent, but not so my friendship and respect for you.

TH. JEFFERSON.

The leaders of different parties bitterly opposed to each other, and living at a time when party spirit ran so high, there is something remarkable, as well as beautiful, in the friendship which existed between these two distinguished men, and which, surviving all political differences and rivalry, expired only on the same day which saw them both breathe their last.*

In the spring of the year 1826 Jefferson's family became aware that his health was failing rapidly. Of this he had been conscious himself for some time previous. Though enfeebled by age and disease, he turned a deaf ear to Mrs. Randolph's entreaties that he would allow his faithful servant, Burwell, to accompany him in his daily rides. He said, if his family insisted, that he would give up his rides entirely; but that he had "helped himself" from his childhood, and that the presence of a servant in his daily musings with nature would be irksome to him. So, until within a very short time of his death, old Eagle was brought up every day, even when his venerable master was so weak that he could only get into the saddle by stepping down from the terrace.

---

* Without meaning the least irreverence in the world to the memory of these two great and good men, I can not refrain here from giving the reader the benefit of a good story, which has the advantage over most good stories of being strictly true:

There was living in Albemarle, at the time of Jefferson's death, an enthusiastic democrat, who, admiring him beyond all men, thought that, by dying on the 4th of July, he had raised himself and his party one step higher in the temple of fame. Then came the news that John Adams had died on the same great day. Indignant at the bare suggestion of such a thing, he at first refused to believe it, and, when he could no longer discredit the news, exclaimed, in a passion, that "it was a damned Yankee trick."

As he felt the sands of life running low, his love for his family seemed to increase in tenderness. Mr. Randall says, in his excellent biography of him, in alluding to this period:

Mr. Jefferson's deportment to his family was touching. He evidently made an effort to keep up their spirits. He was as gentle as a child, but conversed with such vigor and animation that they would have often cheated themselves with the belief that months, if not years, of life were in store for him, and that he himself was in no expectation of speedy death, had they not witnessed the infant-like debility of his powerful frame, and had they not occasionally, when they looked suddenly at him, caught resting on themselves that riveted and intensely-loving gaze which showed but too plainly that his thoughts were on a rapidly-approaching parting. And as he folded each in his arms as they separated for the night, there was a fervor in his kiss and gaze that declared as audibly as words that he felt the farewell might prove a final one.

In speaking of his private life, Dr. Dunglison, in his Memoranda, says:

The opportunities I had of witnessing the private life of Mr. Jefferson were numerous. It was impossible for any one to be more amiable in his domestic relations; it was delightful to observe the devoted and respectful attention that was paid him by all the family. In the neighborhood, too, he was greatly revered. Perhaps, however, according to the all-wise remark that no one is a prophet in his own country, he had more personal detractors there, partly owing to difference in political sentiments, which are apt to engender so much unworthy acrimony of feeling; but still more, perhaps, owing to the views which he was supposed to possess on the subject of religion; yet it was well known that he did not withhold his aid when a church had to be established in the neighborhood, and that he subscribed largely to the Episcopal church erected in Charlottesville. After his death much sectarian intolerance was exhibited, owing to the publication of certain of his letters, in which he animadverted on the Presbyterians more especially; yet there could not have been a more unfounded assertion than that of a Philadelphia Episcopal divine that "Mr. Jefferson's memory was detested in Charlottesville and the vicinity." It is due, also, to that illustrious individual to say, that, in all my intercourse with him, I never heard an observation that savored, in the slightest degree, of impiety. His religious belief harmonized more closely with that of the Unitarians than of any other denomination, but it was liberal, and untrammelled by sectarian feelings and prejudices. It is not easy to find more sound advice, more appropriately expressed, than in the letter which he wrote to Thomas Jefferson Smith, dated February 21st, 1825.*

It was beautiful, too, to witness the deference that was paid by Mr. Jefferson and Mr. Madison to each other's opinions. When as secretary, and as chairman of the faculty, I had to consult one of them, it was a common interrogatory, What did the other say of the matter? If possible, Mr. Madison gave indications of a greater intensity of this feeling, and seemed to think that every thing emanating from his ancient associate must be correct. In a letter which Mr. Jefferson wrote to Mr. Madison a few months only before he died (February 17th, 1826), he thus charmingly expresses himself. [Here follows the conclusion of a letter to Mr. Madison already given, beginning at the words "The friendship which has subsisted between us," etc.]

Mr. Randall gives us, in his work, the following accounts of his last hours and death, written by two of those who were present—Dr. Dunglison and his grandson, Colonel T. J. Randolph. I give Dr. Dunglison's first:

In the spring of 1826 the health of Mr. Jefferson became more impaired; his nutrition fell off; and at the approach of summer he was troubled with diarrhœa, to which he had been liable for some years—ever since, as he believed, he had resorted to the Virginia Springs, especially the White Sulphur, and had freely used the waters externally for an eruption which did not yield readily to the ordinary remedies. I had prescribed for this affection early in June, and he had

* See page 419.

improved somewhat; but on the 24th of that month he wrote me the last note I received from him, begging me to visit him, as he was not so well. This note was, perhaps, the last he penned. On the same day, however, he wrote an excellent letter to General Weightman, in reply to an invitation to celebrate in Washington the fiftieth anniversary of the Declaration of Independence, which he declined on the ground of indisposition. This, Professor Tucker says, was probably his last letter. It had all the striking characteristics of his vigorous and unfaded intellect.

The tone of the note I received from him satisfied me of the propriety of visiting him immediately; and having mentioned the subject to Mr. Tucker, he proposed to accompany me. I immediately saw that the affection was making a decided impression on his bodily powers, and, as Mr. Tucker has properly remarked in his life of this distinguished individual, was apprehensive that the attack would prove fatal. Nor did Mr. Jefferson himself indulge any other opinion. From this time his strength gradually diminished, and he had to remain in bed......

Until the 2d and 3d of July he spoke freely of his approaching death; made all his arrangements with his grandson, Mr. Randolph, in regard to his private affairs; and expressed his anxiety for the prosperity of the University, and his confidence in the exertion in its behalf of Mr. Madison and the other Visitors. He repeatedly, too, mentioned his obligation to me for my attention to him. During the last week of his existence I remained at Monticello; and one of the last remarks he made was to me. In the course of the day and night of the 2d of July he was affected with stupor, with intervals of wakefulness and consciousness; but on the 3d the stupor became almost permanent. About seven o'clock of the evening of that day he awoke, and, seeing me staying at his bedside, exclaimed, "Ah! Doctor, are you still there?" in a voice, however, that was husky and indistinct. He then asked, "Is it the Fourth?" to which I replied, "It soon will be." These were the last words I heard him utter.

Until towards the middle of the day—the 4th—he remained in the same state, or nearly so, wholly unconscious to every thing that was passing around him. His circulation was gradually, however, becoming more languid; and for some time prior to dissolution the pulse at the wrist was imperceptible. About one o'clock he ceased to exist.

Jefferson had the utmost confidence in Dr. Dunglison, and, on being entreated by a Philadelphia friend to send for the celebrated Dr. Physic, he refused kindly, but firmly, to do so, saying, "I have got a Dr. Physic of my own—I have entire confidence in Dr. Dunglison." Nor would he allow any other physician to be called in.

Ever thoughtful of others, and anxious to the last not to give trouble, he at first refused to allow even a servant to be with him at night; and when, at last, he became so weak as to be forced to yield his consent, he made his attendant, Burwell, bring a pallet into his room that he might rest during the night.

"In the parting interview with the female members of his family," says Mr. Randall, "Mr. Jefferson, besides general admonitions (the tenor of which corresponds with those contained in his letter to Thomas Jefferson Smith), addressed to them affectionate words of encouragement and practical advice adapted to their several situations. In this he did not pass over a young great-grandchild (Ellen Bankhead), but exhorted her to diligently persevere in her studies, for they would help to make life valuable to her. He gently but audibly murmured: 'Lord, now lettest thou thy servant depart in peace.'"*

I now give Colonel Randolph's account of his grandfather's death. Having revised this for me, he has in one or two instances inserted a few words which were not in the original.

Mr. Jefferson had suffered for several years before his death from a diarrhœa which he concealed from his family, lest it might give them uneasiness. Not aware of it, I was surprised, in conversation with him in March, 1826, to hear

---

* See Randall's Jefferson, vol. iii., p. 547.

him, in speaking of an event likely to occur about midsummer, say doubtingly that he might live to that time.   About the middle of June, hearing that he had sent for his physician, Dr. Dunglison, of the University of Virginia, I immediately went to see him.*   I found him out in his public rooms. Before leaving the house, he sent a servant to me to come to his room, whereupon he handed me a paper, which he desired me to examine, remarking, " Don't delay ; there is no time to be lost." He gradually declined, but would only have his servants sleeping near him : being disturbed only at nine, twelve, and four o'clock in the night, he needed little nursing.   Becoming uneasy about him, I entered his room, unobserved, to pass the night.   Coming round inadvertently to assist him, he chided me, saying, that, being actively employed all day, I needed repose.   On my replying that it was more agreeable to me to be with him, he acquiesced, and I did not leave him again.

A day or two after, at my request, my brother-in-law (Mr. Trist) was admitted.   His servants, ourselves, and the doctor became his sole nurses.   My mother sat with him during the day, but he would not permit her to sit up at night. His family had to decline for him numerous tenders of service from kind and affectionate friends and neighbors, fearing and seeing that it would excite him to conversation injurious to him in his weak condition.

He suffered no pain, but gradually sank from debility. His mind was always clear—it never wandered.   He conversed freely, and gave directions as to his private affairs. His manner was that of a person going on a necessary journey—evincing neither satisfaction nor regret.   He remarked upon the tendency of his mind to recur back to the scenes of the Revolution.   Many incidents he would relate, in his usual cheerful manner, insensibly diverting my mind from his dying condition.   He remarked that the curtains of his bed had been purchased from the first cargo that arrived after the peace of 1782.

Upon my expressing the opinion, on one occasion, that he was somewhat better, he turned to me, and said, " Do not imagine for a moment that I feel the smallest solicitude

---

* Col. Randolph lived on an estate adjoining Monticello.

about the result; I am like an old watch, with a pinion worn out here, and a wheel there, until it can go no longer."

On another occasion, when he was unusually ill, he observed to the doctor, "A few hours more, doctor, and it will be all over."

Upon being suddenly aroused from sleep by a noise in the room, he asked if he had heard the name of Mr. Hatch mentioned—the minister whose church he attended. On my replying in the negative, he observed, as he turned over, " I have no objection to see him, as a kind and good neighbor." The impression made upon my mind at the moment was, that his religious opinions having been formed upon mature study and reflection, he had no doubts upon his mind, and therefore did not desire the attendance of a clergyman: I have never since doubted of the correctness of the impression then taken.

His parting interview with the different members of his family was calm and composed; impressing admonitions upon them, the cardinal points of which were, to pursue virtue, be true and truthful. My youngest brother, in his eighth year, seeming not to comprehend the scene, he turned to me with a smile, and said, " George* does not understand what all this means."

He would speculate upon the person who would succeed him as Rector of the University of Virginia, and concluded that Mr. Madison would be appointed. With all the deep pathos of exalted friendship, he spoke of his purity, his virtue, his wisdom, his learning, and his great abilities; and then, stretching his head back on his pillow, he said, with a sigh, " But ah ! he could never in his life stand up against strenuous opposition." The friendship of these great men was of an extraordinary character. They had been born, lived, and died within twenty-five miles of each other, and they visited frequently through their whole lives. At twenty-three years old Mr. Jefferson had been consulted on Mr. Madison's course of study—he then fifteen. Thus commenced a friendship as remarkable for its duration as it was for the fidelity

---

* This was George Wythe Randolph, who became an eminent lawyer in Virginia, and who, in the late civil war entering warmly in the defense of the South, was distinguished in both the cabinet and field in the Confederate service.

and warmth of its feelings.   The admiration of each for the wisdom, abilities, and purity of the other was unlimited.   Their habit of reliance upon mutual counsel equalled the sincerity of their affection and the devotion of their esteem.

In speaking of the calumnies which his enemies had uttered against his public and private character with such unmitigated and untiring bitterness, he said that he had not considered them as abusing him; they had never known *him*. They had created an imaginary being clothed with odious attributes, to whom they had given his name; and it was against that creature of their imaginations they had levelled their anathemas.

On Monday, the third of July, his slumbers were evidently those of approaching dissolution; he slept until evening, when, upon awaking, he seemed to imagine it was morning, and remarked that he had slept all night without being disturbed.   "This is the fourth of July," he said.   He soon sank again into sleep, and on being aroused at nine to take his medicine, he remarked in a clear distinct voice, "No, doctor, nothing more."   The omission of the dose of laudanum administered every night during his illness caused his slumbers to be disturbed and dreamy; he sat up in his sleep and went through all the forms of writing; spoke of the Committee of Safety, saying it ought to be warned.

As twelve o'clock at night approached, we anxiously desired that his death should be hallowed by the Anniversary of Independence.   At fifteen minutes before twelve we stood noting the minute-hand of the watch, hoping a few minutes of prolonged life.   At four A.M. he called the servants in attendance with a strong and clear voice, perfectly conscious of his wants.   He did not speak again.   About ten he fixed his eyes intently upon me, indicating some want, which, most painfully, I could not understand, until his attached servant, Burwell, observed that his head was not so much elevated as he usually desired it, for his habit was to lie with it very much elevated.   Upon restoring it to its usual position he seemed satisfied.   About eleven, again fixing his eyes upon me, and moving his lips, I applied a wet sponge to his mouth, which he sucked and appeared to relish—this was the last evidence he gave of consciousness.   He ceased to breathe, without a struggle, fifty minutes past meridian—July 4th, 1826. I closed his eyes with my own hands.

He was, at all times during his illness, perfectly assured of his approaching end, his mind ever clear, and at no moment did he evince the least solicitude about the result; he was as calm and composed as when in health. He died a pure and good man. It is for others to speak of his greatness. He desired that his interment should be private, without parade, and our wish was to comply with his request, and no notice of the hour of interment or invitations were issued. His body was borne privately from his dwelling by his family and servants, but his neighbors and friends, anxious to pay the last tribute of respect and affection to one whom they had loved and honored, waited for it in crowds at the grave.

Two days before his death, Jefferson told Mrs. Randolph that in a certain drawer, in an old pocket-book, she would find something intended for her. On looking in the drawer after his death, she found the following touching lines, composed by himself:

A Death-bed Adieu from Th. J. to M. R.

Life's visions are vanished, its dreams are no more;
Dear friends of my bosom, why bathed in tears?
I go to my fathers, I welcome the shore
Which crowns all my hopes or which buries my cares.
Then farewell, my dear, my lov'd daughter, adieu!
The last pang of life is in parting from you!
Two seraphs await me long shrouded in death;
I will bear them your love on my last parting breath.

As soon as Mr. Madison was informed of the death of his revered friend, he wrote the following handsome letter to a gentleman who had married into Mr. Jefferson's family:

From James Madison.

Montpellier, July 6th, 1826.

Dear Sir—I have just received yours of the 4th. A few lines from Dr. Dunglison had prepared me for such a communication, and I never doubted that the last scene of our illustrious friend would be worthy of the life it closed. Long as this has been spared to his country and to those who loved him, a few years more were to have been desired for the sake of both. But we are more than consoled for the loss by the gain to him, and by the assurance that he lives and will live in the memory and gratitude of the wise and good, as a luminary of science, as a votary of, liberty, as a model of patriotism, and as a benefactor of the human kind. In these characters I have known him, and not less in the virtues and charms of social life, for a period of fifty years, during which there was not an interruption or diminution of mutual confidence and cordial friendship for a single moment in a single instance. What I feel, therefore, now need not, I should say can not, be expressed. If there be any possible way in which I can *usefully* give evidence of it, do not fail to afford me the opportunity. I indulge a hope that the unforeseen event will not be permitted to impair *any* of the beneficial measures which were in progress, or in prospect. It can not be unknown that the anxieties of the deceased were for others, not for himself.

Accept, my dear sir, my best wishes for yourself and for all with whom we sympathize, in which Mrs. Madison most sincerely joins.

JAMES MADISON.

To the same gentleman, Judge Dabney Carr, of the Court of Appeals of Virginia, wrote:

The loss of Mr. Jefferson is one over which the whole world will mourn. He was one of those ornaments and benefactors of the human race whose death forms an epoch and creates a sensation throughout the whole circle of civilized man. But that feeling is nothing to what those feel who are connected with him by blood,* and bound to him by gratitude for a thousand favors. To me he has been more than a father, and I have ever loved and revered him with my whole heart....... Taken as a whole, history presents nothing so grand, so beautiful, so peculiarly felicitous in all the great points, as the life and character of Thomas Jefferson.

After Mr. Jefferson's death there were found in a drawer in his room, among other souvenirs, some little packages con-

---

* Judge Carr was Mr. Jefferson's nephew.

taining locks of the hair of his deceased wife, daughter, and even the infant children that he had lost. These relics are now lying before me. They are labelled in his own handwriting. One, marked "*A lock of our first Lucy's hair, with some of my dear, dear wife's writing,*" contains a few strands of soft, silk-like hair evidently taken from the head of a very young infant. Another, marked simply "*Lucy,*" contains a beautiful golden curl.

Among his papers there were found written on the torn back of an old letter the following directions for his monument and its inscription:

Could the dead feel any interest in monuments or other remembrances of them, when, as Anacreon says,

$$\text{'Ολίγη δὲ κεισόμεθα}$$
$$\text{Κόνις, ὀστέων λυθέντων,}$$

the following would be to my manes the most gratifying: on the grave a plain die or cube of three feet without any mouldings, surmounted by an obelisk of six feet height, each of a single stone; on the faces of the obelisk the following inscription, and not a word more:

HERE WAS BURIED
THOMAS JEFFERSON,
Author of the Declaration of American Independence,
Of the Statute of Virginia for Religious Freedom,
And Father of the University of Virginia;

because by these, as testimonials that I have lived, I wish most to be remembered. [It] to be of the coarse stone of which my columns are made, that no one might be tempted hereafter to destroy it for the value of the materials. My bust, by Ceracchi, with the pedestal and truncated column on which it stands, might be given to the University, if they would place it in the dome room of the Rotunda. On the die of the obelisk might be engraved:

Born Apr. 2, 1743, O. S.
Died —— —— ——.

Folded up in the same paper which contained these directions was a scrap on which was written the dates and inscription for Mrs. Jefferson's tomb, which I have already given at page 64 of this book.

Jefferson's efforts to save his monument from mutilation by having it made of coarse stone have been futile. His grandson, Colonel Randolph, followed his directions in erecting the monument which is placed over him. He lies buried between his wife and his daughter, Mary Eppes: across the head of these three graves lie the remains of his eldest daughter, Martha Randolph. This group lies in front of a gap in the high brick wall which surrounds the whole grave-yard, the gap being filled by a high iron grating, giving a full view of the group, that there might be no excuse for forcing open the high iron gates which close the entrance to the grave-yard. But all precautions have been in vain. The gates have been again and again broken open, the grave-yard entered, and the tombs desecrated. The edges of the granite obelisk over Jefferson's grave have been chipped away until it now stands a misshapen column. Of the slabs placed over the graves of Mrs. Jefferson and Mrs. Eppes not a vestige remains, while of the one over Mrs. Randolph only fragments are left.

GRAVE OF JEFFERSON, A.D. 1850.

Addendum

Index

Addendum from the third edition 1947

EDGEHILL

IT is natural that the Randolph family of ''Edgehill,''
descendants of Thomas Jefferson, should make education
their life work—they were all at home in such matters and
wonderfully gifted; the talk at table was a liberal education, had we younger ones listened and heeded.

The school at ''Edgehill'' began before the Civil War
for the daughters of the family and the neighbors' daughters. After the Civil War the school was greatly enlarged
in scope and usefulness.

It was the best school in the South, much sought after
and patronized by all sections of the country as well as
by well-known Southern families. The standard of the
school was high, as to character and scholastic attainment.

The text books used were for the most part those used
by the University of Virginia—six miles away. Miss
Mary B. Randolph, the oldest sister, was the Principal of
the school. Colonel Randolph had no part in the school,
but was much beloved by the girls, all of whom called him
''Grandpa.''

Miss Sarah N. Randolph taught and took part in all
matters concerning the school work. Miss Carolina R.
Randolph, after her mother's death in 1871, had charge
of the housekeeping; in this she was ably assisted by a
niece, Miss Eliza Ruffin (just grown in '72), who was an
adopted daughter of the house. ''Miss Carry'' had also,
after her father's death in 1875,* the management of the
large farm and garden.

* Later on, in 1884 (when Miss Mary Randolph died and Miss
Sarah had for some years been established as Principal of Patapsco

Mrs. William B. Harrison had no school duties, but through her charm and tact and keen sympathy gave happiness and assistance to everyone. Too much cannot be said of the good these ladies did, together and severally, each in her own way. If there were nephews or nieces who could be helped or given advantages not to be had at home, these aunts at Edgehill were always ready, so far as they were able, to make the way possible.

And their willingness to help reached farther than their family; there often were girls at Edgehill who could not have afforded to be there at school unless the warm hearts of these ladies had made it possible that they go through with their education for less than was usual, or even at no expense.

The school house was very old—it still stands—and was the home of Thomas Mann Randolph and Martha Jefferson his wife.

Mr. Randolph died before the building of the large brick house which occupied the site of the frame building ("our School House"), this having been moved down the hill to make room for the large house.

Martha Jefferson spent her last years in the brick house, Edgehill (the home of her son Thomas Jefferson Randolph), after she was obliged to leave Monticello, her father's beloved home, because it was being sold. This property was named by its first owner, William Randolph of Tuckahoe, "Edgehill" after the battlefield of that name.

It became a beautiful place with large grounds, wide lawns, and fine trees.

At one time it comprised several farms, and was in extent some two thousand acres.

Institute), Miss Carolina Randolph had full charge of the Edgehill School as its principal, assisted by an able corps of teachers. The Edgehill School was discontinued almost at the close of the century.

After many years (1902) Edgehill passed from the ownership of the Randolph family, and since, it has been owned by several people. It was burned in March, 1916, but the walls stood, and the house has been rebuilt.

The views from the house and yard were beautiful— the Blue Ridge Mountains far off lay on the horizon; "Monticello," six miles away, and other low mountains in the foreground, were framed with the fine trees.

As one turned, there was loveliness in every outlook. Edgehill is a beloved spot to many people—to those of the Randolph family, of course, and also to a wide circle of friends, and to the many girls who have spent happy years there, and who went out from its doors with memories to guide them through their lives.

The four sisters who were associated in the school were all so different—and yet all so gifted and fine. The good they did is incalculable.

The influence of their daily and hourly intercourse with the girls in their charge cannot be estimated.

These descendants of Mr. Jefferson, as all of that remarkable family of sisters and brothers, lived the life he inculcated, and he would have approved.

The members of the Edgehill family as the writer knew it in 1872 were—Col. Thomas Jefferson Randolph (Mrs. Randolph having died in 1871), his three unmarried daughters, Miss Mary B. Randolph, Miss Carolina R. Randolph, and Miss Sarah N. Randolph; these soon to be joined by a widowed daughter, Mrs. William B. Harrison of Upper Brandon, and her two young children, Jane and Jefferson. There were also at Edgehill the two youngest children of Mrs. Ruffin (another daughter) who, dying, left her daughter Eliza to Miss Mary Randolph, and the son Cary (an infant) to Miss Carolina Randolph's care.

Later, a niece, Mary W. Randolph, daughter of Thomas Jefferson Randolph II of "Shadwell," came after her parents' deaths to live at Edgehill; she was left by her mother, to "Aunt Carry's" care.

A young nephew, Lewis Randolph, both parents having died, was cared for by his aunts through his short life of eight years.

At Edgehill the vacation months were memorable. There was about the place a touch and feeling of pre-war times.

Then—school being closed—the family, at different times, gathered for short or longer visits. There was, for family and friends, that hospitality for which the old South was famous.

Here came in the 70's and early 80's Colonel Randolph's sisters and their families, the Coolidges of Boston, the Trists and Burkes of Alexandria, Mrs. Meikleham of Washington.

And, too, Colonel Randolph's sons and daughters and their families came—the Randolphs from Charlottesville, from "Shadwell," from "Clover Fields," from "Dunlora"; the Taylors from nearby "Lego" and from near Charlottesville; the Keans from Lynchburg; the Andersons from Savannah; the Masons from King George County; the Ruffins from Danville and Richmond; the Carter cousins from "Redlands"; and the Harrisons and Stones from Washington. To the children who came with their parents on these visits, the country life and the activities of a large farm gave the greatest pleasure and interest—days of happiness never to be forgotten.

These were pleasant times, and there was delightful intercourse, which many, still living, will recall.

M. R. B. McA——

Hampton, Virginia
June, 1939

THE THOMAS JEFFERSON
MEMORIAL FOUNDATION

Monticello is owned by the Thomas Jefferson Memorial
Foundation, a nonprofit organization founded in 1923. It
purchased the property, which now consists of 1800 acres
of land, from the Levy family, who had owned it for over
seventy-five years. The purpose of the Foundation is to
preserve the house and restore the gardens as they were
in Mr. Jefferson's day. The house was renovated in 1954;
renovations included the installation of hidden steel sup-
porting girders under the floors, and systems of heat control and air conditioning, and the exterior walls were
water proofed. The Foundation derives its sole income
from the admission fee and from the profit of the sales in
the Monticello Gift Shop.

INDEX